DATE DUE			

AXUM

AXUM

YURI M. KOBISHCHANOV

Joseph W. Michels, Editor

Lorraine T. Kapitanoff, Translator

THE PENNSYLVANIA STATE UNIVERSITY PRESS

University Park and London

Library of Congress Cataloging in Publication Data

Kobishchanov, Iuriĭ Mikhaĭlovich.
  Axum.

  Translation of Aksum.
  Includes bibliography and index.
  1. Aksum (Kingdom)   I. Michels, Joseph W.
  II. Title.
DT390.A88K6213   963'.4   77-88469
ISBN 0-271-00531-9

Originally published in Russian by:
    Academy of Sciences of the USSR
    Africa Institute
    Moscow 1966

Permission to translate and publish the English version
granted by:
    The Copyright Agency of the USSR and the author

Permission to reproduce illustrations from the *Deutsche
Aksum-Expedition*, Littmann et al., Berlin, 1913,
granted by:
    Walter De Gruyter & Co., Berlin

Contents

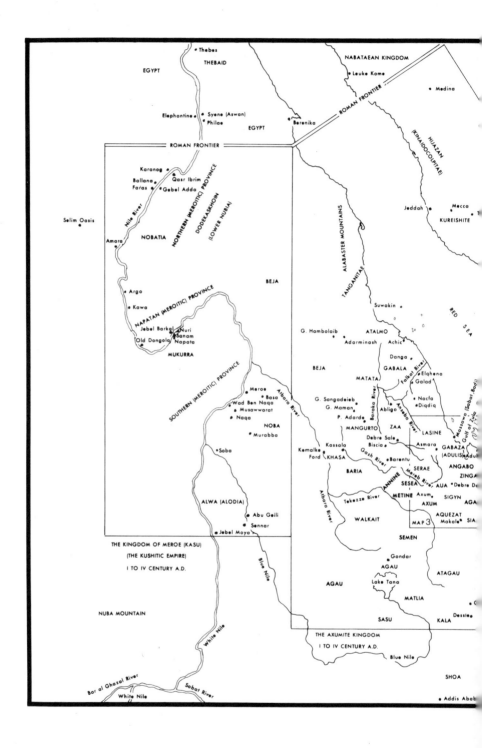

Thebes •

THEBAID

EGYPT

NABATAEAN KINGDOM

• Leuke Kome

ROMAN FRONTIER

• Medina

Elephantine • • Syene (Aswan)
• Philae

EGYPT

• Berenika

ROMAN FRONTIER

HUAZAN
(KINAIDOCOLPITAE)

Karanog •

Ballana • • Qasr Ibrim
Faras • • Gebel Adda

NORTHERN (MEROITIC) PROVINCE

DODEKASCHOIN
(LOWER NUBIA)

ALABASTER MOUNTAINS

TANGANITAE

• Jeddah

• Mecca

KUREISHITE

Selim Oasis •

Nile River

Amara •

NOBATIA

BEJA

RED SEA

• Suwakin

ATALMO

• Argo

• Kawa

NAPATAN (MEROITIC) PROVINCE

Jebel Barkal • Nuri
Old Dongola • Sanam
Napata

MUKURRA

G. Hambolaib •

• Adarminash Achic •

Danga •

GABALA

MATATA

Falkal River

• Elqhena
• Galad

Baraka River

Atraba River

SOUTHERN (MEROITIC) PROVINCE

• Meroe
• Basa
• Wad Ben Naqa
• Musawwarat
• Naqa

NOBA

Atbara River

• Murabba

• Soba

BEJA

G. Sangadeieb •
G. Maman •

P. Adarde •

• Abliga

• Nacfa
• Diqdiq

MANGURTO

ZAA

LASINE

Debra Sale •

Kemalke •

Kassala

Biscia •

• Asmara

GABAZA
(ADULIS)

ALWA (ALODIA)

• Abu Geili
• Sennar

• Jebel Moya

THE KINGDOM OF MEROE (KASU)
(THE KUSHITIC EMPIRE)
I TO IV CENTURY A.D.

Ford

KHASA

Gash River

• Barentu

BARIA

SERAE

ANNINE

METINE

MEREB River

SESEA

Axum

AXUM

ANGABO

ZINGA

AUA • Debra De

SIGYN

AGA

Atbara River

Tekeze River

WALKAIT

MAP 3

AQUEZAT
Makale • SIA

SEMEN

NUBA MOUNTAIN

Blue Nile

White Nile

• Gondar

AGAU

Lake Tana

AGAU

MATLIA

SASU

ATAGAU

• Dessie

KALA

THE AXUMITE KINGDOM
I TO IV CENTURY A.D.

Blue Nile

SHOA

Bar al Ghazal River

Sobat River

White Nile

• Addis Abab

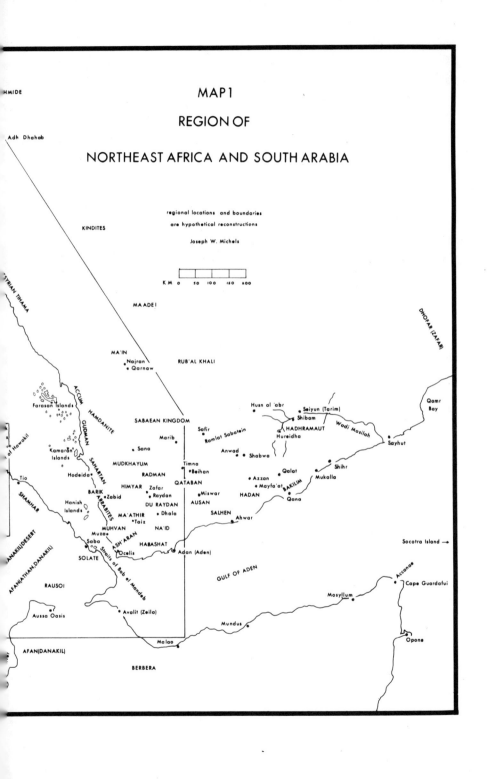

MAP 1

REGION OF

NORTHEAST AFRICA AND SOUTH ARABIA

regional locations and boundaries
are hypothetical reconstructions

Joseph W. Michels

Preface

The rather arduous task of translating a scholarly work is never undertaken lightly or without frequent second thoughts. A compelling need must underlie the decision and be felt strongly enough to overcome moments of weakened resolve. In our case the objective was twofold. Not only did we wish to make Yuri Kobishchanov's distinguished scholarship available to the many Ethiopianists who have no facility in Russian, but we also sought to introduce Axum to the English-reading public. After only a brief acquaintance with the narrative that follows, the reader will surely wonder, as we did, why it has taken so long for Axum to emerge out of obscurity.

Many persons have encouraged us in this endeavor, not least the author himself. Yuri Kobishchanov greeted our proposal with enthusiasm. He prepared very extensive revisions of the 1966 work, *Axum*, as well as the 1968 work, *Sources on the History of Axum*, which is included here as an appendix. (A quick reading of this appendix, before beginning Chapter 1, may give the reader some helpful orientation among the myriads of footnote citations.) As a result, the works fully reflect recent developments in Axumite research. We would also like to thank Yuri Gradov of the Copyright Agency of the USSR for his efficient handling of the necessary translation agreements.

The translation originally was undertaken as an adjunct endeavor to a research project on Axumite archaeology under the direction of Joseph W. Michels, funded by the National Science Foundation. Publication was urged by Thomas Magner, Professor of Slavic Languages and Associate Dean for Graduate Instruction in the College of Liberal Arts at The Pennsylvania State University. We wish to acknowledge his continuing encouragement.

William R. Schmalstieg, Professor of Slavic Languages and Head of the Slavic Languages Department at The Pennsylvania State University, gave unstintingly of his time and expertise in the solution of numerous translation problems. For this we thank him.

The translation of a scholarly work involves fashioning it to a new literary and intellectual milieu. Thus we exercised editorial prerogative in omitting some material which seemed to digress or to be repetitive, as well as in making certain changes intended to insure that terminology is compatible with prevailing anthropological usage. However, every effort has been made to preserve the style of the author of the original works. A similar effort was made to preserve the style and flavor of quotations from authors of antiquity, just as Kobishchanov did. Our overriding wish was to produce an English version as consistent with the original in both form and content as was editorially feasible.

A word or two must be said about spellings of Ethiopian words and of the names of persons and places transliterated from a half dozen different languages. There is little or no consensus in spelling in the literature of Ethiopian studies. This is really not surprising, since spellings are often modified to conform with conventions peculiar to the language in which a person is writing. And since certain proper and geographic names have been transliterated through several languages, quite likely some errors have occurred—few, we trust. Wherever possible we capitalized on existing consensus, but we were more frequently forced to choose among several possibilities. Whatever our choice, we sought to be consistent. Simplicity of spelling was also a consideration. And for ease of reading we avoided diacritical notation except when absolutely necessary.

We wish to express our very special thanks to Willis L. Parker, who performed the arduous task of copy editing this book. His wide knowledge, meticulousness, good judgment, fine sense of style, and above all perseverance and unflagging good humor have been invaluable in completing this work.

Through the generous cooperation of Walter De Gruyter & Co., Berlin, we have been able to illustrate the text with the fine line drawings of Daniel Krencker which were originally published in 1913 as part of the monumental work *Deutsche Aksum-Expedition*.

Finally, we wish to thank Kay McKinley and Carol Leathers of the Department of Anthropology secretarial staff for their admirable patience and good will during the typing of the many drafts through which this manuscript evolved.

J. W. M. and L. T. K.

University Park, Pennsylvania

Axumite Archaeology: An Introductory Essay

Joseph W. Michels

Axumite archaeology has a long and distinguished history, yet among the English-reading public it is virtually unknown to all but a small specialist group. Until very recently all primary sources and all major syntheses were published in French, Italian, German, or Russian. This introduction attempts to remedy the situation by summarizing developments in Axumite archaeology and providing the reader with a comprehensive set of primary source references.

I also want to acquaint the reader with recent efforts at interpreting the archaeological record of the Axumite Kingdom, and, finally, I shall suggest the probable directions Axumite archaeology will take in the near future in the light of current research trends.

Axum, in archaeology and history, is intertwined with South Arabia, Somalia, Nubia, and the northern half of the Ethiopian plateau. Kingdoms from Meroe to Ma'in and sites from Thebes to Marib figure prominently in the historical narrative that Yuri Kobishchanov presents. Site locations can be mapped in a relatively straightforward manner, but historical and paleographic references to tribal regions and ancient petty kingdoms can be geographically ambiguous. Most authors deal with this by omitting regional boundaries in the maps they draw, or by omitting maps altogether. Kobishchanov prepared no maps but did attempt to pull out of the primary sources every shred of geographic information possible. I have taken the liberty of plotting as clearly as I can all geographic references contained in his work; Map 1 presents the results of my reconstruction. The reader should be advised that regional locations and boundaries are entirely hypothetical and any errors rest with me, not Kobishchanov.

I have consulted a number of other sources, especially for geographic references outside the nuclear area of the Axumite Kingdom. Doe (1971),*

---

*A list of References Cited is at the end of this Introductory Essay. The Bibliography and References for *Axum* and Appendix I are at the end of the book.

The lower portion of the ''Giant Fallen Stele'' in Axum.

Phillips (1955), and Bowen and Albright (1958) provided useful information about South Arabia. Pankhurst (1961) was especially helpful with regard to coastal locations on the African Horn. Gann and Duignan (1972), Adams (1974), and Shinnie (1971) were referred to in connection with the Sudan. For Ethiopia in general I benefited from the works of Hable-Sellassie (1972) and Trimingham (1952).

Two key events profoundly affected the development of Axumite archaeology: the German Axum expedition of 1906 (Littmann 1913a, 1913b; Krencker 1913; Lüpke 1913) and the establishment of the Ethiopian Institute of Archaeology by the government of Ethiopia in 1952 (Anfray 1963c).

Adopting a remarkably modern strategy, Enno Littmann, leader of the German expedition, fielded a multidisciplinary team with expertise in paleography, ethnography, archaeology, architecture, technical drawing, photography, and mapping. During a 3½-month sojourn, they laid a systematic, reliable, and comprehensive foundation for all future archaeological research.

The German expedition traveled a circuit from Asmara to Axum and back through the Adigrat/Senafe region. They located and mapped many of the principal Axumite and Preaxumite sites that are distributed along the Tigre plateau. This was the first systematic survey of major archaeological sites within the region and most research undertaken subsequently has been concentrated at sites originally mapped and surveyed by the expedition.

The expedition team recorded numerous inscriptions in Ge'ez, Greek, and South Arabian script, which were subsequently translated and published. This work is the principal corpus of Ethiopian paleographic material which Axumite scholars have worked with until the present. The survey also involved the preparation of architectural plans of the foundations of ancient buildings. Large monumental stone features, such as throne bases, stelae, daises, and altars, were sketched. Site maps, mostly in sketch form, were prepared that showed the location of various ruins on the sites surveyed. Artifacts collected include pottery, coins, objects of bronze, iron, gold, glass, and stone. These were subsequently studied and described and made available to interested scholars through publication.

The expedition team seemed to recognize the dramatic continuity in cultural forms between the Axumite period and the present day. They carefully documented many aspects of the culture and technology of the local population they encountered. Such descriptions can be a paradigm for the interpretation of the archaeological record.

The excavations undertaken by the German expedition at the site of Axum itself generated an enormous volume of information, giving considerable momentum to Axumite scholarship. This expedition was the source of nearly all information on Axum until after World War II, when a sustained campaign of archaeological research was finally inaugurated. This was its most important contribution, but another notable achievement of the expedition was the completeness with which the information derived from fieldwork was made available through publication. A four-volume work published in 1913 contains a complete record not only in narrative form but also in the form of sketches, photographs, site maps, and detailed drawings of individual archaeological features, artifacts, and inscriptions. It also provided comparative studies and one of the earliest attempts at a culture-historical synthesis based on archaeological data. The German Axum expedition, therefore, dwarfs all other efforts until the middle-1950s when a concerted effort was made to investigate Axumite and Preaxumite civilization.

The Ethiopian Institute of Archaeology, established in 1952 by the government of Ethiopia, has led all research on Axum in recent years. The government sponsored the Institute and arranged for it to receive the active professional support of a French archaeological mission provided by the Centre National de la Recherche Scientifique. The Institute publishes a journal—*Annales d'Ethiopie*—which has become the principal source for all Axumite studies. With the inauguration of the Ethiopian Institute of Archaeology and the arrival of talented professional archaeologists affiliated with the French archaeological mission the tempo of research quickened. The French mission included not only archaeologists but specialists in paleography, ethnology, and ancient history. The Institute sponsored excavations at many of the key sites recorded by the German Axum expedition.

The History of Excavation in Axumite Archaeology

The cumulative impact of excavations undertaken by various unrelated expeditions as well as those undertaken by the Ethiopian Institute of Archaeology has been substantial. It seems most appropriate, therefore, to review developments on a site-by-site basis.

Axum (Map 2)   The site of Axum has witnessed perhaps the most ambitious effort at archaeological exploration. Since 1906 it has been the target of no less than 12 seasons of fieldwork, and the quantity of information now available, or in preparation, is impressive.

The first excavation season, lasting $2\frac{1}{2}$ months, was conducted by the German Axum expedition in 1906 (Littmann 1913a, 1913b; Krencker 1913; Lüpke 1913; Zahn 1913). The German team tackled a number of conspicuous targets. They excavated the large dressed-stone thrones located along the foot of Mai Qoho. The Main Group of Stelae attracted their attention. Excavations there were conducted primarily to record as

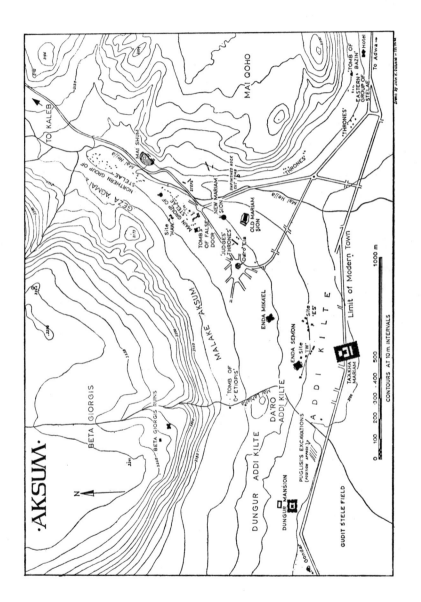

Map 2. Map of Axum. (From Neville Chittick, "Excavations at Aksum, 1973–4: A Preliminary Report." *Azania*, vol. IX, 1974)

fully as possible the giant stelae, the manner in which they were constructed and erected, and their artifact and tomb associations.

Kaleb's tomb, on the northern outskirts of Axum, was also partially excavated. The Christian character of its architecture was noted. A short distance to the east of Axum a structure which is called Menelik's tomb was excavated also.

Perhaps the three most provocative structures excavated, from the standpoint of what they suggest about Axumite society, were the structures named Enda Mika'el, Enda Semon, and Ta'akha Mariam. These were multiroom structures of monumental scale that offered us our first glimpse of elite residential architecture. They were provisionally identified by the German team as palace complexes. The structure with the most extensive remains was that of Ta'akha Mariam. An attempt was made to speculatively reconstruct by architectural rendering the original form of the building, using as a model features from ancient church construction still observable in the area. The architects on the team prepared renderings of a multistoried structure that was impressive in its size and complexity. The reconstruction was corroborated to some extent by documentary references to such structures by travelers in ancient times. The Axum excavations of the 1906 expedition were published in full detail and they stimulated a demand for additional excavation.

The next noteworthy excavation effort undertaken at the site was the 1939 stratigraphic excavation at two sectors by an Italian archaeologist, Puglisi (1941). This was the first attempt to explore the stratigraphy of the site deposit at Axum. One set of trenches located west of Mai Lahlaha yielded a stratigraphic sequence consisting of seven recognizable levels. In the deepest levels Puglisi (1946) noted the occurrence of an abundant amount of "grattoirs" (scrapers). Another set of stratigraphic trenches was dug near Mai Hejja. Here Puglisi recorded the superposition of five levels.

No further excavation of the site was undertaken until after the Ethiopian Institute of Archaeology was founded. Shortly thereafter, in 1954, the Institute undertook excavations at several areas within the site under the general supervision of Jean Leclant. Mikael, a staff archaeologist with the French mission, supervised the excavation of a series of subterranean tombs located in the vicinity of the tomb of Bazin (Mikael and Leclant 1955). Jean Doresse, during the same season, undertook excavations of Axumite ruins located immediately north of the old Mariam Zion church. In addition, he excavated trenches in the area of the Main Stelae Group. He exposed a portion of the area immediately to the west of the Giant Fallen Stele as well as the upper portion of the staircase (and adjacent areas) of the Tomb of the Brick Arches (Caquot and Leclant 1956).

A second season of excavation was undertaken by the Institute in 1955 under the direction of Pironin (Leclant 1959a; Anfray 1965b). The Main

Stelae Group was again targeted for further excavation. The terrace wall (M-1) was partially exposed, and a cemetery complex within the Main Stelae Group area became the primary object of excavation. This was a zone immediately to the west of the Giant Fallen Stele and a zone to the southwest of Nefas Mawcha. Numerous burials were uncovered in the course of these excavations.

Continuing the focus on the Main Stelae Group, Leclant resumed excavations under the sponsorship of the Institute in 1956 (Leclant 1959a). The terrace wall (M-1) first excavated by Pironin was exposed still further. In addition, Leclant undertook excavations of the area that lay immediately west of the flank of the Giant Fallen Stele, as well as a zone to the southwest of the Nefas Mawcha. Finally, he extended excavations begun by Doresse in 1954 of the area east of the Main Stelae Group terrace.

During the following season, the Institute continued its exploration of the Main Stelae Group, this time under the supervision of Contenson (1959a). Contenson innovated to the extent that he laid out the first grid system on that portion of the site which he intended to excavate. The zone selected was north of the Nefas Mawcha and south of the terrace wall (M-1). The excavation revealed three superimposed levels. The uppermost level represented a continuation of the cemetery complex encountered west and southwest of Contenson's excavation area by Pironin back in 1955. Contenson removed the contents of 75 tombs in the course of excavation. The underlying level yielded an assemblage which, on the basis of the associated coinage, could be dated between the V and the VIII centuries A.D. The lowest level contained a rich assemblage including imported amphorae and artifacts of bronze and glass.

The following year, 1958, Contenson shifted his attention away from the Main Stelae Group, which had been the focus of Institute research since 1954, and selected several different targets for exploration (1963a). He extended the 1954 excavations of Doresse in the vicinity of the old Mariam Zion church. In the process he isolated three construction levels, the most recent being Postaxumite. This was underlain by a structural complex dating to between the IV and the VIII centuries A.D. The lowest structural level was identified by Contenson as early Axumite. A short distance from Kaleb's tomb, Contenson excavated a cruciform subterranean tomb named Addi Guatiya after the summit of the hill upon which it is located. Finally, in a small valley cut into the eastern side of Amba Beta Giorgis named Me'elan Debbas, which is located just to the north of Geza Agmai, Contenson put in a test trench at a site that appeared to him to be a collapsed tomb.

The site of Axum was not explored further by the Institute until 1966 when Francis Anfray (1972a) led a three-season campaign to expose a major architectural complex on the western periphery of the site in an area referred to as Dongur-Addi Kilte. The structure occupied an area of approximately 3000 square meters. After three seasons of excavation (1966, 1967, and 1968) a monumental 40-room complex, called the Dongur mansion, was revealed. The complex involved a central structure and a series of interior courtyards that created discrete blocks of rooms. Anfray estimates on the basis of the information gathered during excavation that the structure is of late Axumite age, approximately VII century A.D. He also proposes the interpretation that this is a villa of a member of the elite, not the royal palace.

In addition to excavations at the Dongur mansion, Anfray explored the numerous accumulations of rubble in the immediate vicinity that suggested several other large, palacelike residential complexes. He selected three locations in which to place stratigraphic test trenches, north, northeast, and east of the Dongur mansion, and in all three excavations Axumite architecture was uncovered.

The most recent excavation program at the site of Axum was initiated in 1973 by Neville Chittick (1974), director of the British East African Archaeological Institute. The excavation team led by Chittick consisted of a number of experienced archaeology assistants and a large local labor force. In the course of two field seasons Chittick was able to accomplish a highly ambitious program of excavation that promises to contribute new information on a number of critical monuments which, although the object of previous excavations, continued to resist interpretation. The most noteworthy example of this is the Main Stelae Group, which had been the subject of repeated excavation campaigns. Chittick, utilizing his large labor force, began a series of excavations that unearthed numerous new stelae to be added to the list originally recorded by the German Axum expedition.

In the process of excavation Chittick discovered a series of underground galleries and chambers dug into the bedrock underneath a considerable area of the Main Stelae Group, which he referred to as a catacomb. On the east side of the Main Stelae Group terrace, previously studied by both Pironin and Doresse, Chittick uncovered the Tomb of the Brick Arches, a subterranean complex cut out of rock to a depth of 8 meters below the present surface of the ground.

Another area repeatedly excavated in the past was the Nefas Mawcha, the giant granite slab that had been knocked off its supporting foundation by the force of impact resulting when the Giant Stele collapsed upon it. This feature had been previously interpreted, but Chittick's excavations provided him with new evidence indicating the need for an alternative interpretation regarding the manner in which the structure had been built. He suggested that it was a subterranean structure rather than one on top of the ground and that the vast slab of granite rested on a substructure of smaller slabs providing a central chamber with peripheral chambers all around.

In addition to the reinvestigation of some conspicuous features of the site, Chittick exposed new monuments that are equally impressive. The catacomb complex has already been mentioned. In addition, he discovered the Tomb of the False Door, a subterranean mortuary complex made of beautifully dressed granite connected to a surface structure which appeared to simulate a temple or palace. The mortuary chamber in the subterranean complex contained a stone sarcophagus. Immediately to the west of the Tomb of the False Door Chittick uncovered a small shaft tomb built of stone.

Excavations on the western flank of the Giant Stele revealed a "mausoleum" consisting of multiple subterranean tomb chambers, which were entered through a finely dressed granite door frame. The mausoleum is a monumental mortuary feature that adds to the already vast complex of architecture and to the episodes of major construction previously recorded for the Main Stelae Group sector. Another example of the complexity of this sector is the vaulted-roof structure uncovered by Chittick east of the Tomb of the False Door. Although still only partially exposed, this subterranean feature has doorway arches and a barrel-vault roof made of fired brick. Chittick's systematic and ambitious excavations at the Main Stelae Group ought to provide a firm idea of the nature of constructional developments in this complex and rich portion of the site of Axum upon completion of his analysis.

Chittick extended his excavation program beyond the confines of the Main Stelae Group to include Kaleb's tomb and the Gudit stelae field. Kaleb's tomb had been excavated by the German Axum expedition; Chittick approached the problem of further excavation by placing his trenches against the side of the exposed superstructure and cutting down until he encountered new structural remains. His explorations at the tomb convinced him that extensive and substantial architecture exists beyond what has already been exposed.

The Gudit stelae field, located on the western periphery of the site of Axum and just south of the Dongur mansion (excavated by Anfray), was originally mapped by the German Axum expedition. The area is currently under plow cultivation and the upturned earth reveals very high concentrations of pottery, indicating the presence of a substantial ancient settlement. In addition, however, over 100 stelae—many still upright—have been found. Only a few are dressed; most are somewhat irregular, representing the shapes that they assumed at the time that they were originally cut or split off from the parent rock. Chittick assigned a small excavation crew to excavate at the base of several stelae clusters. They uncovered tombs, one of which contained Egyptian glass goblets dated to the III or early IV century A.D. Numerous objects of iron were also uncovered.

Chittick did not concentrate exclusively on the monumental features at the site but initiated a series of small-scale excavations in portions of the site where he believed there would be a good chance of detecting a less disturbed stratigraphic sequence than that available in the immediate vicinity of the monuments already described. Three sectors were selected. Site ES, located north of the Ta'akha Mariam complex, was an area in which five trenches were placed. All encountered Axumite masonry construction that appeared to date to the VI century A.D. or later. Excavations at site IW, located close to the spot where Enda Semon is believed to have existed, brought about the discovery of a multistoried Axumite structure. Site HAW, located between the Main Stelae Group and the slopes of Amba Beta Giorgis, was less profitable, yielding little of archaeological interest. It is, however, a valuable site since the stratigraphy exposed in the course of excavations provided a vivid record of the erosional history of the Axum area. No additional excavations have been conducted at Axum since the end of the 1974 field season.

Ouchatei Golo   Ouchatei Golo is a site approximately 7 kilometers west of Axum, at the foot of the amba that has been the quarry source for the blue granite used in the fabrication of dressed stone for Axumite construction. It is also the area where large monolithic slabs of granite were cut for the production of stelae. Excavation conducted by Contenson (1959b, 1961a) revealed two connected multiroom structures in an architectural style termed classical Axumite. The structure appears to date to the VII or VIII century A.D. Undressed stelae are located in the immediate vicinity of the structure, which has one distinctive feature, a cistern located in an interior courtyard.

Selaklaka   Cossar (1945) conducted excavations at the site of Selaklaka, approximately 30 kilometers west of Axum, where Axumite architecture has been found. Cossar focused his attention on a pre-Christian necropolis at the site.

Yeha   The site of Yeha, some 50 kilometers east of Axum, has been noted on repeated occasions by travelers coming through the area. It was first mentioned by the Portuguese voyager Alvarez early in the sixteenth century (Anfray 1963b, 1972b, 1974b; Salt 1814). Alvarez mentioned the site as part of his itinerary and described the early South Arabian temple which still stands on the site. In 1769 Bruce (1790) passed through the valley of Yeha, noting the village but not mentioning anything about the archaeological monuments that are to be found there. In 1810 Salt (1814) visited Yeha and discovered the South Arabian inscriptions for which the site is famous. He made copies of a number of these inscriptions and they became the subject of considerable attention upon their publication. In 1893 James Bent (1893) went to the village of Yeha specifically for the purpose of investigating the temple and to secure additional information about inscriptions. The record of his visit includes detailed architectural descriptions.

The first scientifically trained team to examine the site was the German Axum expedition team in 1906 (Littmann, 1913a). The German expedition made a brief visit as part of their return trip to Asmara after completing excavations in Axum. They recorded architectural details of the temple and the ancient Ethiopian church and also reported the existence of a third major structure, which at that time was still only a mound of rubble. They recopied a number of the inscriptions.

Excavations began for the first time in 1960 when Anfray explored a necropolis of subterranean tombs located to the southeast of the temple. Seventeen tombs were excavated (Anfray 1963b, 1973c). Important new information was obtained on Preaxumite ceramics. The Yeha necropolis collection displays remarkable originality. Very fine objects of bronze were recovered along with a host of other distinctive artifact materials.

Over a decade passed before the Ethiopian Institute of Archaeology resumed its excavation program at the site of Yeha in 1971, again under the supervision of Francis Anfray (1972b, 1973c). During the seasons of 1971 and 1972 Anfray accomplished four principal objectives. He initiated excavation of the third structure originally reported by the German expedition, which is now referred to in the literature as the Grat-Beal-Guebri. He surveyed the village and adjacent areas for evidence of habitation which would date to the time of the major Preaxumite structures. He undertook to excavate stratigraphic test trenches at strategic points in the village of Yeha in order to secure a chronological sequence of occupation. These stratigraphic excavations under the immediate supervision of Rodolfo Fattovich (1972) were fairly successful. Finally, Anfray prepared a topographic map of the site for the purpose of maintaining an adequate spatial record of archaeological activity that had already taken place and that was planned for the immediate future.

In 1973 Anfray (1973b, 1973c) continued excavations of the Grat-Beal-Guebri structure, focusing on the central part of the mound. A structure of Preaxumite age that was encountered shows evidence of having been destroyed by a violent fire. According to Anfray the architectural style of the structure had not been reported previously; he dates it somewhere between the V and II centuries B.C. The mound which conceals the third structure is large, and only a portion has been exposed. On the basis of what he has already uncovered, however, Anfray is of the opinion that the structure was a palace. As in the case of Axum, no additional excavation was undertaken at Yeha after 1974.

Haoulti-Melazo   Haoulti and Melazo are two localities which have yielded surprisingly rich remains of the Preaxumite era. Together they refer to the area surrounding the valley of Mai Agazen, where Leclant (1959b), supported by the Ethiopian Institute, excavated two mounds during the 1955 and 1956 seasons. The first mound, referred to as Mound A or Gobochela, was located on the eastern bluff overlooking Mai Agazen. Excavation revealed a small structure which Leclant identified as a sanctuary to the god Almouqah. It contained numerous fragments of dressed stone which had South Arabian inscriptions. The second excavation was of Mound B, located in the vicinity of a village called Ota Kassahoun, east of the valley of Mai Agazen. It revealed a large complex structure with a staircase feature.

Excavations of the eastern side of the valley of Mai Agazen were resumed in 1958 under the supervision of Contenson (1961c). He excavated two mounds, both only a short distance from the Gobochela mound excavated by Leclant in 1955 and 1956. One of the mounds, Enda Cerqos, revealed the remains of two superimposed churches. The underlying structure was built in a basilica plan utilizing fragments of monuments that dated to the pre-Christian era. The overlying structure was built in a circular plan. The second mound examined by Contenson, identified by the place name of Mazaber, contained a small two-room structure.

In 1959 Contenson focused his attention on the western side of the Mai Agazen valley, on a small hill that takes its name (Haoulti) from the presence of large dressed stelae of calcareous tuff. This large-scale excavation involved the exposure of some 3000 square meters of site area, which represented almost complete excavation of the ruins (Contenson 1959b, 1963b). In the process two small temples were uncovered which were made of dressed blue granite, the type found in the vicinity of Axum. Excavation of the deposits in the vicinity of the stelae and temples revealed quantities of Preaxumite objects, including some remarkable seated figures in a South Arabian style. Bronze objects and many other fine specimens were uncovered from this extraordinarily rich deposit.

At the foot of Haoulti hill, to the south of the temple complex at its summit, Contenson discovered a cavity in a section of bedrock in which two basinlike repositories had been constructed. They yielded an abundance of exotic and fine artifacts.

On the basis of these excavations Contenson offered the hypothesis that the ruins represented two constructional phases. Phase I, consisting of calcareous tuff stelae, female statues on thrones, and bull and ibex sculptures and figures, denoted an original sanctuary for the god Almouqah and is believed to date to early in the Preaxumite area. During the second phase, also Preaxumite but later in time, the votive objects from the original sanctuary were reutilized in connection with a new sanctuary consisting of the pair of granite temples, indicating a continuity in worship despite a change in architectural tradition.

Although no additional excavation was undertaken in the Haoulti-Melazo area, interest in the information obtained and controversy over the hypotheses put forward by Contenson continued. In 1961 Jacqueline Pirenne (1970) conducted an on-site inspection of the area to test her suspicion that the South Arabian features recovered at the site of Haoulti and at the site of Gobochela were not found in situ but had been reutilized by later builders who had obtained the objects from some hitherto unknown original location (the early Preaxumite temple). The arguments with which she supported her suspicion included the following: (1) Both the Haoulti and the Gobochela sites were, according to their excavators, only single-component depositions but both yielded mixed assemblages with respect to artifact inventory. The mixed assemblages in both cases consisted of early and late Preaxumite material. (2) The early Preaxumite artifacts from both sites, and from the Enda Cerqos lower church, represent a single collection which had been parceled out over several sites, and they suggest a single structure more ancient in date from which they all originally derived. (3) On the basis of her survey she hypothesized that the original temple was located on the western bluff overlooking the Mai Agazen valley, approximately across from the vicinity of Gobochela, and that the original town which was associated with the early Preaxumite temple was located in the vicinity of Gobochela-Melazo. The two cult statues recovered from Haoulti that are now on display at the Archaeological Museum in Addis Ababa are the subject of a detailed analysis by Pirenne (1967).

Seglamien   A Preaxumite site which shows considerable architectural affinity to the structures excavated at Haoulti-Melazo was the focus of excavations undertaken by Lanfranco Ricci (1974) during the summer of 1974. Large quantities of constructional rubble and heavy concentrations of ceramic material indicate that Seglamien was a principal center during the Preaxumite era. Although the results of Ricci's excavations are incomplete, it is clear that they will reveal a settlement comparable in many respects to the one partially explored at Haoulti-Melazo. The site of Seglamien is located near Medogue, an Axumite site with stelae approximately 9 kilometers southwest of Axum.

Adulis   Adulis is one of the earliest Axumite sites to enter the pages of history and to undergo excavation. An initial survey of the site was undertaken as early as 1840 when Vignaud and Petit, two members of a French mission to Ethiopia, visited the site (Lefebvre 1845; Anfray 1963d). They prepared a map of the site marking the location of three "temples." In 1868 Lord Napier's expedition visited Adulis and exposed several ruins including the foundation of a church built in the Byzantine style with a semicircular apse (Anfray 1963d, 1974). The excavations produced both Axumite pottery and coinage, but they were not scientifically conducted and contributed little of lasting value.

The first scientific excavations were undertaken in the same year as the German expedition to Axum, 1906. During that year two separate parties visited the site for the purpose of excavation. One under the supervision of Sundström (1907; Anfray 1974a) conducted excavations in the northern sector of the site, exposing a large rectangular structure which Sundström called the "palace of Adulis." Axumite coinage of the VIII century A.D. was recovered. Paribeni (1908; Anfray 1974) also explored the site that year. He discovered two additional structures similar in many respects to the one uncovered by Sundström but of smaller dimensions. One he called "altar of the sun" (sanctuary); the other is a basilica with a semicircular apse. In the course of his excavations Paribeni laid out test trenches which encountered a group of ordinary dwellings.

More than half a century passed before Adulis was once again to become the object of archaeological excavation. During the seasons of 1961 and 1962, the Ethiopian Institute of Archaeology fielded an expedition under the supervision of Francis Anfray (1974) which made additional progress. Excavations undertaken during these two seasons uncovered the remains of ancient buildings that utilized fired brick. Masonry pilings used to support upper stories were also discovered. Pottery fragments collected in the course of excavation revealed strong affinities with the late Axumite period, between the VI and VIII centuries A.D., but some of the sherds recovered were clearly of early or Preaxumite provenance. A noteworthy observation made during the excavations was that grinding stones used to prepare flour from cereal grain were characteristically round in shape at Adulis whereas on the plateau they were characteristically oblong in shape. Nearly all coinage uncovered at Adulis is of Axumite origin, yet amphorae and other artifacts of Mediterranean manufacture were encountered. Adulis appears to have been pillaged and destroyed, from the layers of ash and charcoal Anfray observed in the uppermost levels of structures. No additional excavation work has been done at the site of Adulis since the end of the 1961 field season.

Matara Matara is perhaps the most important site on the edge of the Rift Valley escarpment. It lies almost midway between the Axumite port of Adulis and the Axumite capital of Axum and must have played a critical role in the kingdom. The site, just like Axum, Yeha, and Adulis, was commented on by a number of early travelers. In 1868 Denis de Rivoire (Anfray 1963a) reported the existence of the site, noting the stele, pottery, and dressed stone masonry that make up the conspicuous surface indications. In 1903 (Anfray 1963a) amateur excavations were undertaken by an Italian officer in two areas of the sites. No detailed records of the results of these excavations or maps which indicate their location are available, however. In 1905 Dainelli and Marinelli (1912; Anfray 1963a) visited the site and again reported the presence of architectural ruins.

The first scientific survey was, as usual, the product of the German Axum expedition. Having left Yeha, they chose a route of return to Asmara that allowed them to visit the site of Matara as well as other sites. Although they were there only a brief time, they managed to prepare a sketch map of the site which plotted several archaeological features. They also drew a detailed sketch of the Matara stele and of the base of a royal throne.

The Ethiopian Institute of Archaeology launched a major research effort at the site beginning in 1959 with a team under the supervision of Francis Anfray (1963a). The initial effort involved both the 1959 and 1960 field seasons, with the object of excavating Mound A, located 100 meters northwest of the famous Matara stele, at the foot of a small, rocky hill. Excavation exposed a building complex that included tombs and yielded large quantities of artifacts for study.

The next phase of research at Matara took place during the field seasons of 1961, 1962, and 1963 (Anfray and Annequin 1965; Anfray 1963e). Two additional mounds were excavated not far from the mound excavated in 1959 and 1960. One of them, referred to as Mound B in the literature, yielded a single, large, multiroom architectural complex. The other mound contained two distinct architectural groupings, each assigned its own designation: groups C and D. The sprawling multiroom complexes were found to contain not only large quantities of conventional artifact material but also remarkably beautiful exhibition-quality objects of gold, bronze, and stone. Many of the finest pieces in the Axumite collection of the Archaeology Museum in Addis Ababa are from the excavations of Matara.

During the 1964 season Anfray (1967) shifted his strategy and focused his efforts on a cluster of rock-cut tombs on the Goual-Saim hill. The contents of these tombs represent a fine, fully controlled sample for comparisons with tomb contents uncovered at Axum and Yeha during previous seasons.

In 1965 Anfray increased the amount of excavated urban architecture by exploring Mounds E and F. Both yielded the same kind of sprawling multiroom structures that had been found in earlier mounds excavated at the site.

After six seasons of intensive effort Matara has become one of the best-documented archaeological sites in the Axumite Kingdom. Although the final monograph is still being prepared by Anfray, we already know enough to identify some of the more notable features of this very important site. First, it is clearly a key urban center within the Axumite Kingdom. The site is large by Axumite standards, occupying approximately 20 hectares. Excavations have exposed more architecture at Matara than at any other site, and the architecture has surprising variability. Anfray found not only tombs and churches but also elite residences and quantities of ordinary dwellings. This will enable future analysts to examine a number of sociological and economic aspects of the site in a way heretofore not possible, since earlier excavation programs at Axumite sites had concentrated on monumental architectural features.

The site deposit is rich and deep. Some of Anfray's stratigraphic excavations extend down as far as 5 meters. The profiles of his trenches are the only ones so far reported among Axumite sites to yield Preaxumite and Axumite levels in controlled superpositional contexts. Anfray suggests on the basis of his analysis of the stratified deposits that the artifacts which had been derived from them represent two principal phases of occupation: an early phase dating from 500 to 300 B.C., which he classifies as the South Arabian period, and a second phase, separated from the first by a long era of abandonment, that dates to 700 A.D. Excavations here were terminated at the end of the 1965 field season but the quantities of artifacts and features uncovered during the many seasons of work continue to occupy the attention of the staff at the Ethiopian Archaeological Institute. Systematic studies are already becoming available. Anfray (1968b), for example, has published a study of the pottery from Matara.

Inscriptions   The initial corpus of paleographic material to occupy the attention of Ethiopian scholars was the result of surveys, both systematic and casual, conducted over many years. A concerted effort to document available inscriptions at many Axumite sites was undertaken by the German Axum expedition and the publications that ensued offered a thorough presentation of that material. However, the recent dramatic increases in the number of reported inscriptions are a product of the many excavation campaigns sponsored by the Ethiopian Institute of Archaeology.

Virtually all sites that underwent extensive excavation from the 1950s through the 1970s yielded new inscription finds. These have been analyzed and reported upon in the *Annales d'Ethiopie* by two scholars, Drewes and Schneider. In 1959 Drewes published new inscriptions from Melazo. Schneider published new inscriptions from Enda Cerqos in 1961. In 1967 Drewes and Schneider together published new inscriptions from Axum and Matara. Inscriptions from both the Haoulti-Melazo area and Yeha were published in 1970 by Drewes and Schneider. In 1972 they wrote

an article reporting inscriptions from Matara, and in the same year
Schneider published more inscriptions from Yeha as well as from Matara.

This is a highly important by-product of excavation in the Axumite
area, since without this new paleographic material momentum in historical
scholarship cannot be sustained. The value of these inscriptions is made
abundantly clear in the accompanying pages of Kobishchanov's work
where he draws upon them to reconstruct many aspects of Axumite culture
history and Axumite society.

Archaeological Survey

Excavation is not the only strategy of research available to the archaeologist.
An increasingly important role is being played by archaeological survey.
The reasons for this are many and some will become clear in the course of
my review of the results of more recent efforts at survey within the Axumite
Kingdom.

Early Survey Efforts   By restricting ourselves to the survey efforts of
scholarly personnel, the early phase can be regarded as having begun in
the year 1906 when a cluster of archaeological expeditions arrived in
Ethiopia and the colony of Eritrea to undertake systematic documentation
of sites. The surveys were accomplished by the study of surface features,
which were susceptible to ready observation, as well as by modest excavation efforts designed to explore on a preliminary basis some of the ruins
found at the sites. The most productive survey effort during the early
phase was clearly that of the German Axum expedition (Littmann 1913a,
1913b). Documentation of surface features through photography and
artists' renderings and sketches, together with the faithful copying of
selective artifacts and inscriptions, contributed to the high scientific value
of the expedition's effort. In the pages of their publication we have our
first adequate report on Axum, Abba Penteleon, Ashafi, Yeha, Matara,
Kaskase, Tokonda, and Kohaito.

During the same year, Piva (1907) undertook a modest exploratory
excavation at the site of Aratou, northwest of Asmara, which resulted in
the discovery of Axumite ruins. Tokonda was the site of exploratory excavations carried out by Garelli around the same time (Anfray 1963d). Dainelli
and Marinelli (1912; Anfray 1963d) at this time undertook a geological
and ethnological survey of the Italian colony of Eritrea, conscientiously
documenting all archaeological sites encountered during their survey.
Those of notable importance include Deqe Mehari, Rora Laba, and of
course Aratou. By the end of this early phase of survey, a good number of
the principal Axumite-Preaxumite sites had been plotted on regional maps,
and some indication of what they contained was available.

Archaeological Survey in the World War II Era   From the late 1930s through the mid-1940s there was little archaeological activity in the Axumite area of Northern Ethiopia. Only two surveys of any consequence were undertaken during that time, one by Davico (1946) of sites in the Senafe region and the other by Monneret de Villard (1938) of Axum and its immediate vicinity. Monneret de Villard's survey was especially note-worthy since it was concerned principally with recording topographic and related geomorphological observations, and thus represented a new dimen-sion of survey effort, which was to be resumed in the early 1970s by Karl Butzer.

Archaeological Survey in the 1950s   The Ethiopian Institute of Ar-chaeology gave top priority to the systematic and scientific excavation of the principal sites within the Axumite Kingdom, but during this effort a number of important discoveries were made on additional sites not recorded or adequately examined previously. Survey, it seems, was ancil-lary to excavation, and the results of these surveys were published only on an irregular basis in the *Annales d'Ethiopie*.

The incidental surveys were often motivated, as they were in the early phase of survey, by a desire to recover additional inscriptions or other noteworthy monuments. Yet the cumulative result of surveys during the 1950s was substantial. In the Makale region surveys were undertaken by Caquot and Drewes (1955). In the Senafe area surveys were undertaken by Franchini and Ricci (1954), whose efforts led to further examination of Dibdib. In the Adigrat region that lies between the Senafe and Makale regions Miquel undertook a survey in October 1955 (Leclant and Miquel 1959). He discovered three sites of considerable importance to Axumite studies: Etch-Mare, Sabea, and Seglat. At Sabea, Miquel reported the discovery of caches of pottery and bronze not unlike those found at the foot of the Haoulti hill in the Haoulti-Melazo region.

In the immediate environs of the site of Axum, Contenson (1961b) carried on surveys during his excavation seasons at Axum. As a result, four important sites came into the archaeological record. Medebai, located approximately 10 kilometers north of Axum, is almost inaccessible but was visited by members of the Institute's staff, who reported abundant ruins. Medogue, originally reported by Hailemariam (1955), was examined further by Contenson. The site is located 8 kilometers southwest of Axum, only a short distance north of Seglamien, where Ricci was to conduct excavations in 1974. Numerous undressed stelae were observed at the site, together with quantities of pottery. Contenson classified this site as pre-Christian Axumite. Another site reported as a result of Contenson's efforts is Kouhi, 11 kilometers south of Axum. Stelae were also observed there. As in the case of Medogue, Contenson identified the site as pre-Christian

Axumite. A final important site discovered in the environs of Axum during the 1950s is Mahabere Dyagoue, approximately 5 kilometers southwest of the site of Haoulti. An ancient churchlike structure was observed underlying a present-day church. This site was examined after a bronze figure of a bull acquired by Contenson for the museum was reported to have been found there.

In Asmara and its vicinity an amateur named Tringali (1965) had, over the years, conducted archaeological survey that resulted in the discovery of approximately 40 sites both within the town of Asmara and in its immediate outskirts. A good number of these contained Axumite pottery. Tringali's efforts have served the very important purpose of correcting the mistaken impression that there was not much Axumite settlement in the Asmara region.

Archaeological Survey in the 1960s   During the 1960s, the Ethiopian Archaeological Institute still gave archaeological survey a position secondary to excavation. Despite this, however, a number of important sites were reported for the first time in several strategic areas. Reports published by Anfray (1965a, 1965b, 1970) and others (e.g., Ricci 1961) described the new sites.

Most of the excavation during the 1960s was directed at the site of Matara, so most of the new sites uncovered are located in the area between Senafe and Makale, close to the main highway. They include such sites as Enda Maryam-Tsion-Tahot, Bihat (where two stelae were found), and Fekya, which is reported to have remains of a Preaxumite temple. A small mound was observed at Me'erad-Ouorqi. Extensive Axumite ruins are reported from Biet-Abba-Hanni and at Ham. Fired bricks, an uncommon feature, and Axumite pottery were observed at the site of Maryam-Kedi. Additional Axumite ruins were found at Mazret and at Heoula-Tcherqos.

In the province of Eritrea four new sites were reported which date to the Axumite or Preaxumite period. Zala-Bet-Meka is a site comprising an area of more than 4 hectares, with Axumite pottery and remains of dressed stone architecture. Another site, Woqerti, reveals Axumite pottery and an abundance of grattoirs (scrapers). Axumite pottery was also found at a site just outside of Asmara named Mai Melatse. And the site of Ona-Hachel contained both Axumite and Preaxumite pottery.

Archaeological Survey in the 1970s   The pattern already described in the 1950s and 1960s continued into the early 1970s, with survey still an ancillary mission as far as the Ethiopian Institute of Archaeology is concerned. However, even by the early 1970s a number of important sites had come to light. These are reported by Anfray in a recent publication (1973a) in which he also provides an up-to-date map of many of the

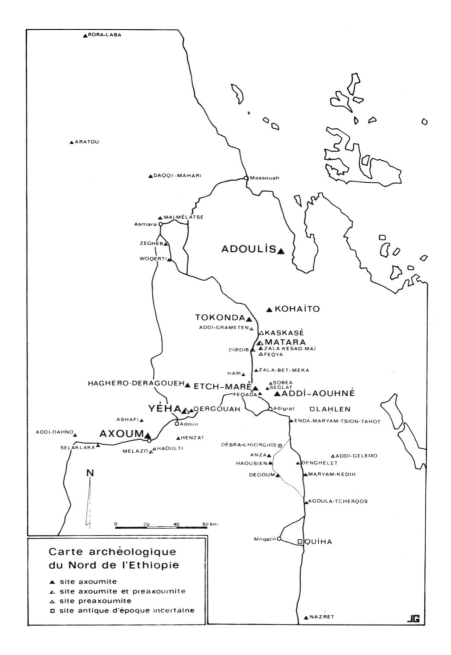

RORA-LABA

ARATOU

DAQQI-MAHARI

Massouah

MAÏ-MÉLATSE
Asmara
ZEGHEB
WOQERTI

ADOULIS

KOHAÏTO

TOKONDA
ADDI-GRAMETEN
KASKASÉ
MATARA
DIRDIB ZALA-KESAD-MAÏ
FEQYA
ZALA-BET-MEKA
HAM
HAGHERO-DERAGOUEH ETCH-MARÉ SOBÉA
SEGLAT
ADDI-AOUHNÉ
FEQADA
YÉHA DERGOUAH
Adoua Adigrat LAHLEN
ASHAFI
ADDI-DAHNO AXOUM ENDA-MARYAM-TSION-TAHOT
HENZAT
SELAKLAKA DÉBRA-GHIORGHIS
MELAZO HAOULTI ANZA
HAOUSIEN DENGHELET ADDI-GELEMO
DEGOUM MARYAM-KEDIH

N

AGOULA-TCHERQOS

0   20   40   60 km

Maqallé QUIHA

Carte archéologique
du Nord de l'Ethiopie

▲ site axoumite
⚲ site axoumite et preaxoumite
△ site preaxoumite
□ site antique d'époque incertaine

NAZRET

JG

Map 3. Archaeological sites in the nuclear area of the Axumite Kingdom.
(From Francis Anfray, "Nouveaux sites antiques." *Journal of Ethiopian Studies*,
vol. XI, no. 2, 1973)

principal Axumite and Preaxumite sites thus far recorded (Map 3 in this book). It is important to realize, however, that the sites selected for inclusion on this map are sites where there is a demonstrable presence of major architecture dating to the Axumite or Preaxumite periods.

The more important sites to be documented during the early 1970s include Lahlen, Addi Aouhne, Haousien, Anza, Degoum, Debre Georgis, and Bietqooqos. The latter was reported by Anfray in a separate paper (1973b). All of these sites are from the Adigrat region. They date to the Axumite period, although exactly when during that period of time they were occupied cannot be determined without further study. The Adigrat group yielded additional stelae: four from Haousien, and one with a Ge'ez inscription from Anza.

The excavation program at Yeha also contributed new knowledge of Axumite and Preaxumite sites in the vicinity of that village, again as a result of incidental survey on the part of Anfray and his excavation staff. Sebra-Aboun, Seqoualou, Sefa-Tourkui, and Haghero-Deragoueh were all recorded in the general area of Yeha. As in the case of the Adigrat group, these sites were variously Preaxumite and Axumite in age. A potentially productive site for further study would be Haghero-Deragoueh, which contained, in addition to Axumite pottery and ruins, fragments of amphorae of Mediterranean manufacture. A final site reported during this period in the Yeha region is Deragoueh. This is an Axumite site at which Anfray observed pottery that appears to indicate that the Yeha area has considerably greater ceramic affinity to Axum than it does to the eastern group of Axumite sites in the area of Adigrat. Around Axum itself the important site of Henzat, containing stelae and Axumite ruins, was revisited by Lanfranco Ricci in 1974 (Ricci 1974).

Systematic Survey   As my previous comments have illustrated, archaeological survey in the Axumite region has undergone two recognizable phases. An early pioneering phase was linked to the recovery of inscriptions and the exploration of prominent Axumite and Preaxumite sites. A second phase was ushered in with the formation of the Ethiopian Institute of Archaeology, when survey became an ancillary activity associated with major excavation programs. During this second phase, the recovery of inscriptions was largely a product of excavation efforts rather than survey efforts, and survey was a nominal undertaking that was concerned principally with filling out the archaeological map, with very little attention spent on analysis.

In the 1970s, however, a third strategy of survey was inaugurated by the work of Karl Butzer and Joseph Michels. Butzer (n.d.) visited Axum in 1971 and 1973 to study certain paleo-ecological features of the landscape that might contribute to our understanding of the impact of Axumite society on the landscape and help to explain the role played by the environment on the development of the Axumite Kingdom. He took advantage of the excellent stratigraphic sections that had been exposed by Chittick's excavation in 1973 to study in detail the history of soil erosion and alluvial processes in the immediate vicinity of Axum, and to use this as a basis for interpreting geomorphological characteristics that could be observed more generally throughout the area. His preliminary study, still unpublished, Butzer considers only a first step in a larger systematic study of the broad ecological systems within which the Axumite Kingdom evolved. He acknowledges that only through a comparison of detailed paleo-ecological studies of a larger number of sites in diverse topographic and climatic environments will we achieve an understanding of the role of ecological factors in the economic vicissitudes of the Axumite Kingdom.

My research is of a somewhat different order (Michels 1975). It begins with the assumption that the dynamics of Axumite society can be understood only in terms of a total picture of the settlement system. With a grant from the National Science Foundation I undertook a settlement-pattern survey during the first half of 1974. The area selected for the survey was a 500-square-kilometer segment of the Shiré plateau (a rolling upland 2100–2400 meters in elevation) that extends from just southwest of Axum to the valley of Yeha, approximately 50 kilometers to the northeast. The limits of the plateau escarpment, to the north and south, placed natural constraints on the width of the survey strip, which thus averaged about 10 kilometers. A stratified random sampling procedure was employed, and a 40-percent sampling of the region was achieved. The archaeological region was grided into approximately 20 zones of 25 square kilometers; each was further subdivided into 25 areas of 1 square kilometer. The 25 areas within each zone were assigned numbers and, using a table of random numbers, approximately half of the areas were selected from within each zone for systematic ground-surface survey. The 40-percent sample actually achieved meant that the surface of 200 square kilometers had been thoroughly surveyed.

During the dry season the Northern Ethiopian uplands are virtually without vegetation; the soils are directly exposed to view in all localities, enabling the archaeologist to detect even modest surface traces of settlement. Local workers were hired to participate in skirmish lines which moved back and forth throughout each 1-square-kilometer area chosen for examination. When a site was located, a collecting unit was defined— usually a square, 10 meters by 10 meters. The workers were then employed to "vacuum" up every pottery sherd or artifact within the collecting unit. If the site were large or complex, several such units would be defined and collected. In a number of cases, where the terrain did not lend itself to the isolation of a collecting unit, a collection would be taken from throughout the site area. Site collections would range in number from 200 to several thousand sherds, but in general the collection averaged about 500 sherds.

In addition to taking collections, a survey report was prepared that included information on site size, topography, vegetation, hydrology, soil, and description of any cultural features at the site such as architectural traces, terracing, or workshop concentrations of lithic artifacts. A photographic record of the site was also prepared. Finally, a local resident would be interviewed with regard to current land-use patterns, agricultural productivity of the soil, types of crops grown, rotation and fallowing schedules, identity of nearest market town, and what (if any) economic specialization characterized the local community, for example, pottery making or the cultivation of a special crop. I hoped that such information would enable me to describe present-day economic networks which could serve as a paradigm in the reconstruction of earlier phases.

All site locations were recorded in 1 / 30,000-scale aerial photographs. The photography was done by the U.S. Air Force in 1963 and generously made available to me by the Ethiopian Cartographic Institute. Since no topographic map of the survey region exists, these same photos in stereo overlays were used to produce by photogrammetric techniques a topographic map with 20-meter contour intervals. The result of the survey was the discovery and documentation of approximately 250 archaeological sites. These sites are indicated on Map 4 and are coded in accordance with the kind of site they represent.

The phasing of survey sites has been accomplished on a preliminary basis as of this writing and the results suggest that eight distinct culture historical phases can be isolated, each with an average duration of approximately 225 years. Preliminary examination of the spatial configurations of settlement for each phase strongly indicates that there are significant differences in settlement patterning and consequently in political and economic networking. This would suggest that the results of a settlement system analysis will contribute to our understanding of developmental processes that are mirrored in the historical narrative of the Axumite Kingdom. As in the case of paleo-ecological survey, settlement-pattern survey needs to be extended to other areas where there is reason to believe key population segments were located.

Recent Synthesis Based on Excavation Data

Perhaps the most prolific interpreter of Axumite archaeology in recent years has been Francis Anfray, currently the head of the French archaeological mission to Ethiopia. In the late 1960s he gave us the evolutionary scheme which is still the most widely applied (Anfray 1967, 1968a). It calls for a three-period development: a South Arabian period, an Intermediate period, and an Axumite period.

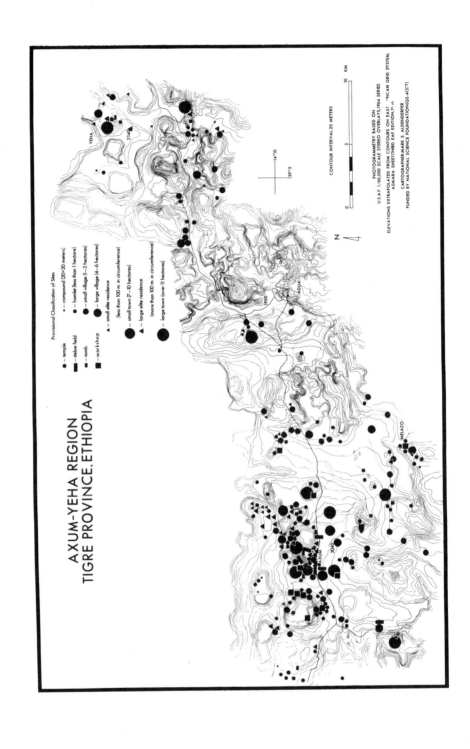

AXUM-YEHA REGION
TIGRE PROVINCE, ETHIOPIA

Provisional Classification of Sites

▲ — temple
▬ — stelae field
■ — tomb
■ — workshop

· — compound (20×20 meters)
● — hamlet (less than 1 hectare)
● — small village (1—3 hectares)
● — large village (4—6 hectares)
▲ — small elite residence

(less than 100 m in circumference)
● — small town (7—10 hectares)
▲ — large elite residence
(more than 100 m in circumference)
● — large town (over 11 hectares)

YEHA

2146

1900

ADUA

AXUM

2046

MELAZO

N

14°10

39°5

CONTOUR INTERVAL 20 METERS

0   5   10   KM

PHOTOGRAMMETRY BASED ON
U.S.A.F. 1/60,000 SCALE STEREO OVERLAYS, 1964 SERIES
ELEVATIONS EXTRAPOLATED FROM CONTOURS ON EAST "RICAN GRID SYSTEM,
ASMARA SHEET(THIRD E.A.F. EDITION),"
CARTOGRAPHER:MARK S. ALDENDERFER
FUNDED BY NATIONAL SCIENCE FOUNDATION(GS 41327)

The South Arabian (or Ethiopo-Sabaean) period extends from the beginning of the V century B.C. to the end of the IV century B.C. During this era indigenous "Proto-Ethiopians" are exposed to South Arabian culture and assimilate it rapidly. Anfray suggests that a truly sedentary settlement pattern may emerge for the first time during this phase. Certainly it represents the first time masonry construction is practiced. The influence of South Arabian civilization is intense. Affinities are overwhelming in cases such as the architecture at Yeha, the sculptures at Haoulti-Melazo, and the boustrophedon-type inscriptions observed at numerous sites. The pottery complex for this period is, however, only poorly controlled taxonomically.

The Intermediate period extends from the beginning of the III century B.C. to the beginning of the Christian era. Although the assimilation of South Arabian culture continues, it does so at a much slower pace; contact between the two regions is considerably weakened. Noteworthy developments during this period are regarded by Anfray as having their basis in the preceding period. Distinctive archaeological traits of the Intermediate period are a less geometric script, red and black pottery of fine quality, and the more common occurrence of bronze and iron artifacts. Sites which are associated with this period include Yeha (the tombs), Matara, Fekya, Zeban-Mororo, Li'Lay-Addi, Gobo-Fenseh, and Haoulti. Anfray reports that as many as 60 inscriptions dating to this phase have been collected from sites in the Akkele Guzai region, suggesting that this area may have been particularly heavily populated. Anfray speculates that it was during this period that the port of Adulis was first established.

The Axumite period is the longest, extending from the beginning of the I century A.D. to about the end of the IX century A.D. Anfray sees this as a florescent stage in the developmental sequence. And although elements of the Preaxumite stage persist—language, writing, religion, religious symbolism—they do so in a modified form. Axumite culture assumes a character peculiarly its own. In architecture, the major structures are rigidly square or rectangular in outline. Foundations are built in tiers which are alternately projecting or recessed. All construction conveys a massive aspect, including the monolithic monuments produced from dressed granite, such as stelae, throne bases, and giant daises. In writing, the Sabaean script is still in use but Ge'ez is flourishing, and Greek is also utilized. Locally minted coinage in gold, silver, and bronze makes its appearance around the III century A.D. Pottery exhibits new vessel shapes and new modes of decoration. Artifacts of foreign manufacture show up in the archaeological record of this phase, demonstrating the important role of long-distance trade.

Anfray tentatively proposes a subdivision of the Axumite period into at least two epochs: Epoch I (III and IV centuries A.D.) and Epoch II (VI to VIII century A.D.). He assigns to Epoch I such features of the site of Axum as Nefas Mawcha, throne bases, Enda Semon, Enda Mika'el, Ta'akha Mariam, and the giant stelae. The features assigned to Epoch II include Kaleb's tomb at Axum, plus the major portion of the Axumite ruins at such sites as Ham, Goulo-Makeda, Matara, Tokonda, Kohaito, Aratou, and Adulis.

Regionalism within the Axumite Kingdom became apparent to Anfray after comparison of archaeological assemblages which had reached a critical mass by the early 1970s. By 1973 Anfray was able to propose a distinction between two archaeological provinces during the Axumite period (1973a): an *eastern* and a *western* province.

The eastern province incorporates all Axumite sites located in the regions of Akkele Guzai and Agame. From Kohaito to Degoum, they constitute an especially dense concentration of major settlements displaying considerable prosperity, occupying a central position in the affairs of the Axumite Kingdom.

The western province includes the sector in which Addi Dahno and Selaklaka are located and extends from there eastward to incorporate the plain of Axum, the region of Adua, and the environs of Yeha. This province, notwithstanding the prestige and importance of its capital (Axum), does not seem, according to Anfray, to have known a prosperity similar to the eastern province's. Major sites appear to be less numerous. Pottery at the sites seems less abundant, and the vessel forms and decorative elements more simple. One possible explanation put forth by Anfray is that the western province reached its zenith in the early Axumite epoch and gradually gave way to the eastern province during the later epoch. This is especially evident with respect to church construction. Anfray observes that there are comparatively fewer church ruins in the western province.

The broad outlines of the history of settlement have been sketched by Anfray (1972a). He indicates that the sites of Kaskase, Matara, and Yeha represent key centers during the original colonization effort on the part of the kingdom of Saba and other South Arabian groups. In the vicinity of these centers, and elsewhere, the South Arabians successfully implanted villages of colonials, who developed a viable economy based on agricultural practices which they brought with them. Anfray (1972b) maintains that the relationship between Marib, capital of the Sabaean Kingdom, and Yeha, capital of the Ethiopian "South Arabian" colonies, is overwhelmingly documented by recent archaeological excavations.

Two inscriptions were found at Melazo which specifically mentioned Marib together with the name of a person also mentioned in an inscription from Yeha. The sites themselves—Marib and Yeha—were fully contemporaneous, on the evidence of a number of stylistic cross-correlations. The technique of dressing stone and the masonry construction techniques were virtually identical. At Yeha as at Marib the same decorative elements were applied to wall panels. The use of pillars of dressed stone in the construction of important buildings is a feature shared by both sites. The inscriptions in high relief found at Yeha are unique within Ethiopia and are not numerous in South Arabia generally. However, they are found throughout the vicinity of Marib.

Despite this evidence, Anfray argues that Yeha should not be considered a replica of Marib. Its similarity with other important sites in the vicinity of Marib, such as Sirwah, is just as great. What this suggests to Anfray is that the colonizing population was drawn from the Marib region, not from Marib itself.

Then, during the I century A.D., the population of the western Axumite province gradually abandoned its Preaxumite towns and villages in preference for new localities—away from the plateau drainage system, which had been a favored setting, and onto the broad plains.

A seeming paradox is evident when one considers that the paramount center for both the Preaxumite and Axumite periods—Yeha and Axum, respectively—are located in the western province, while the archaeological record seems to suggest that the eastern province was considerably more important. Anfray raises the question as to why, and queries whether it could be due to the particular "power" of the people who inhabited the western province. Anfray (1972a, 1974a) makes the observation that neither the power of Axum nor its security was threatened. It had no need, at least during most of its existence, to take steps to preserve its independence. Thus Axumite settlements have a certain permanence, as is clearly seen in Axumite architecture. Anfray notes that practically all important Axumite sites exhibit buildings constructed on a monumental scale.

Of particular interest in this regard are the palace-scale elite residences to be found at such sites as Axum and Matara. Anfray prefers to call them "villas" (1974a) so as to highlight the similarity he and others have perceived between them and comparable structures reported in Syria that date to the same epoch. He argues that the qualities of sobriety, rigidity, and rationality that pervade Axumite architecture appear to have been inspired by the Roman style. The resemblance is believed to be a general one, but nevertheless Anfray believes that the idea of the villa comes from the Near East. The work of George Tchalenko is frequently referred to by Anfray (1974a). Tchalenko (1953) conducted a study of the history of architecture in northern Syria. Many of the comments he makes concerning Roman villas of northern Syria seem to be equally applicable to Axumite villas. Anfray suggests that the source of the Syrian ideas might have been missionaries of Syrian nationality who spread Roman-Byzantine traditions together with Christianity.

Summary

This essay has attempted to provide the reader with an overview of the history of archaeological research on the Axumite region. Future research could profitably continue many of the programs which have already been initiated. By taking this tack, it seems possible to identify approximately a half-dozen principal research tasks that ought to be the focus of future archaeological exploration.

The commitment which the Ethiopian Institute of Archaeology has maintained since 1952 to the excavation of major sites, and especially those portions of major sites which yield monumental structures or artifacts of extraordinary significance, ought to continue. It is the desire to interpret and to relate the impressive achievements of Axumite civilization that motivates most other strategies of research, and it is only through continued exploration of the major sites that achievements of this civilization will continue to be made known. Another very important by-product of excavations at major sites is the recovery of goods of foreign manufacture which help document the larger interaction sphere in which the Axumite Kingdom has evolved. And finally, such excavations continuously unearth new paleographic documents that augment the historical tradition that has so well served Ethiopianists.

Major centers also have zones of habitation which need exploration so that the demographic aspect of these centers can be fully documented. It is only from studying such areas of major sites that we can expect to learn something about craft specialization, community organization, and levels of social stratification. Chittick (1974) in his preliminary report expressed an interest in exploring these areas within the site of Axum as a part of future excavation campaigns. Anfray in his excavations at Matara did in fact explore portions of the site that yielded ordinary habitations, and his research at Yeha involved survey activities designed to identify the location of such habitations.

The still unpublished manuscript by Karl Butzer (n.d.) in which he examines the history of erosion and alluviation at Axum and its immediate vicinity demonstrates the importance of ecological studies. Only through them can we reconstruct the sequence of environmental changes that serve as a framework for the economic, political, and social changes that we may be able to document archaeologically. The role of ecological analysis in the interpretation of cultural evolution is well documented, and it is very likely that key transformations in the historical trajectory of the Axumite Kingdom may be explained in part by environmental factors. It can only be hoped that large-scale paleo-ecological surveys of both the western and eastern provinces of the Axumite Kingdom can be carried out in the near future.

The regional settlement-pattern studies which I conducted in the western Axumite province seem to have been successful in uncovering a history of settlement that can now be correlated with major changes at important sites in the province. When fully analyzed, the data ought to very sensitively document shifts in agricultural strategy and alterations in the organization and distribution of population over the landscape. This will enable us to glimpse the economic, political, and demographic frameworks within which sites such as Axum, Yeha, and Haoulti-Melazo have undergone growth, modification, and, ultimately, abandonment. Similar campaigns of surface survey ought to be conducted at varying parts of the eastern province (in Akkele Guzai and Agame). Only through such surveys can we evaluate the observations made by Anfray suggesting that the eastern province was perhaps more densely inhabited than the western province.

Such surveys will also permit us to explore the phenomenon of regionalism more sensitively, since we can measure it with the artifacts of large numbers of sites rather than being limited to the comparison of only a handful. It may turn out that regionalism that is archaeologically discernible as a result of settlement survey will coincide to some extent with the tribal units that are referred to in the inscriptions, and which appear to have been the basis for much of the political organization of the kingdom, according to arguments provided by Kobishchanov in the accompanying work.

There are, however, certain kinds of comparisons which cannot be made with the characteristically mundane material culture recoverable through survey of ordinary village and town settlements. Comparisons that involve exotic artifacts, artifacts that are utilized in connection with major religious or political events, or artifacts that serve as conspicuous symbols of high social class are simply unavailable in all but the major centers of the kingdom. Such artifacts, including monumental architecture, stelae, and the burial furnishings of elaborate tombs, need further comparative analysis along the lines which have already been explored by the German Axum expedition and more recently by Anfray.

Of utmost importance in the minds of virtually every archaeologist who has worked in the area is the need to construct a sensitive and reliable absolute chronology. The sheer complexity of constructional phases at the major sites, and the large numbers of discrete settlements throughout the landscape, can be properly interpreted only when they have been assigned to phase units that permit reliable comparison. As of this writing no radiocarbon dates have been run on samples from any Axumite sites. This must be rectified at an early date. Anfray has indicated that a charcoal sample from Yeha is in the process of being dated. As Anfray observed, many of the building phases at major sites exhibit evidence—concentrations of ash and charcoal—of having been destroyed violently. These events often represent critical points on a time continuum in the history of a complex society. Chronometric control of these events would be of inestimable value to the preparation of an adequate phase chronology.

The preliminary results of pottery-seriation and of obsidian hydration dating that I have obtained on data recovered during surface survey are very promising. If the preliminary results are supported by more intensive analyses, the result would suggest that even rural village-level sites within the Axumite region are susceptible to dating within a chronological scheme that involves phase categories representing no more than 225 years' duration (Michels 1975). Radiocarbon dating from major sites would be necessary for the evaluation and refinement of any chronological scheme resulting from pottery-seriation and obsidian hydration dating.

Perhaps one of the most provocative aspects of Axumite archaeology is the fact that it has a historical narrative from which it can derive a problem orientation. The opportunity to explore the many provocative hypotheses that are put forth by Kobishchanov in the accompanying work is an exciting prospect. Kobishchanov has offered numerous tentative reconstructions that give focus to Axumite institutions, society, culture, and history. That focus can guide problem-oriented research for years to come. It was this aspect of Kobishchanov's book that impelled me to seek his cooperation in having it published in an up-to-date and fully revised English edition. Many of the speculative reconstructions that Kobishchanov deduces from documentary sources appear to be amenable to archaeological testing. Conversely, much of the patterning that Anfray discerned and which I review in this essay—the more conspicuous period partitions, the notion of regionalism, and even the apparent relationship between Axum and northern Syria—can now be explored in terms of the historical record. Kobishchanov's *Axum* is an important synthesis of a long tradition of historical scholarship. For the archaeologist his book offers an incentive for problem-oriented research.

References Cited

Adams, William Y.
  1974   Sacred and secular politics in ancient Nubia. *World Archaeology*, vol. 6, no. 1, pp. 39–51. London.
Anfray, Francis
  1963a   La première campagne de fouilles à Matara, près de Senafe (novembre 1959–janvier 1960). *Annales d'Ethiopie*, vol. V. Addis Ababa.
  1963b   Une campagne de fouilles a Yeha (février-mars, 1960). *Annales d'Ethiopie*, vol. V, pp. 171–232. Addis Ababa.

1963c   Institut Ethiopien d'archéologie. *Tarik*, no. 1, pp. 17–18. Addis Ababa.
1963d   Histoire de l'archéologie éthiopienne. *Tarik*, no. 1, pp. 17–23. Addis Ababa.
1963e   Matara. *Tarik*, no. 2, pp. 36–40. Addis Ababa.
1965a   Chronique archéologique (1960–1964). *Annales d'Ethiopie*, vol. VI, pp. 3–48. Addis Ababa.
1965b   Note sur quelques poteries Axoumites. *Annales d'Ethiopie*, vol. VI, pp. 217–220. Addis Ababa.
1967   Matara. *Annales d'Ethiopie*, vol. VII, pp. 33–88. Addis Ababa.
1968a   Aspects de l'archéologie éthiopienne. *Journal of African History*, vol. IX, no. 3, pp. 345–366. London.
1968b   La poterie de Matarā. *Rassegna di Studi Etiopici*, vol. XXII, pp. 5–74. Rome.
1970   Notes archéologiques. *Annales d'Ethiopie*, vol. VIII, pp. 31–56. Addis Ababa.
1972a   L'archéologie d'Axoum en 1972. *Paideuma*, vol. XVII, pp. 60–78.
1972b   Fouilles de Yeha. *Annales d'Ethiopie*, vol. IX, pp. 45–64. Addis Ababa.
1973a   Nouveaux sites antiques. *Journal of Ethiopian Studies*, vol. XI, no. 2, pp. 13–27. Addis Ababa.
1973b   Les fouilles de Yeha (mai-juin 1973). *Documents pour Servir à l'Histoire des Civilizations Ethiopiennes*, vol. 4, pp. 35–38. Centre National de la Recherche Scientifique, Paris.
1973c   Yeha. *Archeologia*, no. 64, pp. 34–44.
1974   Deux villes Axoumites: Adoulis et Matara. *IV Congresso Internazionale di Studi Etiopici*, vol. I, pp. 745–772. Accademia Nazionale dei Lincei, Rome.

Anfray, Francis, and Guy Annequin
1965   Matarā: Deuxième, troisième et quatrième campagnes de fouilles. *Annales d'Ethiopie*, vol. VI, pp. 49–142. Addis Ababa.

Beek, G. W. van
1967   Monuments of Axum in the light of South Arabian archaeology. *Journal of the American Oriental Society*, vol. 87, no. 2.

Bent, James Theodore
1893   *The Sacred City of Ethiopians being a Record of Travel and Research in Abyssinia in 1893. With a Chapter by Prof. H. D. Müller on the Inscriptions from Jeha and Aksum*. London.

Bowen, Richard LeBaron, and Frank P. Albright
1958   *Archaeological Discoveries in South Arabia*. Johns Hopkins Press, Baltimore.

Bruce, James
1790   *Travels to Discover the Sources of the Nile in the Years 1768–1773, vol. I–III*. Edinburgh.

Butzer, Karl W.
n.d.   *Soil Erosion and Alluvial History at Classical Axum*. Unpublished manuscript, University of Chicago.

Caquot, André, and A. J. Drewes
1955   Les monuments recueillis à Maqallé (Tigre). *Annales d'Ethiopie*, vol. I, pp. 17–41. Addis Ababa.

Caquot, André, and Jean Leclant
1955   Arabe du sud et Afrique. Examen d'une hypotèse récente. *Annales d'Ethiopie*, vol. I. Addis Ababa.
1956   Rapport sur les récents travaux de la section d'archéologie. *Comptes*

Rendus de l'Académie des Inscriptions et Belles-Lettres, p. 228.

Chittick, Neville
1974   Excavations at Aksum, 1973–4: A Preliminary Report. *Azania*, vol. IX, pp. 159–205. Nairobi.

Contenson, Henri de
1959a   Les fouilles à Axoum en 1957. *Annales d'Ethiopie*, vol. III, pp. 25–42. Addis Ababa.
1959b   Aperçus sur les fouilles à Axoum et dans la région d'Axoum en 1958 et 1959. *Annales d'Ethiopie*, vol. III, pp. 101–106. Addis Ababa.
1961a   Les fouilles à Ouchatei Golo, près d'Axoum, en 1958. *Annales d'Ethiopie*, vol. IV, pp. 3–14. Addis Ababa.
1961b   Trouvailles fortuites aux environs d'Axoum (1957–1959). *Annales d'Ethiopie*, vol. IV, pp. 17–38. Addis Ababa.
1961c   Les fouilles à Haoulti-Melazo en 1958. *Annales d'Ethiopie*, vol. IV, pp. 39–60. Addis Ababa.
1963a   Les fouilles à Axoum en 1958. *Annales d'Ethiopie*, vol. V, pp. 1–40. Addis Ababa.
1963b   Les fouilles à Haoulti en 1959. *Annales d'Ethiopie*, vol. V, pp. 41–86. Addis Ababa.

Cossar, B.
1945   Necropoli precristiani di Seleclaca. *Studi Etiopici*, edited by Conti-Rossini. Rome.

Dainelli, G., and O. Marinelli
1912   *Risultati di un viaggio nella Colonia Eritrea*. Florence.

Davico, A.
1946   Ritrovamenti sud-arabici nelle zona del Cascasé. *Rassegna di Studi Etiopici*, vol. V. Rome.

Doe, Brian
1971   *Southern Arabia*. McGraw-Hill, New York.

Drewes, A. J.
1959   Les inscriptions de Melazo. *Annales d'Ethiopie*, vol. 3, pp. 83–99. Addis Ababa.

Drewes, A. J., and R. Schneider
1967   Documents épigraphiques de l'Ethiopie—I. *Annales d'Ethiopie*, vol. VII, pp. 89–106. Addis Ababa.
1970   Documents épigraphiques de l'Ethiopie—II. *Annales d'Ethiopie*, vol. VIII, pp. 57–72. Addis Ababa.
1972   Documents épigraphiques de l'Ethiopie—III. *Annales d'Ethiopie*, vol. IX, pp. 87–102. Addis Ababa.

Fattovich, Rodolfo
1972   Sondaggi stratigrafici (Yeha 1971). *Annales d'Ethiopie*, vol. IX, pp. 65–86. Addis Ababa.

Franchini, Vincenzo, and Lanfranco Ricci
1954   Ritrovamenti archeologici in Eritrea. *Rassegna di Studi Etiopici*, vol. XII. Rome.

Gann, Lewis H., and Peter Duignan
1972   *Africa: The Land and the People*. Chandler, San Francisco.

Hable-Sellassie, Sergew
1972   *Ancient and Medieval Ethiopian History to 1270*. Addis Ababa.

Hailemariam, Ato Gezau
1955   Objects found in the neighborhood of Axum. *Annales d'Ethiopie*, vol. I.

Addis Ababa.

Krencker, Daniel
1913   Ältere Denkmäler Nordabessiniens. *Deutsche Aksum-Expedition*, vol. II.
        Georg Reimer, Berlin.

Leclant, Jean
1959a   Les fouilles à Axoum en 1955–1956. Rapport préliminaire. *Annales
        d'Ethiopie*, vol. III, pp. 3–25. Addis Ababa.
1959b   Haoulti-Melazo (1955–1956). *Annales d'Ethiopie*, vol. III, pp. 43–82.
        Addis Ababa.

Leclant, Jean, and André Miquel
1959   Reconnaissances dans l'Agamé: Goulo-Makeda et Sabéa (octobre 1955
        et avril 1956). *Annales d'Ethiopie*, vol. III, pp. 107–130. Addis Ababa.

Lefebvre, Théophile
1845   *Voyage en Abyssinie exécuté pendant les années: 1839–1843, vol. I–III.* Paris.

Littmann, Enno
1913a   Reisebericht der Expedition / Topographie und Geschichte Aksums.
        Deutsche Aksum-Expedition, vol. I. Georg Reimer, Berlin.
1913b   Sabäische, Griechische, und Altabessinische Inschriften. *Deutsche Aksum-
        Expedition*, vol. IV. Georg Reimer, Berlin.

Lupke, Theodor von
1913   Profan- und Kultbauten Nordabessiniens aus älterer und neuerer
        Zeit. *Deutsche Aksum-Expedition*, vol. III. Georg Reimer, Berlin.

Michels, Joseph W.
1975   *Archaeological Survey of the Axumite Kingdom, Tigre Province, Ethiopia.*
        Paper presented at the meeting of the Society of Africanist Archaeologists
        in America, Boston University.

Mikael, K. and J. Leclant
1955   La section d'archéologie, 1952–1955. *Annales d'Ethiopie*, vol. I, pp. 1–6.
        Addis Ababa.

Monneret de Villard, Ugo
1938   Aksum: Ricerche di topografia generale. *Analecta Orientalia*, vol. 16,
        pp. 1–138. Rome.

Pankhurst, Richard
1961   *An Introduction to the Economic History of Ethiopia.* Lalibela House, Addis
        Ababa.

Paribeni, Roberto
1908   *Ricerche nel Luogo dell'antica Adulis.* Rome.

Phillips, Wendell
1955   *Qataban and Sheba.* Victor Gollancz, London.

Pirenne, Jacqueline
1967   Haoulti et ses monuments: Nouvelle interprétation. *Annales d'Ethiopie*,
        vol. VII, pp. 125–140. Addis Ababa.
1970   Haoulti, Gobochela (Melazo) et le site antique. *Annales d'Ethiopie*,
        vol. VIII, pp. 117–127. Addis Ababa.

Piva, Abele
1907   Una civiltà scomparsa dell'Eritrea. E gli scavi archeologici nella regione
        di Cheren. *Nuova Antologia*, pp. 323–335. Rome.

Puglisi, Salvatore
1941   Primi risultati delle indagini compiute dalla missione archeologica di
        Aksum. *Africa Italiana*, vol. VIII, no. 3–4. Rome.

Puglisi, S. M.

1946   L'industria niolitica di Axoum. *Rassegna d'Science Preistoriche*, vol. II. Rome.

Ricci, Lanfranco
1961   Antichità nello Agame. *Rassegna di Studi Etiopici*, vol. XVII. Rome.
1974   Scavi archeologici in Etiopia. *Africa*, vol. XXIX, no. 3, pp. 435–441. Rome.

Rivoire, Denis de
1868   *Bulletin de la Société de Géographie.* Paris.

Salt, H.
1814   *A Voyage to Abyssinia, and Travels into the Interior of that Country, executed under the orders of the British Government, in the years 1809 and 1810.* F. C. and J. Rivington, publishers, London.

Schneider, Roger
1961   Inscriptions d'Enda Čergos. *Annales d'Ethiopie*, vol. IV, pp. 61–65. Addis Ababa.
1972   Documents épigraphiques de l'Ethiopie—IV. *Annales d'Ethiopie*, vol. IX, pp. 103–113. Addis Ababa.

Shinnie, Peter L.
1971   The Sudan. In *The African Iron Age*, edited by P. L. Shinnie, pp. 88–107. Clarendon Press, Oxford.

Sundström, R.
1907   Report of an expedition to Adulis. In "Preliminary Report on the Princeton University Expedition to Abyssinia," edited by E. Littmann. *Zeitschrift für Assyriologie*, vol. XX, pp. 171–182.

Tchalenko, George
1953   *Villages antiques de la Syrie du nord.* Paris.

Trimingham, J. Spencer
1952   *Islam in Ethiopia.* Barnes and Noble, New York.

Tringali, G.
1965   Cenni sulle "ona" di Asmara e dintorni. *Annales d'Ethiopie*, vol. VI, pp. 143–161. Addis Ababa.

Zahn, Robert
1913   Die kleinfunde. In *Deutsche Aksum-Expedition*, vol. II, by Daniel Krencker, pp. 199–231. Georg Reimer, Berlin.

I

The Political History of Axum

The Axumite Kingdom arose toward the end of the II century A.D., although the first mention of Axumites is dated to the middle of that century and could have been borrowed from a work dating even earlier. The first mention of Adulis, also possibly borrowed from an earlier source, dates to the second half of the I century A.D.

Adulis and the Tigre plateau

The rise of Adulis may have been connected with the Hellenic-Egyptian colonization of the shores of Northeast Africa under the first Ptolemies. In the VI century A.D. Cosmas Indicopleustes found there a Greek inscription[1]* allegedly composed in the name of Ptolemy IV Philopator (222–205 B.C.). This inscription is a falsification more or less contemporary with the ruler to whom it is ascribed. In the colophon of the inscription, which has not been preserved, "evidently there was contained a reference to the founding of Adulis or to the relationship of Ptolemy IV to this city."[2] Pliny asserts that Adulis was founded by Egyptian slaves. The tradition cited by Pliny is based on the etymologizing of the name Ἀδούλις from the Greek δοῦλος ("slave") and the alpha privative ("non"). In comparison with the old centers of the Preaxumite epoch, such as Yeha and Kaskase, Adulis and Coloe (Matara) were young towns whose development occurred primarily in the Axumite Period.

The western part of the Tigre plateau appears to have been colonized largely by Axumites. The Axumite inscriptions do not speak of the subjugation of tribes of the Ethiopian plateau west of Axum. Evidently this territory, right up to the country of Baria located in the vicinity of the Tekezze River, already entered into the composition of the Axumite Kingdom at the dawn of its existence. The mastering of new lands and the growth of population connected with them led to an intensification of Axum's role at the end of the Preaxumite epoch. The Axumites became the most numerous people of Northern Ethiopia. The migrant communities did not break up into rival scattered territorial groups, but rather continued to participate in the organizational framework which had evolved locally

*See Bibliography for complete references.

over many centuries, and whose origins date back to the initial South Arabian colony of Yeha.

The continuity of a number of civic centers during the transition from Preaxumite to Axumite time suggests that the decline of the very ancient South Arabian culture (V–IV centuries B.C.) did not lead to the destruction of state organization. It remained in the form of rather small "kingdoms" bounded by the territory of a tribe or a tribal union with a common civic center. Indeed, the rather small (initial) Axumite "kingdom," which it is impossible to equate to the future Axumite Empire, constituted just such an entity.

In the II century A.D. an expansion of Axumites was begun in the reverse direction; not to the west but to the east, not into the sparsely populated "new" lands but into the originally settled regions of Preaxumite Ethiopia from where in former times the ancestors of the Axumites themselves had come. It appears, therefore, that the central geographical position of Axum in the growing Northern Ethiopian periphery played an important role in its rise to power. However, the remoteness of Axum from the maritime regions impeded the development of long-distance trade.

An explanation for the rise of Axum, therefore, cannot be sought, as is done by many authors, in the growth of Red Sea trade. The development of long-distance trade in the region of the Bab el Mandeb Gulf began in the III century B.C.—400 years before the rise of Axum! Furthermore, although Axum was located on trade routes leading from the seacoast into the interior of the African continent it was neither a sea nor river port. Finally, there were many other towns located on important trade routes in Northern Ethiopia. Many of them, not to mention sea ports, continued to have greater trade significance than the town of Axum even after the Axumites seized control of long-distance trade throughout Ethiopia. In fact, it was precisely the evolution of the Axumite Kingdom that promoted the rise of certain trading towns, such as Adulis.

Trade, including Red Sea trade, played an important (but by far not the paramount) role in the development of ancient Ethiopian society. However, it cannot explain the rise of Axum at the expense of other Northern Ethiopian communities. This continues to be true even if one focuses upon inland caravan trade.

The ascendency of Axum among other urban centers of Ethiopia progressed rapidly and with surprising parallels to the ascendency of Rome. What role, if any, was played by political events dating to the Preaxumite Period remains unknown because of the rather negligible amount of study so far undertaken of that period.

At the time of its emergence (end of the II century A.D.) the Axumite Kingdom had two large states as its neighbors: Meroe in Nubia, Saba in Southern Arabia. Both were in a deep decline and shortly thereafter col-

Reconstruction of the top of the "Giant Fallen Stele" in Axum.
(All illustrations in the text are from Enno Littmann et al.,
Deutsche Aksum Expedition, vol. II. Walter De Gruyter & Co.,
Berlin, 1913)

lapsed altogether. The Roman Empire also was experiencing a crisis
caused by its enduring struggle with another world power—the Persian
Empire. Rome needed Axum's help in its struggle with the Persians. Rome
also called upon Axum to protect its ships from attacks by pirates and to
protect the boundaries of Egypt from the inroads of the Beja nomads.

Berber piracy and the inroads of the Beja

Piracy near the shores of Ethiopia and Somalia was born about 100 B.C. as a result of the establishment of a direct route from Egypt to India and East Africa. Prior to this, piracy had scarcely existed. Originally, foreign ships arrived at African Red Sea ports especially for trade. Goods which they brought could be acquired by means of exchange. The local inhabitants themselves conducted direct trade with India, Ceylon, and Indonesia, and served as intermediaries between them and the peoples of the Eastern Mediterranean.

A different situation began to take shape toward the end of the II century B.C. Now only a rather small part of the passing ships arrived for trade in the ports of Ethiopia and Somalia. The majority of them simply made provisioning stops here, saving their best goods for the ultimate ports of their voyage. Piracy evolved as a response to this change.

Agatharchides[3] and Strabo[4] (evidently also based on Agatharchides) mention the suppression of Red Sea pirates by the Ptolemaic fleet. In 78 B.C., a mariner from Thebais named Callimachus received the title "protector of the Indian and Eritrean Seas" (τῆς ’Γνδιχῆς χαί ’Ερυθρᾶς θαλασσῆς).[5] This probably meant the protection of Egyptian ships from pirates since no one was threatening Egypt from the direction of the Red Sea. After the conquest of Egypt by the Romans, the protection of seafarers from Red Sea and Indian Ocean pirates passed into the hands of the Roman authorities. Octavian Augustus fitted out expeditions against the pirates, but his successors shunned a systematic struggle with them. Roman captains therefore had to take archers on board their ships in order to be protected from the brigands of the Red Sea and Aden Gulf.[6] The reasons for such a passive policy by Rome in relation to her subjects will be discussed below. Meanwhile, it is important for us to note that in the II and I centuries B.C. seafarers from Egypt and the Mediterranean feared the pirates who operated near the shores of Ethiopia and Somalia. One more communication concerning Ethiopian pirates has been preserved; this is a tale about the fate of the merchant Yambul who was taken captive by them, which was cited by Diodorus.[7] The name Yambul is probably Nabataean and the story about him is a romantic tale of the Nabataeans. However, this episode faithfully depicts the dangers of sailing the "Eritrean Sea" where piracy flourished. Indeed, the Nabataeans themselves preyed upon the trading vessels.

Such an event also befell a certain Meropius of Tyre as related by Tyrannius Rufinus.[8] The incident dates to around 420 A.D., and the harbor at which the ship of Meropius called lay somewhere in modern Eritrea, probably to the south of Adulis on the seacoast of the Danakil desert or near the Dahlak Archipelago.

Pseudo Arrian speaks of the fact that local tribes frequently attacked passing ships. According to his words, "ships which are sailing there (to Adulis) now put in at the island of Orien (Dahlak el Kebir), which lies opposite Adulis, because of the raids from the mainland. Formerly they put in at the innermost part of the gulf [Zula] on the so-called island of Diodorus, near the mainland itself where a foot bridge existed by which the barbarians who lived there made raids on this island."[9] Just as in the case with Meropius, the Ethiopians attacked the ships not on the open sea but when they put in to shore.

The title "protector of the Indian and Eritrean Seas" was unknown in the Roman and Byzantine periods. Evidently there was no need for this position in the new political situation which involved the emergence of a strong power in the southern part of the Red Sea—the Axumite Kingdom. Axum took upon itself the preservation of order in these waters. The ancient inhabitants of Somalia recognized the hegemony of Axum only to a modest degree, but followed the orders of the Axumite ruler. The authority of Axum was felt far more strongly near Adulis. Rufinus says directly that Berbers pillaged Roman ships only when "the neighboring tribes informed them of the dissolution of the [Axumite] alliance with the Romans." Only the Axumite Kingdom was able to come forward as an ally of the Romans. Consequently, while the alliance remained in force the Axumite king forbade the coastal tribes to engage in piracy. One Axumite king (the author of the Adulis inscription) relates: "I subjugated the Solate people and ordered them to protect the seacoast. Having dispatched a war fleet, I subjugated the rulers who lived along that side of the sea, Arrabites and Cynaedocolpitae [literally dog wombs] having commanded them to pay tribute and conduct affairs peacefully on land and sea."[10]

The order "to protect the seacoast" could only mean a commission to carry on a struggle with piracy and the order to "peacefully conduct affairs on land and sea" could only mean the prohibiting of raids and sea plundering. From the text of the inscription it is clear that the inhabitants of South Arabia were also engaged in piracy. Pseudo Arrian also speaks of this.

Arab rulers enjoyed the support of Roman merchants as an incentive in their struggle with the pirates. Pseudo Arrian speaks of constant embassies and gifts to the Arab rulers on the part of the Romans.[11] In another place are enumerated the goods imported especially for these rulers.[12] Quite possibly the embassies and gifts could have originated not only with the Roman government or Roman vice-regents but also with provincial and local authorities, even with town magistrates who were not infrequently engaged in trade.

It is almost inconceivable that an embassy of the central Roman government could have been sent to Axum prior to the beginning of the IV century A.D. On the other hand, provincial and local authorities were able at an earlier date to send their representatives with gifts to the Axumite ruler. In particular the prefect of Egyptian Berenika was able to do this. Diplomatic relations with Axum were essential to provincial authorities since they looked after the interests of Roman subjects whose ships plied the waters located under Axum's control. The power of the Axumite Kingdom prevented Roman authorities, both provincial and expeditionary, from actively and directly struggling with pirates in the Axumite sphere of influence. Roman authorities were therefore obliged to recognize the hegemony of Axum in the southern portion of the Red Sea and to leave to the Axumite monarchy suppression of piracy.

Mommsen rightly noted that "the Axomide [Axumite] and the Safar [Himyarite Zafar in Arabia] governments already on the strength of geographic conditions were obliged to allot still greater attention to the struggle with piracy than the Romans in Berenika and Leuke Kome; it is possible that precisely this circumstance contributed to the fact that the Romans in general preserved good relationships with these necessary, albeit weaker, neighbors." [13]

Roman-Byzantine Egypt suffered from the plundering raids of the Beja, nomadic tribes of the Nubian desert, even more than from the Berber pirates. The Beja carried out their first raid on Roman possessions in Egypt as early as the reign of Claudius (the successor of Augustus). In the reigns of Claudius and Nero they harrassed the boundary of the empire between the Nile and the Red Sea. In Egyptian Berenika, Syene (Aswan), and Dodekaskhoin, the Romans placed garrisons in defense against Beja raids. A corps of meharists (dromedary cavalry) was created in support of the garrisons and operated in the eastern desert. Punitive expeditions were undertaken against the Beja (for instance under Hadrian in 137 A.D.). Prior to the middle of the III century A.D., Roman forces successfully restrained the onslaught of the Beja. But from 249 A.D. raiding intensified. The raids of the Beja on Egypt followed one after another and became progressively more devastating and deeper in their penetration. During the period from the middle of the III to the middle of the VII century A.D. the Beja held all of Upper Egypt under the threat of their attacks. They reached north as far as the Tiran islands and the Sinai Peninsula, where they killed several monks. In the south, Roman (Byzantine) forces drove the Beja first from Dodekaskhoin then from Berenika and the Alabaster Mountains with their emerald mines.

Roman-Byzantine governments in their struggle with the Beja relied upon the tribes of the Noba (Nubians) but they were not always able to oppose the onslaught of the Beja. The help of a more powerful state which bordered upon Beja territory was needed. Axum was such a state in the period of maximum expansion of the Beja along the Egyptian frontier. It was becoming continually more evident that the Beja attacked Egypt either when they were not subjugated by Axum or when they received permission for war from the latter. Lesquier[14] adheres to this point of view as do the contemporary authors Drewes[15] and Cerulli.[16]

A similar situation had taken shape in Arabia. Here the spheres of influence of Rome, Axum, and Persia were contiguous. Attacks by the Arabians on Roman possessions compelled the empire to seek help from a powerful state—Himyar or Axum.

The Roman-Byzantine Empire was therefore interested in the existence of a strong power on the shores of the Red Sea which would be able to defend its boundaries and guarantee the safety of trade.

"The alliance with the Romans" signified for Axum first of all an alliance with merchants (that is, with private individuals), secondly with provincial authorities, and only in the last place with the central Roman government.

It is possible to speak of a genuine alliance of the Roman government with the government of Axum only from the beginning of the VI century A.D. Meanwhile many sources, beginning with the III century A.D., attest to Axum's alliance and friendship with Romans or Roman subjects.

The suppression of piracy was dictated by the economic interests of the Axumite monarchy itself. It received incomparably greater benefits from the development of trade than from sharing in pirates' spoils. Moreover, under the pretext of the struggle with piracy the Axumite monarchy was able to tighten its authority on the inhabitants of the shores of the Red Sea. We can only speculate that since Axumite rulers took upon themselves the protection of Roman merchants, affording them safety of movement in the southern part of the Red Sea, Roman merchants may have, in turn, aided Axum in its overseas campaigns. Only one undertaking of such a sort (525 A.D.) is reliably reported and then only because the help from the Romans originated from the central government. How frequently Roman and other foreign merchants helped the Axumite rulers in their struggle with insurgents and neighbors for the purpose of uniting many peoples and countries under an imperial Axumite authority can only be conjectured.

Whatever the specific circumstances, enough seems clear to suggest that international pressures which built up near the borders of Ethiopia around the end of the II century A.D. facilitated the creation of a strong and farflung Axumite Kingdom.

First information about Axum

Prior to the II century A.D., epigraphic and narrative sources do not mention either Axum or the Axumites. Pliny the Elder (about 60 A.D.) mentions Adulis and its trade with the Romans but says nothing about the subjugation of Adulis to any sort of state. Pliny refers to Adulis as the trade center of the Troglodytes.[17] Toward the middle of the II century A.D.[18] Claudius Ptolemaeus not only recognizes Adulis but also identifies the Axumites (Αξουμῖται) among the peoples of Northeast Africa. It is said of them that they are at the cultural level of the tribes of the Nubian desert.[19] It is possible that this information was obtained by Ptolemaeus from a lost writing of Marinus of Tyre (about 100 A.D.). Neither Ptolemaeus nor Marinus, however, says anything about the Axumite dominance either on the Ethiopian plateau or in the Nubian desert and indeed both allot scant attention to the Axumites. The city of Meroe and the Meroitic Kingdom are far better known to them.

Wissmann, analyzing Claudius Ptolemaeus' communication concerning Arabia,[20] proposed that the Cynaedocolpitae (in contemporary Tihama or 'Asir Tihamat on the Hijaz-Yemen coast) were subject to the "ruler of the Habashat" (Abyssinians), possibly as early as the time of Marinus of Tyre (about 100 A.D.).[21] However, the text of Ptolemaeus provides no basis for such a conclusion. In any event, the Axumites could scarcely have been able to extend their dominion onto the Arabian peninsula at such an early date.

The first information about the ascendency of Axum and its entry into a wide political arena dates to the end of the II century A.D. At that time the military and political might of the Axumite Kingdom had grown so great than an invasion of Arabia was undertaken.

An Adulis inscription copied in the VI century A.D. by Cosmas Indicopleustes (and later lost) speaks of the rapid and spectacular rise of Axum. The date of the inscription has not been precisely established and its author is unknown. Dillmann[22] considered the author of the inscription to be the ruler Zoskales. Drouin[23] argues that the legendary ruler Ella Awda, known only from the medieval lists of Axumite rulers, is its author. Glaser at first (in 1890) maintained that the inscription was left not by an Axumite ruler but by a Himyarite ruler, but under the influence of criticism retreated from this position and subsequently identified an Axumite ruler who reigned after Zoskales[24] as the author of the Adulis inscription. One of Glaser's arguments deserves attention: the territorial possessions of the author of the inscription were more extensive than those of Zoskales.

At present Pirenne[25] and Drewes[26] ascribe the Adulis inscription to Sembruthes and date it to the beginning of the IV century A.D. Wissmann[27] dates the inscription to the time interval between the writings of Ptolemaeus and those of Pseudo Arrian (end of the II century A.D.). The new dating of Sabaean inscriptions proposed by Loundine has altered former notions about early Axumite chronology. Therefore the dating of the Adulis and Sembruthes inscriptions still remains an open question. Only one thing is clear: both inscriptions, composed in Greek and dedicated to the gods, appeared prior to the middle of the IV century A.D., at which time Axum was beginning to be Christianized and the Greek language was replaced by the Ethiopian language.[28]

The Axumite ruler, the author of the Adulis inscription, reports: " . . . Having commanded the peoples closest to my kingdom to preserve the peace, I bravely waged war and subjugated in battles the following peoples." In Tigre they included Aguezat, Agame, Sigyn, Aua, Zingabene, and Angabo; Tiama [Siamo or Tziamo], Atagau, Kala [Kaila?], and Semen to the south and southwest of Tigre. The country of Semen is characterized as consisting of inaccessible mountains with mists, cold and snow; and as being situated along that side of the "Nile"[29] (Tekezze-Atbara) which approaches the modern region of Semen. Thus, even tribes in close proximity were not identified with the Axumite Kingdom. Moreover, between the land of the original "kingdom" (of the author of the Adulis inscription) and the regions of Aguezat, Aua, and Agame lay the "nearest peoples," who had preserved the "peace" or neutrality. All of this information is compatible with either the rise of Axum or with its regeneration after a deep decline. It seems more reasonable to propose the former, the more so since in the inscription there is no allusion to the *former* might of Axum. On the contrary, its author maintains that no ruler before him carried out similar conquests. However, this latter assertion can refer only to expeditions beyond the boundaries of Northern Ethiopia.

In order to subjugate the tribes enumerated above, the Axumite ruler had to carry out at least three campaigns: to the northeast, to the south, and to the southwest. Subsequently, a campaign was directed to the northeast districts of the plateau, where Axum subjugated the Lasine, Gabala (Gabala in the Danakil desert or Gambela in Enderta, or perhaps Gabaza-Adulita?), and Zaa (Saho?) peoples. Adulis, the main port of Northern Ethiopia, had by now become fully surrounded by Axumite possessions, and as a sign of his authority the king commissioned the Adulis monument.

At a later date the Atalmo were subjugated. Evidently this was a nomadic people who lived north of Adulis. The inscription speaks of the subjugation of "Atalmo ('Ατάλμω), Beja (Βεγά) and all peoples who [lived] alongside them." "Having subjugated of the Tanganitae (Ταγγαΐτων), those who live near the borders of Egypt, I again made the road from the districts of my kingdom to Egypt a thoroughfare." The Beja (or Blemm) were at that time the main people of the Nubian desert, and the Tanganitae were evidently one of their northern tribes. The inscription speaks about the subjugation of "all the peoples" of this region; from the boundaries of the Ethiopian plateau to the Roman possessions in Egypt and Northern Nubia. But this still does not mean, as Turayev proposed, that the "Kingdom of Meroe" was also subjugated by Axum.[30] If this were actually so, the author of the Adulis inscription would certainly have mentioned the conquest of this very great kingdom, or at least the campaign into its territory.

Reconstruction of the commemorative throne of an Axumite king.

The sixth military campaign was ended with the conquest of the Annine, Metine, and Sesea tribes. All three tribes evidently lived somewhere in the mountains farther to the west of Axum. It is possible that the Axumites invaded their districts while returning from a victorious campaign against the Beja.

The seventh expedition of conquest was directed toward the southeast, into the deserts of the Horn of Africa. Here the Axumites subjugated "the Rausoi (Ραύσων) barbarians (Berbers), who lived far from the sea-coast on broad, waterless plains and who traded in incense." Undoubtedly a people of the Somali Desert is being spoken of. The Solate (Σωλατέ), a coastal people, were also subjugated and ordered "to protect the seacoast," possibly in the region of the Bab el Mandeb Gulf. Evidently this is the limit of the conquests of the author of the Adulis inscription to the southeast. In the course of this expedition, it is likely that along the way the Danakil desert tribes, tribes of the Aussa oasis, and tribes of the fertile Chercher highlands (modern Harar province) would have also been conquered.

Seemingly, this concluded the expansion of early Axum on the African continent. The author of the Adulis inscription says with pride that he was the first among all the rulers who came before him to have "subjugated all of the neighboring peoples; in the east right up to the Incense Land [Somalia] and in the west right up to the land of the Ethiopians [i.e., the Negroes] and Sasu." The latter was located in Southwest Ethiopia, in the Blue Nile valley.

Having conquered Semen and the neighboring territories to the south of Tekezze, the Axumite king found himself at the frontier of Sasu. But did he invade? It is difficult to hypothesize whether a ruler might have shunned a description of this undertaking, notable for both its difficulty and the possible results. Indeed, Sasu was the principal gold-producing country in Ethiopia.[31] Consequently the expression "right up to Sasu" could even mean "right up to the countries located *almost at the boundaries* of Sasu," with "almost" being omitted from the boasting. Another explanation has also been proposed: Cosmas Indicopleustes, who was interested in the gold-bearing country of Sasu, may have made an error, reading a name "familiar" to him instead of the correct one. Psychologically this is possible, although in Cosmas' work *no other paleographic errors have been observed*. Instead of Sasu, Glaser[32] (and after him Kammerer[33] and others) suggested reading *Kasu*; that is, the Meroitic Kingdom. This correction remains unproven even though quite recently Kirwan insisted on it.[34]

Even if we accept this correction it does not give us the right to maintain that the Adulis inscription attests to the conquering of Kasu by the Axumites. Indeed, among the listing of campaigns carried out by the author of the inscription not a single word is said about a campaign to Kasu. And only with complete failure of the expedition would its description not have been reflected in the inscription. Consequently, even with Glaser's correction it is possible only to speak of the establishment of a common boundary between Axum and Meroe, evidently located in the Nubian desert.

As far as Berbera (or the Incense Land) is concerned, Pseudo Arrian assigns at least part of it to the possessions of King Zoskales. Part of the Nubian desert also belonged to Zoskales. Another part was under the influence of Meroe, which Pseudo Arrian calls "the mother country."[35] The possessions of Axum under Zoskales were therefore not as extensive here as under the author of the Adulis inscription. Such information reveals how unstable Axumite authority (and also that of Meroe) was in the reaches of the Nubian and Somali deserts. All the conquered tribes were assessed tribute or tax.

Finally, the last campaign (or series of campaigns?) by the author of the Adulis inscription was directed against Arabia. He communicates "Having dispatched a fleet, I subjugated the rulers of the Arrabites and Cynaedocolpitae who lived along that side of the Eritrean [Red] Sea. . . . I made war from Leuke Kome up to the lands of the Sabaeans."[36] The land of the Sabaeans is the Sabaean Kingdom in South Arabia; Leuke Kome is a port in Hijaz at the southern boundaries of the Roman possessions. The Cynaedocolpitae are the population of 'Asir Tihamat or Tihama on the Hijaz coast. It is probably not the Arab-Bedouins but the Arhabites (one of the Himyaritic tribes of the Bab el Mandeb Gulf region), who are called Arrabites. Thus all of Tihama—the Red Sea coastal area of South and Central Arabia—and both shores of the Gulf proved to be under the control of the Axumite king.

A vast power, the largest on the African continent (after the Roman Empire), was thus created as a result of these successful military campaigns. Axum shared with Rome and Iran major spheres of influence on the huge Arabian peninsula.

The author of the Adulis inscription says, in conclusion, that he erected it in the twenty-seventh year of his reign. He was a very remarkable ruler. The conquests carried out under his command attest to his military talents. Some of the campaigns were led by him personally. Others were led by faithful agents. Huge spoils were taken during each campaign, part of which the king kept for himself. The tribute levied on the conquered peoples increased his wealth and augmented his authority within the Axumite Kingdom. The king exhibited concern over the development of trade. He made the road to Egypt and the sea routes safe, and he made sacrifices to Poseidon "for those who sail the sea."

Two more Greek inscriptions of Axumite kings are dated to approximately the same time as the Adulis inscription. One of them was found at Abba Penteleon in the immediate vicinity of Axum, the other at Deqe Mehari on the route from Adulis to Axum. The first inscription is in very poor condition; the name of the king who left it has not been preserved. But the dedication "to Ares, god of the Axumites" attests to a pre-Christian time period. Some sort of events in "the country on that side of the sea"[37] (i.e., in Arabia) are spoken of in the inscription. Gratitude, evidently for a successful campaign into that country, was expressed to Ares-Mahrem.

The other inscription, from Deqe Mehari, belongs to King Sembruthes, who calls himself "the great king" and "king of kings of the Axumites." He says that he left the inscription in the twenty-fourth year of his reign.[38] The long period of his reign and the magnificent title indicate the growing power and significance of Axum.

The name Sembruthes is unknown in the "Lists of Kings." One can find in the lists only a certain Ella Shemera or Ella Shamara,[39] whom Littmann tried to identify with Sembruthes.[40] However, Conti-Rossini resolutely[41] objected. Drewes found it possible to identify Sembruthes with Shamir Yuhar'ish (II or III?). In Drewes' opinion this is not at all difficult; allegedly they both lived at approximately the same time and their names are consonant; Drewes is inclined to consider the name Sembruthes as South Arabian. He proposes that the dethroned Shamir could have found asylum in Ethiopia and the Axumite kings allied to him could have made him the heir of their throne.[42] Recently it has been proven that in South Arabia at least three Shamir Yuhar'ishes[43] ruled, one of whom reigned at the beginning of the III century A.D. and another in the last quarter of the III century A.D.[44] to the beginning of the IV century A.D. This still further complicates attempts to synchronize Shamir and Sembruthes.

It is possible to allow that the South Arabian name ŠMR YHR'Š could have been transmitted in Greek as Σεμβρύϑης, but in what kind of document? Such a distortion of the ruler's name is *possible* in a narrative source but *improbable* in his own inscription, even in the Greek language (compare the transmission of the names of Ezana and Kaleb or Ella Asbeha in inscriptions on stone and coins). Historical considerations also mitigate against identifying Sembruthes with Shamir Yuhar'ish II or III.[45] In South Arabia each of them ruled about ten to twenty years; then, according to Drewes' hypothesis, one of them fled to Ethiopia. How long he was at the royal palace in the position of an emigré or guest is impossible to state. He then allegedly inherited the Axumite throne and after a twenty-four-year reign left the inscription in which he called himself Sembruthes. This seems too long a life for one person. Shamir Yuhar'ish would have been too advanced in years by the time of Asbeha's death to have ascended to the foreign Axumite throne, especially in light of the preference for healthy and young kings. And then to have him rule for no less than twenty-four years contributes to one's skepticism. All this makes identification of Shamir Yuhar'ish with Sembruthes a very remote possibility.

Drewes also advanced the hypothesis that the Adulis inscription was left by Sembruthes and that it is three years later than his inscription at

Deqe Mehari.[46] Essentially, what is being proposed is the common identification of two individuals about whom it is known that: (1) they ruled more than 23 years (24 and 27); (2) they marked the year of their rule in the inscriptions (in contrast to other Axumite kings); (3) they ruled during one distinctive epoch (Greek and pagan inscriptions); (4) they considered themselves extremely remarkable rulers. These very general similarities make common identification probable but not proven. Until new facts become known the question of the authorship and dating of the Adulis inscription remains open.

Possibly the answer to it will come from South Arabia. The Arabian campaigns of the author of the Adulis inscription must have found reflection in South Arabian epigraphics, which records all such important political events.

II and III century A.D. Sabaean inscriptions concerning Axum

The first Axumites appeared in Arabia under King Gedara, about whom several Sabaean inscriptions from Marib (and the Ge'ez inscription from Asbi Dera) speak. In these sources the name Gedara is given by several consonants; in the inscription in the Ge'ez language he is called GDR, but in the inscriptions in the Sabaean language GDRT. It is true, perhaps, that two different individuals are being spoken of, but it is more probable that GDR and GDRT are one and the same person. Pirenne and Drewes, for example, consider it possible to date the inscriptions which mention GDRT and GDR to one and the same time—the middle of the III century A.D.[47] The newest investigation of Loundine and Ryckmans dates the sources which mention Gedara as the end of the II or the beginning of the III century A.D. In Sabaean inscriptions GDRT and his successor are called "king of the Habashat,"[48] "nagashi," "nagashi, king of the Axumites,"[49] and "king of the Abyssinians and Axumites" (*mlk 'ḥbšt w'ksmn*).[50] It is clear that an Axumite king is being spoken of. The name GDR could have been given in Sabaean as GDRT if it was interpreted as being feminine in gender. This is possible since the Arabs also include proper masculine names within the feminine gender (for example, Antara[t], Umaiya[t], Muawiya[t], etc.). In the medieval "Lists of Axumite Kings" the name Gedur or Za Gedur Za Ba Nukh[51] is encountered. This may very well be the same name as the GDR–GDRT of the inscriptions, and that at the base of the legend of Za Gedur there is the historical personage of King GDR. Usually this name is read in the inscriptions as Gadar or Gadarat; I propose the spelling *Gedara*.

Our knowledge of the Axumites at the end of the II century A.D. comes primarily from inscriptions of their foes—the Sabaean kings and princes.

The only inscription in the Ge'ez language of the Axumite king Gedara was found in 1954 in Havila Asserai (on the border of Tigre and the

Danakil desert, in the region of Asbi Dera). The inscription was marked
on a votive object of bronze (a scepter in the form of a plow). The inscription written in the Ge'ez language was executed in archaic Ethiopian
script (without vowels). In the archaic script the word "nagashi" in
"status constructus" was written ፍንሠ, *nagaŝya*[52] instead of the classical
nagaše. A similar *status constructus* form of names [ending] in *"ya"* is encountered in the ethnic name of Ezana (*be'esya* instead of *be'esē*). Of all
of these arguments on the relative antiquity of the inscription put forth
by Drewes and his successors, only the one concerning the archaic form
of the script is compelling.

The inscription reads thus: *gdr ngŝy 'ksm tb'l mzlt l'rg wllmq.* According
to Jamme's translation[53] it means: "Gedara, king of Axum is humbled
before the [gods] Arg and Almouqah." Arg is unknown but Almouqah is
very well known both in Ethiopia and Arabia. This was the Sabaeans'
national god whose cult the Sabaean colonists transplanted in ancient
Ethiopia (from the V century B.C.). The scepter which bore the inscription
was found in a secret hiding place of the sanctuary of Almouqah together
with objects of the Preaxumite period. In the epoch of Axum's florescence
the cult of Almouqah was not widespread. Thus the dedication of the
inscription to Almouqah is weightly proof of its antiquity. The very form
of the name of this god—LMQ—is characteristic of Sabaean inscriptions
of the III century A.D. (for example, of Ilsharah Yahdib and his brother
Ya'zil Bayin).[54] Pirenne and Drewes date the rule of Gedara to approximately 250 A.D.[55] Loundine's investigation dates the epoch of Gedara as
occurring at the end of the II or the beginning of the III century A.D.[56]

Why did Gedara turn not to the Axumite tribal god Mahrem, nor to
the gods of the astral-agricultural triad, but rather to the archaic Almouqah,
whose sanctuary was preserved in remote Havila Asserai? Probably
Mahrem, whose incarnation the Axumite king was considered to be,
proved to be impotent before a god who had helped the king's opponents.
As a token of humbleness before Almouqah, Gedara donated the bronze
scepter to the sanctuary. The scepter was probably a sign of authority of
the sacred king. The cult of Almouqah remained extremely popular in
South Arabia. The inscription possibly therefore attests to the defeat of
Axum in its struggle in the south of Arabia. All of this lends support to
our argument that Gedara—the author of the inscription under consideration—and Gedara-Gadarat of the Sabaean inscriptions are one and
the same person.

All our information about Gedara-Gadarat has to do with the bitter
struggle for power which flared up in South Arabia in the second half of
the II century A.D. in connection with the decline of the Sabaean Kingdom.
The power and the throne of the Sabaean king was being contended for
by the kings of neighboring Hadramaut and Qataban, by the sovereign

princes of Raydan and by the tribal leaders of the Himyarites and Hamdanites. First the Arab-Bedouins and then the "Abyssinians" (ḥbšt), who had sailed to Arabia from the African continent, became involved in their struggle.

"Abyssinians" are first mentioned in an inscription of the Hamdanite prince Abikarib Yuhaskir and his brothers.[57] The inscription was composed around 183 A.D. in gratitude to the god Ta'lab for the victory of the Hamdanites over their foes, the Himyarites (the tribes of Barik and Marad). The Hamdanites, supporters of the old Sabaean dynasty, carried out raids on the lands of the Himyarites. In turn the Himyarites invaded the territory of the Hamdanites and of the Sabaean king, Alhan Nahfan II, but suffered a defeat. Battles took place in the south, in the region of Na'id. Among all of these skirmishes and raids there is mentioned also "a campaign against the Abyssinians." The name of the region in which the campaign took place has not been preserved. Afterwards, the Hamdanites joined with the Arab-Bedouins and together they attacked the Himyarites. The Ethiopians, together with the Himyarites, emerged as opponents of the Sabaean king. The bloodshed resulting from the struggle should not be exaggerated. In each battle one or two men were killed. The size of the armies involved was not great. The Hamdanites campaigned with a detachment of 150 to 200 troops. Their Bedouin allies sent a detachment of 60 men.

A poorly preserved inscription by Alhan Nahfan II[58] speaks about more significant military actions. Probably it tells about battles in which the Sabaeans came against an army fielded by a coalition of South Arabian kingdoms (Hadramaut and Qataban), of principalities (Mudkhayum and Radman), and of "the king of the Habashat." The main battlefield was Du Raydan. The forces of each of the opponents included the community militia, the royal detachments, detachments of vassal princes, and Bedouin nomads. But the main force of the coalition, evidently, was made up of "princes and leaders and communities of the Habashat king" ('qwl w'qdm w'š'b mlk ḥbš [t]). Wissmann hypothesizes that the latter expression reveals the extensiveness of the Ethiopian possessions in South Arabia. It is possible that the Ethiopians had already taken possession of the Asiatic shore of the Bab el Mandeb Gulf, which had earlier belonged to the Himyarites.[59]

If such were the case, the Axumites would have been a real threat to Himyar, which was becoming the main pretender to supremacy in South Arabia. Alhan Nahfan and the Hadramaut king, Yada ab Ghaylan, concluded an alliance with each other against the Himyarites.[60] The joint struggle against Himyar brought Saba and Axum into an alliance which was officially concluded about 190 A.D. Two inscriptions of Alhan Nahfan II and his son (and co-ruler) Sa'ir Awtar, which have been preserved in many copies,[61] speak of it. The Sabaean kings brought their god a gift of 30 statues in celebration of the alliance. The inscriptions reveal that the Habashat were ruled by a king named GDR who lived beyond the sea (i.e., in Ethiopia) in a place by the name of Zar'aran.[62]

In still other inscriptions Gedara is called "the king of the Axumites." Also, the region of Ash'aran on the banks of the Bab el Mandeb Gulf, which turned out to be under the complete command of Axum, belonged to him. Military detachments of "Abyssinians," with their leaders, were located in the Arabian possessions.[63]

The Axumite king was the strongest ally of Alhan Nahfan and, consequently, the strongest ruler in the southern part of the Red Sea.

After the death of Alhan Nahfan II, his son and co-ruler Sa'ir Awtar (about 190 A.D.) remained the Sabaean king. The alliance between Axum and Saba was canceled during his reign. The reason for this can be seen in the revival of the power of the Sabaeans and their expansion toward the sea coasts which were at that time in the hands of Himyarites and Hadramauts in the south and in the hands of the Ethiopians in the west. The inscriptions speak of five victorious campaigns of Sa'ir Awtar against Hadramaut and the Habashat.[64] He conquered Hadramaut (inscription *CIH*, 334) despite the fact that the Ethiopians advanced on the flanks of the Sabaean forces in an effort to help their Hadramaut allies. Sabaean inscriptions tell of this but Conti-Rossini did not know of their existence and therefore spoke about "the faithfulness [of Gedara] to the end" to the alliance with the Hamdanites.[65] Rabib Ahtar and Asad 'As'ad, leaders of the Bakilim tribe and supporters of Sa'ir Awtar, headed the Sabaean army in the region of the Hadramaut city of Qana. They successfully conducted military operations against Hadramaut and took prisoners. The poorly preserved text speaks unclearly about "armies and oppressions of Abyssinians (in the Bakilim region?) at the same time as they [the Sabaeans] made war against Hadramaut before this inscription was made."[66] Not a word is said about the victories of the Sabaeans over the Ethiopians. The Himyarites entered into an alliance with the Sabaeans.[67]

An inscription of gratitude by a certain Himyarite, dedicated to the god Almouqah who delivered his country from the enemy,[68] dates to the same time. Only the Ethiopians could have been "the enemy."[69] Nevertheless, Zafar (capital of Himyar) and Ma'aphir (a key point on the route from Zafar to Marib and Aden) were taken by Africans. In the opinion of Wissmann and Höfner,[70] with whom both Jamme[71] and this author agree, not only the Habashat who had settled in Arabia but also the African subjects of Axum took part in the invasions of Saba and Himyar.

An inscription[72] of the Himyarite chief Qatban Awkan tells about this. He fought on the sea and land under the command of Sa'ir Awtar. Evidently the campaign of King Gedara against the "land of the Habashat" (the Hàbashat and the Axumites) was carried out on both land and sea. Although in Jamme's opinion this campaign was carried out on the African continent,[73] Wissmann's position, that the military operations were carried out in 'Asir Tihamat / Tihama, is the more probable.[74]

The allied South Arabian force, gathered in the city of Na'id, then moved to free Zafar. The city and its outskirts were occupied by "*bygt wld ngšyn* and by the expeditionary forces (*mṣr*) of Abyssinians." The simplest translation of the term *bygt wld ngšyn* is "Bigat (or Beigat) son of the nagashi"; Jamme insists upon this.[75] However, other Sabaeanists see in *bygt* (*bigat*) Beja (Blemm).[76]

One can advance the following argument in support of the latter view. Actually, as Jamme indicates, in Sabaean inscriptions the word *wld* signifies the relationship "son of the father," sometimes a relationship equivalent to this (e.g., Saba wld Almouqah). However, one is compelled to suggest that the word *nagashi* is not Sabaean but Ethiopian terminology. In the Ge'ez language, *waled* (plural, *welud*) means not only "son" but also "slave" and "dependent."[77]* Thus, "the people of the nagashi" is expressed as somebody's "son," similar to the *wld* of the Qatban inscription. Evidently, "the Beja, subjects of the nagashi," was meant. Consequently, the Beja were conquered by Axum and took part in its overseas expedition.

During the night the South Arabian forces approached Zafar but did not succeed in taking the Ethiopians by surprise: the latter hid in "the citadel of the god (Upp Ilan) in the center of the city." A siege of the citadel was begun. New forces came to the aid of the besieged, yet the Ethiopian garrison was finally dislodged from the city and settled into a camp, evidently having been united with other detachments. Meanwhile new reinforcements joined the Sabaean-Himyarite force and together they carried out a night attack on the Ethiopian camp within three days after the capture of Zafar. The Axumites were betrayed by their South Arabian allies. By the end of the battle the Ethiopians had lost 400 troops— a comparatively large number. The corpses of the slain Africans were beheaded and desecrated. The remnants of the Ethiopian force hid in the camp but their food supply was exhausted. After three days, the Ethiopians carried out an unsuccessful sortie; and within two more days, tortured by hunger, they abandoned the Zafar region and went to Ma'ahiratan (probably the center of the Ma'ahir region). Finding themselves in a hostile country, the Axumite army remained without provisions. The South Arabian forces, on the other hand, received constant help from the populace. An allusion to the organization of this aid is contained in an inscription of the Himyarite leader Abikarib Ahras[78] dated 207 A.D.[79]

Another inscription[80] speaks about a campaign of Sa'ir Awtar against

---

*Translator's note: "dependent" is an adjectival form in the Russian text.

the region of Ash'aran in the vicinity of the Bab el Mandeb Gulf, a region which had been captured by the Ethiopians. Afterwards, the Sabaean forces set out northward, reaching Najran and compelling the Habashat (who had evidently penetrated from 'Asir Tihamat), to fall back.[81] From Najran Sa'ir Awtar carried out a campaign against the young Kindite Kingdom of Central Arabia. Among the foes of the Sabaean king are also mentioned the Romans ("Greeks," *yawa[n]um*). Wissmann is therefore correct in postulating an anti-Sabaean coalition of Hadramaut, the Kindites, and Axum under Rome's protection.[82] The military encounter resulted in the defeat of Rome's allies and further territorial expansion of Saba. Ethiopia, however, held on to the Red Sea shore of Arabia.

Between 207 and 210 A.D. Sa'ir Awtar died and the Hamdanite dynasty of "kings of Saba and Du Raydan" was interrupted. Yasrum Yuhan'im I in co-rulership with his son, Shamir (or Shammar) Yuhar'ish II, turned up on the Sabaean throne. Shortly thereafter, the father died and Shamir ruled alone. But pretenders (descendants of the ancient Sabaean dynasty) Ilsharah Yahdib (or Yahdub) II and his brother Ya'zil Bayin contended for the throne. The brothers forced Shamir out of Marib and proclaimed themselves "kings of Saba and Du Raydan."

In his struggle with them Shamir depended upon the Himyarites, especially on the Radman and Mudkhayum tribes, and in part on the Qatabans. He finally turned to Axum for help after having achieved no success with these allies. A whole series of inscriptions refers to this event, including an inscription by the leaders of the Bakilim tribe (Rabšams Yazid and Yakbayyam Ya'zil[83]) dating to 213 A.D.:[84] Shamir requested help from the Habashat against Ilsharah and Ya'zil, and the "people of Habashat" took part in the war. The inscription of Yakbayyam relates that Shamir, the Himyarites, and the Habashat sent ambassadors to the brother kings of Saba (Ilsharah and Ya'zil), proposing peace and their submission. Evidently by 213 A.D. military operations had ceased. Consequently this particular war involving Axumites in Arabia occurred between 210 and 213 A.D.

Judging by inscriptions [*Ja*, 574, 575 (*Ry*, 539), 576 (*Ry*, 535), 577, 585, 590 and *CIH*, 314+954] the coastal regions of Sahartan, Gudman, Accum (in Yemenite Tihama), Ash'aran and Ma'aphir (including the city of Sayyam and the capital of Himyar, Zafar) were located at that time in the hands of the Axumite king. King Wazeba I (WDBH) ['Azbah ('DBH) of the Sabaean inscriptions] was the head of the Axumite state at the time. His title was "king of the Axumites" (*mlk'ksmn*).[85]

Only Axum's aid allowed Shamir Yuhar'ish III at the end of the III century A.D. to resume the struggle for the throne.[86] Judging by the inscriptions, the Sabaeans first attacked the Ethiopian possessions in Yemenite Tihama, closest to the Sabaean kingdom.[87] They carried out two campaigns in which both ground troops and the fleet participated. The Habashat who lived there, and the coastal tribes of Sahartan, Gudman, Accum, and Barik who were subject to them, suffered great losses. Their villages, camps, and fields were ravaged; many were killed, others were taken away into captivity. Nevertheless, the Sabaeans did not succeed in capturing the seaside fortress of Wahidat ("Alone") in spite of the presence of the fleet.[88] The Gudman tribe subsequently sent ambassadors to Saba with a request for peace. The king of the Habashat also concluded peace with the Sabaeans, although Axum kept its possessions in Yemenite Tihama. The Sabaeans went on to crush the Kindites, taking their king prisoner, and then brought Shamir to defeat.

Shamir, as was indicated above, had called on the Axumite king, Wazeba I, for help. This may have happened even prior to the beginning of the Sabaean campaigns against the Ethiopian possessions in Tihama. Shamir with his Himyarites, the king of Hadramaut, the Axumite king and the tribes of Tihama subject to him formed a coalition against the Sabaeans. The purpose of the coalition evidently was the preservation of existing boundaries in Arabia (which the hegemony of the Sabaeans threatened), and the placing of Shamir on the Saba throne. The Ethiopian forces, together with the Sahartan troops, attacked the Sabaeans. Another Ethiopian detachment occupied Najran, which had joined the anti-Sabaean coalition. The Hadramaut king also promised help to Najran. Nevertheless, the Sabaean kings, surrounded on all sides by foes, crushed them one after the other.

The Ethiopians used ground forces and the fleet and fought on a broad front from Najran in modern Saudi Arabia to the southern extremity of Arabia. They dispatched garrisons to the cities of allies who had come over to their side.[89] As Wissmann suggests, only the death of Wazeba saved the Sabaean kings from inevitable defeat.[90] The coalition disintegrated and, as mentioned above, the Ethiopians concluded peace with the Sabaeans. Soon at least a part of the Axumite possessions in Arabia passed under the authority of the united Himyarites and Sabaeans. Nevertheless, the Axumite kings preserved the pretense of domination not only over the coastal lands but also over all of the Sabaean-Himyarite state.

Axum under Ze Haqile

Information about the Axumite Kingdom and its king Zoskales (Ζωσχάλης), whose name can be identified with Ze Haqile (or Za Hakala) of the "Lists of Axumite Kings,"[91] is given by Pseudo Arrian's *Periplus*. One should not attach significance to information from the lists concerning the length and dates of Ze Haqile's reign, especially since they are contained only in certain lists of version C. In other versions Ze Haqile is generally not mentioned.

According to Pirenne and Altheim's investigation, "Periplus" describes events during the years 208 to 210 or 225 A.D.[92] Pseudo Arrian calls Kharibael (king of the Himyarites and Sabaeans) and Eleaz[us] (king of Hadramaut) contemporaries of Zoskales in Arabia. They identify the former [Kharibael] with Karib'il, the opponent of Ilsharah Yahdib II, who is thought to have reigned in Himyar after Shamir Yuhar'ish II. Eleaz was probably the Hadramaut king, Il'azz Yalut, also an opponent of Ilsharah. Thus Ze Haqile could be a contemporary of Ilsharah (whom *Periplus* passes over in silence) and a successor of Wazeba I. Wissmann proposes that Zoskales usurped Axumite authority after Wazeba's death.[93] This hypothesis remains unproven. Considering the dating of Sabaean inscriptions proposed by Loundine (in particular *CIH*, 314+954) and the fact that Shamir Yuhar'ish II ruled before Karib'il, it is possible to move the beginning of the reign of Ze Haqile from 208–210 A.D. to several years later.

Describing the tribes and markets of the seacoast of contemporary Eritrea and the Sudan, Pseudo Arrian remarks: "Zoskales—miserly in living and tending toward accumulation, but in other respects a worthy man and one versed in Hellenic sciences, rules over those places—from the land of the Moschophagi (in the region of Suwakin) to the rest of Berbera (Somalia)."[94]

To the Graeco-Egyptian merchant who was the author of *Periplus*, Ze Haqile seemed "miserly in living," i.e., living far from luxuriously in comparison with other eastern rulers. Such "simplicity" in royal life style is, of course, only relative.

Gold and silver vessels were brought to Adulis especially for the king (Ze Haqile). They were fashioned in conformity with local style out of what was evidently low-purity metal, and were not very artistic in execution. Outer garments worn at court—the abollas and kaunaks—were also somewhat ordinary.

The relative simplicity of Ze Haqile's life in comparison with the luxury of later Axumite kings indicates the youthfulness of the Axum monarchy and its recent rise. In *Periplus* the reference to Axum as "the capital of the so-called Axumites" indicates the same thing. The author of *Periplus* in no way projected the name "Axumites" onto other tribes which had been incorporated into the kingdom of Ze Haqile, i.e., the Axumite Kingdom. In fact, *Periplus* does not call Zoskales (Ze Haqile) the Axumite "king," since his kingdom was so obscure. Yet *Periplus* is the first Graeco-Roman work after Ptolemaeus' to mention the Axumites. If one compares the commentary of *Periplus* about the Axumites and about Meroe[95] it is clear that the Meroitic Kingdom at the beginning of the III century A.D. was represented as the more important.

The information of *Periplus* about the personal qualities of Ze Haqile is interesting. Ze Haqile "tended toward accumulation." He knew the value

Stele No. 31, Axum.

of wealth and how it could be put to use. He did not neglect his taxes nor his trade interests, nor the trade interests of his subjects. He, or one of his predecessors, made Adulis an "officially established market" which facilitated the collection of trade duties and the enforcement of his monopoly on several articles of trade, such as gold and ivory. However, Pseudo Arrian, when describing in detail the trade of Ethiopia and neighboring countries, mentions the monopolies of South Arabian kings and the trade duties of the Nabataeans but does not say a word about the trade duties or monopolies of the Axumite kings. But then neither does he mention the export of Ethiopian gold. Evidently such omissions are attributable to the shortcomings of *Periplus*.[96]

It is unclear whether the port of Avalit, in the north of Somalia, which was already familiar to Claudius Ptolemaeus, belonged to the Axumites. The making of Adulis into "an officially established market" was favorable not only to the Axumite kings but also to the city. The move was probably in payment for the aid Adulis extended the Axumite kings in connection with their subjugation of the Ethiopian plateau, neighboring plains, and South Arabia. The Adulites continued to be faithful allies of Axum in the expansion and preservation of the Axumite state.

Ze Haqile is called "a person versed in Hellenic sciences," i.e., not a stranger to Greek learning. No other ruler is similarly characterized in *Periplus*. Probably no others were in as close contact with the Graeco-Roman merchants as Ze Haqile. The basis of "Hellenic sciences" was a knowledge of the Greek language. All of the inscriptions of the early Axumite kings which have come down to us, except one inscription of Gedara's, were composed in Greek. Even Ezana I and Ezana II used the Greek language in their bilingual inscriptions. Greek inscriptions on Axumite coins were retained still longer. Graeco-Roman influence is also noted in early Axumite architecture and sculpture.[97] The Axumite monarchy tended toward a cultural and ideological rapprochement with the Graeco-Roman world.

Pseudo Arrian speaks of Ze Haqile with great respect. The merchant does not like the king's economy but hastens to add that "in other respects [Ze Haqile] is an entirely worthy person."

From *Periplus* it is evident how the trade of Adulis with the Roman Empire, South Arabia, and India blossomed under Ze Haqile. Roman traders even penetrated into the interior regions of the kingdom. Pseudo Arrian himself was only in Adulis but he knew the distance to Coloe (Matara) and Axum. A Greek dedicatory inscription of a certain Aurelius and two persons named Antonianus was found near Axum; one of the two is called a saint (genitive case αγιου).[98] Judging by the names and paleography, these were emancipated Roman slaves of the first half of the III century A.D. During excavations of the town of Matara, just south of

Senafe, a necklace of 14 Roman coins of the II–III centuries A.D., primarily of the dynasty of the Antonines, was discovered.[99]

A cache of Kushan coins, discovered in 1940 at the Debre Damo monastery (northeast of Axum), has been dated to the reign of Ze Haqile. This was an extremely ancient Christian monastery which had already flourished in the early Middle Ages. The cache consisted of 104 gold coins. Five of them turned out to be double gold denarii of Vima Kadphises II, five were gold denarii of Kaniska, 88 were minted by Huviska, and the six most recent were gold denarii of Vasudeva I.[100] Thus approximately 84 percent of all of the coins in the cache belonged to Huviska, and to his successor Vasudeva I only a little more than 5 percent. Such a ratio can be explained only by the fact that the cache was accumulated in the first years of Vasudeva I's reign when still only a few coins of his minting were in circulation. Vasudeva I ascended the throne around 220 A.D. The Kushan coins were therefore probably exported from India soon after this date, around 222 A.D. After some time, the money found its way to Debre Damo and was hidden here. Neither Roman nor Persian coins turned up with them; consequently the interval of time between acquisition and concealment of the coins was probably short.

The remains of a gold-decorated box were discovered in association with the coins. Judging by its description the box was typically Axumite in style. Undoubtedly the owner of the cache was an Axumite. Most likely he had journeyed to India, sold his goods there, and brought home the money he made on them. Why did the cache turn up at Debre Damo? It is difficult to believe that a Christian monastery already existed there before 230 A.D. Christianity reached Ethiopia about a hundred years later. Most likely, the location of the future monastery was the site of a mountain pagan sanctuary not unlike those known in South and Central Arabia. The box with the coins was either brought as a gift to the god of the mountain or it belonged to a priest who had made a journey to India. The high value of the cache more readily speaks in favor of the latter assumption. The 104 coins totaling 109 gold denarii plus the precious metal box was a fortune with which one could acquire an estate of medium value.

In any event, the find of Kushan coins attests to the trade links of the young Axumite Kingdom with India as early as the first quarter of the III century A.D.

Pseudo Arrian mentions Indian goods and Indian merchants who had traveled to East African ports situated south of Adulis. Similarly, there is evidence of trade voyages of Axumites to India. Numerous archaeological finds, including the box from Debre Damo, indicate the high development of handicrafts in Northern Ethiopia during the II–III centuries A.D.

Ze Haqile's coastal possessions, according to Pseudo Arrian, stretched from the land of the Moschophagi (near contemporary Suwakin) to the "rest of Berbera," possibly to the Bab el Mandeb Gulf. The *Periplus* makes no note of Axumite possessions in Arabia, but Karib'il ruled in Southern Tihama. It is not known how far the possessions of Ze Haqile extended into the interior of the African continent: *Periplus* did not mention the Ethiopian plateau beyond the "mother country of the Axumites."

The Axumite Kingdom around 270–320 A.D.

The period of Axumite history from 220 to 270 A.D. is not illuminated by written sources. It is not known which of the monumental structures of Axum and other North Ethiopian cities can be dated to this period. The same can be said of the inscriptions.

The subsequent period, around 270–320 A.D., is known somewhat better. The western group of Axum palaces, the platform of Beta Giorgis with gigantic stelae, and possibly the Cyclopean slab—the greatest of the monolithic structures of Axum—probably date to this time. Perhaps at this time the fame of Axum first reached Iran. In a Coptic translation of *The Chapters* of the prophet Mani (216–276 A.D.) to the apostle of Manicheism are attributed the words: "There are four great kingdoms on earth: the first is the kingdom of Babylon [Mesopotamia] and Persia; the second is the kingdom of Rome; the third is the kingdom of the Axumites; the fourth is the kingdom of the Chinese." [101] Thus the Axumite Kingdom was placed on a par with the great empires of the world of that time: Chinese, Persian, and Roman. If the relative position of Axum actually dates to the period of the Mani sermon or could even have been figuratively evoked by the events of that time, it illustrates the prestige of Axum in Iran around 270 A.D.

At the end of the last quarter of the III century A.D., Axum began minting its own coins. Up to that time only foreign coins had circulated in Ethiopia: coins of the Roman Empire,[102] of the Kushan Empire (the cache at Debre Damo), and of the Sabaean Kingdom.[103] Minting of coins had a political significance. Many cities of the Roman empire and vassal kingdoms issued copper coins. Vassals of the Persian realm issued silver coins. However, the issuing of gold coins was a privilege restricted to the Roman, Persian, and Kushan emperors. Only an independent, powerful and rich state had its own gold money. The Axumite kings, at the outset, placed in circulation three metals: gold, silver, and copper (bronze). By this act they placed themselves on a par with the greatest monarchs of the world of that time.

The beginning of Axumite coinage can be dated only by the form and weight of the coins. Coins of the first Axumite kings imitate Roman coins minted during last quarter of the III century A.D. and the beginning of the IV century A.D., especially the coins of Diocletian and the vassal kings of the east. Another method of dating the beginning of coinage, although

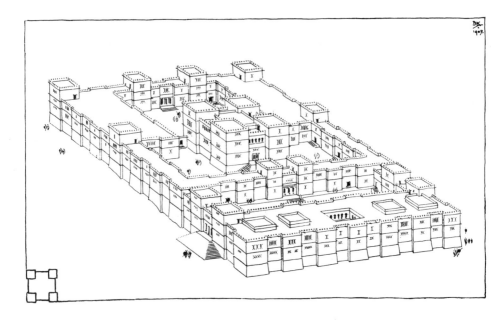

The palace Taʻakha Mariam, Axum (a reconstruction).

less reliable, is as follows. Ezana I came to the throne about 325–330 A.D. Coins of two of his predecessors are known: Endubis (Ενδύβις) and Ousanas I (Ουσάννας, Ουσανας). Such a chronological order was established in recent years by J. Pirenne's investigations. Thus Ezana I was the third Axumite ruler to mint coins. Probably Ousanas I was the father of Ezana I. Tyrranius Rufinus mentions him.

In 249 A.D. the Beja made an attack on Thebais [the Roman province of Upper Egypt] and were turned back with difficulty by the forces of the Emperor Decius. Did the Axumites not stand behind their neighbors and vassals the Beja? In 268 A.D. the Beja again invaded Egypt, probably in collaboration with anti-Roman forces.[104] In Egypt and Syria war was going on between the armies of the Palmyran Queen Zenobia, the Arabs, the Beja, and the Egyptian rebels headed by Firmus on the one side and the Roman legions on the other. However, the Emperor Aurelian defeated the anti-Roman coalition which was supported by Persia, put down the rebellion, and destroyed Palmyra. In 274 A.D. he returned to Rome, where a triumphal celebration was arranged, described much later in this manner:

"First came twenty elephants, two hundred different tamed wild animals from Libya [Africa] and Palestine . . . four tigers, a giraffe . . . eight hundred pairs of gladiators not counting captives from the barbarian tribes,

Blemm [Beja], Axomites [Axumites], Happy Arabs [Southern; Yemenite; "Arabia Felix"], Indites, Bactrians, Iberians, Saracens [Northern Arabs], and Persians with products of their countries." [105]

The Beja, Saracens, and, in part, the Persians were among Zenobia's allies. They could have been taken prisoner on the battlefield. But it was impossible to speak of battles with Caucasus peoples (Albanians and Iberians), Indites, Serians, and Axumites. Evidently these peoples participated in the triumphal celebration as delegates of congratulatory embassies and therefore they also carried "products of their countries" as gifts for the emperor. Flavius Vopiscus later maintained that the authority of Aurelian was extremely high among the eastern peoples. Not only the subjects of the empire but also "Saracens, Blemm [Beja], Aksomites [Axumites], Bactrians, Serians, Iberians and Albanians [of the Caucasus], Armenians and even Indic peoples revered him almost as a god incarnate." [106] Aurelian, in fact, was the first of the Roman emperors to proclaim himself a god.

Flavius Vopiscus is repeating some source or other which has not come down to us, and in his communication there is much that is unclear. The Emperor Aurelian ruled so short a time (270–275 A.D.) that by 272–273 A.D. neither the Serians of China or Central Asia nor the Indites or Bactrians would have been able to send their embassies to him. The reign of his predecessor was also very brief. In the course of the entire second half of the III century A.D. not the Roman emperors but the king and queen of Palmyra personified Roman authority in the east, and evidently the embassies of Axumites, Serians, and others were directed to the king and queen of Palmyra.

Conti-Rossini proposed that the Axumites, together with the Beja and Arab-Saracens, were allies of Zenobia. The Adulis inscription dates to this time in his opinion. He considered the Axumites who participated in Aurelian's triumphal celebration to be prisoners.[107] Later authors identified the Axumite king—Zenobia's ally—with Sembruthes. All these hypotheses, however, must be dismissed since the authorship of the Adulis inscription is unknown and the time of its composition scarcely coincides with the reign of Zenobia.

In spite of the defeat of Zenobia, part of Thebais remained in the hands of the Beja right up to 280 A.D. Even later, driven out of Egypt by Probus, they continued the onslaught on its borders. In 284 A.D. Emperor Diocletian ordered the Roman forces to leave lower Nubia (Dodekaskhoin), where the Nubians (Noba), allies of Rome in the struggle with the Beja, lived. The Romans paid a subvention to the latter for eschewing raids on Egypt. But even later the Beja continued to penetrate the frontier of Egypt, reaching Sinai in the north. About 290 A.D., Arab raiding became more frequent. In 297 A.D., when the Persians and Arabs entered Syria and

Palestine, Diocletian gave up the land south of Syene (Aswan) to the Nubians. In what way, if any, the offensive by the Beja and Arabs was connected with Axumite politics is not clear.

Information has been preserved indicating that the Axumites were entering Nubia at the same time. At the juncture of the III–IV centuries A.D. there appeared Heliodorus' novel *Aethiopica*. The events of the time of Persian domination in Egypt which Heliodorus read about in Herodotus served as the historical background for the novel. The Meroitic Kingdom was represented at the height of its power (which had long ago become a thing of the past). The embassies of various southern peoples brought gifts and congratulations to the Meroitic king: "And now, when almost all the ambassadors had passed before his eyes, the king rewarded each one with gifts of equal value and very many of them with still more valuable gifts. The ambassadors of the Auksiomites [Axumites], who were not obliged to pay tribute but were always friends and allies of the king, appeared before him last. Expressing their favored position in connection with the successes gained, they also brought gifts. Among others there was some strange species of animal of surprising bodily structure..."[108] (a detailed description of a giraffe follows).

The similarity of the description of the triumphal celebration and the reception of ambassadors in Heliodorus' novel and the corresponding places in Flavius Vopiscus' work attracts one's attention. If we disregard the Caucasus peoples, the Persians, Bactrians, and Saracens, then in Heliodorus' novel there are enumerated all the embassies of the eastern peoples who participated in Aurelian's triumphal celebration (counting also those who are said to have considered him [Aurelian] virtually as a god incarnate). These include the Serians, the "Happy" [Southern] Arabs, the Beja, and the Axumites. Only the "Indic peoples" were absent; probably simply as an omission by the novelist (but they were replaced by the Troglodytes). This similarity is scarcely accidental. Heliodorus was a younger contemporary of Aurelian and undoubtedly had heard about his triumphal celebration.

A communication of Heliodorus' concerning the friendship and alliance between Axum and Meroe at the end of the III century A.D., right on the eve of the Axumite campaigns into Meroe during which Nubia was annexed to the Axumite Kingdom, is interesting. At that time the Meroitic Kingdom was in the last stage of its decline.

The final mention of the Meroitic king, Teceridamani, dates to 254 A.D. Six more kings whose names have not been precisely determined reigned after him.[109] About 300 A.D. Meroe was abandoned. A stone stele with a victory inscription (in Greek) of an unknown Axumite king was the last written memorial found in the city.[110] The author or hero of the inscription calls himself "the king of the Axumites and Omerites (Himyarites)"; consequently, this unknown Axumite king nominally ruled over South Arabia. The term "Himyarites" incorporates all of the South Arabian population, thus supporting a relatively late date for the inscription: the end of the III century to the beginning of the IV century A.D. Separate words preserved on the stele indicate victories of the Axumites, the taking of booty, the ruination of the country (undoubtedly the Meroitic Kingdom is being spoken of). The inscription also refers to destruction of houses or temples and to the submissiveness of the inhabitants who brought tribute and recognized the authority of the Axumite king. Evidently, the Meroitic Kingdom was not able to recover from the crushing defeat.[111]

An attempt has been made to attribute the inscription from Meroe to Ezana I or II, but this is improbable. The title of the inscription's author is different from the magnificent titles of Ezana I and Ezana II. Evidently one of the predecessors of Ezana I, perhaps Ousanas I from whom he received in inheritance the title of king not only of Axum and Himyar but also of Kasu or Meroe, erected it.

Besides this inscription, two others composed in archaic Ethiopian characters in the Ge'ez language were found at Meroe. These inscriptions have not been completely deciphered.[112] They were discovered on the exterior walls of temple T in Kawa and on pyramid A–19. This indicates (as do the language, characters, and content of the inscriptions) their "lower class" and "domineering" origin. Whether they were left by troops of the author of the Greek inscription or by Ezana's troops remains unclear.

The hypothesis of the ascending of Shamir Yuhar'ish (II or III?) to the throne in Axum logically entails the view that Ella Amida, the father of Ezana II, and Ezana I (who was formerly confused with Ezana II) are descendants of Shamir.[113] Drewes proposes that the very name "Ella Amida" is South Arabian. It is actually encountered in Sabaean inscriptions in the form of 'L'MD in *CIH*, 29 and is unusual for the Ge'ez language. Drewes views the fact that his (Ezana II's) early inscription and one of the Ethiopian texts of the bilingual inscription are written with the Himyarite alphabet as further evidence of the Sabaean origin of Ezana II.[114] This evidence is not convincing. There can be a completely different explanation. Indeed, the Greek language of the Axumite inscriptions in no way attests to a Hellenic origin of the Axumite kings and the Sabaean nature of the name Ella Amida (or Ale Amida) still requires proof. The name "Ella Amida" belongs to the second (or ethnic) names of the Axumite kings known to us from different sources. To the same type belongs the second name of Kaleb, Ella Asbeha, and also the names of the kings Ella Sahel, Ella Gabaz, Ella Saham, etc.

By the end of the period described, all the principal countries later subjected to it in the IV–VI centuries A.D. had actually or nominally entered into the Axumite Kingdom. Axum had entered the arena of world politics: this became evident in the reign of Ezana I, about 330–360 A.D.

The reign of Ezana I

Ezana I actually was the first Axumite king about whom we have a knowledge both from his inscriptions and from works of foreign authors. The years of Ezana I's reign can be established only approximately. A letter was addressed to him by the Roman emperor Constantius II (the son of Constantine the Great), presumably in 356 A.D. How long Ezana I had reigned before and after this date remains unknown. It is proposed, on the basis of the work of Tyrranius Rufinus, that he came to the throne about 330 A.D. The "Lists of the Kings of Axum" do not mention Ezana I.

We can judge which territories the Axumite Kingdom included at the beginning of Ezana I's reign by his title, which is given in the well known bilingual inscription of this king. Besides Axum and Northern Ethiopia, several other countries were listed in Ezana's title—part of them African, part of them South Arabian. Ezana calls himself "king of Axum and Himer [Himyar] and Raydan and Saba and Salhen and Habashat and Siamo and Beja and Kasu."[115] Apparently, the order in which these countries are listed in the royal title reflects the succession of their conquest. The Axumite king who left the Greek inscription at Meroe called himself only king of the "Axumites and Omerites," of Axum and Himyar.

Later on, the names of the rest of the countries appeared in the title of the Axumite kings. Of them, Saba with the royal residence of Salhen, and Himyar with the residence of Du Raydan encompassed at that time all of South Arabia except Hadramaut. Siamo was situated on the eastern slope of the Ethiopian plateau. The Beja were subject to Axum as early as the reign of the king who built the Adulis monument. Meroe, the capital of Nubia (Kasu), was conquered last. Thus by the time of Ezana I's accession to the throne, the Axumite Kingdom nominally included an enormous territory as a result of conquests by early Axumite kings: the author of the Adulis inscription, the author of the Meroe inscription, etc.

Axum was located in the center of this territory. Here the Axumite king exercised his authority more completely than in the extra-Ethiopian possessions. All of these lands represented one country even though divided into Axum proper and vassal "kingdoms." Evidently the royal title calls this whole country "Axum."

In the Ethiopian texts of Ezana I's bilingual inscription, "Habashat" is mentioned among the Arabian countries. This name is given as "Ethiopia" in the Greek text. At that time Nubia and all of tropical Africa was called Ethiopia. This term began to be applied to modern Ethiopia only from the time of Philostorgius, Cosmas Indicopleustes, and Procopius Caesarensis (V–VI century A.D.). The Habashat of the Sabaean inscriptions is the district which belonged to the Ethiopians and was situated on the Arabian coast of the Red Sea. Since Habashat is mentioned in the Arabian part of Ezana I's possessions, evidently this Arabian district was meant.

One of the political problems which from time to time, with astonishing regularity, confronted the rulers of the empires of Northeast Africa (i.e., the Meroitic pharaohs, the kings of kings of Axum, the kings of Great Nubia, the sultans of the Mamelukes, etc.) was the subduing of the freedom-loving tribes of the Nubian desert. Virtually all of the Axumite rulers were obliged to dispatch their forces; and Ezana I was no exception. The greatest of the desert tribes at that time were the Beja. Ezana I's inscription speaks of their pacification.[116]

Ezana I was now so strong that he could change the traditional methods of "pacification." When the Beja rebelled, he sent a force against them under the command of his brothers—She'azana and Hadefa[s]. Ezana did not go on the campaign personally as he had formerly done. The Beja "laid down their weapons"; even this numerous people did not consider opposition to Axum possible now. Under an escort of Axumites, six tribes of Beja in full strength with their "kings," wives, children, and cattle were brought to Ezana. The migration lasted the whole of four months. On the way, the migrants received food and drink according to a precisely determined quota. In Axum they appeared before Ezana I and, evidently, again repeated their submission. Now the mercy of Ezana I had no bounds; he not only did not sell the Beja into slavery, not only did he let them keep their families, cattle, and their tribal unity, but he also ordered 25,140 head of large-horned cattle, clothing, and food to be given to the six "kings." These six tribes which constituted a significant portion of the Beja were resettled into the "land of Matlia" (of the Greek text)[117] or into the "land of BYRN" (both Ethiopian texts).[118] It is possible that this is the territory of the medieval and present-day Begemdir (which literally means "land of the Beja") on the eastern bank of Lake Tana. This was the southern boundary of the Axumite Kingdom. Thus the Beja were settled in a frontier district economically connected with Axum in the surroundings of loyal tribes (Agau, Semen, etc.). The Beja who remained on their native land were weakened by the migration of part of their people and for a long time refrained from rebellion.

Ezana I stands at the summit of his power in the following inscription: "Rebellious tribes were subdued, renouncing the prolonging of the struggle. The king resettled them at enormous distances, lightly gave yesterday's rebels great riches (land, cattle, clothing). By one word of Ezana the migrants were supplied with food in a sufficient quantity on the way;

to the gods he brought valuable gifts—gold, silver, and bronze statues, a parcel of land."

Of all of Ezana I's inscriptions, the bilingual one has the most obvious propagandistic character. Moreover, the propaganda is directed primarily to a foreign audience. We see this in the fact that the Greek text occupies a place of honor. It is executed most carefully in both stylistic and paleographic respects. In the content of the bilingual texts there are also significant differences. In the Greek text there is less overt boasting. Only the god Ares (Mahrem) is extolled. In all the remaining instances the text avoids laudatory epithets. It concludes with a communication about the bringing of gifts to the gods. The Ethiopian versions, however, indulge in more flowery expressions and personal details which emphasize the generosity of the king.

Moreover, in the Ethiopian texts of the bilingual inscription there is an addition which is not present in the Greek. First comes a sacro-juridical formula. Punishment threatens that person who scrapes off the inscription in order to write a new one or who moves the stele to another place or overturns it. That person who honors it will be blessed. Then there follows a message about the purpose of the inscription ("we have erected it, so that it would speak about us, about us and about our city") and about the dedication to Mahrem of a strip of ground and a stone throne. This latter element is not found in the Greek text; only the dedication of metal statues and the inscription itself is mentioned. In the concern demonstrated by the king over the fame of the city it is possible to see the rudiments of demagoguery.

We can judge the authority of Ezana I in Meroe and South Arabia by his title of supreme ruler of these countries, but probably the South Arabian kings who were considered his vassals also preferred to preserve the best possible relations with Axum, not directly rejecting his claims and not attracting his wrath on themselves. They needed the support of the Axumites against an outside foe—the Persian world power and its Arabian allies. In Ezana I's inscriptions nothing is said about his wars in South Arabia. A hint about them is contained in only one Latin source contemporary to Ezana I. This source, *The Complete Description of the World and Its Peoples*, was written, as is evident from the events mentioned in it, in 350 A.D.[119] The first twenty paragraphs of the *Description* are given in the form of an itinerary and, evidently, are an additional translation of a Greek itinerary. In §18 the route from India to South Arabia and Axum is shown. South Arabia is called Little India (India Minor). The name of the Axumite Kingdom is distorted; however, it is easily restored by its appropriate place in the itineraries. The Axumite Kingdom is presented as a strong military power imposing its influence on India Minor, which asked for military aid (*auxilium*) from Axum when Persia began a war against it.[120]

The character of the communication shows that recent events were being spoken of since recollections were still fresh. Altheim and Stiehl are inclined to think that Ezana I actually possessed a part of the Red Sea coastal area of South Arabia.[121]

Ezana I protected the traditional religion of the Axumites, especially the cult of the god Mahrem. In both Ethiopian texts of the bilingual inscription the giving of a strip of land (?) to the god Mahrem is mentioned.[122] All the texts of the bilingual inscription speak of giving Mahrem gold, silver, and three bronze statues.[123] Probably these were the gigantic bronze statues (with a height up to 5 meters), the base of one of which was discovered by the German Axum expedition.[124] With respect to the astral-agricultural triad—the gods Astar, Beher, and Medr—the king limited himself to good wishes.

Because of confusion of Ezana I and Ezana II it was formerly thought that the first of these kings adopted Christianity about 350 A.D. and made it the state religion. Actually the propagation of Christianity in Ethiopia did not assume the form of a single-occasion act or a compulsory mass baptism. It proceeded gradually and voluntarily over the whole course of the evolution of the Axumite state. This is suggestive of the well known "democratism" of earlier Axumite society, indicating that strong traditions of an older social structure still existed.

By the middle of the IV century A.D. Christianity had become a genuinely world religion. The entire Roman Empire was almost completely Christianized. Christianity was recognized officially and received the support of government authority. By this time it was spreading beyond the boundaries of the Empire; to the northern and southern Arabs, into Persia, and even into South Arabia. In Ethiopia, Christians could have appeared even before the middle of the IV century A.D. but information about them has not been preserved.[125] Under Ezana I, a Christian community was organized in Axum. Frumentius became its bishop.

Undoubtedly Frumentius was a historical personage. Completely reliable documents mention him: *Apologia of the Emperor Constantius*, by Athanasius, a letter of the Emperor Constantius II to Ezana I, and also the *Historia ecclesiastica* of his younger contemporary Tyrranius Rufinus.

Rufinus tells of the appearance of Frumentius in Axum and of his life in that country. According to him, Frumentius and his brother Aedesius were taken as captives to Ethiopia and given to the king. Both young boys were pupils of the Tyrian philosopher Meropius. The king made them his own servants, whereupon Frumentius "was entrusted with his [the king's] exchequer and his correspondence" (there is nothing improbable in this). After the king's death his very young son became his successor. Frumentius and Aedesius received their freedom but remained in Axum ostensibly at the urgent request of the queen. Rufinus maintains that Frumentius "took the rule of the state into his own hands." In my view, this is an exaggeration. It is possible that as a confidant and adviser of the queen he did acquire considerable power. Now he "undertook earnestly to find out whether there were not Christians among the Roman merchants. He wanted to give them the very greatest advantages and to persuade them to meet in specified places where they would be able to conduct divine services according to the Roman rite. Frumentius conducted himself in such a way that he influenced others by his example, and with praises and favors induced them to do everything necessary in order to prepare places for the erection of God's temples and other purposes, being in every way possible concerned about the propagation of the seeds of Christianity." In other words, he undertook the conversion of the local populace. In Ethiopia, "numerous Christian communities appeared and temples were erected." Most likely this is an exaggeration. However, the appearance of at least one organized Christian community and the construction of at least one church (or the remodeling of a private home) is undoubted. It is entirely probable that there was not just one community and church but two or three, but not as many as Rufinus indicated. The version of the Ethiopian synaxarion, that Frumentius instructed the young king in the Christian faith, is at most the conjecture of medieval monks.[126]

After the young king grew up and was able to conduct government affairs on his own, Aedesius and Frumentius left Axum and set out for the borders of the empire. Rufinus says that both the king and the queen-mother repeatedly asked them to remain, especially Frumentius who far excelled his brother. Aedesius returned to his native land in Tyre but Frumentius set out for Alexandria. There he appealed to the bishop, Athanasius the Great, to initiate a bishopric in Axum. Athanasius appointed Frumentius himself and sent him back to Ethiopia. In conclusion, Rufinus says that he received all this information directly from Aedesius of Tyre, the brother of Bishop Frumentius.[127]

Tyrranius Rufinus was a person who deserves credence. He could have become acquainted with Aedesius in Tyre. In Alexandria, Rufinus was on friendly terms with Athanasius the Great and people who knew Frumentius personally. Therefore, there can be no doubt that he received his information firsthand. It is true, as Bolotov showed, that the chronological and geographical coordinates of Rufinus' story are muddled, "but Rufinus transmitted fact itself truthfully."[128] Up to the present, not one investigator has doubted the veracity of the basic information communicated by Rufinus. It is possible to blame him, over and above the geographic and chronological confusion, for exaggeration of Frumentius' authority and the successes of Christian evangelism; but in this respect Aedesius could also be guilty. All of the historical and social conditions of the story are completely reliable or probable and find confirmation in sources which differ in nature.

We can present the propagation of Christianity in the Axumite Kingdom in the following manner. Prior to the middle of the IV century A.D., individual Christians from the Roman Empire and, in part, from other countries came to Ethiopia for a more or less prolonged period of time. Some of them were slaves. Only the king and upper nobility were able to possess expensive European and Asian slaves. Literate and intelligent slave-Christians not infrequently succeeded in attaining considerable influence. One of them, Frumentius, tried to create his own religious community and set it in opposition to the tribal communities of his rivals. As a confidant of the king, he was able to utilize the economic privileges of the monarchy for his own purposes and, in Rufinus' words, actually did so. At first Frumentius gathered Christians from among the Roman subjects and foreigners in general, mainly from among the merchants. They readily came into the union which, although fraught with certain political dangers, undoubtedly was in their economic interests. Thus the foundation of the Axumite Christian community was laid. Accompanying the merchants and travelers were Christianized slaves who also came into the community. The community had considerable means at its disposal, the major part of which the merchants provided. It was able to construct a stone church, to decorate it luxuriously, to dispense free meals after divine services, and to give material help to the poor. This was the beginning of widespread promulgation of Christianity. One cannot doubt that Frumentius used all of his influence in order to attract as many individuals as possible to the Christian community and convert them to his faith. It is not known whether the Axumite nobility, tied to traditional ancestral and tribal cults, supported him from the very beginning. But all outcasts, those deprived of civil rights, and indigent persons were obliged, naturally, to seek entry into the community. Thanks to Frumentius' activity, Christian communities appeared also in other cities, including of course Adulis where there were especially many foreigners. Christianity gradually became a real force in Ethiopia and it was able to attract individual representatives of the Axumite nobility, along with their families. The king had no reason to fear his trusted slave and he did not hinder Christian evangelism. Moreover, Frumentius and Aedesius were sufficiently prudent and sensible, as Rufinus emphasizes, not to provoke the hostility or suspicion of those who were in power. The vaguely monotheistic ideas which had been propagated among the educated Axumites created a favorable soil for the acceptance of Christian doctrine. The Axumite king quickly comprehended what sort of political benefits the new teaching would bring to him. From this time on the Christian community could count on the monarchy's support.

As Rufinus relates, Frumentius organized the Axumite Christian community at the beginning of the reign of a young king who could only have been Ezana I;[129] when he was sufficiently grown, Aedesius and Frumentius left Axum. Frumentius arrived in Alexandria between 346 and 356 A.D. (more likely closer to the latter date). At this time he was appointed by Athanasius as the Orthodox (Monophysite) bishop of Axum and returned to Ethiopia in that capacity. In 356 A.D. new persecutions of Orthodox (Monophysite) believers had begun and Athanasius was again deprived of his eparchy. Between February 24, 357 A.D., and October 2, 358 A.D.[130] he wrote the *Apologia*, addressed to Constantius II (the protector of Arianism), wherein he says the following: "Understand, for the third time there has come to me a rumor that letters have been received by the Axumite sovereigns in which they are asked to look after the sending back from there of Frumentius the Bishop of Axum. They would have to track me also to the very boundaries of the barbarians in order to lead me to the so-called legal protocols of the prefects and also to incite the laymen and bishops to submit to the Arian heresy."[131]

In order that, by the time of the writing of the *Apologia*, a rumor about the letters could have reached Athanasius for the third time they would have had to be sent at least a year before this, i.e., in 356 A.D. Athanasius speaks of "letters" and not just about one letter, correctly or mistakenly thinking that several diplomatic missions were sent to Axum. We know of only one of these. In proof, Athanasius cites in the *Apologia* the text of a letter which came from the Emperor Constantius and was addressed to the rulers of Axum, Ezana I ('Αιζανᾶ) and his brother Sezana (Σαιζανᾶ). In the latter, it is not difficult to recognize the brother of the king—the She'azana of the bilingual inscription of Ezana I.[132] In the Greek text of the bilingual inscription he is called Seazana (Σαιαζάνας).[133] It is difficult to say whether Athanasius or Constantius' secretary distorted the name She'azana-Seazana into Sezana; however, the name of the Axumite king "Ezana" is given with utmost precision for the Greek language.

There are letters addressed to the Axumite rulers demanding that they join in the persecution of the Orthodox (Monophysite) believers. Athanasius is reviled as a blasphemer and villain, Frumentius as his dangerous accomplice. The emperor expresses concern about the souls of the Axumites: " ... It follows to fear that he [Frumentius], since he arrived in Axum, has corrupted you with blasphemous speeches and not only has he been disturbing the clergy, hampering it and blaspheming, but also thereby he is becoming a perpetrator of the crime of tainting and ruination of all your people."[134]

Constantius demands that Frumentius be returned to Egypt without delay and receive a new ordination in the Ethiopian order from the Arian bishops. The emperor did not wish to hear any kind of excuses from the

Axumite rulers. Constantius' letter resembles a tactless meddling in the affairs of the Axumite Kingdom which moreover could not be backed by either economic pressure or military force. The arrogant and demanding tone of the letter is startling.

It is not difficult to imagine how it was met. For the Axumite king and for the nobility, with their protection of different cults and highly indefinite religious views, the dogmatic zeal of Constantius was completely alien. Ezana I and the Axumite nobility were, evidently, absolutely indifferent to the struggle of the Arians with the Athanasians, which was being waged around dogmatic formulae. None of them, except perhaps the personal enemies of Frumentius, intended to get mixed up in this struggle. On the contrary, they knew Frumentius well and they sided with him. The demand of the emperor with respect to Athanasius was impracticable since he was not residing within the limits of the Axumite Kingdom. The demand to return Frumentius to Egypt for a new appointment proved simply absurd.

In the circumstances created, the Axumite king and his council (advisers) were obliged to turn to Frumentius for elucidation. As an interested party he, of course, gave an interpretation to the events and commented upon the letter in a manner in no way to Constantius' benefit. To Frumentius and his partisans it was not difficult to prove that the Roman emperor was addressing in an unworthy manner the Ethiopian "king of kings," a person of rank equal to his. They also suggested that he was striving to spread his authority into the Axumite Kingdom and meddle in Axumite affairs. Frumentius had full opportunity to make a copy of the letter and send it to Athanasius. One cannot doubt that the letter did not produce favorable consequences for the Roman emperor. The authority of the Roman government certainly suffered. On the other hand, the Axumite king once again saw what kind of political possibilities the new religion bore. The very letter of Constantius shows what kind of authority the "Axumite rulers" enjoyed in Alexandrine church circles. The Athanasians considered them as their defenders.

In Philostorgius'[135] *Historia ecclesiastica*, information is contained on the Roman embassy headed by Bishop Theophilus Indusius. The embassy pursued religious aims. Theophilus was sent by the Emperor Constantius to the Himyarites and Axumites. At first the embassy arrived in the "Sabaean Kingdom called Himyar." It brought rich, indeed royal, gifts, including 200 Cappadocian horses of the best blood. The gifts were delivered to the Himyarite ruler, whom Philostorgius called an ethnarch (i.e., a ruler of the people but not a king). As a result of negotiations, the Himyarite king "was inclined toward piety" (i.e., he accepted Christianity in the Arian doctrine). He agreed to the construction of churches, the more so since the emperor allocated resources for them: money, smalt, and marble. One church was built in Tafar (Zafar), the capital of Himyar, another at Adan (Aden), a third in the so-called Persian market in the south of Iran. Probably in addition to religious matters, questions of trade were also discussed, for example those concerning protection of the interests of Roman merchants. But primary attention was allotted to religious policy.

From South Arabia Theophilus "set out for the Axumites who were called Ethiopians," where he also carried out some sort of diplomatic errands. Judging by the nature of his mission in Himyar, these errands concerned religious matters. Perhaps Theophilus himself delivered the letter of the Emperor Constantius, mentioned above, to Ezana I. Philostorgius did not mention the name Ezana, but Ezana I *was* the Axumite king at the time of Constantius II. The king of the Axumites was not called βασιλεὺς (king), like the Roman emperor, but τυράννος (tyrant), which nevertheless is a rank above the Himyarite ethnarch.

Philostorgius' work is preserved in fragments. It is difficult to judge in how much detail the whole embassy of Theophilus Indusius is described. However, the impression is created that the diplomatic negotiations in Himyar were allotted great attention, while the mission to Axum was spoken of less readily. Probably the results of the mission to Axum were not as significant as those of the one to South Arabia. This is understandable. The Axumite king was in no way inclined to carry out the demands of the Roman emperor. Moreover, the embassy in Himyar, which had given rich gifts to Ezana's vassal (to the Himyarite king who agreed to the demands of the Romans and for this received their political support), unavoidably compelled Ezana I to be on the alert. The Roman-Axumite relations under Ezana I were therefore extremely contradictory. On the one hand, the acceptance of Christianity by the Axumites and inhabitants of South Arabia connected the Axumite Kingdom more closely with the Roman Empire. On the other hand, Rome's policy in the region of the southern seas not infrequently was seen as an encroachment on Axum's rights. This led to those "abrogations of the alliance with the Romans" of which Rufinus spoke. Usually the community of trade interests prevailed and similar "abrogations of the alliance" were a temporary occurrence. However, they show how jealously the Axumite Kingdom guarded its privileges and sovereignty. This political line was also followed by the successors of Ezana I: the kings of the end of the IV through the beginning of the VI century A.D.

Under Ezana I there appeared the rudiments of a written literature in the Ge'ez language. Along with this were introduced letters of the Byzantine-Greek type which are used even now in Ethiopia. Undoubtedly Frumentius played a direct role in connection with this innovation as the king's secretary and the head of the royal chancellery. The Greek text of the bilingual inscription of Ezana I, evidently, is also the fruit of Frumentius' creativity.

However, the first translations of Christian books into the Ge'ez language could scarcely have appeared in the reign of Ezana I. The language of his inscriptions is somewhat more archaic than the language of the Ethiopian Bible. Littmann considered that the first translations of Christian texts into the Ge'ez appeared a century after the activity of Frumentius.

The Axumite Kingdom at the end of the IV to the middle of the V century A.D.

The development of the Axumite Kingdom continued even after Ezana I's death. Excavations and eyewitness accounts (those of Cosmas and Nonnus) indicate the previously unparalleled luxuries which surrounded the Axumite king.

The condition of the country in this period is known to us only from brief descriptions of Roman-Byzantine authors. Many of them visited the Axumite Kingdom in the course of a journey passing through Adulis into India and Ceylon. This attests to the significance of Adulis in the Roman Empire's trade with India, Ceylon, and Southeast Asia. The role of the sea route to India continued to grow. The protracted Roman-Persian wars had for a long time closed the trade route from India via the Euphrates and the Syrian roads. The route via the Red Sea and the Indian Ocean was far more dependable. Moreover, here the Roman subjects could trade with peoples of the tropical Asian countries without Persian and Arab middlemen. The trade route from the Red Sea to the East African coast continued to function; Cosmas Indicopleustes was familiar with it.

Unfortunately, in the IV–VI centuries A.D. peripluses similar to the *Peripluses* of Agatharchides and Pseudo Arrian were not composed. Instead there appeared itineraries, one of which was utilized in the first paragraphs of *Complete Description of the World*. In the Greek texts of two itineraries which are very similar to each other,[136] not only is the route from Ceylon to the Axumite Kingdom indicated but also the religious affiliation of the inhabitants. Peoples of different countries are characterized as Christians, "Hellenes" (i.e., pagans), Magi (Zoroastrians). The piety of the Physon Indians, who are not Christians but who also do not worship idols as the "Hellenes" do, is especially noted. The Indians of the Malabar Coast are called "Christians and Hellenes" (Χριστιάνοι χαὶ Ἑλληναις). The inhabitants of "Axomia" (i.e., the Axumite Kingdom), on the other hand, are called "Hellenes and Christians." Evidently there were more pagans among them than Christians.

"Axumites and Adulites" and Taino (Siamo) are mentioned in Epiphanius' book *De duodecim gemmis*, written soon after 394 A.D.[137] Their religious affiliation is not noted. They are simply called "Indian peoples."

Narrative sources permit one to maintain that foreign merchants from the Roman Empire, India, Ceylon, South Arabia, and Socotra Island[138] (which played a prominent role in the trade of the northern part of the Indian Ocean right up to the nineteenth century) were found constantly in Adulis and Axum during this period.

The Axum and Adulis merchants also carried out overseas journeys. In Arabia, they traded not only in the port cities but also in the interior areas of the peninsula. Among the foreigners who inhabited Najran (a very large caravan trade center) *The Book of Himyarites* names a certain "Abyssinian" Yona, who was a deacon.[139] If one considers the tendencies of merchants of that time to associate with fellow countrymen, then it can be proposed that Yona was the head of a rather populous trade colony; otherwise he would not have had a leadership title such as "deacon." Numerous caches [finds] of Axumite coins recovered in South Arabia also indicate trade links with Axum.

An Ethiopian inscription recently discovered in Egypt dates to the IV–V centuries A.D. It was discovered in Wadi Menih, on the ancient road from Berenika to the Nile Valley, together with Egyptian hieroglyphic, Graeco-Roman, Graeco-Christian, Nabataean, and early Arabic inscriptions.[140] The author of the inscription, the Axumite Abreha, probably arrived in Berenika by sea and from there set out by caravan road for the Valley of Egypt.

Mention of Axumites in a letter of Synesius of Cyrene (circa 355–414 A.D.), written about 410 A.D. (not long before Synesius accepted the position of bishop of Cyrenaican Ptolemais), dates to the beginning of the V century A.D. He tells of the struggle of the Christians with barbarians (or Berbers) somewhere in the south of Cyrenaica—in the Jalu oasis, according to the opinion of investigators of Synesius.[141] This is ancient and early medieval Augila (modern Awjidah). Deacon Faustus, who fought with his bare hands "heaping up" around himself the corpses of the Berbers, is especially eulogized in the letter. Faustus is called Μελάμπυγος ("Black-assed"). Synesius, as a Byzantine erudite, is alluding to Hercules' famous epithet. For the brave deacon such a comparison is flattering. But the coarse epithet is appropriate only if Faustus actually was black-skinned. Evidently this was so. A native inhabitant of Augila would hardly have appeared "black" to a Cyrenaican inhabitant.

The remark on Faustus' origin in the concluding wish of the letter therefore does not in itself seem unexpected: "A thousand successes to the priests of the Axumites!" (Αὐξουμιτων-, in Migne's publication;[142] Αξωμιτων, in Ershe's publication).[143]

Not merely a single individual is being spoken of but a group of Axumites sufficiently strong so as to independently, albeit in an alliance with Byzantium, carry on a struggle with the Berber tribes in the depths of their country. This was a whole community with their own divine votaries. How did the Axumites turn up in an Eastern Sahara oasis? Research indicates that at a later time, in the XVI to the XX century, a caravan route ran from the banks of the Nile to Barka (Cyrenaica) via the oases of Salim, Kufrah, and Jalu. This was the most easterly of the trans-Saharan routes. Probably the Axumites arrived in Jalu via this route from the south, from Nubia. Such a hypothesis, advanced by Caquot and Leclant, agrees well with the fact that the penetration of Axumites into Nubia on the eve of the V century A.D. is well known.[144]

Other hypotheses do not appear so probable. If the Axumites had been slaves they would not have been able to emerge as one of the parties in the struggle with the Berbers. On the other hand, Axumites can scarcely be considered as conquerors: Byzantine and Ethiopian sources say nothing about Axumite conquests to the west of the Nile. Indeed, the likelihood itself of such a distant military expedition via the sands of the Eastern Sahara is virtually excluded. One can think only that it is a trade colony which is being spoken of. In such an event, the unexpectedly broad scope of Axum's foreign trade on the African continent is revealed and, what is more, as early as the beginning of the V century A.D.

The work of Pseudo Callisthenes (Palladius?), who visited the Axumite Kingdom at the beginning of the V century A.D., has special value. He knew a certain Thebaidian law teacher (scholastic) who made a journey into India. This law teacher set out for Adulis from Thebais, on a ship with a certain "holy man" (priest?). Having seen the city, the law teacher made a trip to Axum "where the kinglet ($\beta\alpha\sigma\iota\lambda\dot{\iota}\sigma\chi\circ\varsigma$) of the Indians abides." From here the scholastic again set out, via Adulis, for the Troglodytes who lived near the cape of the Aromats (Guardafui Ras Asir), and from there across the Indian Ocean to India, to the country of the Brahmins (i.e., into India proper). He made this part of the journey with "Indians" with whom he had become acquainted in Axum. Judging by the fact that the Axumite king is called the "kinglet of the Indians," the scholastic's fellow travelers were Axumites. The Latin version of Pseudo Callisthenes' work mentions Axumite ships in Ceylon.[145] Cosmas Indicopleustes speaks of the same thing. Pseudo Callisthenes also visited India. Moisei, the bishop of Adulis, accompanied him on the journey. The bishop's journey to India is scarcely explained by curiosity alone. One can speculate that the bishop was visiting his spiritual flock, which was sojourning in India most likely for trade purposes. Perhaps Moisei counted on collecting alms from among the flock for the needs of the Adulis eparchy. In any event Pseudo Callisthenes provides varied material about the journeys to India and Ceylon not only of Egyptians but also of Axumites.

It is significant that besides the Axumite eparchy there also appeared references to an Adulis eparchy. In 451 A.D., the Adulis bishop was present at the Chalcedonian council.[146] This attests to a further spread of Christianity in the Axumite Kingdom. Four learned travelers figure in Pseudo Callisthenes' work: he himself, two priests, and the law teacher. All of them, for one reason or another, turned up in the territory of the Axumite Kingdom. No doubt the organization of Christian communities in Northern Ethiopia made possible journeys into that country not only for merchant-adventurers but also for scholars wishing to examine strange cultures.

The Axumite king is called "kinglet" by Pseudo Callisthenes. This term was usual in the V–VI centuries A.D. for foreign, i.e., non-Byzantine monarchs. For example, the king of the Nobatie (Silko) in the VI century A.D. calls himself "kinglet of the Nobatie and all the Ethiopians."[147] However, in Ezana I's bilingual inscription only vassal "kings" of the Beja[148] are called "kinglets" (βασιλισχοί); Ezana I himself is called "king" and "king of kings."

How often Roman subjects made journeys to the Axumite Kingdom in the V century A.D. can be judged from a Codex of Theodosius II (408–450 A.D.); one of the articles focuses upon those "who travel to the Homerites (Himyarites) and Axumites" (*Codex Theodosianus*, XII, 2, 12). Significantly, the Himyarites are mentioned first and only after them are the Axumites mentioned. Theophilus Indusius first visited South Arabia and from there went to Axum. Sources of the VI century A.D. directly mention that "Roman merchants visit in the interior areas of the Himyarites called Indian Auzelis (Adulis) and then in the area of the Indians and Kushites" (Ethiopians),[149] and that "Roman merchants pass through [the land] of the Himyarites to Axum and the country of the Indians."[150] Philostorgius, whose work was concluded between 425 and 433 A.D., also mentions the location of the Axumites in reference to the ports of South Arabia. In his words, the Axumites lived "on the left shore of the Red Sea" [on the left if one sailed to the Axumites of Adulis from Adan (Aden) or Muza (Moha); if one sailed along the Red Sea from Egyptian harbors or from Palestinian Ela (Elat), Adulis and the Axumites proved to be on the right shore of the sea]. Philostorgius' information about the Syrians who at this time supposedly lived on the shores of the Indian Ocean to the east of the Axumite Kingdom is extremely interesting: "Before these Axumites, in a direction to the east up to the Outer [Indian] Ocean, live Syrians who bear this name also among the local inhabitants. Alexander (the Macedonian) led them out of Syria and settled there. Even now they use the native language but under the sheer rays of the sun became black."[151] The "blackness" of these Syrians indicates that they were confused with equatorial races; evidently the Christians of Kerala (Malabar Coast of

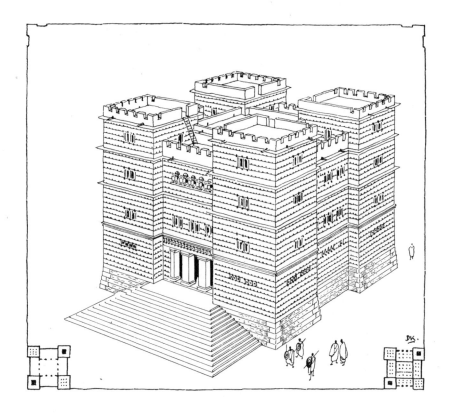

Reconstruction of the central structure
of the palace Enda Mika'el, Axum.

India) are being spoken of. They actually are of Syrian origin. Philostorgius notes the spreading of Syrians (South Arabian Christians) "up to the Axumites," i.e., up to the borders of the Axumite Kingdom. Evidently South Indian Christians, whose traces are noted also on Socotra Island, traded and settled on the African shores. It was certain that they could be encountered in Adulis, the largest station on the route from Syrian-Palestinian Elat to South India.

The most valuable information about the Axumite Kingdom of the V and beginning of the VI centuries A.D. is communicated by Cosmas Indicopleustes.[152] He visited Adulis and described its sights.

Besides Adulis, Cosmas made a journey to Axum, where he even visited the palace and saw the feeding of giraffes in the presence of the king.[153] In Axum he gathered information about the gold-bearing country of Sasu in Southwest Ethiopia. According to his testimony, trade links of the Axumite Kingdom stretched to the southwest as far as Sasu and to the northeast as far as Persia, Ceylon, and the country of the Ephtalites (White Huns) in Northern India. Cosmas says that Ceylon "is visited by ships . . . from Ethiopia" and Ceylon's goods "are sent into Persia, Omeritia (Himyar), and Adulia (Adulis)." Also that the Ethiopians of the Axumite Kingdom acquire emeralds from the Beja and supply them to the Western Indian Barigazi and to the White Huns. Cosmas encountered inhabitants of Socotra Island in Ethiopia who arrived there for trade purposes. Their bishop having received ordination from the "Persians," they were Christians of the Nestorian rite.

In Ethiopia, Cosmas found not only individual Christians but also Christian communities and churches with bishops. He writes: "Among Bakter ('White') Huns and Persians, and other Indians and Persarmens (Armenians) and Medes (Medians) and Elamites and along all the land of Persia there is no end to the churches with bishops and very many Christian communities and also a multitude of martyrs and monks who live as hermits; likewise in Ethiopia and in Axum and in the whole country around it." Just how important Axum's trade with Persia was at the beginning and middle of the VI century A.D. is indicated by the fact that in his letter to the Axumite king the Emperor Justinian insisted that the Axumites cease trade with the Persians.[154]

The relative significance of coastal cities and countries in Ethiopian trade at the beginning of the VI century A.D. can be determined on the basis of a list of ships which had gathered in the summer of 525 A.D. in the harbor of Gabaza. The list is contained in *Martyrium sancti Arethae* . . .[155] and has been analyzed in detail by N. V. Pigulevskaya.[156] From India 9 ships arrived; however, it is not known what *The Martyrdom* means by "India." Seven ships came from the "Island of Farasan," i.e., from the islands of Farasan al Kabir, where the South Arabian Christian Farasan tribe lived. This tribe played a large role in Yemen and Hidjazan trade. From Palestinian Ela (Elat), the main Red Sea port of the Syrian-Palestinian region, came 15 ships. From Egyptian ports (Clysma, Berenika) came 22 ships, 20 of them from Clysma and only 2 from Berenika, which indicates that by the beginning of the VI century A.D. the route from Thebais to Berenika (and farther by sea to Arabia, Ethiopia and the countries of the Indian Ocean) had fallen into disuse. Prominence among the Red Sea ports of Egypt had passed to Clysma, which under the name of Culzum flourished in subsequent centuries also. Moreover, 7 ships arrived from the Island of Iotab (Tiran).

Procopius Caesarensis describes the Ethiopian ships: "They do not smear them with pitch nor anything else; the planks are not held together with iron nails but are joined with ropes."[157] The cargo capacity of such ships was not great but they served for long sea voyages, including those to India and Ceylon.

Information of Cosmas Indicopleustes, Pseudo Callisthenes, Synesius, *The Book of the Himyarites* (and others) attests to the fact that at the end of the IV through the beginning of the VI centuries A.D. Christianity had attained great successes in the Axumite Kingdom. This does not completely dispute Bolotov's[158] opinion that paganism prevailed in the V century A.D. in Ethiopia as before. Perhaps the majority of the populace remained non-Christian, but the influence of Christianity was growing steadily even in formally non-Christian circles. The king probably continued to perform traditional rites, but he protected the churches. Nothing is known about persecutions of Christians in Ethiopia. On the other hand, many facts indicate a flourishing of Christian communities in the IV–V centuries A.D. under the aegis of the Axumite monarchy.

Judging by Axumite coins the following kings ruled between Ezana I and Ezana II: Aphilas (Αφιλας), Ousanas II (Ουσανας), Wazeba II (WZB), and possibly also one of the "anonymous" ones. Nothing more is known about these kings. We cannot with certainty even identify the father of Ezana II, who is called Ella Amida in the inscriptions, with one of these kings: Wazeba II or the "anonymous" one.

About 370 A.D. the Himyarite king Asad Abukarib embraced the Jewish religion. A group of Judaeo-Himyarites emerged. They were connected, ideologically, first of all with the Arabo-Judaic tribes of the Hijaz oases, and through them with the Jews of Syria and Mesopotamia, who in political relations were oriented toward Iran. This group was irreconcilably hostile to Byzantium and Axum. The Himyarite kings of the second half of the IV century A.D. to the second half of the V century A.D. said nothing in their inscriptions about dependency on Axum. Their power grew directly since Himyar emerged as an intermediary in the trade between India, Byzantium, and Iran on the one hand, and with Axum and East Africa on the other hand. In this period the Axumites could scarcely have realized their old pretensions to hegemony in South Arabia. As far as Roman-Byzantine sources are concerned, they speak of Axum and Himyar as states equal in significance and status.

In spite of the prolonged flourishing of Axum, its political fortunes suffered a series of setbacks. In countries located within Axum's sphere of influence—South Arabia, Northern Nubia, and Beja—strong government alliances of Beja, Noba, and Himyarites were formed. In the V century A.D. the Beja and Noba intensified their onslaught on Roman-Byzantine Egypt. They devastated and even conquered frontier territories (part of Northern Nubia and the region of the Alabaster Mountains). The raids of 429 and 450 A.D. were especially destructive. Heading the Beja was a king (a tyrant) who according to Olympiodorus'[159] testimony placed "arhonts" over individual tribes. It is unknown whether he was (even formally) subject to the Axum king. In any event, the Byzantines communicated with the Beja without the instrumentality of Axum. In contrast to the Axumites, the Beja firmly adhered to pagan cults (in particular, the cult of Isis) and did not accept Christianity. The Noba also had their own kings independent of Axum since Axum's influence no longer reached so far to the northwest. But to make up for it they were under the political influence of Byzantium.

In South Arabia supremacy finally passed over to the Himyarites. At the end of the IV–V centuries A.D. the Himyarites possessed all of South and part of Central Arabia. As before, the Axumite kings pretended to hegemony in South Arabia.

The reign of Ezana II

Ezana II was the best known of the Axumite kings. Much reliable information on his reign is contained in his inscriptions. His father was King Ella Amida. The "ethnic name" of Ezana II was Be'ese Halen. His reign appears to have been a long one. This is evidenced both by the marked development of script observable in his inscriptions and by the production of large quantities of coinage, exhibiting considerable stylistic variability (in particular the Greek transcriptions of his "ethnic name" and the treatment of religious symbols). The name of Ezana II is not on the "Lists of Kings." One encounters a similar name, Tazena, the son of Ella Amida (versions A and B). In version "C" the son of Ella Amida is Ella Ahayawa, who reigned for only three years. The sons of the latter are Abreha and Asbeha, or Ella Abreha and Ella Asbeha, under whom the baptism of Ethiopia took place. They reigned 27 years and 3 months. According to another tradition, the baptism of Ethiopia took place under King Ella Asguagua, who ruled for 76 or 77 years. In all of these versions there is a certain amount of historical truth, and behind the enumerated names stand at least two figures: a king who is named in one or another variant of the lists, and Ezana, who is confused with this king.

Ezana II's title was extremely close to the title of Ezana I. Among the names of the countries subordinate to the king only "Ethiopia" or "Habashat" is absent. Among the Arabian countries, Ezana II's title names Saba and Himyar with Salhen and Du Raydan. It is possible that the authority of Ezana II on the Arabian Peninsula was purely fictional. But on the African continent he ruled with a firm hand; carrying out campaigns against unruly vassals. Ezana II's inscriptions, which F. Altheim and R. Stiehl date to the second half of the V century A.D., show that right up to that time even on the outskirts of the Tigre plateau the authority of the

Axumite king was unstable. The king could feel confident only in Axum itself. As happened not infrequently in the Axumite kingdom (let us recall the Adulis inscription), the beginning of Ezana II's reign was marked by an increase of anarchy and separatism, by defection of dependent tribes and "kingdoms," even those closest to Axum.

A hint of this is contained in the earliest of Ezana II's inscriptions concerning the resumption of personal tribute collection. The king "set out [making the rounds of his possessions] in order to restore his kingdom and bring about order in it. And he spared whoever submitted but he killed whoever refused to submit."[160] Thus the MTT (Matata?) tribe which dwelt somewhere on the Sudan border paid tribute only after an armed encounter from which it "bore a bloody defeat."[161] The majority of tribes with their kings submitted and brought gifts. Ezana II dealt mercifully with them; in the inscription he clearly flaunts his magnanimity. The entire inscription has an edifying nature; it was erected in Axum as a warning to his vassals and as a stern reminder to his subjects about the power of the king who did not know defeat and before whom the rebellious tribes were submissive. The official purpose of the inscription, just as of the other victory inscriptions of Axum, however, was to express gratitude to the gods for victories gained. Nowhere in the inscriptions of Ezana II's predecessors (with the exception of Sembruthes, who limited himself to a simple praising of the king) does the "secular" element play so conspicuous a role. The inscriptions of Ezana II, beginning with the very earliest, bear a secular ideological loading. Hence it is evident what significance Ezana II attached to the ideological factor in consolidating his royal authority.

The following inscription of Ezana II[162] tells about the utter defeat of the Aguezat principality somewhere on the northern or northwestern edge of the Ethiopian plateau. The Axumite king mounted a campaign against Atagau, a neighboring principality, strengthening his authority on the outskirts of the plateau. The Aguezat with their king Abba Alke'o were obliged to accompany the Axumite force. But during the campaign their "perfidy" was discovered. Having taken advantage of some kind of insubordination on the part of the Aguezat as a pretext, Ezana II sent his "armies" to ravage their country. Abba Alke'o was arrested and was bound with a chain to the "bearer of his throne." Even if Abba Alke'o was set free at some point his position as a vassal of Axum could not but have changed. In the middle of the VI century A.D., the Axumite king Wazeb, son of Ella Asbeha, again was obliged to bring the rebellious Aguezat tribe to submission.

The destruction of the Aguezat Kingdom had a most important significance for the consolidation of Ezana II's authority. After the destruction of the greatest of the local principalities, the Axumites began more fully to control the situation in Northern Ethiopia. No longer fearing broad coalitions, they were able one by one to suppress the separatism of the outlying tribes. Some of these tribes probably were absorbed by Axum and were included in the composition of the Axumite people. It seems, for example, to have happened to the Metine people. Urban trading communities, especially, seemed to have benefited from union with Axum and the creation of the Axumite state.

Ezana II undertook the subjugation of the tribes of the eastern desert with an iron hand. Ezana II's third inscription tells of a punitive expedition against the Afan.[163] Characteristically, the event that served as a pretext for the campaign was the Afan's plundering of an Axumite trade caravan, involving the massacre of the people accompanying it. Undoubtedly this caravan was going to the salt lakes of Danakil, from whence the caravan route proceeded via the oasis of Aussa and the fertile Chercher highlands region of Harar to the Incense and Cinnamon Bearing lands.

In response, Ezana II sent armies which destroyed the Afan (or at least a quarter of them). The alite (evidently the title of the ruler) with his children were taken captive and enormous spoils—prisoners and cattle— were seized. The inscription concludes by describing a sacrifice to the god Mahrem and the consecration of a stone throne to the gods, etc.

The last stage of Ezana II's conquests is described in his bilingual inscription, the Greek and Pseudo-Sabaean texts of which were found recently. Having consolidated his authority within the territory of Northern Ethiopia, and having subjugated the neighboring desert countries, Ezana II turned his weapons and his diplomacy to the west, into Nile-Nubia. As is evident from Ezana II's title, he considered himself the sovereign of Kasu.

By this time the Noba (Nobatie or Nubians) occupied this country (which had been destroyed by the Axumites and threatened by the Beja). They evidently arrived from the southwest, from modern Kordofan, where tribes who are related to them continue to live even today.

Probably Shinnie is incorrect in laying stress on their forcible conquest of the country.[164] Kirwan, following Shinnie, mistakenly attributes to Ezana II's inscription the assertion that the Noba were the foes of Kasu. In reality, according to the inscription, there were no other peoples in Kasu besides the Noba. The cities of the former Meroitic Kingdom are called "the cities of the Noba." Completely different peoples—but not the Kasu-Meroites—emerged as foes of the Noba. This indicates what significance the influx of foreign groups had upon Nubia as early as the middle of the IV century A.D. Archaeological data confirm the "Nubianization" of the Meroitic Kingdom by the middle of the IV century A.D. In the north, where the Meroitic population suffered less from Axumite inroads, the Meroitic element was more significant. And in the local culture of that time (the so-called culture of group X), Meroitic and also Roman-Egyptian traits were observed along with Negro-Sudanese traits.[165] K. Mikhalovsky considers the culture of the tribes of "group X" as the direct heir of Meroitic culture and he also considers the dominant group of the population of Lower Nubia of the early Middle Ages to be the posterity of the old Meroitic[166] nobility.

The old Meroitic cities, in particular Alva, Meroe, Daro (mentioned by Pliny [Historia naturalis, VI, 191] according to Aristocreon), Fertoti (undoubtedly Fer Tuti, the city or temple of the god Thoth), etc., were the centers of the new government unions. In them evidently was preserved the old Meroitic populace, in particular peasants and priests. Eventually they merged with the Nubians. These latter were divided into two basic groups: Northern and Southern. Afterwards, part of one or the other group split off to form still another ethnographic unit.

To the north were based those whom Ezana II called the "Red Noba." Undoubtedly these were the creators of the "culture of Group X," Procopius' "Nobatie." Silko, the author of the Greek inscription from Elephantine, [167] later became their ruler. Silko called the Southern Noba the "other Nobatie." For Ezana II, whose subjects had dealings mainly with the Southern group, they were simply the "Noba." It is interesting to note that in the title of Kaleb (Ella Asbeha), Noba and Kasu are listed as two different countries (or do we have before us simply a striving to represent the object of truth as fully as possible, which is a common practice in the Middle Ages?). In addition to the Noba, the Beja also began to settle in Nile-Nubia as early as the III century A.D. Silko also mentions the Beja in Nubia, in an inscription.[168]

Its wealth, combined with political weakness, made Nubia tempting prey in the eyes of the Axumites, and the celebrated historical name of Kasu gave to the capture of Nubia special political meaning. Here were located extensive fertile lands ("the islands" of Meroe), the real granary of the Eastern Sudan; here were rich and ancient cities, including Alva and Daro; here passed the trade routes to the west and south, into the countries of Black Africa. Alva and Daro were becoming Axum's rivals for influence on the frontier peoples and in trade with Southwest and West Ethiopia. This rivalry was not only one of the reasons but also the handiest pretext for Ezana II's campaign.

In the words of the inscription the "peoples of Noba rebelled and grew proud." "They attacked the peoples of Mangurto and Hasa and Baria and everyone else.[169] And twice and thrice they broke their vows and killed their neighbors without compunction." These neighboring peoples resided in the area of the modern Ethiopian-Sudanese border, to the north and south of the oasis of Kassala. Ezana II considered them his subjects and took them under his protection. He dispatched his representatives and confidential agents "for the investigation of their (the Noba's) offenses." Regardless of what kinds of results the investigation would lead to, the very fact that Axumite representatives had been sent had important political significance; the Axumite king advanced himself as the supreme arbiter and hegemonic power of the quarreling parties. The Nubians rejected the king's claims; they drove his representatives off ignominiously after having taken away their weapons and clothing. Ezana II again sent "a warning" to them, demanding "cessation of their criminal acts"; probably the Axumite king reminded the Nubians also of his claim to supremacy in Kasu and demanded their complete submission. They again refused to submit, and moreover in an insulting manner. Ezana II's inscription—the sole source which describes these events—mentions all of this. As we see, Ezana II was trying to show himself as a generous and just ruler who was striving for the peace and well-being of the peoples subject to him. But the enemies and insurgents by having exasperated him brought his wrath upon themselves: "And when they preferred war, I made war on them."

The Nubians considered themselves out of reach of Axumite arms. In the words of the inscription: "The Noba peoples [said]: 'They [the Axumites] will not cross the Tekezze (Atbara).'" The Noba sent a strong force, attempting to prevent the Axumites from crossing the river. On the bank of the Atbara at the Kemalke ford the first battle occurred. The Nubians were utterly defeated: "And I fought with them on the Tekezze at the Kemalke ford," relates Ezana II. "Here I put them to flight. And I, not pausing, chased those who were fleeing for 23 days, killing, taking prisoners and taking spoils." On the way, the Axumite forces pillaged and destroyed the country, burning towns and villages. They emerged on the bank of the Nile, and at the confluence of the Nile and the Atbara a new battle ensued. The Nubians were again defeated; many were taken captive. The Axumites sank Nubian ships overcrowded with women and children, looted stores of food and cotton, and threw the surplus of these products into the river. Four leaders were killed, and a priest or "lord" (evidently an ecclesiastical king). Temples were destroyed, statues of the gods were smashed, a large quantity of precious and other metals was seized. Cattle, slaves, clothing, and other riches were also seized. Two leaders who came to the Axumite camp were arrested as spies.

Then Ezana's army split up. On the day following the battle at the mouth of the Atbara, separate detachments were sent upstream along the Nile into Southern Nubia. They destroyed the "brick" cities of Alva and Daro and a large number of "straw" cities. They seized spoils and safely returned to the north, "having frightened the enemies and having subjugated them." Then some of the returned detachments and some new

ones were sent downstream along the Nile into Central Nubia. They captured Tabito, Fertoti, and the "royal" city (evidently Kawa), and also
four "straw" cities. During the campaign they reached the borders of the
"Red Noba" (in the north) and returned with great spoils. Ezana II
returned to Axum, having erected a consecrated throne at the confluence
of the Atbara and the Nile, opposite the city "built of brick . . . on an
island." A frightened and ravaged Nubia [170] (at least Southern and Central
Nubia) was obliged to recognize his authority. However, Ezana II does
not say whether the country was assessed tribute.

In this campaign Ezana II showed himself to be a talented general. He
acted decisively, boldly, and rapidly; and his experienced troops proved
themselves invincible. He could declare in truth: "I do not have a foe
either overt or secret; there is no foe subordinate to me" (literally: "There
is no foe who would stand before me and behind me; there is no foe who
would follow").[171]

On Ezana II's coins a "demagogic slogan" is encountered, supplanting
the "ethnic name" of the king (although in the inscriptions the "ethnic
name" is also encountered later). In the inscription about the campaign
into Nubia (in the Ethiopian text) there is a sentence reminiscent of the
"demagogic slogan." "My people enjoy justice and law and there are no
burdens on them." [172] In the far shorter Greek text the corresponding slogan
is absent, and the "Pseudo-Sabaean" text is far too decayed to be able to
judge this even tentatively. Judging by the Ethiopian text of the bilingual
inscription concerning the campaign into Nubia, Ezana II was extremely
concerned if not about the people then about his popularity among the
people.

Two of Ezana II's inscriptions [173] are dedicated to Mahrem, the tribal
and dynastic god of the Axumites. Another [174] is dedicated to the triad of
agricultural gods: Astar, Beher, and Medr. It is possible that this indicates
an attempt at broadening the limits of the official cult.

The inscription about the campaign into Nubia, however, also contains
information denoting a shift in the religious ideas of the king. This shift
shows one of the stages in his religious quest, and may indicate a reform of
the official religion.

This inscription is definitely monotheistic. In it, a single god called
"Lord of the Heavens," "Lord of Earth," and "Lord of All" is mentioned
twelve times. He is "for all Eternity," "most perfect," and "invincible."
Thanks to him the Axumites and the king gained victories. They give
thanks to him for the defeat of the foes, the annihilation of Nubian men and
women, the driving into slavery of those who remained alive, and for the
rich spoils and their safe return. The impression is created that the author
of the inscription is trying persistently to suggest to the readers that for all
the successes of Axum they were indebted to a single god. This is nothing

more than propaganda for a new religious idea—the idea of monotheism. Simultaneously this is propaganda for royal authority. Ezana II declares that a single and invincible god made him king, vanquished his foes, and renders to the king constant and all-powerful protection. "May the Lord of the Heavens strengthen my kingdom!" This is the sole desire of Ezana II. The god also gives protection "to the peoples" or communities of Axum but does this through the king. The king appears as the deputy of god on earth; but not just any king, only the Axumite king. In the beliefs of the Axumites and other African subjects of Ezana II, the king was a living god (the incarnation of the sun or the sun-moon deity) but he remained one of many gods, including god-kings, and not necessarily the most mighty one. The role of deputy of the sole and all powerful god was far more significant. Therefore the introduction of a monotheistic cult led to an unprecedented strengthening of the Axumite monarchy.

What did this monotheistic religion of Ezana's represent? Up to 1914 all investigators called this last inscription Christian. Turayev was the first to note that it was simply monotheistic and not necessarily Christian.[175] Littmann[176] and also Doresse[177] came to a similar conclusion.

In my opinion, judging from formal indications, it is not Christian. In the first place, except for acknowledgment of a sole and all-powerful god there is nothing Christian in his image. Neither the Trinity nor Christ nor Mary is mentioned. In the second place, this sole god, as Littmann correctly noted, retained many traits of Mahrem (the national and dynastic god of the Axumites) and also of Astar.[178] Ezana II dedicated two thrones to him just as to the pagan gods; one in Meroe, and one in Shado—close to Axum. But this is no longer the former Mahrem and indeed he is not called Mahrem. This is the god of a vaguely monotheistic religion in which both Christianity and Judaism and all other monotheistic cults are syncretized. This same god also figures in the inscription of the Axumite Abreha from Wadi Menih, and in several South Arabian inscriptions of the IV to VI centuries A.D. To crown the resemblance of this new god with Mahrem, the inscription of Abreha refers to him as "The Lord of the High Heavens" and in many South Arabian inscriptions—"Lord of the Heavens and Earth."

Evidently this patently monotheistic religion had been growing over a long period of time, and under Ezana II it was vigorously propagated throughout Axumite society. Therefore the author of the Ethiopian text of the bilingual inscription about the campaign into Nubia made use of the terminology of monotheism for propagandizing his own religious views.

However, the late coins of Ezana II have the sign of the cross, attesting to his conversion to Christianity. The religious terminology in the Greek text of the inscription on the campaign against Nubia undoubtedly bears a Christian, or more precisely, a monotheistic character. The designation *mambar* for Christian stelae as well as for the altars ("thrones") of pagan gods represents a tradition within Axumite religion.[179]

Deserving attention is the disparity between the religious terminology in the Ethiopian and Greek versions, respectively, of this inscription. For Graeco-pagan readers, i.e., primarily Byzantine Christians, the Axumite king emerges as a co-religionist and for his countrymen he emerges as an indirect monotheist. Evidently, under Ezana II, Christians did not make up the majority of Axumites and in Axumite society there were sufficiently influential non-Christian elements which Ezana did not wish to annoy openly with Christian propaganda.

It is possible that in Axum of the IV–V centuries A.D., just as in South Arabia in the V–VII centuries A.D. (prior to the complete victory of Islam over Hanifism), there existed a similar, more or less formalized, monotheistic religion. But its historic role consisted primarily in its preparing the soil for the Christianization of the Axumites.

Beginning with the time of Aedesius and Frumentius, the language of the clergy of the Axumite Church was Greek (just as it was in Nubia up to the X century A.D.). However, the conversion of Christianity into the state religion of the Axumites necessitated the translation of the Old and New Testaments into the Ge'ez language. The translation was accomplished no later than the beginning of the VI century A.D., when quotations from the Psalm book (Psalter) appeared in Axumite inscriptions. Possibly by this time, i.e., during the reign of Ezana II, the reform of the old consonantal Ethiopian alphabet was carried out.

The new religion was indebted for its ideas to the world religions then existing and to the monotheism of neighboring Arabia.[180] But in the affirmation and propaganda of the new cult, the will of the king is visible. One can speak of the first "monotheistic reform" in Ethiopia. However, this religion did not take root; it served only as a transitional stage to the complete victory of Christianity. If toward the end of his life Ezana II himself did not become a Christian, then he was very close to it. On his later coins there appeared the sign of the cross instead of the sun-moon symbol. It is known that Ezana II gave protection to the Christians, and the Roman emperor addressed him as if he were a co-religionist. The propagation of Christianity in Ethiopia did not take the form of a single-occasion act or compulsory mass baptism. It proceeded gradually and voluntarily over the entire period of the evolution of the Axumite state. This suggests the well known "democratism" of earlier Axumite society indicating that strong traditions of an earlier social structure still existed.

The reform of the ancient Ethiopian script is closely connected with the development of Ethiopian literature; including perhaps Christian literature. Before Ezana II the Ethiopians wrote down only the consonantal sounds of their speech, not designating their vowels, nor their length, nor diphthongs, nor the doubling of consonants. They used script only in short dedicatory inscriptions, mottoes on coins, legislative "monuments" (*tazkar*), and presumably in business transactions. All these varieties of writing were extremely stereotyped in form, meager and monotonous in content, grammar, and vocabulary. They were very easily read and understood by those for whom they were intended—an extremely limited circle of readers. Under Ezana II, the circle of readers broadened and inscriptions became complicated. Thus reading of the Ge'ez writing was facilitated by the introduction of vowels.

Searches of the new systems of writing have already revealed two of the earliest of Ezana II's inscriptions (*DAE*, II, no. 8, 6). Both are unvocalized (i.e., they are written without vowels), just as are the inscriptions of Ezana II's predecessors. They are, however, composed in the Ge'ez language but in Himyaritic script with characteristic orthography ("mimation," etc.). It was formerly thought that in Ethiopia the Sabaean script was used right up to 300 A.D. and that Ethiopian script proper was developed only in Ezana II's reign. In recent years ancient Ethiopian unvocalized inscriptions of the III century A.D., composed in Ge'ez and not following the Sabaean tradition, have come to light. Evidently, Ezana II *returned* to Sabaean script and orthography in their Himyaritic form.

Traces of "Sabaeanization" are noted in the third ("Ethiopian") text of the bilingual inscription (*DAE*, IV, no. 7), which is distinguished from the second "Sabaean" text (positioned above it) primarily by script and orthography.

In Ezana II's late inscriptions this experiment was abandoned since the letters were supplemented with symbols for the designation of vowels. This was the most radical and original reform in the history of Ethiopian writing, not being equaled either before or after. The reform was brought about by the necessity to designate in writing the vowel sounds. Ge'ez is richer than other Semitic languages in short vowels, long vowels, and diphthongs. The reform now permitted distinction in the writing of words differing in sound and meaning as well as certain grammatical forms which had formerly appeared identical in the unvocalized written form.

The earlier consonantal letters, for which the pronunciation in the single variant "consonant + short *a*" had been retained, were taken as the fundamental form. Ligatures of a single type were formed for all possible combinations of "consonant + vowel" in the Ge'ez language. This was accomplished by means of adding a ligature of one of the ten symbols (for long vowels and diphthongs: $\bar{a}, \bar{o}, \bar{u}, \bar{\imath}, \bar{e}, \breve{e}, \breve{u}\bar{e}, \breve{u}\bar{a}, \breve{u}a, \breve{u}i, \breve{u}e$) to the fundamental form or by a small alteration in the writing of this fundamental form itself.

The main principles of vocalized Ethiopian script do not have an analog anywhere in the Semitic-Hamitic world, yet they are characteristic of Indian alphabets. In the nineteenth century, at the same time that Müller[181] and other historians thought that the reform of the ancient Ethiopian script was the work of Christian missionaries who transported the Greek idea of transmitting short and long vowels to Ethiopian soil, such scholars as W. Jones and R. Lepsius linked the Ethiopian letter-syllabic alphabet with India.[182] In 1915 A. Grohmann emphasized the principal similarity between the very idea of the vocalized Ethiopian alphabet and the principles of construction of the ancient Indian Brahmi and Kharoshti alphabets.[183]

The Indian influence on the reform of the ancient Ethiopian script is more than likely. However, the reformed alphabet so precisely transmits the phonetic system of the Ge'ez language that its creator could only have been an Axumite. Unfortunately we know neither the time of its creation nor the name of the brilliant reformer. In the light of recent studies on the chronology of Axumite inscriptions the opinion has been spread that the vocalized alphabet appeared in Ethiopia only in the second half of the V century A.D. (formerly it was considered that it was invented in the middle of the IV century A.D.). However, it could have been created one or two generations earlier than the time of its appropriation by official epigraphers.

In recent years the hypothesis has been advanced that soon after its appearance the Ethiopian letter-syllable vocalized script exerted an influence on the development of the alphabets of three major peoples of the Caucasus region: the Armenians, Georgians, and Agvan (Caucasus Albanians, the ancestors of the Azerbaidjanians of Shirvan). Modern-day Armenian scholar Gurgen Sevak first directed attention to the similarity of the Armenian and Ethiopian alphabets.[184] D. A. Olderogge advanced the hypothesis according to which Mesrop Mashtots, the creator of the Armenian alphabet and a teacher of the creators of the Georgian and Agvan alphabets, used symbols of the vocalized Ethiopian script. It is possible that not long before (at the end of the V century A.D.) it was introduced into Armenia by the Syrian Bishop Daniel.[185]

Up to now all investigators have considered the introduction of vocalization to be a single act. Actually, in both of Ezana II's vocalized inscriptions we already find all categories of ligatures. Nevertheless, one circumstance indicates that it is more likely that a period of development of ligature script took place which preceded its appearance in the inscriptions. Vocalization of ligatures was carried out (and is still being carried out) in multiple form; there are not many exceptions but they do exist. Ligature writing must have been developed by scribes of the royal chancellery, where exceptions in the formation of the ligatures were assimilated and established. It is possible to see in ancient Ethiopian monograms, which also are a ligature of sorts, predecessors of vocalized symbols. The earliest of the monograms are represented on coins of the Axumite kings of the early IV century A.D. and in some stone inscriptions.

In any event, there is no doubt that the reform of the Ethiopian alphabet was connected with the reforming activity of Ezana II and his retinue, and was the product of the general economic and cultural rise of the Axumite Kingdom beginning at the end of the III century A.D. and continuing through the middle of the IV century A.D. Such factors as Ethiopia's cultural development, the birth of Ethiopian literature, the needs of the royal chancellery, and the spread of foreign monotheistic religions (Christianity, Judaism, South Arabian monotheism, and possibly also Buddhism and Manicheism) all contributed to the success of the reform. Vocalized writing did not acquire dominance all at once. Even on coins of Ezana II's successors (as well as those of himself), mottoes were stamped with unvocalized script. Likewise, Christianity was not at once victorious. Nevertheless, the cultural attainments of Ezana II's reign entered forever into the flesh and blood of Ethiopian civilization, preserved over the courses of several millennia.

The Axumite Kingdom at the beginning of the VI century A.D.

The rather short reign of King Tazena or Tezena, the father of the famous Kaleb (Ella Asbeha), opens the history of Axum in the VI century A.D. Very little is known about him. Probably Tazena, with a greater basis than his predecessors, pretended to hegemony in South Arabia; evidently some Himyarite kings recognized his authority. Thus King Ma'adikarib (Ma'adkarim), who ruled at the beginning of the VI century A.D., was considered by the Syrian tradition to be Christian and a protegé of Ethiopia. A characteristic assertion is contained in that version of *The Letters of Simeon Betharsham*, which Joannes Ephesius quotes. In his words, the Himyarite Jew, King Dhu-Nuwas, supposedly wrote to the Lakhmide King Al Munzir III: "It will be known to you that the king whom the Kushites (Axumites) placed in our land has died; the winter has passed and the Kushites have not been able to come to our land and establish a Christian king as usual."[186] However, in Simeon's *Letters* the words "as usual"[187] do not exist. Perhaps the whole assertion is a tendentious exaggeration but it undoubtedly contains a germ of truth: the fact of the connection of Ma'adikarib with Axum and possibly his dependency. It is more probable that Ma'adikarib was a usurper and was obliged to seek support from without and that the interference of the Axumites in the affairs of South Arabia had long ago become traditional. Nevertheless, Ma'adikarib's inscription says nothing of his dependence on Ethiopia.[188]

In the first half of the VI century A.D. the Axumite monarchy made a final attempt to firmly subjugate Himyar. This was the beginning of the Ethiopian wars in Arabia, which terminated with the capture of the south of the peninsula by the Persians, with the destruction of the Himyarite Kingdom, and with the weakening of Axumite influence.

Axumite wars in Arabia: 517–537 A.D.

The Ethiopian wars in Arabia have been investigated far better and in more detail than any other question of the history of pre-Islamic Arabia and the Axumite Kingdom. It is therefore sufficient to draw only a general picture of the military, diplomatic, and ideological struggle in South Arabia in which the Axumite monarchy took part. Moreover, the facts which relate primarily to Ethiopian, and not to South Arabian, history have been more carefully analyzed.

At the beginning of 517 A.D. the Himyarite King Ma'adikarib was overthrown by 'Arib As'ar Masruk Dhu-Nuwas,[189] who had embraced Judaism under the name of Joseph (Yusuf). The political orientation of the Himyarite monarchy again changed. The policy of Dhu-Nuwas was directed against that part of the Himyarite nobility which received trade benefits from Ethiopia and the Roman Empire and which confessed the Christian religion. Dhu-Nuwas occupied a clearly hostile position in relation to Axum and the Romans.

Sources which go back to Nonnus and Joannes Antiochus say that the Himyarite king confiscated goods of the Roman merchants and "curtailed trade" between Ethiopia and Byzantium.[190] In addition to political losses Axum bore economic ones.

The South Arabian Christians turned to Axum for help. The Najran Bishop, Thomas, set out for Ethiopia asking the Axumites to render military help against Dhu-Nuwas. No doubt Thomas promised them the support of the local populace, primarily the Christians in whose name he was acting. A special chapter of *The Book of the Himyarites* was devoted to this embassy. Only the title "Story about How Bishop Thomas Came to the Abyssinians and Told Them that the Himyarites Were Persecuting the Christians"[191] has been preserved.

The Axumite king acted swiftly. With the beginning of favorable winds in May-June 517 A.D., the Axumites crossed the sea and landed on the shore of Tihama. Dhu-Nuwas' authority was still so unstable that he was not able to exert serious resistance. The Axumites occupied Zafar, the capital of the Himyarite Kingdom, and other very important cities. Dhu-Nuwas fled to the mountains.[192] All of South Arabia found itself under Axum's authority.

Who led the Axumites in this campaign? *The Martyrdom of Arethius* names Ella Asbeha, but this source confuses facts connected with the first campaign. A description of the campaign has not been preserved in *The Book of the Himyarites* but the title of a corresponding chapter, "Story About the First Visit of HYWN' (Hywana or Hayawana) and the Abyssinians,"[193] remained. Not another word about this HYWN' is contained in *The Book of the Himyarites*. This name is reminiscent of the name Ella Ahayawa of the "Lists of Kings," who reigned for only three years and who was the predecessor of Ella Asbeha.[194] *Who was he?* It is scarcely possible to explain the appearance of this name as a paleographic error. The scribe could not have so distorted the name of King Kaleb, or Ella Asbeha, who is repeatedly mentioned in other places. HYWN', most likely, is not Kaleb but some other Axumite king or general (more likely a king). "The Lists of Kings" distinguishes Tazena and Ella Ahayawa, but is it possible that Ella Ahayawa was Tazena's second name? If this supposition is true, then a predecessor of Ella Asbeha is being spoken of. Consequently, Ella Asbeha came to the throne after 517–518 A.D. Nevertheless, while it has not been proven, the version about the identification of HYWN' with Kaleb remains in force.

In the winter, with a fair wind, part of the Axumites departed for their homeland and part remained in South Arabia. A detachment of approximately 600 men was stationed in Zafar.[195] Smaller detachments evidently remained in other places. Undoubtedly the Ethiopian troops brought no little burden to the local populace. This inevitably must have given rise to displeasure among Himyarites directed at the occupying troops. The relatively neutral or unstable groupings of pagans and Nestorians now supported Dhu-Nuwas while the Axumites, because of the eastern winter monsoons, could not send reinforcements into Arabia.

Dhu-Nuwas quickly took advantage of the favorable situation and took active measures. First of all he tried to seize Zafar, where the Ethiopian garrison was located. Loundine thinks that "in the city a considerable Christian population existed which showed Yusuf (Dhu-Nuwas) stubborn resistance."[196] However, neither the inscriptions nor *The Book of the Himyarites* nor *The Letters of Simeon Betharsham* nor other sources which speak about executions and slaughter in Najran and Muha (Muhvan) ever mention a word about repressions against the Zafar inhabitants. They speak only of the annihilation of the Ethiopian garrison by Dhu-Nuwas (Masruk). Furthermore, slaughter among the Zafar townspeople would have had to be mentioned, if not by the inscriptions in any event by *The Book of the Himyarites*. Although there were many Christians in Zafar the inhabitants suffered from the Ethiopian occupation and were scarcely unanimous and decisive in their hostility toward Dhu-Nuwas. Therefore the Axumites in Zafar were obliged to feel insecure.

However, Dhu-Nuwas was not able to take Zafar by storm, or decided not to. He resorted to a ruse. We may conjecture that he took into account the fact that the Axumites would be happy to set out for their homeland from this alien and hostile country. Dhu-Nuwas sent a letter to Zafar in which he promised the Ethiopians complete safety if they would abandon the city. Their leader allowed himself to be cruelly deceived. According to the expression of *The Book of the Himyarites*, "when the Abyssinians received his (Dhu-Nuwas') letter and moreover heard the words of his ambassadors who confirmed his oaths, they, in the simplicity of their souls, believed his oaths and came out to him [and especially] Abba Abavit their leader . . . with three hundred [troops]." At night the Axumites were treacherously slaughtered and their corpses were dumped in one place. The 280 Ethiopians remaining in Zafar were locked up in a church and burned together with it. The story of *The Book of Himyarites* about these events is greatly damaged and only partially reproduced in the Arab-Christian *Chronicle of Seert*.[197] The preserved fragments, however, permit one to imagine the picture of treacherous nocturnal slaughter, the profanation of the corpses, and the burning alive of people in the church where they worshiped. Then the Ethiopian church in Zafar was rebuilt and converted into a synagogue. (I. Guidi, 1881, p. 480.)

The inscriptions of Sharakh'il Yakbul briefly mention that the Himyarites "upon the return . . . of King Yusuf As'ar (Dhu-Nuwas) did battle 'against the Abyssinians in Zafar' ('ly ḥbšn bẓfr) and burned the church (wdhrw qlsn)" (*Ry*, 508, 3). (G. Ryckmans, 1953, pp. 295–296; J. Ryckmans, 1953, pp. 319 et suiv.; J. Ryckmans, 1956; A. G. Loundine, 1961, pp. 34–35; M. Rodinson, 1969, pp. 26–34.) Evidently this is the same as in the inscription *Ry*, 507, 4: "when they burned the church (kdhrw qlsn) and killed the Abyssinians in Zamu(?) (whrgw 'ḥbšn bẓmw)." (G. Ryckmans, 1953, pp. 294–295.) A. G. Loundine reads "in Zafar" instead of the unclear "in Zamu(?)" and instead of *wtsn* he reads ·*qlsn* ("church"). A third inscription, *Ja*, 1028, 3, reads: "when they burned the church and killed the Abyssians in Zafar." (A. Jamme, 1966.) The second letter of Simeon Betharsham gives similar information.[198]

Sharakh'il Yakbul was a most outstanding general of Dhu-Nuwas. *The Book of the Himyarites* mentions him under the name of "General Dhu-Yazan."[199] Sharakh'il belonged to the very noble family of Yazan, which at that time provided political leadership for the South Arabian pagans. Consequently, the pagans came over to Dhu-Nuwas' side. Even some of the Christians sided with Dhu-Nuwas. Among the ambassadors sent to Zafar by Dhu-Nuwas were two Jewish clergymen from Tiberias and two "Christians in name only."[200] According to J. W. Hirshenberg's hypothesis, which N. V. Pigulevskaya supports, they belonged to the Nestorian sect[201] (which was being persecuted in the Eastern Roman Empire but which had found asylum in Persia). The Nestorian patriarch was based in Ctesiphon. Here there was more tolerance toward the Nestorians and they occupied a pro-Iranian or neutral position in the Roman-Iranian struggle. There were many Nestorians in Arabia's trading cities, especially in the eastern but also in the southern part.[202] Clergymen of Socotra Island, according to Cosmas' words, also received ordination "from Persia,"[203] i.e., from the Nestorian patriarch. Probably the South Arabian Nestorians, if they did not render military aid to Dhu-Nuwas, maintained neutrality in spite of the anti-Christian policy of this king.

Thus Yusuf Dhu-Nuwas was able, in the winter of 517 A.D., to unite around himself all elements who were dissatisfied with Ethiopian domination. However, a series of Himyarite districts showed resistance to him. These districts were Muhvan (with the port city of Muha or Moha, ancient Muza), Ash'aran (in the region of the Bab el Mandeb Gulf), and also the city of Najran (in the north of the country). Here Christians predominated, who were connected by trade interests with Africa and the Roman Empire. Dhu-Nuwas (Masruk) and his generals (as Sharakh'il Yakbul's inscription indicates) "destroyed Muhvan and Ash'aran, burned churches, and annihilated all the inhabitants of Muhvan."[204]

Having dealt with the tribes of the southern coast, Dhu-Nuwas sent Sharakh'il Yakbul north to the city of Najran, while he remained on the coast with part of the troops, fearing a new landing of Ethiopians. Sharakh'il's armies carried out a thousand-kilometer march and reached Najran. The Najranites surrendered and delivered hostages, but at the first opportunity they were ready to revolt. Late in the autumn of 518 A.D. when, because of unfavorable winds, the Ethiopians were no longer able to sail across to Arabia, Dhu-Nuwas arrived in Najran. He seized the city and brought repressions down upon the inhabitants. Massive slaughters began, the infamous November slaughters of the Najran Christians. According to *The Martyrdom of Arethius* 770 people were killed.[205] The sources cite the names of many of them. The slaughters continued for several days. First there were slaughters of monks and nuns, deaconesses, clerics, then men from noble families, and finally women and children. But there was no total extermination of inhabitants at Najran as there had been at Muhvan. This is explained by the lesser resistance of the Najranites to Dhu-Nuwas and also by the relatively greater antagonism between the urban nobility and the common people.

The persecution of Christians and the burning of churches continued in other areas: in Hadramaut, Marib, and Hajaran.[206] Many Christians fled beyond the borders of the Himyarite Kingdom.

Dhu-Nuwas tried to find support among the Persians and their vassals, the Lakhmides. He dispatched an embassy to Hira (Al·Hirah) with a letter to the Lakhmide king, Al Munzir III, calling on him to deal with the Christians. For this, 3000 denarii were promised to the self-interested Al Munzir. Dhu-Nuwas' letter was read out in the presence of the Lakhmide court, army, and foreign ambassadors. Among them were prominent representatives of Christian sects. At that time in Hira there were the presbyter Avraam, the ambassador of the Eastern Roman Empire, the Monophysite bishop of Persia (Simeon Betharsham), the ambassador of the Persian ruler, the Orthodox bishop (Sargis Rusaphius), and the Nestorian bishop Sila. Among them only Sila, it seems, tried to justify Dhu-Nuwas. If *The Martyrdom of Arethius* does not slander him, Sila "wanted to play up to the pagans and Jews."[207] The remaining ambassadors, even the Persian Simeon, and also the local Christians resolutely judged Dhu-Nuwas

(Masruk). The Christian Lakhmides compelled Al Munzir to renounce support of Dhu-Nuwas. The Lakhmide king concluded a peace treaty with Byzantium.

At this time the Najran refugee Christians began to arrive in Hira. Christian circles headed by bishops and priests, having gathered in Hira, unleashed an energetic agitation against Dhu-Nuwas. Simeon Betharsham wrote the two *Letters*[208] which told about the events in Himyar and glorified the Najran martyrs. Simeon wanted "all true believers," Monophysites and representatives of other Christian trends, to find out about the evil deeds of Dhu-Nuwas (Masruk). Simeon proposed taking immediate measures against the Tiberias Jews in order to isolate Dhu-Nuwas and to offer him gifts of money so that he would refrain from further persecutions of the Christians.[209] In Simeon's *Letters*, as P. S. Devos so astutely noted, there is contained a thinly veiled appeal to the Axumite king (which is repeated three times in one of the letters) to stand up for the dissenters—the Christian Monophysites who were being persecuted by the "Romans, Persians, and Himyarites." Almost simultaneously with Simeon Betharsham, another Syrian author, Jacob of Serug,[210] wrote *An epistle to the Najranians*. Joannes Psaltes from Beth Autonius composed a poem about the Najran martyrs, and Paul of Edessa translated it from the Greek into Syrian.[211] No doubt propaganda against Dhu-Nuwas came out all over Syria, Palestine, and Mesopotamia. Letters and verses in Syrian and Greek penetrated into Egypt, Constantinople, and Ctesiphon and were propagated over the entire Near East. Presbyter Avraam and Bishop Sargis also promoted agitation against Dhu-Nuwas. To a considerable degree, thanks to their efforts and also the efforts of all of Byzantine diplomacy, Dhu-Nuwas actually was isolated and received no real aid from outside. Himyarite trade, even without being disrupted by the persecution of the Christians, proved to be in the most deplorable condition. The Byzantine emperor, Justin I, began to look for measures to take against Dhu-Nuwas. It became clear that the sole power capable of overthrowing the Himyarite king was Axum. However, Byzantine diplomacy and the church by no means immediately turned to Axum. This is even more strange since it was precisely from Ethiopia that a swift reaction to the activities of Dhu-Nuwas was bound to follow. After all, Dhu-Nuwas had come out against the Axumite state first; his first killings were carried out on Axumites and their allies. The Zafar killings and the Muhvan slaughter had to produce a greater impression in Ethiopia than the Najran massacres. However, neither in 518 A.D. nor in the following six years did the Axumites begin military actions against Dhu-Nuwas. Meanwhile he could not count on outside help and indeed even inside the country he did not enjoy universal support. Why didn't Axum act? Evidently some sort of internal events, most likely civil war, prevented war with Himyar.

It is possible that Joannes Ephesius wrote about it but the text of his work is badly damaged. An inscription of Kaleb (Ella Asbeha), which was discovered recently, tells of his war against the rebellious tribes of Aguezat and Hasat (probably in the semidesert regions of modern day Northern Eritrea). In addition to detachments of Axumites (in the badly damaged text of the inscription no less than six "armies" of Axum proper are listed), militias of the Agau, Atagau, Gabala, and Azabo (probably Kushites in language, and dwelling west and southwest of the Axumites) were joined to the royal force. The raids of the Aguezat, who were joined also by the neighboring Hasat (the Hasa or Has of other sources), preceded the war.

King Kaleb was obliged to advance his forces (which he headed personally) to suppress this rebellion. Ultimately the Axumite king was the victor, having seized 400 captives, 300 cows, and 200 camels, but the struggle with the cattle-breeding tribes so close to the capital of the region evidently occupied his forces for a long time. In the concluding part of the inscription (line 34) it is possible to see a hint of the preparation of a marine expedition against Himyar.[212] It would be tempting to date the events of which this inscription speaks (and which has at present not been completely deciphered) to 519–523 A.D.

In our opinion, Cosmas Indicopleustes, who visited Adulis and Axum at the very time when Ella Asbeha was preparing for the campaign against the Judaeo-Himyarites, has in view the campaign of 525 A.D. At that time, in Cosmas' words, Ella Asbeha had only just emerged from his early youth.[213] It is possible that the internal strife in Ethiopia was connected with Ella Asbeha's coming into power after the death of Tazena who, we suggest, also carried out a campaign into Arabia in 517 A.D.

The brutality of Dhu-Nuwas, directed at the extermination of pro-Axumite and pro-Byzantine elements in Himyar and at the blockading of Axum, severed the trade routes to India, to Iran, and in part to the Byzantine possessions which were so important to the Axumites. This also was bound to contribute to the increase of social tension in the Axumite Kingdom. All of this created a highly favorable atmosphere for the rebels, who launched internal war in Ethiopia, ceasing, evidently, only by 524 A.D., when the young King Kaleb (Ella Asbeha) finally consolidated his authority in Axum's African possessions.

After this he dispatched an embassy to Alexandria to the local Monophysite patriarch. Evidently the Axumite bishop had died. As a result a new bishop was appointed, called Euprepius[214] (in *The Book of the Himyarites*) or Joannes (in the chronicles of Joannes Malalae and Theophanes the Byzantine, and in *The Martyrdom of Arethius*), who had formerly been prosmonarios of the Alexandrine church of Joannes Predtechius.[215]

Hence it is evident that the bishops of Axum and Adulis, the successors of Frumentius, continued to originate from Alexandria. Moreover, they were not natives of Ethiopia but native Egyptians or other Monophysite clergymen who were in Egypt's capital.

There is no doubt that Kaleb and Ella Asbeha are one and the same person. Like many medieval Ethiopian kings he had two names (if not more). Ethiopian historiography likes to emphasize the symbolic significance of this name.[216] Ella Asbeha ruled at the dawn of Christianity in Ethiopia. Under him the sun of Christian faith ascended, evolving into a state religion. However, the religious policy of Ella Asbeha had its own pluses and minuses, its victories and defeats. The wars which he and also his vassals waged did not, in the final analysis, give the desired results.

All sources unanimously depict Ella Asbeha as an enlightened, inquisitive, and wise ruler, as the protector of scientific and religious knowledge. Some authors contemporary to him relate interesting details. Cosmas Indicopleustes describes Ella Asbeha's palace; this "four-turreted palace of the king of Ethiopia" was, up to 1938, preserved in the center of the Ta'akha Mariam complex. Here Cosmas saw "four bronze figures of unicorns," a rhinoceros, stuffed with chaff, elephants, and one or two giraffes. They were placed in the palace at the order of the young king for his amusement. Joannes Malalae (according to Nonnus) describes four domesticated elephants harnessed to Ella Asbeha's chariot.[217] We may thus imagine not only the luxury of the Axumite palace of the V–VI centuries A.D. but also the personality of the most prominent of the kings of this period. If the keeping of wild animals in captivity was the custom of Axumite kings, then the keeping of the stuffed rhinoceros can attest to his special interest in natural history. Ella Asbeha displayed the same such interest in history. In Cosmas' words, he ordered the Adulis ruler to send him copies of the Greek inscriptions on the throne of Ptolomaeus and the stele—the famous Adulis monument. For a king who had finally gone over to Christianity, a pagan dedicatory throne could not have had religious value. Obviously Ella Asbeha collected memorials of the country and ancient art works. *The Book of Himyarites* attributes to him a very characteristic remark: he spoke about the Himyarites as if they were barbarians, considering them far beneath himself and his compatriots in respect to spiritual culture.[218] Ethiopian historical tradition depicts Ella Asbeha as the protector of Christian "enlightenment." "Seven saints" allegedly lived under his patronage.

Under Ella Asbeha, probably, many parts of the Old and New Testaments and also other Christian books were translated into the Ge'ez language. Just as were his immediate predecessors, Kaleb [Ella Asbeha] was a Monophysite. It is not without reason that the Monophysites of Syria looked to him with hope in spite of his youth. Moreover, one can speculate that in the framework of the acute conditions of the struggle with the Heterodox, Ella Asbeha abruptly altered the religious policy of the Axumite monarchy. The former broad tolerance and moderate protection of Christians changed into active propagation of Christianity, which had been proclaimed as the state religion. The sharp turnabout of the official

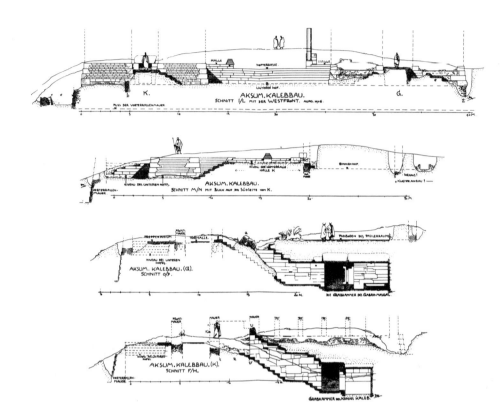

Kaleb's tomb, Axum.

course found reflection in the mottoes of Axumite coins. Instead of the former demagogic slogan, Kaleb's [Ella Asbeha's] coins contain the inscription: Θὲου ’ευχαρίστια — "In gratitude to God!" (in the inscriptions of the Axumite kings similar slogans were encountered earlier). The strengthening of religious antagonism in South Arabia, and probably in Ethiopia, compelled the Axumite king to define clearly his attitude toward one or another religion, having backed it with the all of the state authority.

The Ethiopians adopted Christianity, not in the Orthodox form, the official religion of Byzantium, but in the Monophysite form—now persecuted, now tolerated in the East of the Empire. The Axumite bishop Joannes was chosen by the Monophysite patriarch of Alexandria. The Alexandrine patriarch was the main spiritual authority for Ella Asbeha. This was fostered by the long-standing ties between Axum and Egypt and between the young Ethiopian church and the Egyptian Monophysite church,[219] and moreover by the policy of the Axumite kings, who aspired simultaneously to both a strengthening of ties with Byzantium and toward independence of it.

After Ella Asbeha subjugated the rebellious vassals on the African continent and made firm his authority in Ethiopia, it became clear that Axum could in the very near future begin military operations in South Arabia. Both sides were preparing for war. It was sometime then, toward 524 A.D., that a political and military alliance of the Eastern Roman Empire, the Axumite Kingdom, and the South Arabian Christians was formed, directed against Dhu-Nuwas.

Byzantium and Axum persistently sought a diplomatic rapprochement. The initiative was not only Byzantium's, as is usually thought, but also existed on the Ethiopian side. A church embassy of Axumites to Alexandria would have been obliged to talk over urgent political questions. The results of any negotiations would have been reported to Emperor Justin I by the Alexandrine patriarch. Subsequently, it appears, Justin directed an embassy to Axum with a letter to Ella Asbeha. Timothy, the Alexandrine patriarch, did the same thing at the request of the emperor. He transmitted to Ella Asbeha the blessing of the Nitria and Scitia monks and also his own blessings and gifts.[220]

The Byzantine emperor proposed to Ella Asbeha a joint invasion into Himyar. The invasion plan envisioned movement into Ethiopia of Byzantine forces for union with the Axumites. The movement would be over dry land via Egypt, Egyptian Berenika, and the lands of the Beja and Noba. This plan was not adopted, probably partly because of the route's difficulties,[221] but mainly because the Axumites did not wish to accept foreign forces albeit as "allies." Therefore the Byzantine expeditionary corps was not sent to Ethiopia either by dry land or by sea. The Byzantines did not land their forces in Himyar, also because of the resistance of Axum. The emperor was constrained to limit his role to simply supplying ships to help the Ethiopian fleet and was forced to abandon any idea of direct intervention in the affairs of the Himyarites and Axumites. Axum thus occupied a main place in the tripartite coalition of 524–525 A.D.

The forces of Dhu-Nuwas were so large that for a successful struggle with them the usual Axumite detachments, formerly sent to Arabia on local ships, were not sufficient. Ella Asbeha was able to gather an army of many men but he did not have a fleet big enough for transporting it.

Besides the Axumite army, the South Arabian Christians who had fled into Ethiopia were prepared for the invasion. By 524 A.D. a multitude of emigrés from the Himyarite Kingdom had gathered. Among them were representatives of the nobility, including Sumafa Ashwa of the Yazan family—the brother of Sharakh'il Yakbul. He was one of the richest, most distinguished and influential of Dhu-Nuwas' subjects and in Ethiopia he became the acknowledged head of the Himyarite emigrés. In 517–518 A.D.,

Sumafa Ashwa together with his brothers and kinsmen had fought on the side of Dhu-Nuwas. In the inscriptions of the 520's (A.D.) the names of the brothers of Sumafa Ashwa disappear and he himself emigrated. A conflict occurred between Dhu-Nuwas and the heads of the Yazan family. Some Yazanites paid with their lives; others fled abroad. Even those who had accepted Judaism (the inscriptions mention them) [222] scarcely really supported Dhu-Nuwas. Evidently, the centralization and unification policy of Dhu-Nuwas alienated the South Arabian nobility and also the community members who were connected with the nobility. Dissatisfaction with Dhu-Nuwas' rule grew in the country and was further aggravated by economic difficulties. Dhu-Nuwas' regime was nearly ripe for a fall. For Ella Asbeha and his allies the time to take decisive action had come.

About 524 A.D. a plan of invasion into South Arabia emerged. It represents a remarkable example of Axumite strategy. Direct invasion of the Ethiopian forces had to be preceded by a landing of South Arabian emigrés, who were to disorganize the home front of the Himyarites and to break loose from the king all who were vacillating. In turn, they were to get the dissatisfied to rise up in rebellion, tearing down the carefully prepared defense of the sea coast. Finally, they were to divest the struggle of Dhu-Nuwas with the Axumites of any patriotic character and to prepare for the landing of the Ethiopian forces.

In the spring or summer of 524 A.D., the South Arabian emigrés landed in the south of the Himyarite Kingdom and consolidated their forces in the mountain fortress of Mawiyat. Dhu-Nuwas proved powerless to cope with the rebels. The local populace supported them. Probably the Christians and the other dissatisfied elements from all over Yemen made their way to them. Judging by the inscription from Husn al Gurab, counted among the emigré-rebels were representatives of many tribes and cities—from Najran in the north to Hadramaut and the borders of Oman in the south. [223] With his noble status and religious-political affiliation, Sumafa Ashwa (then not formally a Christian) was precisely that person around whom the most diverse elements of Himyarite society were able to unite. The problem of the Ethiopian invasion which faced Dhu-Nuwas was compounded by civil war. Moreover, the majority of his subjects either remained neutral or went over to the side of his opponents. At the same time the rebels holding the fortress of Mawiyat attracted the forces of Dhu-Nuwas, thereby weakening the defense of the sea coast.

In the summer of 525 A.D. everything was ready for the invasion. In the harbor of Gabaza a large transport fleet made up of seventy ships was gathered. *The Martyrdom of Arethius* describes it in detail, saying how many ships each of the islands or cities sent. A corresponding passage of the *Iliad* clearly served as a model for this listing of the ships. The ships were gathered from various "Roman, Persian, and Ethiopian harbors" and from the islands of Farsan (Farasan) and Iotab (Tiran). However, in another listing Persian ships are absent and probably were originally mentioned in error. The majority of ships named in the list came from Roman-Byzantine ports. Ethiopian ships are not named because they did not have to gather in Adulis from distant ports. Finally, seven ships were sent by the Farasans,[224] who were rebellious subjects of Dhu-Nuwas. A combined Ethiopian-Byzantine-South Arabian fleet was thus formed. The Axumite forces were put on the ships. The fleet was divided into two squadrons;[225] one of them was directed farther to the south so as to make its landing at a considerable distance from the first one. Part of the ships were wrecked but the remaining ones reached the points designated for the landings all right.[226] A Himyarite inscription uses the form of a dual number in speaking about the landing of the Ethiopian forces.[227] *The Book of the Himyarites* also knows of two simultaneous landings of Axumites; one detachment was commanded by Kaleb and the other by his general Z'WNS (Dhu Awnas). However, this could be a distortion of the name of King Dhu-Nuwas (a transposition of letters).

The purpose of this maneuver is not entirely clear. Moreover, its success was possible only in the event that Dhu-Nuwas could not count on unconditional support of the princes of the coastal tribes. Evidently their position depended on whether the Axumite forces or Dhu-Nuwas' forces appeared on their territory. The inscription from Husn al Gurab says that in battles with the "Abyssinians" the Himyarite king received support only from the Himyarite and Arhabite princes proper.[228] The leaders of other tribes did not support Dhu-Nuwas. Arabian tradition also says that the leaders of the tribes refused to obey him.[229] The fate of South Arabia hung now on one or two battles; they had either to strengthen Dhu-Nuwas' position or show that his cause was lost.

The Book of Himyarites and *The Martyrdom of Arethius* tell of a battle which was waged on the seashore. In it the Himyarites fought on horseback but the Ethiopians were not mounted. The Himyarites bore great losses, were broken up, and fled. Their king was killed by an Ethiopian soldier who carried his body through the shallow water to the shore and chopped off the head with a sword.[230] Arabian sources contain vague echoes of this battle.[231]

As a result of it, and possibly, one or two additional small battles, the Himyarites' resistance was broken. The Axumite forces easily occupied Zafar, Najran, and other cities. Sumafa Ashwa and the rebels of the Mawiyat fortress did not take part in the military operations—so brief was the war. All of South Arabia again found itself under the authority of Axum.

Sources describe the victory procession of Ella Asbeha about the conquered country. A kinsman of the Himyarite king escorted him into Zafar. Here the Axumite king seized the palace, harem, and treasury of Dhu-Nuwas.[232] Soon Sumafa Ashwa and also probably the other emigrés arrived in the capital. Everywhere Ethiopians destroyed pagan temples and synagogues, restored and built churches anew, and restored divine services in them.[233] Clergymen were not lacking; some of them had arrived with the Axumite army, others, such as the Misium Grigentius, were sent to Himyar by the Byzantine church authorities. Ella Asbeha was extremely concerned about the propagation of Christianity in the country where only yesterday Jews had ruled. His victory inscription placed in Marib bears a pious Christian character.[234]

To all former Christians it was proposed that they return to the bosom of the church in the course of a year. Sumafa Ashwa became a Christian;[235] Ella Asbeha himself became his godfather. This strengthened, on a new basis, the personal tie between the Axumite king and the leader of the South Arabian rebels. Local Christian emigrés who had returned from Ethiopia and other countries occupied very important posts in the traditional institutions of authority. Thus Ella Asbeha made the son of "saint" Arethius of Najran an ethnarch, or tribal head. Sumafa Ashwa received the title of king and occupied the Himyarite throne as a vassal of Ella Asbeha.[236]

Ella Asbeha was not given to repressions. He understood that after the bloody dominion and fall of Dhu-Nuwas, the Himyarites expected customary religious tolerance, civil peace, and the restoration of trade connections from their new rulers. Sources tell about the killings of Himyarite Jews by the Ethiopians, but these brutalities were not carried out at the order of Ella Asbeha. The Himyarite nobility complained to the Axumite king about the killings and the violence of the troops. In order to protect themselves local Christians tattooed the sign of the cross on their arms. In spite of the oppressions, Jews and pagans remained in the territory of South Arabia. This attests to the well-known tolerance of Ella Asbeha and his deputies.

After a stay in Arabia of about seven months,[237] the Axumite king returned to his home country, leaving behind a reorganized system of government in his overseas possessions.

Himyar changed into an autonomous state although dependent on Axum. Sumafa Ashwa (the king of Saba, Du Raydan, etc., etc.) was considered its head. Above him stood Ella Asbeha—king of Axum, Himyar, Saba, Raydan, etc., etc. In his inscription King Sumafa calls Ella Asbeha "his lords, nagashis of Aksum"[238] (the words "lords" and "nagashis" are *plurals* in this inscription).

The Himyarite king subjugated local princes and all the native populace. An Ethiopian administration was created side by side with the local one. Ella Asbeha placed Axumite troops in Himyar. Ethiopian military leaders were at least *de facto* independent of the local authorities and perhaps even independent of Sumafa Ashwa himself. Moreover, they formed under him a special [advisory] council which, according to the official version, was obliged "to protect the king from enemies."[239] The Himyarite king was obliged to take into consideration the decisions of this council. Possibly a special representative of the Axumite king (perhaps the Ariat of the Arabian sources) was the chairman of the council of Ethiopian military leaders.

Thus as a result of the 525 A.D. campaign, a unique "dual government" was established in South Arabia. Side by side with the Himyarite king and the princes-kails, an administration of Ethiopian military settlements or colonies which were subject only to their own military leaders existed. The royal inscription of Sumafa Ashwa calls them "deputies of the nagashis of Aksum ('qbt / lngš / 'ksmn).[240] They possessed great military power and consequently greater actual power than the Himyarite king. Therefore the rule of Sumafa Ashwa is mentioned by Procopius Caesarensis only. Sumafa Ashwa ruled approximately up to 535 A.D. In 531 A.D., according to a majority of investigators,[241] a Byzantine embassy was sent into Ethiopia to Ella Asbeha and into Himyar to Sumafa'. Procopius Caesarensis, who was excellently informed in affairs of this sort, mentions it. A certain Julian, "the brother of the strategos Summus," headed the embassy. The emperor (the famed Justinian) gave him two separate commissions. The first was to find out whether the Himyarites and the Arab-Maadei who were their dependents, and also, of course, the Ethiopians who dominated them, were beginning military actions against the Persian power. The second commission was of a purely economic nature: to induce the Ethiopians to take into their own hands the Chinese silk trade which was conducted via ports of Ceylon and South India by Persians who had brought the silk into the boundaries of the Roman Empire. The emperor, in Procopius' words, did not wish to enrich his Persian enemies.[242]

The first commission was evoked by the difficult military situation in which the Byzantine Empire then found itself. From 529 to 531 A.D. (when the Padishah Kavadh died), the Persians inflicted a series of defeats on Byzantium. Their campaigns followed one after another. The Arab Lakhmides, who were subject to the Persians, appeared in the environs of Antioch and at the borders of Egypt. The Himyarites, and the Arabs of Central Arabia (Kindites, Maadei) who were subject to them, were able to divert the Lakhmides, having struck them from the rear.[243] The world-wide Roman Empire partially restored by Justinian was now in need of Axum's aid, the aid of its vassals and of the vassals of its vassals. However, it never did receive real help. The economic part of the mission also failed. Here is how Procopius Caesarensis tells of the embassy's failure:

"Ellistheei (Ella Asbeha) and Esimithius (or Esimithaios, i.e., Sumafa Ashwa) promised to fulfill the request [of Emperor Justinian] and sent the [Byzantine] minister back, but neither one of them fulfilled the agreement. [To the Himyarites] it would be difficult, having crossed the wilderness and having traversed a very long route, to attack a people who were far more warlike [or more capable militarily] than they were. The Ethiopians were not in a position to buy silk from the Indians since the Persian merchants, inhabiting the land bordering the Indians and arriving in the ports where the Indian ships put in, usually bought up the whole cargo from them."[244]

Procopius' explanation seems probable. It proposes that Ella Asbeha made an attempt to organize a silk trade. If such were the case his agents went to Ceylon and South India. Here they tried to buy silk in addition to the staple, traditional goods. Were the Axumites capable of competing with the Persian merchants? Hardly. Besides, the silk trade was a new business for the Axumites, whereas the Persians had conducted it in an exemplary fashion and had come to monopolize it. Procopius also mentions this correctly. From his story it follows that the Axumites did nöt acquire even a small quantity of silk. This can hardly be explained solely by the fact that the Persians outcompeted them. More likely the Axumites did not seriously try to engage in trade with this commodity. Besides, most silk fabrics were obtained by the Persians along caravan routes through Central Asia.

In Joannes Malalae a description of another embassy is preserved. Joannes Malalae does not give the name of the ambassador, but it was Nonnus—son of Avraam. Nonnus, as is evident from the correspondence of Photius, was sent first to the Arabs and Himyarites and then to Ethiopia, to Axum.[245] Joannes Malalae relates the following about the embassy.[246] Justinian sent a letter to Ella Asbeha in which he proposed that he cease trading with the Persians and begin a war with the Persian ruler Kavadh. Ella Asbeha allegedly carried out his proposition. Actually, no kind of war took place between Ethiopia and Persia. In the proposition to cease trade with the Persians and to direct it along the Nile route we may discern a distortion of the information concerning the attempt to take over the Chinese silk trade from the Persians. The mention of the name Kavadh compels one to date the embassy of Nonnus to the period prior to 531 A.D. Like Julian, Nonnus had a commission relative to the Kindite king Kais (Kais ibn Salyama ibn al Haris). However, while Julian was obliged to obtain the forgiveness of Kais in Himyar, Nonnus was obliged "if possible" to bring Kais to the emperor....[247] Theophanes the Byzantine retells Joannes Malalae's text about the embassy to Axum but calls the ambassador Julian, and dates the embassy itself to 571 A.D.[248] The latter is an obvious error. As far as the name Julian is concerned, it probably was taken from Procopius Caesarensis. If one believes Theophanes, then the notes of the ambassador (used by Joannes Malalae and after him by Theophanes) would have to be ascribed to Julian. However, impressive arguments force one to recognize that Nonnus was the author of the notes on the embassy.

Evidently Theophanes and Joannes Malalae confused two Byzantine embassies to Ethiopia and Arabia—those of Julian and of Nonnus. This confusion is easily explained; both embassies pursued similar goals and both concluded unsuccessfully. In such a case, the name of Kavadh could have mistakenly gotten into Joannes Malalae's text.[249]

The fact that the embassies of Julian and Nonnus were *not* one and the same can scarcely be doubted; but just as undoubted is the fact that they were very close in time; literally, they followed one after the other. Whether Nonnus journeyed to Ethiopia prior to 531 A.D., earlier than Julian, or after this time remains unknown. In the latter case Joannes Malalae is mistaken, dating the embassy to the time when the Padishah Kavadh was still alive. It is more probable that Nonnus journeyed to Ethiopia prior to 531 A.D. (i.e., between 526 and 530), between the restoration of Axumite domination in Himyar and Julian's embassy. In 532 A.D. peace was concluded between Byzantium and Iran and the necessity of intervention by the Ethiopians in the Byzantine-Persian struggle was considerably lessened.

The persistence and fruitlessness of attempts by Byzantine diplomacy to draw the Axumite Kingdom and its vassals into war with Persia should be noted. Approximately at the same time we see in Ctesiphon an Axumite ambassador, a Monophysite by religion, who by his intercession rescued his famous co-religionist Simeon Betharsham from a dungeon where he had been thrown at the order of the Padishah, who had heeded the slander of the Nestorians. They had accused Simeon of adherence to Byzantium.[250] This episode demonstrates that the Sassanides clearly distinguished complex relations with Axum from hostile relations with Constantinople. The Ethiopians did not break off normal ties with Iran, and in its turn the Persian power did not exhibit hostility toward them. As has been noted above, Persia refused to give Dhu-Nuwas help against Axum and did not push its vassal Lakhmides toward war. On the other hand, the Byzantine-Axum relations left much to be desired in spite of the officially demonstrated friendship of these two Christian powers. Byzantine diplomacy clearly was not strong enough to exert pressure on Axum. An example in point was the attempted blackmailing of the Axumite king by rapprochement with his unreliable vassal. The Byzantines tried to establish contact with Sumafaʿ Ashwaʿ. At their intercession, Sumafaʿ permitted the Kindite king, Kais, to again occupy the throne. However, between 532 A.D. and 535 A.D. Sumafaʿ was overthrown and imprisoned in a fortress. Abreha, a common soldier or junior commander of the Ethiopian troops stationed in South Arabia, occupied the Himyarite throne.

Ella Asbeha tried to restore order but suffered defeat. In Procopius' words, "he sent under the leadership of one of his kinsmen an army consisting of 3000 men but this army did not want to return to its native land and intended to stay in this fine country [i.e., Arabia Felix]. It entered into dealings with Abram [Abreha], kept secret from its leader; at the beginning of the battle it killed him, joined with the enemy army, and settled in this country. Ellistheii [Ella Asbeha] in great annoyance sent another army against Abram [Abreha] which entered into battle with Abram's army but was smashed and hastily returned to its homeland. Now fear restrained the Ethiopian king from any attempts to fight with Abreha-Abram."[251]

In this communication, which Arab tradition confirms,[252] Abreha led common soldiers ("many servants of the Ethiopian army and all who had an inclination toward crime")[253] in their struggle with the military-tribal nobility. The social contradictions in Axumite society were already so great that they led to open revolts albeit beyond the borders of Ethiopia. How this struggle was reflected in Ethiopia itself remains unknown.

At first, Byzantine diplomacy treated Abreha with hostility. Class sympathies were not so much involved as was straightforward political calculation. Abreha had overthrown Sumafa, with whom Byzantium had established contact. Moreover, the Byzantines did not have faith in the stability of the rebels' position and did not want, because of them, to quarrel with Ethiopia.

The hostile tone in which Procopius speaks of Abreha's rebelliousness is characteristic. However, with the consolidation of Abreha's authority the situation changed. Byzantium sought rapprochement with him and actually established a close political and ideological bond. Abreha obtained Byzantine aid in building churches.[254] Embassies from the Byzantine Empire arrived in Himyar, one of which is mentioned by a Marib inscription.[255] In counterbalance to the Monophysites of Ethiopia, Abreha supported Orthodoxy[256]—the official ideology of Byzantium. Flirting with local patriots, he composed inscriptions in the Sabaean language and dedicated them now to the Christian Trinity, now to the directly monotheistic Rahman.[257] It may be true that the Axumite monarchy was not delighted by the intrigues of Byzantine diplomacy; even if the rapprochement of Byzantium with Abreha occurred after his conciliation with the Axumite king. Ella Asbeha, evidently to the end of his life, refused to acknowledge the usurper as the Himyarite king. But his successor did so.

To Procopius it was known that "after the death of Ellistheei, Abreha was obliged to pay tribute to the successor of his royal authority in Ethiopia and thereby consolidated his own authority."[258] Arabian writers communicate approximately the same thing.[259] In his inscription of 543 A.D., Abreha also refers to himself as a vassal-tributary (?)—'azlī—of the Axumite king,[260] and in an enumeration of embassies mentions the embassy of the latter to Abreha in the very first and thus most honored place.[261] Even the embassy of a world power—the Roman Empire—is named after the Ethiopian one. Evidently all the embassies took place in the same year—543 A.D.

Although acknowledging the hegemony of Axum and sending tribute to Ethiopia, Abreha, de facto, carried out an independent policy. He strove to restore the might of the Himyarite Kingdom and to spread its influence into

Central and Northern Arabia. He carried out campaigns on Mecca and Central Arabian Halaban. These campaigns, at least the first of them (the campaign of 547 A.D.), were carried out by Abreha in alliance with the Byzantines.

An Arab legend relates that one of the Ethiopian soldiers of Abreha who had lost a battle near Mecca fled to Ethiopia with the sad news.

Soon after his death, legends were created about the outstanding personality of Abreha. Three literary-historical traditions were enriched by them: Arabic, Byzantine, and Ethiopian. No Arabian writings touch upon the events of the VI century A.D., or upon the history of Himyar, which do not also recognize Abreha. In Byzantine literature, especially in literary works connected with the name of Bishop Grigentius, Abreha assumed the image of a pious, Orthodox king. In *The Life of Saint Grigentius* was first contained the assertion that Ella Asbeha himself appointed Abreha as the king of the Himyarites directly after the overthrow of Dhu-Nuwas.[262] Thus, both kings allegedly experienced the very best of relationships. Ethiopian tradition went still further. It made Abreha and Ella Asbeha blood brothers. Moreover, under the influence of Arabs and Byzantines particular attention was alloted to Abreha. According to the "Lists of Kings," he was the elder of the two brothers and died earlier than Ella Asbeha. During the life of Abreha, Ella Asbeha was his co-ruler and after Abreha's death he reigned alone. This joint reign supposedly lasted 27 years and 3 months (in reality Abreha reigned about 23 years and Ella Asbeha about 20 years). After the death of his "brother," Ella Asbeha reigned 12 more years. According to the lists, these kings had an honorary name—Eguala Anbasa (Sons of the Lion). Perhaps the etymologizing of this descriptive name explains the legend about their being relatives. Abreha himself calls himself Rumahis Zabiyaman. This descriptive name figures in the Marib inscription[263] and in the recently published *Ry* 506, and *Ja* 544–547. Drewes translates it as "Spear of the Right Hand,"[264] which is far from indisputable, although it can be connected with Ethiopian customs and representations. Abreha died around 558 A.D., having outlived Ella Asbeha by 15 to 20 years.

In essence, Ella Asbeha did not succeed in turning South Arabia into a fully integrated component of the Axumite Kingdom. It maintained significant independence even while remaining under the political influence of Axum and while paying yearly tribute to it. In Northern Nubia, local rulers grew stronger. However, the more fertile and richer south evidently remained under the hegemony of Axum. The victory of militant Christianity did not lead to a change in the foreign policy of the Axumite Kingdom. Ella Asbeha, although demonstrating amicability toward Byzantium, continued to shun all attempts at foreign influence on the affairs of his country. Ethiopia became Christian but not Orthodox. It developed friendly ties with Byzantium while maintaining normal relations with Persia, which remained Byzantium's main enemy in the east. The ancient ties of Ethiopia with India continued to develop. Evidently, Axum continued to expand its influence into the interior of the Ethiopian plateau. In spite of individual political failures, the reign of Ella Asbeha constituted one of the most brilliant epochs in the history of the Axumite Kingdom.

The Axumite Kingdom: VI–VIII century A.D.

The development of the Axumite Kingdom continued even after Ella Asbeha's death (about 540 A.D.). Up to the middle of the VIII century A.D. Axumite kings minted their own coins, although gold gradually disappeared from the coinage, yielding to copper and in part to silver. The imprints on the coins changed so as to imitate contemporary Byzantine images. The construction of stone buildings continued. The appearance of Christian churches and the first monasteries on the outskirts of the Axumite Kingdom, far from the old urban centers, is extremely indicative. In the extreme north of Ethiopia a church was founded at Danga (in the country of the Tanganitae?), on the trade routes from Axum and Adulis into the country of the Beja and the Valley of the Nile. Somewhat further south in Aratou are also preserved churches of the VII–VIII centuries A.D. Near Danga the Hagar-Najran (literally "city of Najran") monastery arose. This area is today in Northern Eritrea, on the border of historic Ethiopia and Eastern Sudan. The "city of Najran" was named either in honor of the Najran martyrs of 518 A.D. (as legend maintains) or in honor of the Najran Christians driven out of Arabia after the death of Muhammad. The Ethiopian legend says that 40 Najranians and 32 Ethiopians were the founders of the monastery. According to another version a total of 40 men were the founders. Like the Arabian Najran, Hagar-Najran was situated on the border of a continental desert at the intersection of important caravan routes. Another monastery situated farther south of Hagar-Najran was founded according to the medieval Ethiopian book *Gadla Sadkan* (*The Lives of the Saints*) by 8 Syrians and 62 Ethiopians.[265] It is difficult to say to what degree the above cited figures are true. In the extreme south of the Axumite Kingdom the Nazre (i.e., Nazareth) monastery was founded, of which the church is preserved. In direct proximity to the capital and other cities of the central part of the kingdom arose the Debre Damo monastery, possibly on the site of an ancient pagan temple.

In some localities on the outskirts of the Axumite Kingdom, grottoes are preserved which display traces of habitation and brief rock inscriptions that contain ancient Christian names. They belong to monk-hermits of the VII–VIII centuries A.D. It is significant that the monastic laws of Pachomius[266] were promulgated during this time.

It is possible as B. A. Turayev (p. 67) thinks that monasticism penetrated simultaneously into Ethiopia in two different forms: monastery monasticism with the communal regulations of Pachomius the Great (whose center became the Debre Damo monastery founded according to tradition by Za-Mikael Aragavi) and secluded monasticism with the ascetic regulations of Shenuta (whose center in Axum became the secluded Madar monastery founded by Isaac).

The impression is created that the end of the period of Axum's development was marked by a "monastic movement" in which Ethiopian Christians in large numbers renounced the world and went off to adopt the hermit life or entered monasteries.

Under the cross-influence of Byzantine Egypt and Ethiopia, Nubia was Christianized. An apocryphal legend tells of the baptism of a eunuch of the *candace* (Meroitic queen) who, having returned to Meroe from Jerusalem, began to preach the new religion. Tertullian considered the Meroitic Kingdom as one of the countries where Christianity attained some propagation. Eusebius wrote that Egyptian Christians fled here from the persecution of Galerius and Maximinus (the beginning of the IV century A.D.). However, Meroe remained primarily a pagan country. The invasion of the Meroitic Kingdom by the Noba simultaneously weakened both the growth of Christianity and local traditional religion. The latter had evolved under the influence of the ancient Egyptian religion of the New Kingdom and of later periods.

Despite this, however, Christianity continued to make inroads into the country. Barhebraeus speaks of Christians in Nubia under Emperor Constantine. Between 407 A.D. and 427 A.D. Olympiodorus visited here. The natives, however, remained pagans. The Beja were also pagans as they never had recognized Christianity.

The Nubians adopted Christianity during the second half of the VI century A.D., after the arrival of spiritual-political missions sent by the Byzantine emperor Justinian and the Empress Theodora.

The Christian inscription of the Nubian king found in Kalabshah[267] dates to this time. He ruled in Northern Nubia. After a long struggle he subjugated the Beja and Southern Nubians. Silko never said anything about his dependence on Axum. Indeed, the sovereign of such a large state could scarcely have been dependent. Furthermore, he does not speak of clashes with Axumites; yet his conquests could scarcely have avoided touching upon the interests of Axum. The successes of Byzantine diplomacy in Nubia are understandable. Just as did the rulers of the Himyarite Kingdom, the rulers of Nubia of the VI century A.D. strove to gain independence from Axum by strengthening their ties with Byzantium.

A description of Upper and Lower Nubia of the VI century is contained in Joannes Ephesius' *Historia ecclesiastica*. He made use of letters of the Monophysite missionaries from Nubia. Having arrived in Saba, the capital of Alwa in 581 A.D., the missionary Longin found Christian Axumites, many of whom were followers of the heresy of Julian of Halicarnassus. Longin argued with them from the position of orthodox Monophysitism and was able to make them change their minds, whereupon he received a letter from them renouncing the heresy.[268] Joannes Ephesius and Longin did not indicate the social position of the heretics; therefore, we do not know who was being spoken of: military colonists of Axum in the sphere of which Alwa was then located or merchants, etc. It is most significant that the king of Alwa invited Longin from Lower Nubian Faras to be the bishop of his country rather than [someone] from the more closely located Axum, even though a Christian community whose nucleus was made up of Axumites existed in his capital. This most likely attests to the striving of the Alwa king to gain independence from the Axumite Kingdom.

Arabian sources which contain communications about the struggle of the Muslim conquerors of Egypt with the Northern Nubians say nothing about the dependence of the latter on Axum. In the chronicle of the Alexandrine Coptic patriarchs a communication is preserved about a war which was waged by the "Abyssinian" king against the Nubian king around 686–688 A.D. From a subsequent exposition it is evident that it is not the ruler of Ethiopia who is being spoken of but the king of North Nubian Mukurra.[269]

An Arab author of the VIII century A.D., Al Fazari, cited by Al Mas'udi, mentions "the state of the Nubians which belongs to An Najashi" (لنجاشى عمل النوبة), the largest of the African states, which occupies the whole of 1500 farsahs in length and 400 farsahs in width.[270] Such an extensive possession had to include all of Nubia and Northern and Central Ethiopia. However, it cannot be ruled out that in this matter the text of Al Fazari is faulty. The size of African states is being spoken of. From west to east are listed Ghana, the principalities of the Sahara oases, and the "country" or "province" (عمل) of the Nubians (النوبية), which belongs to the nagashi. Why then is Ethiopia not mentioned? Perhaps its name was simply omitted? Context would seem to indicate this. In such a case not Nubia but Ethiopia would have had to figure as a possession of the nagashi. On the other hand, Nubia is called, as other African countries also are, not مملكة (kingdom) but عمل (province, region); dependent countries are usually named in this manner. In that form in which it is preserved, the text of Al Fazari speaks of the dependence of Nubia on Axum in the VIII century A.D.; but this evidence is not indisputable.

Important political shifts occurred in South Arabia at the end of the VI century A.D. and during the beginning of the VII century A.D., which completely excluded this region from the sphere of Axumite influence. After Abreha's death, his son Yaksum, the grandson of Sumafa Ashwa, called Saif (Saif Dhu Yazan), and Masruk, the second son of Abreha,[271] succeeded each other on the Himyarite throne. In this struggle the Yazanites [Saif's supporters] turned for help first to Byzantium, which declined to support them, and then to Iran. The Persian Padishah Khosru II (590–628 A.D.) agreed to send, for the conquest of Himyar, ships on which were placed a detachment of 800 criminals recruited in the jails of Persia. This detachment, headed by the Persian general Wahriz, succeeded in 577 A.D. in subjugating all of South Arabia. Yaksum was deposed. Saif became the Himyarite king. However, the Ethiopian military colonists remained in their previous situation. They hatched a plot and killed Saif "with their own spears."[272] Masruk, the son of Abreha, occupied the throne. But around 599 A.D. he was overthrown by a new Persian detachment. South Arabia was turned into a marzpanate—a frontier province of the Sassanide power. The Arabian sources which alone tell about these events say nothing about the participation of Ethiopia in the struggle which was going on. Different groups inside the Himyarite Kingdom acted, as did Iran and Byzantium, but not the Axumites. Axum's position is presented as neutral, or in any event extremely passive. Evidently the Axumite monarchy consciously turned away from participation in extra-African affairs.

Axum occupied the same position at the beginning of the VII century A.D., in the period of Muhammad's preaching. The political significance of Axum was still so great that both Muhammad and his opponents repeatedly appealed to the Axumite king, took refuge in his possessions, and asked for his support. Information about these events was preserved by early Muslim tradition written down by Arab historians of the VIII century A.D. and preserved in the works of At Tabari.[273] It can be summarized as follows:

In the month of Rajab of the fifth year of the prophecy of Muhammad (i.e., in 615 A.D.) the first group of Muslims headed by Usman, a nephew of the prophet, who was married to his daughter Rukaya, fled from Mecca to Ethiopia. Rukaya and several prominent Muslims, a total of eleven men and four women, were in this group. The authenticity of the tradition is supported by the fact that all the emigrés were listed by name with an indication of origin and family connections. The prophet himself allegedly advised them to flee to Ethiopia: "the friendly country whose king oppresses no one." The sources quote the words of the Muslims who returned later from Ethiopia: "We came into the land of Abyssinia and lived in it as good neighbors, confessed our faith and praised Allah, we were not subjected to insults and hearing nothing which discredited him." This indicates a considerable tolerance in the Axum of that time.

The emigration lasted for several years. To the first group of Muslim refugees were added new ones. Some emigrés arrived as whole families with wives and children. Others made their way one by one. Among the newly arrived, Ja'far, the son of Abu Talib, the cousin of the prophet, turned up. A total of no less than a hundred Mecca refugees gathered in the Axumite Kingdom, among them 82 men and also their children and wives.

Kureishite pagans sent an embassy to Ethiopia with a request to hand over the emigrés. The sources name the full names of the ambassadors. Evidently the Muslims who had fled to Ethiopia had been preparing for military action against Mecca, as had those who later settled in Medina. The embassy of Kureishites concluded unsuccessfully. The nagashi allegedly "protected those [of the Muslims] who had come to his country [Axum]." The Muslim emigrés in Ethiopia, however, maintained ties with their co-religionists in Hijaz. Consequently, the dealings of the Axumite Kingdom with Mecca and Medina were not disturbed. After the conciliation of Muhammad with the Kureishites, some of the emigrés returned to Mecca. Others, however, remained in Ethiopia several more years, up to the time of the embassy of Amr ibn Omayyah ad Damri.

In 6 A.H. [after the Hegira] (627–628 A.D.) Muhammad sent to Ethiopia an official embassy headed by Amr ibn Omayyah ad Damri. Amr delivered a letter of the prophet to the Axumite king. At Tabari, citing VIII century A.D. sources, quotes the text of this letter. It is, undoubtedly, a fabrication. However, the fact of the embassy and of Muhammad's letter is undoubted. Amr, in the context of his embassy, probably pursued those very goals of which the Muslim tradition speaks: the prophet was trying to convert the Axumite king to his faith, which he allegedly succeeded in doing. The tradition, preserved by At Tabari, quotes a letter of the Axumite king to Muhammad, written in the Muslim spirit and containing the assertion that the king actually had embraced Islam. He says also that he sent his son to the prophet. The name of the son is given sometimes as أرمى and sometimes as أرما (undoubtedly this is the name أرماح "Armah" distorted by the copyists). The Axumite king Armah I, well known from coins and the "Lists of Kings," is the person in question. Ibn Ishaq says the following about him: When Armah in the company of 60 Ethiopians was sent by his father to Mecca, the ship on which he was sailing sank, and all passengers perished. This allegedly happened in the month of Rajab (October-November), 630 A.D. Actually, Armah ruled happily and long, which is evident from the abundance of his coins. Evidently the tale of his journey to Mecca is nothing more than a pious fiction. The version of the death of Armah is a compromise between the version of his hadj in Mecca and doubts concerning the existence of this hadj. Moreover, 16 Muslims of the early emigrants who had settled in Ethiopia returned with the ambassador Amr to Mecca.

The fact that Muhammad actually sent a letter to the Axumite king is confirmed by the following considerations: first, the tradition which goes back to the communications of several writers notes the full name of the Muslim ambassador; second, it notes the name of the addressee, the king of Abyssinia, whom they called الاصحم بن أبخر —Ella Saham, son of Abgar. The name of Ella Saham is recorded in the "Lists of Kings." Moreover the legends of the Saho tribe[274] mention a King Saham. This name is connected with North Ethiopian toponymics similarly to the names of other Axumite kings; in Southern Tigre there is a Saham district. The name Abgar is not recorded in the "Lists of Kings" and does not appear on Axumite coins. However, أبخر could be a distorted spelling of the name الجبز, "Ella Gabaz," which *is* recorded in the lists, where he figures as the father and immediate predecessor of Ella Saham.

Not only Muslims but also their opponents fled to Ethiopia, where they counted on finding asylum and "an abundance of the means of living." V. V. Barthold first paid attention to a certain story of early Muslim tradition preserved by Ibn Hisham and At Tabari. One of the Prophet's foes, Ikrim ibn Abu Jahlya, fled from Mecca after its conquest by the Muslims. He headed for the sea coast and tried to get over into Ethiopia. Obviously, if the Axumite king had become a passionate follower of Islam, as Muslim tradition believes, or even if he had turned away from neutrality in the internecine struggle of the Meccans, Ikrim would not have counted on asylum in the Axumite Kingdom. Ikrim ibn Abu Jahlya supposedly said: "I wanted to set out to sea in order to join the Abyssinians. When I came to the ship in order to board it, the ship's master said, 'Slave of God, do not get on my ship until you acknowledge God's unity and renounce all gods but Him; I fear that if you do not do this we will perish on the ship. . . .'"[275] Concerning this, Barthold remarks: "It is possible that the sea communication between Arabia and the opposite coast of the Red Sea was in the hands of Christian Abyssinians."[276] There is nothing improbable in this, although the ship's master did not necessarily have to be an Ethiopian. He is not called an Abyssinian and only indicated as a monotheist, most likely a Christian. But in the VI century A.D., Christianity was professed by the Arabs of the Red Sea coastal area in addition to the Ethiopians, for example by the Farasans, who were traditional seafarers. The ship's master to whom Ikrim turned could have belonged to their number.

Tradition, connected with the beginning of Muhammad's activity, indicates that the Meccan Kureishites carried on an extensive trade in the Axumite Kingdom. "And the land of the Abyssinians (at the beginning of the VII century A.D.) was a place of trade for the Kureishites, who traded in it, finding an abundance of the means of living and safety and a fine trading place." The reference to the safety of trading within the

borders of the Axumite Kingdom of the VII century A.D. is interesting.
This indicates the strength of the central authority and its striving to
encourage foreign and domestic trade.

Sources also contain other curious details. The Muslim refugees—the
first group of 15 persons—sailed to Ethiopia from the Hijaz port of Shu'aïba
"on two trading ships which brought them to the land of the Abyssinians
for half a dinar (per person?)." [277] Although these facts were written down
in the VIII century A.D., they could fully convey comparatively recent
recollections about the beginning and middle of the VII century A.D.
The poets of pre-Islamic Arabia, Amru-'l Kais and Labid, mention "good
spears" from Shamhar (coastal area to the south of Adulis). Tarafa mentions
large ships from Adulis. Kusaiir compares the pile of saddles of the hero
of Kasida, whose praises he is singing, with the Adulis ships that in the
morning leave Dahlak (an Ethiopian island in the archipelago of the same
name). A Meccan legend says that the four sons of Abd Manafa (juncture
of the VI–VII centuries A.D.) traded with different countries: the eldest,
Abd Shams, traded with the king of Abyssinia. Al Baladsori communicates
that on the eve of Islam gold coins were imported into Mecca: Byzantine,
Sassanide, and "Himyarite" coins. Conti-Rossini is inclined to interpret
"Himyarite" as "Axumite," since the Himyarites by this time had ceased
coinage. [278] However, Axumite money has not yet been found in Mecca.
In the IX century A.D. Al Mas'udi heard about the past glories of Adulis
and the trade journeys of the Arabs to this city.

We know almost nothing of the reigns of the Axumite kings who were
the successors of Ella Asbeha and the predecessors of Armah. According
to Byzantine and later Ethiopian sources, [279] Ella Asbeha voluntarily
renounced the throne in favor of his son Atherphotam, or Gebre Meskal
[Gabra Meskal]. Ella Asbeha went off to be a hermit on the "mountain
of Ophar" (in the Afar desert?), or to Abba Penteleon (in the vicinity of
Axum), where long before the Christianization of Ethiopia there existed
an ancient Sabaean sanctuary. Ella Saham, according to Muslim tradition,
also renounced his authority. Having turned to Islam and having given the
throne to his son, he allegedly wrote to the prophet: "I have sent to you
my son Armah and in truth I myself do not rule. . . ." [280] Significantly,
both kings, Ella Asbeha (Kaleb) and Ella Saham, supposedly gave their
authority to their successors and became proselytes of a new religion. If
this is not the repetition of one and the same legend, then one can speak
only of the voluntary transfer of their authority. Ella Asbeha and Ella
Saham were strong kings who left the throne after earning great reputa-
tions, and who enjoyed an enormous esteem beyond the borders of their
state. Such kings are not deposed from the throne.

One of the most interesting finds of recent years is an inscription of
Wazeb, the son of Ella Asbeha. The inscription was discovered at Axum

and has not yet been fully deciphered. It tells of his victorious war on the African continent, probably to the south of the Tigre plateau.[281] It is possible that the second descriptive name of Wazeb was Ella Uzena. According to a South Arabian inscription from Marib, *CIH* 541, the Himyar king, Abreha, submitted to a successor of Ella Asbeha whose name can be read as Ella Uzena[282] (if this spot in the inscription is not the name of the people of the "Ge'ez"). Whether he was Ella Asbeha's son remains unknown. Procopius Caesarensis does not call this king's successor his son; he speaks only of the "successor of his authority,"[283] which in and of itself is significant, but does not permit one to make definite conclusions. The "Lists of Kings" consider Ella Asbeha's successor to be his son, who was named Asfeh. The successor of Asfeh was his brother Arfed, and then still another brother Amsi. Thus three brothers reigned in succession.[284] Since the lists treat Kaleb or Ella Asbeha as two different people, then Kaleb's successor is called Gebre Meskal (Slave of the Cross) or Kwastantinos (Constantine). These two names are encountered in all versions of the lists except C, but in the majority of cases the second name is ascribed to a particular ruler—to the son of Gebre Meskal. In Axum, a folk tradition continues to identify the tomb and the palace of Gebre Meskal. He is considered the founder of the ritual of coronation and a series of rites connected with it, and is also known as the builder of churches.

Numismatic data do not confirm a single one of these names, but Ella Uzena of the Marib inscription can be connected with Ousanas II (Ουσανας) and also with Ousas ('Ουσας), (contracted from 'Ουσανας ?), of the Axumite coins, which belong to the same type as that of Kaleb's coins. Nezana's coins also belong to this type. It is possible to date them to the middle of the VI century A.D. The coins of Anaeb (or Ebana), Alalimiris, Ioel, Israel, Gersem I, and Ella Gabaz date from the late VI to the beginning of the VII century A.D.

The coins of Ella Saham have not been preserved. The successor of Armah I may have been Iathlia, and subsequently Hataz I. On the coins of Armah I and Hataz II the demagogic slogan is revived. The king is depicted on the throne with state and religious attributes. This may indicate some sort of change in the status of kings of the VII century A.D. in comparison with the preceding period. The coins of Za Wazen or Wazena, Za Ya'abiyo la Madhen, Armah II, next an unknown king, Hataz I, Gersem II, and Hataz II reveal a clear decline in monetary affairs. Their coins were not very artistic and were made of bronze and silver but not of gold. Three or five of the latter kings ruled in the VIII century A.D. By that time traces of the decline of the Axumite Kingdom were clearly appearing. The names of these kings are completely unknown to the "Lists of Kings." The lists contain the names of individuals, some of whom possibly never occupied the throne, together with others who perhaps reigned during the Late Axumite period (VIII–IX centuries A.D.). The "Lists of Kings" (version C), however, do give the name of Ella Sahel.[285] His coins have not been preserved but an inscription from Ham is dated to his reign.[286] Unfortunately, there are no chronological references in the inscription. Paleographic indications permit one to date it between the second half of the VI and the beginning of the VIII century A.D.

Political events of that time are little known. Only the Arabic tradition written down by historians of the VIII century A.D. and preserved by At Tabari communicates anything at all. In 10 A.H. (July–August 630 A.D.— since the month is indicated), Muhammad received the news that the Ethiopian flotilla had attacked the port of Shu'aïba. The prophet sent a detachment of 300 Muslims under the leadership of Alqama ibn Mudjazziz al Mudlidji to help Shu'aïba. According to Ibn Ishaq, the detachment returned with nothing, not even having entered into contact with the enemy. According to Al Waqidi, the Muslims gained a victory, having run the Ethiopian ships aground. In that same year Muhammad spoke about the death of the nagashi as if it were a sad occurrence for the Muslims. Perhaps the death preceded the attack on Shu'aïba? Later, in Medina, a spear was shown, allegedly given as a gift to the prophet Muhammad by the Ethiopian nagashi.

In 20 A.H. (640–641 A.D.) Caliph Omar was again forced to send Alqama ibn Mudjazziz against the Ethiopians since the "Abyssinians carried out a villainous act against the Muslims (of Arabia)."[287] This time Alqama was accompanied by four ships and 200 troops. But even this military expedition of the Arabs against the Axumites ended in failure. In Conti-Rossini's opinion the Red Sea remained in the complete control of the Ethiopians.[288] The following year, 21 A.H. (641–642 A.D.) "the Yemenites came up out of their own Yemen and set out for Abyssinia for their own protection." However, it is not known whether or not their campaign was a victorious one. In any event, in 31 A.H. (651 A.D.) "the black ones" carried out a new raid on Arabia.[289]

In subsequent years the raids were probably repeated. In 702 A.D. a final, large-scale attack by the Ethiopians on Hijaz took place. Their fleet unexpectedly seized the port of Jedda, thus creating a direct threat to Mecca, the religious center of the Caliphate. In Mecca panic reigned. Abdallah the son of Amr ibn al Assa persuaded the Meccans to abandon the city and to block the road to the Kaaba against the invasion of "blacks as innumerable as ants."

Probably in response to this raid, the Arabian fleet seized and destroyed Adulis. Archaeologists Sundström and Paribeni report traces of the destruction of Adulis which, in their opinion, can be attributed to Arabs sometime during the VII or beginning of the VIII century A.D. Adulis

was later rebuilt but was not again able to attain its former size or prominence. In the VIII–IX centuries A.D. its population, according to archaeological data, was composed of Christians and Muslims, with a numerical
and probably a political predominance of the latter. The neighboring
Dahlak archipelago and probably the environs of Massawa were occupied
by Arabs. Later new settlers from Arabia were added to them.

Massawa is called by neighboring people Batse (among the Tigre) or
Bade (among the Beja). Medieval Arabs called this place Badi. A communication has been preserved which says that in 634 A.D. Caliph Omar
sent a rebel named Abu Mihgan to Basi (Badi with a paleographic error—
باصع instead of باضع ?). In any event, after 702 A.D. Dahlak was turned
into a place of political exile by the caliphs.

About 715 A.D., the poet Al Akhias, who had written a satire on Caliph
Suleiman ibn Abd al Malik, was exiled on Dahlak, where he remained
until 720 A.D. In 718–719 A.D., Yazid ibn al Mukhallib was also exiled
there. Caliph Mansur exiled Abd al Jabbar, son of the Khorasan vice-
regent (753–775 A.D.), to Dahlak. During this time, neither sea raids of
Ethiopians nor trade voyages of Ethiopian Christians on their own ships
were even mentioned. Evidently the Arabs almost completely annihilated
the entire Axumite fleet. New information concerning the Ethiopian fleet
does not appear again until the beginning of the XIV century A.D.

On a wall of the palace of the Omayyads in Quseir-Amrah, the Axumite
nagashi is depicted among the four most powerful rulers of the world side
by side with the Byzantine and Chinese emperors and the Visigoth king
of Spain. This fresco, which was executed about 705–715 A.D., attests to
the fact that the Axumite Kingdom still retained remnants of its former
power.[290]

Recently M. V. Krivov turned his attention to the mention of Ethiopia
in *The Revelation* of Pseudo-Methodius, a Byzantine literary monument of
the second half of the VII to the VIII century. Judging by the sentiments
displayed by the author of *The Revelation*, the Byzantines, hard-pressed
by the Arabs, hoped for help on the part of the distant but co-religionist
Axumite Kingdom whose forces "having come out of the Ethiopian Sea"
inflicted a defeat on the Muslims and forced them to abandon and return
all Christian lands up to Yatrib (Medina) itself. (V. Istrin, pp. 17, 20, 22;
M. V. Krirov, pp. 120–122. [In Russian]) M. V. Krivov (pp. 121–122)
proposes that the Byzantines not only knew about the victories of the
Ethiopian fleet on the Red Sea but also sent their envoys to Axum.

The Late Axumite period

The Late Axumite Period begins around the middle of the VIII century.
It was characterized by a gradual weakening of royal authority, a decline
of cities and trade, growing isolation, and progressive political fragment-

ation. However, the outlines of decline are clearly noticeable even at the beginning of the century. Gold disappeared from monetary circulation within the Axumite Kingdom. The strengthening of the Beja in the north and of the Falasha and Agau in the south cut the Axumites off from the main gold-bearing districts and excluded them from the profitable gold trade.

The reasons for the decline are not entirely clear. Some contributing factors are recognizable but they cannot be considered paramount. The decline of Axumite trade, which began at the end of the VI century and continued throughout the VII century, is one such factor. Even more important was the loss of all extra-Ethiopian possessions. However, the internal economic processes which went on in late Axumite society remain unknown.

Cross section of fortification embankment, Axum.

The external political circumstances which changed from the middle of the VII century A.D. to the beginning of the VIII century A.D. played an important role. In the Near East, during this time, instead of a system of two great empires hostile to each other there appeared a world power (the Arabs), which had absorbed the whole of Persia, the greater part of Byzantium, and a series of other large states. For the first time not only peripheral possessions but also main centers of a great power (Mecca and Medina before the transfer of the capital to Damascus) were in close proximity to Ethiopia. The previous competition between the two giant empires, each of which had tried to attract Axum and Himyar to its side, was superseded by the almost absolute domination of a new world power. This new world power was disrupted only by internal disturbances.

In the northern part of the country the Beja expanded their sphere of influence. The Nubians and the Beja gained strength, of course, at the expense of a weakening Axumite Kingdom. Arab authors speak of complete independence of the Beja from Nubia and from Axum. Moreover, the possessions of the Beja in the IX–X centuries A.D. embraced the greater part of modern-day Eritrea, including the Baraka River valley and the region of Hamasien. Here are found numerous burial places of the Beja dating to the VIII and following centuries.[291] Only from the XI century A.D. does resettlement of these places by Ethiopian Christians begin: first the Bogos-Agau, then the Tigre-Tigrai (descendants of the Axumites).

The Agau peoples also became active in the Late Axumite Period. The Falasha Jews, whose language belongs to the Agau group, formed their own state. The first, very vague, stories about them were brought by the adventurer Eldad Danit, who presented himself before the Cairo Jews as being by birth from the Jews of "Kush" (tropical Africa). The information communicated by Eldad bears a legendlike character,[292] but nonetheless is the first information about the Ethiopian Falasha. Eldad, no doubt, found out about them through Arab merchants. Ethiopian legends even tell of the temporary domination of the Jews over Northern Ethiopia after the fall of the Axumite Kingdom.

Arab authors of the IX century A.D. communicate little information concerning the Ethiopia contemporary with them. The Nubians and the Beja were at the center of their attention. Al Hashimi (who quotes Al Biruni) speaks of the participation of "Abyssinians" in the traditional fairs of Ukaz "in Nejd." [293] Al Yak'ubi conveys the most valuable news about the Ethiopians of IX century A.D. "Their capital is Ka'bar and the Arabs continually journey to it for trade. They [the Ethiopians] have great cities and their coastal area is Dahlak. Those who are kings in the countries of Al Habasha [i.e., Abyssinia] stand under the authority of the great king and are subject to him and pay to him *haraj* (tax). An Najashi [nagashi] adheres to the Christian faith of the Jacobite doctrine." [294]

It is difficult to say what this city of Ka'bar is. In earlier and later times, no such city has been reported in Ethiopia. It is reasonable to speculate that in the text of Al Yak'ubi, which has come down to us, a mistake was made. Conti-Rossini first proposed that Ka'bar was a distortion of Gondar. Then he came to the conclusion that only Axum could have figured under this name. *Ḥudūd al-'Alam* and the inscription of Hadani Dan'el give other names of Ethiopian capitals of that time.

Ḥudūd al-'Alam (The Regions of the World) [295] is a Persian geographical work of the IX century A.D. One of its sections is devoted to Ethiopia. The Persian geographer asserts that the Ethiopians are a people of "lofty feelings and obedient to their king; merchants from Oman, Hijaz, and Bahrein come here." Among the Ethiopian towns mentioned are Suwar, where the royal armies were stationed; Rasin, a town on the seashore (the residence of the Axumite king); and Rin, where the Ethiopian commander-in-chief and his army dwelt. This latter place abounded with gold. Rasin, according to Minorsky, is an incorrect spelling of Badi, and Rin is an incorrect spelling of Zeila. In any event none of the cities named can be identified with Axum. Evidently the Persian geographer did not know the ancient capital of the Ethiopians, which attests to the sharp decline of its role. It is interesting that *Hudūd* names two high individuals in Ethiopia, the king and the commander-in-chief, who had residences in different places. This is one more piece of evidence of the decline of the Axumite Kingdom.

I propose that only one Ethiopian source of that time can be considered reliable. This source consists of three inscriptions of Hadani Dan'el, carved on a stone throne in Axum.

The first inscription (*DAE*, IV, no. 12) tells about battles of the troops of the hadani with the people of Baria, and about a campaign into the Kassala district (now in the Sudan Republic) that involved seizing of spoils. The second inscription (*DAE*, IV, no. 13) speaks about a war of the hadani with the Walkait people, who had evidently settled the contemporary district of that same name. The Walkait pillaged Axum but Hadani Dan'el brought them to defeat, seized huge spoils, and made the area into his own hereditary possession—Maiya Salasala. Consequently Axum was not his residence. The last of the three inscriptions of Hadani Dan'el (*DAE*, IV, no. 14) tells about his conflict with the Axumite king, who looked extremely wretched. Actually he became the vassal of the Hadani and accepted from the hand of the latter authority over Axum "as a land of the kingdom" of Hadani Dan'el. An attempt of the king to achieve independence from the Hadani was considered a mutiny. On the other hand, Hadani Dan'el emphasized that he had received his authority over Axum from his father Dabra Ferema.[296]

The Axumite Kingdom was in the final stage of decline, although the old dynasty evidently continued to exist. The ancient capital still was inhabited and enjoyed respect but had ceased to be the political center of Ethiopia. The head of the Ethiopian state bore the title "hadani."[297]

One way or another, a ruler with the title "king of Axum" gave way to another who bore the title of "hadani" in medieval Ethiopia. This fact is established by all Axumite and Postaxumite sources. According to written Ethiopian tradition, the late Middle Ages witnessed the replacement of the Axumite kings with the Zagwe dynasty. This dynasty ruled Northern and Central Ethiopia right up to 1268 or 1270 A.D., a total, according to tradition, of 372 years. Thus the Axumite dynasty ceased, according to Ethiopian tradition, in 896 or 898 A.D. In any event, by the end of the IX century A.D., the Axumite Kingdom had finally ceased to exist.

Conti-Rossini argues that the inscriptions of Hadani Dan'el reflect the replacement of the ruling dynasty in Ethiopia at approximately the indicated time.[298] It is impossible to prove this but there is nothing improbable in it. In any event, even if the kings of the Zagwe dynasty were not descendants of Hadani Dan'el, they did bear his title.

Ethiopian tradition further maintains that the descendants of the royal dynasty of Axum found refuge in Northern Ethiopia in the Shoa region, where they even established their own state. If nothing else, this legend attests to the pretenses of the kings of the Shoan Solomon dynasty (who overthrew the Zagwe dynasty at the end of the XIII century A.D.) to a "legal" descent from the Axumite kings. Therefore the events of 1268–1270 A.D. are called the "restoration of the Solomon dynasty."

Nonetheless it is undoubted that in Shoa, and in other regions of Central Ethiopia which did not enter into the composition of the Axumite Kingdom, a Northern Ethiopian Christian culture created by Axumites was propagated in the Middle Ages. Probably such a diffusion of culture is connected with some shifting of the populace. In the case being considered, it may have involved the resettlement of Axumites into Central Ethiopia. Monks and priests (advocates of Christianity) and also merchants must have been found among the settlers. But it is not known whether peasants and, what is more important, members of the ruling house migrated with them.

Why did the Axumite Kingdom perish? The expansion of the Beja, Walkait, Falasha, and other peoples who had at one time been subject to Axum was more likely the consequence than the reason for its decline. The crushing defeat of Adulis by the Arabs severely restricted Axum's trade with Asiatic countries and with Egypt, but by no means ended it entirely. It is true, however, that under the new conditions it was more difficult for the Axumite kings to preserve their relative trade monopoly; this led to a decrease in the flow of profits and duties to Axum, and a simultaneous enrichment of its rivals and former vassals. But is it possible to explain the decline of an ancient and previously powerful kingdom by simply a change in trade conditions? Only after having carefully studied the economic basis of Axum and its government can one put such a question.

Stele, Axum.

II

Economic Resources

Very little is known about the economic resources of the Axumite Kingdom, partly because of the scarcity of written sources and partly because
of insufficient archaeological study. However, by summarizing the scanty
data, it is possible to give a review of certain fundamental elements of
economic behavior and of the economic system.

Population

The population of the largest towns—Axum, Adulis, and Coloe (Matara)
—judging by the area they occupied, was numbered (even in their most
flourishing period) in thousands or a few tens of thousands of persons.
Some notion of the numbers of Axumites is given by the size of their army.
According to At Tabari, in 525 A.D., 70,000 Ethiopian troops were landed
in Arabia.[1] *The Martyrdom of Arethius*, the source closest in time to the
events, indicates a significantly smaller number: 15,000 troops.[2] But even
this, undoubtedly, is exaggerated. From that same *Martyrdom of Arethius*
it is known that the Ethiopian army was transported to Arabia on 70
ships. If one takes into account the insignificant cargo-carrying capacity
of ships of that time, then it is clear that they could not have transported
even half of these 15,000 men.[3]

Usually far fewer troops took part in the campaigns of the Axumite
kings. Having conquered Himyar in 517 A.D., the Axumite king Ella
Asbeha garrisoned his "occupation army" there. In the city of Zafar, the
capital of Himyar, a garrison of about 600 Ethiopians was subsequently
annihilated by Dhu-Nuwas: first 300 men, then 280[4] men were killed.
Moreover, Ethiopian detachments probably of smaller size were stationed
in other localities of South Arabia. *The Martyrdom of Arethius* communicates
that the Ethiopians stationed their troops in Najran, and Dhu-Nuwas
threatened "all who were left by the Ethiopian king in my realm."[5] The
entire "occupation army" of Axum could not have exceeded 1500 troops.
However, such a garrison comprised only part of the Axumite army that
participated in the campaign in Himyar. The greater part of the Axumites
returned to their homeland. In any event the Axumite army did not
exceed several thousand men.

When the Axumite king sent troops against Abreha, the Axumite Army consisted of a total of 3000 men. Abreha did not do battle with them, but tried instead to attract them to his side.[6] Evidently to both himself and to the Axumite ruler, these 3000 troops seemed a fully sufficient force for the suppression of the rebellion in Himyar.

The numerical strength of the Axumite army can be judged by the size of the losses inflicted on its opponents; undoubtedly these figures are comparable. In battles with the Aguezat and Hasat tribes the forces of Ella Asbeha killed a total of 400 enemy men, not counting several hundred women and children.[7]

The Axumite army was no larger under Ezana II than it was in the VI century A.D. One can judge this in the same way, that is, by the number of foes beaten by detachments of Axumites (in one case 705 and in another case 1387 men, women, and children). Judging by the tone of the inscriptions, the cited figures seemed very large and could have exceeded the number of victors.

Thus the size of the Axumite army was measured in thousands of men. If one takes into account that basically it represented a people's volunteer corps, then all the population of Axum proper (the city and surrounding area) can be estimated at several tens of thousands of persons (but not more than 80,000 to 100,000).

In other areas of Northern Ethiopia the population was smaller than in the dominant community of Axum, but also on the order of thousands and tens of thousands of persons. Some notion of the numbers of the Agabo tribe in the area of Akkele Guzai is given by an inscription from Anza,[8] which speaks of the building operations of the Agabo. The inscription does not indicate how many men were occupied in the operations. Let us attempt to determine their number by the quantity of bread given to them. In the course of 15 days the workers received 20,620 loaves; consequently an average of 1374 or 1375 loaves daily. In Ezana I's bilingual inscription it is said that to the Beja who were being resettled (a total number of 4400 persons) were given 22,000 loaves daily,[9] i.e., 5 loaves apiece. However, the bread requirement of the Agabo and the Beja could have been different since the Agabo were farmers whereas the Beja were cattle breeders, and extremely frugal with food, especially with vegetable food. Also, those Agabo occupied in construction operations were grown men, whereas among the Beja being resettled there were men, women, and children. Therefore, for each worker mentioned in the Anza inscription more bread had to be supplied than the average for each of the Beja being resettled. In an inscription from Safra there are other norms of bread distribution. The king received 12 pieces or portions (less probable, 22 pieces), the priest who carried out the sacrifices 6 pieces, and the donor

9 pieces.[10] Evidently the last norm was the most usual, since the donor performed "sacred" jobs. Moreover, 9 loaves is the arithmetic average of all three distribution norms—$(12 + 6 + 9) \div 3 = 9$. Consequently, it is most probable that in the activities at Safra (if the norms were carried out), each worker would have received an average of 9 loaves daily. It is not known, however, whether the loaves in Axum, Safra, and Anza were of one and the same weight. But let us assume that this *is* so. Then each worker in Anza received 9 loaves (as in Safra), or 5 loaves (as with the Beja), which is less probable. In the former case, 1374 or 1375 bread loaves daily would have been required by 153 persons (excluding the king, etc.) and in the second case by 275 persons.

We have thus obtained two estimates of the number of healthy, grown men among the Agabo. For one grown and healthy man there were approximately four women, children, very aged persons, and cripples. Consequently, in order to determine the total number of the Agabo it is necessary to multiply the number of grown men by 5. Thus, if all of our previous assumptions are close to the truth, then in the beginning of the Axumite period the total number of Agabo equaled 765 (that is, 153×5) or 1375 (that is, 275×5), probably closer to the first figure.

Nomadic and seminomadic tribes of cattle breeders were still smaller in numbers than the agricultural Agabo tribe. In the six "peoples" of the Beja, enumerated by Ezana I, there were 4400 persons.[11] Judging by context this was the number of all the mouths to feed: men, women, and children. Consequently in each tribe there was an average of 733 or 734 persons. This is somewhat less than the proposed number of Agabo, and by far less than the number of Axumites proper (the members of the urban community).

Groups of settled fishermen, hunters, and gatherers of wild plants each numbered a few hundred or even less. And groups of nomadic hunter-gatherers did not exceed 30 to 40 persons each. Authors of antiquity write about rather small groups of "Ichthyophagi" (fish-eaters) who were scattered along the shores of the Red Sea. Strabo speaks of "a well-populated island" in Lake Psebo (Tana), where since olden times lived the Waito, settled hunters of the hippopotamus. One medieval Ethiopian source describes a group of nomadic hunters in northwestern Ethiopia near the western boundaries of the Axumite Kingdom: it numbered only 16 persons.[12] In the VI century A.D., Nonnus visited the Icthyophagi on one of the Red Sea islands. He describes them as an extremely poor and primitive tribe.[13]

The total size of the population of the Axumite Kingdom (urban and rural, settled and nomadic), without Arabia and Nubia, could scarcely have exceeded 350,000 to 400,000, at the outside a half million.

Land and agriculture

The ecological conditions of the northern part of the Ethiopian plateau, where the Axumite Kingdom arose, were exceptionally favorable for agriculture. Abundant precipitation falls in the rainy seasons, of which there are two in Ethiopia. Cosmas Indicopleustes wrote about the "great rains" which pour down in Western Ethiopia from the month of Epiphi (July) to the end of the month of Thoth (September), according to the Egyptian calendar. "And during all three of these months there were extremely heavy rains from which a multitude of rivers are formed."[14] Nonnus clearly describes the climate of that part of the Axumite Kingdom which he visited (i.e., the lands between Adulis and Axum): from Adulis to Aua there was aridity and summer heat, but from Aua to Axum rainy weather occurred from midday, when the sky was covered with storm clouds and a heavy rain fell. At another time of year, supposedly, the "land of the Adulites" was flooded by rains right up to Aua, but from Aua to Axum the weather was dry: "then the land produced ripe fruits."[15] From Nonnus' observations the conclusion can be drawn that when he was in Ethiopia the region of Adulis was dry but closer to Axum the weather was rather wet. This is natural: the Red Sea coast was and remains more arid than the plateau. However, according to the evidence of geologists, this wet zone was then wider than it is now. The boundary of desert lands was farther removed to the north and east. Mention of "ripe fruits" indicates that the Axumites were engaged in agriculture.

The soils of Northern Ethiopia are very fertile. Academy Member L. I. Prasolov[16] has investigated the soils of Northern Ethiopia. He describes them as stony, with a color from light to dark brown and from gray to almost black. Of the samples, 71 percent were classified as average to highly acidic (pH 6.0); 27 percent were classified as weakly acidic (pH 6.1–7.3). This latter category is most favorable for the growing of the majority of plants. Moreover, 2 percent of the samples were classified as slightly alkaline (above pH 7.3). Fifty-eight percent of the samples were rich in phosphorus, and almost all contained a sufficient quantity of magnesium and potassium. The Ethiopians, themselves, categorize the soils into black and red ones. The former are located primarily in valleys and the latter on the mountain slopes. The black ones, as a rule, are more fertile and permit cultivation of the earth up to twelve years without a rest; the red ones, no more than four to five years. As a whole, the soils of Northern Ethiopia are extremely fertile. Prasolov compares them with the red soils of India and the Mediterranean and with the chernozems of the Ukraine.

It is possible that the Axumites (like their descendants in the Middle Ages and their eastern neighbors the Himyarites) gathered two harvests a year.

Evidently wheat was one of the main agricultural crops. The spikes of the long-bearded Ethiopian wheat are depicted on Axumite coins; wheat bread and flour figure in Axumite inscriptions. This cereal grain is still widely cultivated in Ethiopia. A startling diversity of extremely original and archaic[17] varieties is observed.

Academy Member N. I. Vavilov, having carefully studied thousands of samples of Ethiopian wheats, came to the conclusion that the Abyssinian plateau is one of the two main centers of their domestication. More recently, it has been felt that the Northern Ethiopian plateau (or Tigre plateau) is a very ancient but *secondary* focus of wheat domestication: *Triticum durum* Desf. subsp. *abyssinicum* Vavilovi, *Triticum turgidum* subsp. *abyssinicum* Vavilovi, and *Triticum polonicum* L. and others. One cannot doubt that wheat cultivation appeared in Northern Ethiopia long before the beginning of the Axumite period.

Barley and spelt-emmer are cultivated in Ethiopia, in addition to wheat. All of these are very ancient cereals. The northwestern and northern parts of Ethiopia are considered an ancient but secondary focus of their domestication. That they were not authenticated for the Axumite epoch indicates only the paucity of our knowledge.

Other cereals grown in Ethiopia which are closer to millet include sorghum, finger millet, and t'eff. T'eff (*Eragrostis t'eff* Trotter *Ethiop.* ጣፍ) is cultivated only on the Ethiopian plateau, where it is native.[18] T'eff goes into the baking of black bread.

The northern and central parts of Ethiopia are the homeland of finger millet or dagussa (*Eleusine coracana* Gaerth). This grain enters into beer making. The word *dagussa* is international, not Ge'ez or Amharic, though related to Amharic *deggese*, "to celebrate." Portères cites related words in several languages: the Gurage of south central Ethiopia, *dagasam*, "to prepare a holiday," and *deges*, "holiday"; the Amharic *tej*, "honey wine"; the Tuareg *dakno*, with the same meaning; the Arabic *dohn*, "sweet sorghum" or "finger millet." He conjectures that beer from finger millet was considered the "honey wine of the poor";[19] honey wine gave the name to the beer and the beer gave the name to the cereal.

Of the numerous species of sorghum whose homeland is Africa, several are propagated in Ethiopia. Neighboring Nubia or Eastern Sudan is the homeland of the following species of sorghum: *Sorghum durra* (durra), *S. rigidum*, *S. cernuum*, *S. subglabrescens*. Some of them have been preserved in the wild state in Ethiopia. It is even possible that Northern Ethiopia entered into the make-up of the "cradle of sorghum domestication." This pertains especially to *Sorghum aethiopicum* Rupr., which is encountered here in the wild state. Unfortunately, t'eff, finger millet, sorghum, and millet have not as yet been detected in the settlements of the Axumite period.

The cultivation of flax is very widespread in Ethiopia and extremely ancient. Flax is grown exclusively for the sake of its oily seeds; the fiber is not used. Chick peas, peas, and other legume plants are also raised. Sources of the Axumite period do not mention them, although this by no means indicates that the Axumites did not cultivate oil and legume plants. For example, judging by the inscriptions, they did have vegetable oil.

The columns of buildings of the Axumite period (in Adulis and Tokonda) are decorated with representations of grapevines and grape clusters. In the inscriptions, wine (Greek οἶνος; Ge'ez ወይን)[20] is mentioned. This indicates viniculture. It came, no doubt, from Arabia—probably early in the Preaxumite period.

Axumite agriculture was a plow and irrigation agriculture. Up to recent times only indirect evidence attested to the existence of the plow among the Axumites (for example, the word "plowing" in the Ethiopian descriptive name for rhinoceros was correctly deciphered by Cosmas Indicopleustes as (Αρουὴ 'Αρίσι,[21] i.e., አርዌ ፡ ሐረሰ —the beast of the plowing). This descriptive name, authenticated also in the Ethiopian Bible,[22] has been preserved also in modern Ethiopian languages. Thus the word for plowing among the Axumites was ሐረሰ (compare the Arabic حرِيث).

Recent archaeological finds have provided examples of agricultural equipment and its depiction, dated to the Axumite period and to the end of the Preaxumite period. In Haoulti, Melazo, and Yeha, bronze sickles were found, probably for ritual reaping. They have openings for nails by which, evidently, they were fastened to a wooden handle. In Haoulti, clay figurines of either a bull or pair of bulls under a yoke were found. On the cliffs of Amba Focada (or Dakhane near Gulo Makeda) are preserved engraved images of a pair of bulls harnessed to a plow.[23] This plow does not differ from the modern Ethiopian one; it consists of five wooden parts without moldboards. Such a plow did not turn over the soil. A field probably had to be plowed two to three times before sowing.

Apparently the plow was the main agricultural implement of the Axumites. Along with it must have existed other auxiliary hand tools which are preserved in modern Northern Ethiopia: the mattock, for the raising of heavy virgin soils against which the primitive Ethiopian plow was powerless; hoes, extremely different in Northern and Northwestern Ethiopia; digging sticks, for planting seeds; and also the sickle and different threshing and winnowing tools. Unfortunately neither literary allusions nor archaeological finds have been preserved, which would permit us to become acquainted with examples of these implements.

The greatest achievement of Ethiopian agriculture was the use of artificial irrigation. The primary elements include a basin for collecting water from temporary streams and rains, dams, irrigation canals, terraces on the mountain slopes and sometimes on the flat summits of mountains (*amba*). In Northern Ethiopia numerous artificial terraces surround the remains of settlements of the Axumite period. In Axum and Kohaito, Axumite and Preaxumite dams and cisterns for the collection of water of temporary rain-fed streams are preserved.

Not a single description of the agricultural operations of the Axumite period has been preserved. However, some notion of them is given by sources of the XIV–XVI centuries A.D. *The Life of Aaron Mankerava* (XV century A.D.) tells how Aaron and his followers visited in the "land of Zango which is in Esterana" to the south of the Awash River. The monks spread soil on the rocks, made irrigation canals, sowed wheat, beans, peas, lentils, planted almond trees and grapevines, mandragora and bananas. "And the land of Zango in Esterana which was a burning desert became a garden."[24]

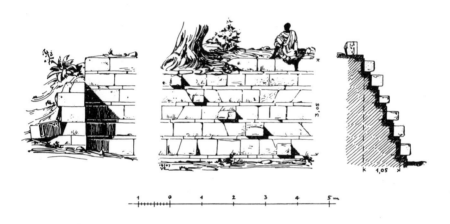

The Kohaito dam.

On the whole, Axumite agriculture was on a high level of development for Africa. One can compare it with the ancient agriculture of Meroe. However, the Axumite irrigation system was closer not to the Meroitic and Egyptian but to the South Arabian system, which had reached its climax in the irrigational art of the Sabaeans, Himyarites, and Nabataeans. Irrigation in the Axumite Kingdom was on a somewhat lower level than among the three latter peoples, but this was compensated for by more favorable natural conditions, greater resources, and greater productivity of labor. The use of draft animals for plowing and probably for threshing linked Axumite agriculture with livestock breeding.

Animal breeding

In Preaxumite Ethiopia, certain wild and domestic animals were sacred to the gods. Among these would be included the wild mountain sheep and the toro antelope, and domesticated bulls, sheep, and goats. In the sanctuaries of Preaxumite towns are found depictions of bulls, sheep, goats, and camels. Statuettes of bulls made of bronze and alabaster with dedicatory inscriptions to the gods Almouqah and Astar have been preserved, as well as others without inscriptions. They date to both the Preaxumite and Early Axumite periods. The cow, *Bos africanus*, is pictured on bas-reliefs of Deir el Bahri that illustrate the life of the country of Punt (middle of the II millennium B.C.). To this same breed, evidently, belong the humpless bulls pulling plows which are depicted on the cliffs at Amba Focada.

The zebu is rather widely propagated in modern Africa (over all Eastern and Western Sudan, in Ethiopia, and Eastern Africa). Depictions of the zebu on the cliffs of Eritrea date to Preaxumite time: in Addi Kanza, Beth Sema'iti, Temalika, Za'ara (the Akkele Guzai region) and Ba'ati-Meskal (Serae region). A sculpture of a humped bull with an archaic Ge'ez inscription from Zeban Kutur (Eritrea) dates to Early Axumite times. And two statuettes of red clay possibly date to the VI–VIII centuries A.D.[26]

One must compare the rock drawings of a zebu (or half-zebu—sanga) in the Harar region with these depictions. Evidently, the zebu was cross-bred with *Bos africanus* in Ethiopia during antiquity, and hence a new hybrid cattle breed was propagated all over savannah Africa.

Besides bulls, about which Cosmas Indicopleustes also speaks,[27] the Axumite inscriptions name the domestic animals of Table 1 within the territory of Northern Ethiopia.

Table 1. Inscription References to Domesticated Animals

On the Statu-ette from Zeban-Kutur	From Safra	Bilingual of Ezana I	DAE IV, Nos. 10, 21, 30	The Axum Inscription of Ella Asbeha	Wazeb's Inscription
Young bullock (*lg'*?)	Cow (*lhm*) Sheep (*bg'*)	Cows (*lhm*) Sheep (*bg'*) Pack animals* (*'nss*)	Cow (*lahm*)	Cows (*lhm*)	Cows (*lhm*)

*Pack animals are also mentioned among the spoils seized in the country of Afan (*DAE*, IV, No. 10, 22).

It is not clear what is meant by "pack animals"—camels or asses? Domestication of the wild (Nubian) ass occurred in the regions of Nubia and Ethiopia. On the bas-reliefs of Deir el Bahri are depicted the pack asses of the inhabitants of Punt and also a Puntian woman riding on an ass. It is not known if the Axumites knew how to produce mules; it is not even known whether they bred horses.[28]

Breeding of camels was possible only in the desert region of Ethiopia.[29] On the cliffs of Northern Eritrea (the valley of the Baraka River) are encountered depictions of riding camels of the Axumite period.[30] The Romans created a detachment of meharists (dromedary cavalry) for the struggle with the Beja in Berenikan Egypt. Arab authors speak of camel cavalry of the Beja in the middle of the VII century A.D.[31] The first mention of camels in Axumite inscriptions dates to Ezana II's reign; in one of his inscriptions are mentioned camels (ገማል) in Atagau,[32] in another are mentioned riding camels (አርበብት) in Nubia.[33] Camels (*gml*) in Aguezat are mentioned in the inscription of Kaleb (Ella Asbeha).[34] In the inscriptions of the Hadani Dan'el are mentioned *mahr*, *'amhar*—camels, according to Littmann's interpretation.[35] It is reasonable to speculate that just as in the Middle Ages, the Axumite merchants acquired camels for trade caravans.

In its evolution, animal breeding was oriented toward the production of meat and milk. The inscription from Safra attests that cowhides were also used and possibly also horns. Nothing is known about the methods of pasturing cows. Similarly, sheep and goats were raised for the sake of their hides and milk. The meat of rams and goats, castrated at an early age, was valued highly. This was true in the Middle Ages and is true today. In the inscription from Safra we encounter the expression *bg'zgb*. Drewes translates this as "adult ram,"[36] although he is not convinced of the translation of the word *gb*. This word can be connected with the Arabic root جبّ "to cut," "to castrate"; hence مجبوب "eunuch." In such a case *bg'zgb* possibly means "wether." The ability to castrate animals indicates a considerable development of animal breeding.

In the deserts which surround Northern Ethiopia, livestock breeding was nomadic or seminomadic. Authors of antiquity communicate the details of the life style of the nomads: songs of the Troglodyte shepherds at the campfire where they whiled away the night while keeping the flock; quarrels because of pastures; and night crossings when the Troglodytes hung little bells on the necks of the males of the pack animals (camels or asses?) in order to scare away predators.[37] Perhaps the tale of Al Baladsori about the victory of Muhammad ibn Abdallah al Kumma over the Beja in 855 A.D. is an echo of this custom: the Arab military leader fastened little bells on the necks of the horses, whereupon the camels of the Beja fled, having been frightened by their sound.[38]

The Axumites, and peoples subject to them, kept many cattle (large-horned and small-horned). Unfortunately the data which are at our disposal pertain only to the spoils of war and to the royal household. The campaign of Ezana II against Afan yielded the following booty: 31,957 head of large-horned cattle and 827 "pack animals";[39] the campaign into Nuba, 10,560 head of large-horned cattle and 51,050 sheep.[40] Kaleb (Ella Asbeha) seized from the Aguezat and Hasat tribes 300 cows and 200 camels.[41] Wazeb also stole many large-horned cattle from his foes.[42] Hadani Dan'el seized from the Baria 120 cows and 200 sheep, and then from another opponent 17,830 camels (?) and 10,030 cows. Earlier he had seized from that same opponent 10,000 cows, 130 bulls (?), and 608 camels (?). From the Walkait people Dan'el seized 5,000 camels (?) and 802 cows and then 10,000 sheep and 3,000 cows[43] (these figures are clearly rounded off; magical significance is ascribed to the number 30).

Part of the cattle went into the rations of the troops; part were given as a sacrifice. But the major part, probably, went into the herds of the participants of the campaigns, especially of the king and nobility. After the campaign on Afan only 100 head of large-horned cattle were sacrificed to the god Mahrem[44] (1/320 part of the spoils). The king and nobility must have possessed enormous herds of cattle. Ezana I was able at one time to supply the Beja with 25,140 cows.[45]

Nothing is known about Axumite poultry raising. Domestic chickens (still the sole domestic poultry) were authenticated as early as the XV century A.D. in Ethiopia. Wool production was unknown to the Axumites.

Bee raising is widespread in Ethiopia. It is reasonable to assume an ancient tradition for this industry. Honey and a honeyed drink are mentioned in the inscription from Safra (A, 9 and 22) but it is not known whether the honey was obtained from domesticated or wild bees. Prins and Drewes are inclined toward the latter opinion,[46] although they do not support it with arguments. In my opinion it is more natural to assume the former.

Gathering, fishing, and hunting were occupations that characterized small, marginal tribes. Hunting played a certain role in the life of cattle breeders in semidesert regions and perhaps a minor role in the life of the farmers on the plateau.

Handicrafts

A principal source of information on local handicrafts is the various forms of representational art. Locally produced items, intended primarily for the Axumite elite, are often easily distinguished from items of foreign manufacture.

One of the earliest forms of clothing used by the inhabitants of Northeastern Africa is the leather loin cloth or apron. Among some of the peoples of Southern, Western, and Eastern Ethiopia this article constitutes one of the main elements of female dress. On the bas-reliefs of Deir el Bahri are depicted the double leather aprons of the ancient inhabitants of Punt, both men and women. The womens' aprons were somewhat longer.

Sculptures of the V–IV centuries B.C. found in Ethiopia depict fabric clothing. Statues from Asbi Dera and Haoulti, and the smaller of the figures on the bas-relief of the stone throne from Haoulti, depict (evidently) women dressed in heel-length shirts with sleeves. It is possible to distinguish folds, wide bands along the lower edge (probably colored), and a pattern in the form of flowers (whether painted or stitched is not known). The larger figure on the Haoulti throne depicts a bearded man in a knee-length half-skirt (a type of Indian dhoti) and a short cloak thrown over the shoulders. The ends of the cloak are fastened by a knot on the exposed chest.

The same type of clothing also existed in South Arabia; the borrowing is undoubted. It remains unknown whether this clothing (1) was completely fabricated in Ethiopia on the South Arabian model, or (2) was imported from South Arabia, or (3) was sewn in Ethiopia from imported fabrics. The first assumption is most probable, but the other two should not be ruled out.

During the Axumite period a sharp class differentiation in clothing was noticeable. Unfortunately it is necessary to rely exclusively on iconographic sources for this information since archaeological data are unavailable. On Axumite coins the king is pictured in a shirt, a shamma, and a head scarf, on top of which a crown is worn. Joannes Malalae (according to Nonnus) describes lighter clothing for the Axumite king; only a linen loin cloth and linen and gold turban.[47] The linen fabric for the loin cloth and the turban was, of course, imported from Egypt, which was famed for its linen cloth. In Ethiopia, flax was grown only to obtain oil and for the baking of flat cakes from flax seeds.

Only Cosmas Indicopleustes left us a description of ordinary Axumites: the soldiers and peasants. They were bare to the belt in loin cloths alone, of white color, hence, made of cloth. In the inscription from Safra, and in the bilingual inscription of Ezana I, clothing (lbs) is mentioned, but precisely what kind is not known. Pseudo Arrian describes in detail the ready-made clothing and fabrics imported into the Axumite Kingdom.[48] This permitted Mommsen to assert "The usual clothes of the inhabitants of Habesha [he means the Axumite Kingdom] were of Egyptian manufacture."[49] Mommsen is clearly exaggerating since even from *Periplus* it is evident that not only Egyptian but also Indian fabrics were imported. At the same time it is necessary to note that Pseudo Arrian was not interested in local craft production if it was not directly connected with foreign trade. Therefore the tale of *Periplus* about the importing of clothing should not be taken to indicate the Axumites did not know how to make clothing. However, until spinning, weaving, and tailoring implements are found it will be impossible to prove the presence of these crafts.

Unfortunately, no Axumite leather articles have come down to us. But ethnographic data permit us to think that in Axum wineskins, leather pouches, shields, and clothing were produced.

Salt making, mining, and metallurgy

Few data are preserved concerning the extraction and processing of minerals in the Axumite Kingdom. It is possible, however, to make a few observations. Salt making, the gathering and washing of precious stones (emeralds, sapphires, etc.), and panning for gold were all undertaken. In addition, obsidian was quarried, as was building stone. Iron ore may have also been extracted. Most likely, the Axumites extracted salt in the northern Danakil desert, where there are salt lakes. In the Middle Ages the local inhabitants of this region prepared blocks of salt for shipment to regional markets.

Cosmas Indicopleustes[50] speaks of the Axumites exporting salt to Sasu but not a single source speaks of the import of salt into the Axumite Kingdom. Consequently, we may infer that the Axumites extracted sufficient salt not only to satisfy their own needs but also to export into the interior of the African continent.

Obsidian was quarried in Ethiopia from ancient times. A principal source was the shore of the Red Sea, especially in the region of the Hawakil Gulf. Laboratory analysis has shown that obsidian of ancient Egyptian and Nubian articles is of Ethiopian origin.[51] Ancient obsidian mines in Eritrea were investigated by G. Tringali.[52] Pliny[53] speaks about the export of obsidian from Ethiopia. Pseudo Arrian communicates that obsidian was extracted ("which was encountered only here") in the sandy alluvia of the Hawakil Gulf.[54] Evidently local "barbarians" (ancestors of the Saho and Danakil) extracted it. Obsidian was also used in Ethiopia. At the site of Matara were found obsidian cutting tools.[55]

In the shallows of the Red Sea it was possible to gather pearls. Excavations in Haoulti-Melazo revealed pearl beads of two types which date to the Preaxumite or to the beginning of the Axumite epoch.[56]

The most important mining district of ancient northeast Africa was located in the northern region of Axumite possessions, in the country of the Beja. Rich deposits of gold in gold-bearing sands and ores were worked by local inhabitants. Ancient Egyptians exploited these deposits. And during the VIII–IX centuries A.D. Arab prospectors worked the gold mines. However, the Beja themselves were comparatively little occupied with extraction of gold. Besides gold, the Beja district yielded precious stones (emeralds, sapphires, etc.). The Beja extracted the precious stones and sold them to the Egyptians and the Axumites.[57] Another gold-bearing (and platinum) region exploited by Axum was located in Southwestern Ethiopia, in the country of Sasu. However, on the northern outskirts of the Tigre plateau there also were deposits of gold, for example, farther north and northwest of Asmara, where they were worked in Preaxumite and possibly also in Early Axumite times.[58]

We do not know when iron ores began to be extracted in Ethiopia. Sources of the III–IV centuries A.D. speak of the fact that the Ethiopians did not have their own iron and imported it from Roman possessions, India, and Arabia.[59] However, in neighboring Meroe iron mines were worked beginning from the I century B.C. right up to the VIII century A.D., i.e., to the end of the Axumite period (data of the Ghana archaeological expedition in Sudan).

Pseudo Arrian informs us that Ethiopia imported (via Adulis and Avalit) different metals (including finished goods). He lists iron, light-yellow copper in strips, brass in bars, and tin. Moreover, he points out that brass in Adulis "is used for [fabrication] of decorations." Strips of copper "go for casting or are cut up into arm and leg bracelets for ... women; iron is used in the [fabrication] of spears against elephants and other wild animals and also against foes."[60]

Thus, in Pseudo Arrian's works, the Ethiopians of the Axumite period knew how to work the following metals: iron, copper, tin, brass, and bronze as well as precious metals. Iron was subjected to forging; copper and bronze to smelting; copper and brass were cut, bent, and of course underwent forging and incising. Military and hunting spears, including a spear for elephant hunting, were fabricated from iron, while decorations were made of copper and brass. Even if one is limited to the information of Pseudo Arrian it is possible to speak of a significant development in metallurgy by the beginning of the Axumite period.

Excavations of stratified Axumite and Preaxumite archaeological deposits yielded numerous finds of metal objects of local origin. There were votive and ritualistic objects of bronze, small statues of bulls[61] and a lion, iron in the form of a plow (Asbi Dera), stamps of fine open work (Sabaea,[62] Haoulti,[63] and Yeha[64]), a bronze earring,[65] rings and bracelets,[66] and beads and crosses worn on the body (Axum[67] and Yeha[68]).

Excavations at Axum in 1957 revealed finely executed decorations of gilded bronze, a cover plate and pendant which mounts a plate of colored glass.[69] They were undoubtedly of local workmanship. The cover plate has, as a central element of ornamentation, the representation of an Ethiopian bull አ . The glass was imported from Egypt. Judging by the outline of አ and the stratigraphic position in which the artifacts were found they can be dated to the V–VII centuries A.D.

In Preaxumite deposits at Haoulti, Melazo, Yeha, Sabaea, and Mai Mafales were found specimens of weaponry and work tools of bronze: pole axes, the tips of spears or daggers, pots, sickles, chisels, beads, rings, needles, and knives (or adzes). During the Axumite period, however, bronze went primarily into the fabrication of art objects—decorations and sculpture. During prospecting at the Axumite town of Matara a multitude of bronze artifacts of local production were found: knives, blades, needles, pins, rings, stamps of Preaxumite time, and also many plates and a cup (18.8 cm. in diameter) of the Axumite period.[70]

Casting of bronze articles was carried on in Ethiopia but it is not known if the bronze was imported, since neither its composition nor its source has been adequately determined. Judging by the color of the patina, Preaxumite bronze is not uniform.[71] The casting process used is not known. Nevertheless, the separate importing of copper and tin permits one to assume that the Axumites knew the secret of making bronze.

Specimens of iron-forged articles have been discovered: short swords, a chisel, rings and bracelets,[72] chains, and various fragments. In addition, bronze, silver, and gold Axumite coins indicate not only the development of coinage in metal, but also smelting of precious metals and medal art. Unfortunately, tools of the forging, foundry, and jewelry crafts have not yet been found, with the exception of stone crucibles for the smelting of gold in ancient mines close to Asmara.[73] In Haoulti a piece of a gold wire —a jeweler's material—was found. A cache of two pairs of gold earrings and gold rings of two types also turned up there.[74] Gold rings and a necklace were also found in the burial grounds of Yeha.[75] In 1940, a III-century-A.D. Axumite art object of considerable complexity was discovered. It is a wooden box decorated with 23 gold plates of different

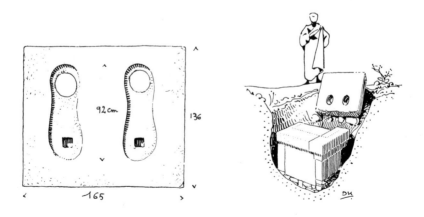

The "socketed" stone base of an Axumite statue.

form and size (rectangular, square, and six-sided), covered with a fine relief chasing depicting grapevines and flowers, and by thin slabs of green stone (marble?). The plates were fastened to the box with gold nails; 31 nails were found.[76]

Evidently the masterpieces of Axumite craftsmen have not come down to us. Cosmas Indicopleustes speaks of bronze unicorns which decorated the "four-turreted palace" in Axum.[77] Joannes Malalae (according to Nonnus) describes Ethiopian gold articles with which the king adorned himself and his chariot. He also describes the silver decorations on the chariots of the district rulers.[78] In Ezana I's bilingual inscription it is said that the king erected five statues to the god Mahrem: one gold, one silver, and three bronze.[79] The statues, of course, have been destroyed. Only the stone base of one of them has been preserved; each foot of the statue equaled 92 cm.[80] In such a case the height of the statue was not less than 5 m.

Ceramics

Excavations at Axum in 1906, 1938, 1955, 1957, and 1958–1959, in Tokonda in 1906, in Adulis in 1907, in Rore in 1922, in Debre Damo in 1943, and in Matara in 1906 and 1959–1960[81] yielded a comparatively large number of ceramic finds. These data allow us to assess the role pottery production played in the life of the Axumite Kingdom.

The majority of Axumites used only local ceramic wares. Axumite vessels of different appearance, size, and use have been preserved. These include cups with straight sides and flat bottoms or with a short hollow foot; rather small, hemispherical cups; cylindrical vessels with flat bottoms and, sometimes, with rather small, horizontal handles; large vessels; large long-necked pitchers with carved sides and ornamented handles. In addition, there are pitchers of medium size with a molding below the rim, and a large flat handle which joins the molding with the shoulder of the vessel; small wide-necked pitchers of cylindrical or slightly conical form, frequently with a small semi-cylindrical handle (sometimes perforated in the upper part) which joins the molding with the shoulder of the vessel; round-bottomed vases of streamlined form with small horizontal handles; vases on a support with straight sides and a broad base; and basins thickly decorated from top to bottom with engraving.

Adulis developed a special ceramic dishware made out of white clay and decorated by engraving. It is found in all towns of the Axumite Kingdom so far excavated: Adulis, Axum, Matara, and Yeha.

All of the above-mentioned vessels continued to be manufactured throughout the Axumite period. Ethiopia did not have a similarly elaborate and diverse ceramic complex at any other time either before or after this period. Axumite ceramic vessels were fabricated carefully and richly embellished with tasteful decoration. Ornamentation varied: geometric, representational, incised, etc. The vessel base was sometimes executed in the form of a human foot or the paw of an animal. Sometimes the ornamentation is in relief, though more often incised. The vessel color is red and black. Some dishware is covered with a well-fired glaze.[82]

Axumite ceramics were produced by one of three methods: drawing out of the clay material, building up of clay cord, or sculptured modeling. However, all ceramics were prepared without the use of a potter's wheel. The richness of the ceramic complex denotes craft specialization, the singling out of potters from the general mass of small manufacturers.

Axumite potters fabricated not only dishware decorated with modeled and painted elements, but also actual sculptures. In Adulis, Paribeni found a clay statuette of a female torso. Anfray discovered two similar statuettes at Matara. One was made of fired clay and the other of sandstone.[83] These three rather small sculptures are highly reminiscent of images of the goddess of fertility or Earth Mother in various archaeological cultures of the world. In 1955–1959, Pironen and Contenson discovered, in Axum, several clay sculptures of a single type. They depict with striking realism and expressiveness the heads of Ethiopian women with long hair falling to the shoulders.[84] In the Late Axumite deposit at Haoulti were found statuettes.[85] All clay sculptures were subjected to careful firing.

Another art object of the potters was a miniature clay model of an Axumite house with windows and all construction details.[86] For the paving of part of the floors in the palace of Ta'akha Mariam, fired brick was used.

Carving on stone, wood, and bone

The craft of Axumite stone carvers appears still more laborious, developed, and specialized. It was they who fabricated the colossal monolithic stelae in the form of structures with extensive architectural detail. They also carved the dedicatory thrones and altars. Stone cutters rough-hewed and polished the multi-ton basalt and granite blocks. They cut out graceful inscriptions, bas-reliefs, miniature flacons of mica, plates of colored stone for decorating boxes, crosses worn on the body, signet rings, beads, large and small stone cups, statuettes, and water drains in the form of wild-animal heads. They worked in basalt, granite, sandstone, alabaster, mica, semiprecious and probably precious stones. Unfortunately the technology of the Axumite stone cutters has not been studied. The names of some of them—the only names known to us of Axumite craftsmen—have been preserved. Evidently the craft of the stone cutters was an honored one.

The earliest examples of wood carving are to be found in ancient churches of Debre Damo and Yeha, and date to a comparatively late period when the Axumite Kingdom was in its decline or had already perished. But even at this time the work of the Ethiopian carvers demonstrates an impressive mastery.

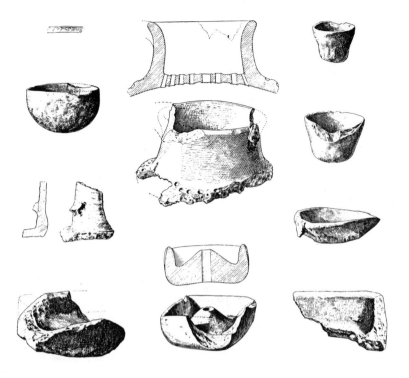

Axumite stone vesselware.

Examples of bone artifacts of the IV–VIII centuries A.D. were discovered by excavators in Axum in 1958. They include a carefully chiseled spoon, a small four-cornered chest, two carved hilts, and two awls.[87]

The quarrying of building stone and stone for making artifacts constituted an important branch of mining. Principal materials sought included limestone (primarily white), sandstone, bluish and black basalt, granite, and marble of different colors (especially white and green).

Architecture

It is possible to judge the art of Axumite builders by the intact foundations of ancient buildings, by the platform of Beta Giorgis with stelae which depict the multi-storied Axumite buildings, and by clay models of houses. In addition, we can make use of architectural descriptions in Cosmas Indicopleustes[88] and later authors.[89] Finally, we can examine stone funeral basilicas of the Axumite kings, temples and early churches, and also dams and cisterns for collection of water (Mai Shum and Ashafi,[90] etc.). Defensive structures are virtually undiscovered (in 1958 a defense wall with

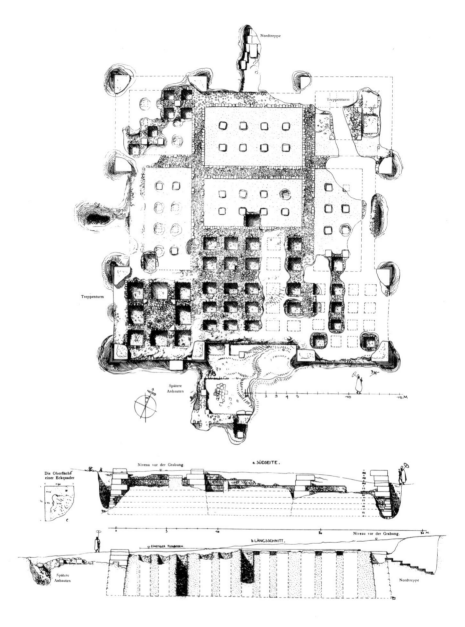

Palace Enda Mika'el, Axum (central structure).

bastions which protected the temple precinct of the town of Axum[91] was discovered).

This enumeration already indicates the range of Axumite construction. The Axumites transported over many kilometers huge, sometimes multi-ton, blocks of basalt, granite, white and green marble, and limestone into their towns. The working of these types of stones, especially the very hard bluish and black basalt (Axum, Adulis, Coloe [Matara]), required considerable skills; the underlying processes and technology are still unexplained.

In Axum, Adulis, and Coloe (Matara) a multitude of one-storied and two-storied buildings were constructed; usually five rooms were placed in each story. The main body of the palace of Ta'akha Mariam (the royal residence of the VI[?] century A.D.) in Axum was reconstructed as eight storied. The largest of the stelae shows a palace building of 14 stories. Relatively early Axumite palaces (prior to the IV–V[?] centuries A.D.) are Enda Mika'el and Enda Semon, which were built on a square plan. Each side of Enda Mika'el was 27 m. and each side of Enda Simon was 35 m.

The royal residence of Ta'akha Mariam was an ensemble of buildings[92] forming a closed rectangle with dimensions of 120 m. × 80 m. It had three inside courtyards arranged at different levels, many hundreds of rooms, peristyles, dozens of staircases. In the center of the ensemble was raised an eight-storied castle; evidently the "home of the King" himself (beta nagashi). It was square in plan with a basal area of 24 m. × 25 m. This was not only a dwelling place with household accommodations but also an impregnable fortress.

In 1966–1968 Ethiopian and French archaeologists under the direction of F. Anfray discovered still another Axumite palace complex—the so-called Dongur, which dates to the VII century A.D.

The ensemble occupies an area of nearly three thousand square meters. It has the form of an irregular square. In the center rises the main building with monumental staircases and luxurious chambers. A closed ring of large and small structures surrounds it. A considerable number of these structures are grouped into four basic blocks where there are forty chambers, four interior courtyards, and four more courtyards between the main building and the structures which surround it. According to F. Anfray, this was both a castle and a villa.[93]

On the territory of the historic city of Axum a multitude of hillocks are visible which indicate still unexcavated ruins of such villas.[94]

In Adulis and Matara, other urban villas of the Axumite period (particularly of the VI–VIII centuries A.D.) have been investigated primarily via F. Anfray's excavations.

In the southwestern part of Adulis as early as 1868 the English cleared off several ancient ruins. In 1906 Sundström discovered a monumental rectangular building of basilica plan with dimensions of 38 × 22.5 m. in the northern part of the city. He thought that this was the "palace of the Adulis ruler." In that same year R. Paribeni discovered to the east and west of this building several more structures. One of these proved to be very similar to Sundström's "palace." As in Axum and Matara, the main building in each case was surrounded by other less luxurious structures forming a complex together with the main building. Paribeni made excavations also in the southwestern part of the city where the English had previously dug. In 1961–1962 the Franco-Ethiopian Archaeological Expedition worked and uncovered still another ensemble which was reminiscent of the one that had been excavated earlier.[95]

In Matara four villas, three churches, and the quarters of the ordinary citizens (where up to thirty families lived) were discovered. Each of the four villas has at least one main building and a series of secondary structures. Of them, villa "B" very much resembles the classical Axumite complexes of the same type. There are also compounds and buildings of a type intermediate between the villa and the common man's urban home.[96]

Buildings, burial vaults, and reservoirs were equipped with stone staircases of at least three types. Besides surface structures there were underground ones. The buildings were illuminated via doorways, window openings, and light shafts (square and rectangular openings left in the middle of the flat roofs). The doorways were equipped with wooden doors with metal fastenings and handles. Window openings were equipped with wooden grilles. The inside and sometimes the outside walls and also the roofs of homes and temples were decorated with carved wooden friezes, with appliqués of ivory, metals, and colored stone. The floors (in Axum and Coloe [Matara]) were inlaid with polished stone slabs or bricks. The "parquet," in Ta'akha Mariam, of alternating white and green marble slabs produced a powerful impression. All the remains of the palace complex were destroyed by the Italians in 1938.

The Axumites, in contrast to the Ethiopians of the Preaxumite period, practiced mixed construction. That is, they combined wooden beams, framings, and supports with monolithic stone panels, columns, slabs, and large-scale and medium-sized polished blocks. They laid undressed stone with an earthen grout, whereas the Preaxumites used dressed stones and no grout. The mixed construction was less stable than purely stone masonry but very sophisticated and relatively cheap. However, despite the use of a cementing solution, Axumite buildings were relatively unstable. The Axumites did not know the arch. They made ceilings of stone panels or wooden frames.

III

The Socio-Economic System

System continuity over time

The view of the Axumite Kingdom as a feudal one is rather firmly held (some authors invest this word with an exclusively political content[1]). Only Loundine calls the "Axumite Kingdom" a slave-holding one, but he refrains from developing arguments in support of his position.[2]

The specific nature of the sources and their scantiness does not permit one to proceed to a systematic description of purely economic relationships such as societal division and cooperation of labor (including exploitation and distribution). These latter processes express the economic relationships of property. More approximately, property is expressed through forms of social structure. These include those social relationships (juridical relationships of property, of law, of obligation, privileges, familial and marital relationships, the belonging to a class, the belonging to a caste, etc.) which express in a concealed, complicated and indirect form the actual accumulated or disappearing relationships of exploitation (or mutual aid) and inequality (or equality).

I shall try, even though in a fragmented way and in the most general outlines, to reconstruct the picture of social and economic relationships which prevailed in the Axumite Kingdom.[3] In some cases the problem remains forever insoluble, whereas in others its solution must be postponed.

Over the expanse of the II–VIII centuries A.D. the productive basis of Ethiopia underwent many changes. They can be successfully traced only in a few cases because of the uncoordinated and fragmentary nature of the information which has come down to us. However, we can maintain that an overall continuity in social structure from Early to Late Axum clearly prevailed over minor system transformations. To a significant degree this is also true of the following period. The persistence of the social structure of the Axumite Kingdom into the Medieval period is undoubted.

The family

Very little information has been preserved about the family and about marriage among the ancient Axumites. In one of the Sabaean inscriptions of the III century A.D. "wives and children" are mentioned of South

Arabian Abyssinians.[4] In Ezana II's inscriptions a "family" (**ሐ⌒ደ·**)[5] is mentioned.

Nothing is known about marriage regulations among the pagan Axumites. It is also unknown to what extent Christian marriage regulations were observed after the adoption of Christianity. In the XIV–XV centuries A.D. we find polygamy among the Ethiopian Christians (especially among the kings and nobility). In addition, we find different forms of "civil marriage," traces of lineage exogamy, and other violations of Christian norms. But it is not known whether such practices remained from the Axumite period or were introduced from Central Ethiopia, which was settled by the Amhara and Kushites and Christianized later.

In the Axumite period the closest relatives of a criminal bore the responsibility for his crime. Ezana II's inscription speaks of this: "... If anyone overturns it [the victory inscription] or moves it, then let this person, his land, and his family be overturned, moved, and driven out of the country."[6] Similar formulae are found in recently discovered inscriptions of Kaleb (Ella Asbeha) and his son Wazeb.[7] Although only the confiscation of the land of the criminal is mentioned, the driving of the family out of the country means also confiscation of land of the whole family. This attests to the existence of familial (lineage?) land possession. In modern-day Tigre, the more distant relatives of a peasant retain a certain right of possession to such a farm. One cannot doubt that similar norms existed also in antiquity, and indeed could have been more strongly manifested than now.

It is not known what kind of position women occupied in the Axumite family. One of the Sabaean inscriptions speaks about the fact that women accompanied the Ethiopian troops on campaigns;[8] this custom was preserved up to the beginning of this century. It is possible that they, just as in the XIV–XIX centuries A.D., took part in military operations.

Tribalism

Up to the present the Tigre population has been divided into territorial (tribal) communities. Now only vestiges of the tribal structure are preserved, but 500 years ago it unquestionably had great significance. The population of the Axumite Kingdom (at least the nuclear area) was divided into tribal groups (*'angād, 'aḥzāb*). In the Axumite inscriptions the names of the tribes or tribal alliances which settled the Northern Ethiopian plateau are preserved. One such tribal group was the Axumites proper.

The word *'aḥzāb* or *'ěḥzab* in classical Ge'ez (singular *ḥezb*) signified in the Ge'ez language ethnic, political, and social communities of the most diverse nature. It should be translated by the word "peoples" (lineages?).

The Ge'ez, Walkait, Gabaza, Metine, Axumites, and other tribes were divided into such *'aḥzāb*. SWSWT, the king of the Ge'ez, appeared to Ezana II "with his peoples," [9] but his successor King Abba Alke'o came to Ezana II "with his people";[10] the king of the Gabaza named SBL came to Ezana II "with his peoples"; King WYLQ (Walkait?) says to Ezana II: "Our peoples came . . .";[11] in the inscription about the campaign into Nubia[12] and in the inscriptions on coins[13] "peoples" of Axum proper are spoken of. At the same time, concerning the meeting of Ezana I with the Metine, it is said: *baṣha 'angāda meṭin kwellu* ("all the peoples of the Metine came"), where the word *angād* (peoples) is used evidently with the same meaning as that of the word *'aḥzāb*. The same expressions are encountered in inscriptions of Kaleb (Ella Asbeha) and Wazeb. In the Axumite inscription, Kaleb says that he has divided his peoples (having in view the militias or "armies") and sent them on raids.[14] In the Marib inscription, he says that he entered battle "with his peoples" and twice mentions that he sent one half of his peoples to one place and the other half of his peoples to another place. He evidently means the landings in South Arabia and subsequent battles and raids. Here also is mentioned the fact that the Axumites also pursued the hostile "peoples."[15] In Wazeb's inscription the term *'aḥzāb* is used four times: three times in the meaning of "militias"—"and my peoples were victorious," "with his peoples"; and as written in the psalm, "all peoples," "god preserved me and my peoples. . . ."[16] In the inscriptions of Hadani Dan'el, where they tell about the "subjugation of 30 peoples"[17] and about the inroads on "the tribes of the Walkait," the word *'angād* clearly has that same meaning.

It is possible to conclude that in the Axumite period the terms *'aḥzāb* and *'angād* were of the same meaning and were used for designating different tribal or lineage communities. When the Axumite king spoke about his subjects, then he called them *'aḥzābya* ("my peoples"). This word usage is characteristic for Ezana II's inscriptions,[18] for the Ethiopian inscription from Marib, and for mottoes on coins of the Axumite kings.[19] It corresponds to the Himyaritic where the word *'ś'b* ("peoples") designated primarily tribal or lineage communities, probably of different degrees.[20] An analysis of the names of the "armies" of Ezana II shows that the communities were called by family (lineage?) names. It is significant that in the Axumite inscriptions the word "people" figures only in the plural. The fact that the Axumite inscriptions constantly mention communities, and that the word "peoples" itself was applied first of all to communities, speaks about their role in the social life. In this respect the "demagogic slogans" on Axumite coins are especially indicative.[21]

The Axumite kings clearly courted the tribal communities, trying to obtain their favor. The very title of the monarch, "King of the Axumites," i.e., of the people and not the territory, is a remnant of the tribal relationships.

Privileged communities

Powerful vestiges of the primitive system led to the fact that the privileges acquired by the feudal nobility were extended (to one or another degree) to its kinsmen. Evidently the most privileged group of Axum was the royal family. Next came the king's more distant relatives, the royal lineage. There is virtually no information about Axum's royal lineage and its privileges.

All of Axum, evidently, constituted a privileged community similar to the Athenians in the Athenian alliance, or to Rome in the Roman state. Adulis, which under Ze Haqile (210–220 A.D.) was already an "officially established market," was another privileged community. Here trade privileges were present. Evidently military colonies which were set up by Axumites beyond the boundaries of their own community (in Africa and Arabia) were privileged communities.

The first mention of them dates to the second half of the II century A.D. when "Abyssinians" of South Arabia headed up the tribes of Tihama. Ethiopian military settlements appeared here again at the beginning of the VI century (in 517 A.D. and 525 A.D.) and existed until the end of that century. Authority over the colonists was vested in the sovereigns of South Arabian indigenous tribal communities. The Marib inscription of Abreha[22] mentions the Ethiopian names Garah, Waṭṭah, and 'Awdah. The latter two are called "sovereigns of Gadan," a well-known Himyarite tribal community. The majority of the colonists were occupied in productive work. No wonder Procopius emphasized that Ethiopian armies remained in South Arabia because of the fertility of the lands of that place.[23] Just as were the local community members, they were enlisted into labor conscription. Loundine speaks of the fact that the Ethiopian colonists in Arabia constituted a stratum of minor nobility.[24] However, there are more grounds to consider their settlements as privileged communities. In comparison with the local population, the military colonists were able to enjoy a series of advantages but were obligated to military service.

It is possible to assume that the resettlement of colonists into Arabia had precedents on the territory of Ethiopia itself. Perhaps here the setting up of colonies was organized almost analogously to the resettlement of the six Beja tribes under Ezana I. *Kebra Nagast* describes the setting up of colonies headed by the legendary Ethiopian king—the founder of the Axumite Kingdom—David, the son of Solomon.[25] At the time of the writing of *Kebra Nagast* (XIV century A.D.) and later, the Ethiopian kings practiced widely the settlement of military colonists on the boundaries of the kingdom or in rebellious districts.

Deserters and exiles

The tribal bonds among Axumites were not indissolubly firm in the second half of the II century A.D. and even less so in the VI century A.D. Information about Ethiopian deserters in South Arabia dates to this time. One of the inscriptions of the Sabaean king Ilsharah Yahdib mentions "some of the Abyssinians," who had evidently come over to the side of the Sabaeans in the period of the war with the Ethiopians.[26] Procopius mentions that Abreha, about 535 A.D., enlarged his army because of the Axumite deserters; the switchover was massive.

The common law of Axum stipulated as a punitive measure the exile of citizens with their entire family and confiscation of their property. It is not necessary to think that the banished exiles were obliged to leave the boundaries of the Axumite Empire, including the vassal kingdoms. Probably they were exiled only from the capital and from the region of Axum. Exile could have been an especially effective measure of punishment if neighboring communities did not permit the exiled person to occupy the same property and legal position which he had enjoyed in his native land.

Organization of communal labor

Construction and irrigation operations were never carried out in Ethiopia on a scale comparable to that of such neighboring countries as South Arabia, Nubia, and Egypt. However, the Axumite stelae and the monolithic [rock-hewn] churches of Lalibela belong in the company of the greatest of similar structures in the entire world. Although the latter were not created in the Axumite period, they came from an epoch close to it and in the same tradition.

During the course of the entire Axumite period, palaces, temples, and churches were built, stone thrones and stelae were raised, and irrigation canals were constructed. Building and artifact stone was obtained from long distances. Stone quarries of granite and basalt were discovered by Bent 6 km. northwest of Axum.[27] From these quarries, multi-ton stone blocks (monumental, monolithic stelae up to a height of 34 m.), a gigantic stone slab (with dimensions of 17.3 × 6.7 m.), and miscellaneous stone construction parts were brought into Axum. Cosmas Indicopleustes related that Ella Asbeha demanded of the Adulis ruler the relocation to Axum of the famed Adulis monument.[28] The stele, which depicts Horus with crocodiles, was transferred to Axum from Adulis. All of these operations, as well as the construction of the palace complex of Ta'akha Mariam and the terraces of Beta Giorgis, required large work gangs. Judging by the nature of the construction operations and by the technique of construction, unskilled peasant laborers could have performed the work. However, some operations would have required craft specialists.

OBERER QUERSCHNITT

0,20

0,62

5,68.M.

0,32

0.93

UNTERER QUERSCHNITT.

The stele of Matara.

The form of organization of labor could only have been simple co-operation. It is important to resolve the question of what the relationship of the worker-builders was to the institutions benefiting from their construction efforts. What was their place in Axum's social structure?

In this respect two inscriptions are extremely interesting; from Matara and Anza—one dated to the beginning, the other to the first half of the IV century A.D. The inscription from Matara is carved on a granite stele. The Ge'ez ('gz) composed it "for the sake of their fathers" (l'bwh). The community transferred the granite stele with the help of the neighboring communities of Subli and Aw'a Ilfi.[29] The inscription from Anza was also carved on a stele and composed in the name of Bazat, the king of the Angabo. Tribal members (Angabo) labored 15 days to transport the stele. Upon the completion of the work a holiday was arranged. The workers received bread and beer.[30] In both cases, the operations were carried out by the community members. In the second case, the tribal king (negus) supervised them directly. Construction operations were the affair of the whole tribe and participation in them was a sacred obligation of tribal members before their ancestors. Upon completion of operations the dedication of the object to a god in the presence of the whole army followed.

The king who left the inscription on the Adulis monument says: "Having summoned and having gathered my armies I have raised this throne (to the god Mahrem-Ares)."[31] Perhaps the army took part in operations connected with the building of the victory throne? At least in Yemen, the Axumites acted thus. The South Arabian inscription from Marib, dated 657–658 of the Himyarite era (542–543 A.D.), speaks of the restoration of the Marib dam. The operations were carried out at the order of King Abreha and under his supervision. Local community members and the royal troops—not only Himyarite but also Ethiopian—carried them out.[32] If other customs had existed in Ethiopia, the Axumite armies would not have begun to carry out construction operations in a country conquered by them. Abreha strove in every way possible to gain the favor of his Ethiopian army but still did not free it from labor conscription. Consequently, even at home in their native land, in Axum, the Ethiopian armies must also have taken part in construction. Another description of construction operations carried out by Axumites in Yemen is contained in *The Life of St. Grigentius*. The Axumite king Ellesboam (Ella Asbeha) restored and built anew in Yemen a multitude of churches, after having destroyed a large number of pagan temples [and synagogues]. Construction operations were organized in the following manner: "Having placed the troops in the city of Atarfa [Zafar] and in the closest cities and having forced the local populace to work, he [the king] everywhere restored churches, having set up his nobles as the supervisors of the operations."[33] It may be assumed that not only the local inhabitants but also the Axumites themselves took part in the operations. Another detail is also interesting: the Axumite "nobles," who were simultaneously the leaders of the military detachements quartered in corresponding towns, directed the operations. In Medieval and more recent periods, Ethiopian kings directly led the construction operations. During the clearing of a road or building of a temple the king laid the first stone. After him, according to seniority, all the nobles, the military leaders, the retinue, and the soldiers did the same thing. Neither lay nor clerical persons were exempt from construction operations if the king participated in them. This undoubtedly was a very ancient custom. It is possible that it existed also in the Axumite Kingdom.

Thus the data preserved permit one to think that construction operations in Axum were carried out on the order of a collective labor conscription. Probably the king himself, tribal leaders, and lineage heads directed the operations and took a symbolic part in them. Nothing is known about the use of slave labor in construction.

Undoubtedly only experienced tradesmen-builders could carry out certain of the operations. The stonemasons from Axum who left the inscription "That which they did is pleasing to the stonemasons (lwqrt)" probably were among such specialists.[34] How their labor was recompensed is not known. Perhaps it was not generally rewarded and the stone masons were obliged to work gratis in the capacity of labor conscription or corvée.

In summary, we see that the organization of construction operations in the Axumite Kingdom attests to the preserved remnants of a primitive egalitarian system. At the same time it reveals typically feudal traits: operations were begun at the order of the monarch or his deputy, and were carried out under supervision and under the leadership of representatives of the king, even if such persons were not members of the laboring tribe.

Personal dependency and slavery

In the inscriptions of the Axumite kings, in Greek sources contemporary to them, and in later Arabic and Ethiopian sources there are indications of the fact that slavery existed in ancient Axum. Slave holding, exploitation of slave labor, and slave trading must necessarily have played an important role in the stratification of Ethiopian society and in the emergence of the first political states on the Ethiopian plateau. Slavery formed a necessary part of the economic base of Axum and continued to exist in Ethiopia for more than a thousand years right up to the recent abolition of slavery. However, one must not exaggerate either the degree of development of slavery or its significance in Axumite life.

There are comparatively numerous communications about the capture of slaves. The Axumite king, the hero of the Adulis inscription, tells about the seizing of spoils: "I did battle with the Ge'ez people, then with the Agame and the Sigyn, and when I was victorious over them I took away from them their property and of their people I took half, as my share . . . I did battle with the Sesea people who went off to a very high and inaccessible mountain. I surrounded them and forced them to come down and I took for myself as many as I wanted of young men and young women, youths [teenagers] and young [teenaged] girls and all of their property"[35] ("half" can mean any significant part). The royal share of the spoils cannot be considered as "a tax in slaves"; this was indeed the lion's share, "half" of the captured spoils. Consequently not all of the property and not all of the people of Sesea are being spoken of but only that part which one way or another fell into the hands of the Axumites.

The Axumite king who left the Greek inscription at Meroe mentions children ($\tau\acute{\epsilon}\chi\nu\alpha$)[36] in the make-up of the spoils. Three of the four inscriptions of the Axumite king Ezana II mention the capture of slaves. In the inscription about the punitive expedition against the country of Aguezat, Ezana tells how the Axumites "robbed" [the people] of Aguezat who arrived with Abba Alke'o, king of the Aguezat: "And all whom we robbed we took [into captivity] and put into chains. And we also kept naked Abba Alke'o, king of the Aguezat, and chained him together with his throne bearer." Then the warriors of Ezana "crossed the Nada River and killed whomever they found. From here they went into the country of Agada, killing and taking into captivity people and animals."[37]

In another inscription a campaign on Afan, whose inhabitants had attacked an Axumite trade caravan, is spoken of. "We sent our warriors [says Ezana] and they killed and took slaves and spoils from them (i.e., from the Afan tribes). We eliminated . . . four tribes and took the *alite* (king) with his two children into captivity. And 503 Afan men and 202 women, a total of 705 were killed. Taken captive were: 40 men, 165 women and children, a total of 205."[38] "And after we arrived in Alaya, a settlement in the country of Atagau, we obtained camels and pack animals (asses or mules) and men and women and provisions for 20 days."[39] These men and women of Alaya were temporarily mobilized just as were their pack animals. The inscriptions speak about the pillaging of the country, the driving away of cattle, and the capture of slaves in other expressions.

The campaign into Nubia is spoken of in the third inscription. This was a punitive expedition against the Nubians, who had attacked the allies of Axum and who had insulted the Axumite ambassadors. King Ezana II "followed the fleeing [foes] for 23 days, killing [some], taking [others] into captivity, and seizing spoils. . . . And there were many drowned [Nubians in the Nile]. . . . [The warriors of the king] sank their boats, which were overfilled with people—men and women—in the river." "And I [Ezana II continues] took into captivity two leaders who had come as spies. . . . And in Angabe I seized Nawi, a noble person. . . . There were five leaders who were killed and one priest. And I arrived in Kasu and killed in battle and took into captivity the people [of Kasu] at the point of confluence of the rivers Sida [Nile] and Tekezze Atbara. . . . And they [the Axumites] killed and took captives and threw people into the water [of the Nile]. . . . And they returned whole and unharmed, having taken captives and having killed the Noba [Nubians] and having taken spoils from them. . . . [There were taken] captive: 214 men, 415 women, a total of 629 captives. Killed: 602 men, 156 women and children, a total of 758 killed. The killed and captured totaled 1387." [40]

In his Axum inscription Kaleb (Ella Asbeha) says: "And we took captive . . . / more than ten / s of hundreds / and the number / of Aguezat and Ḥasat killed / was: / about 400 men, hundreds of women and children; / a total / of hundreds captured . . . ; killed and captured / a total / of hundreds / " (the figures are damaged). [41] In Wazeb's inscription there is a similar passage: "The armies which I sent pillaged and killed and seized captives and spoils . . . Captured: men . . . , women and children . . . , a total of . . . , was captured; Killed: men . . . , women and children . . . ; a total of . . . was killed; a total of . . . , captured and killed" (the figures are damaged). [42]

In a communication of At Tabari, the capture of Himyarites by the Ethiopians is spoken of. The nagashi (Ella Asbeha) ordered his military leader Ariat to "kill one-third of their men, destroy one-third of their country, and take into captivity one-third of their women and children." And Ariat, following the order of the negus, "killed one-third of the men of his [Yemen], destroyed one-third of their country, and sent to the nagashi [that] third which he had taken captive." [43] The veracity of these communications is confirmed by the story of Procopius Caesarensis and the Syrian *Book of the Himyarites*. The *Book* mentions that the Ethiopians seized many captives in Himyar, including 50 persons "of the royal family" (i.e., representatives of the royal tribe). All of them were driven into Ethiopia. [44] The Ethiopian inscription from Marib, devoted probably to those same events, also mentions taking into captivity [45] (capture of the Himyarites by the Ethiopians is implied).

In the royal inscription of Sumafa Ashwa it is said of the Himyarites: "And they were reduced to slavery for the king of Axum." [46]

Late Axumite sources give evidence about the taking of captives. In one of Hadani Dan'el's inscriptions the "capture of thirty tribes" [47] is spoken of. Most likely these tribes were assessed tribute. In another inscription about the war with the Walkait it was communicated that the warriors of the Hadani "attacked and took captives." [48] In the third inscription the capture of the Axumite king himself and his subsequent freeing [49] is spoken of; but these are troubles of civil war which had flared up between the king and the Hadani and cannot be considered as the driving of the captured into slavery. It is necessary to note that while the number of captured horses, bulls, and sheep is always indicated, the number of people taken into captivity is not spoken of. Evidently they represented a qualitatively insignificant and not very valuable spoil which can be explained by the decline of slave trading by the time of the Hadani Dan'el.

The fact that the capture of slaves was by no means the main purpose of Axum's military expeditions attracts attention. In the period of the Axumite Kingdom the subjugation (and the obligation to tribute) of neighboring countries was becoming the purpose of the campaigns. The taking [of people] into captivity occupies an incomparably less important place. The cattle driven off from the foes represented a more valuable part of the spoils than the captives. In those inscriptions that talk about the capture of slaves and the taking of tribute, the communication concerning tribute occupies a more important place. As a rule, the assessment or payment of tribute is spoken of in the concluding part of the inscriptions irrespective of whether or not it was mentioned earlier. Only in two of Ezana II's inscriptions (in the inscription about the raid on Kasu and in the inscription about the punitive expedition against Afan) is the seizure of captives mentioned while the levying or payment of tribute is not mentioned. We may therefore speculate that the campaigns against Himyar, Kasu, and Afan were first of all dictated by a propensity to levy tribute on them and were only to an insignificant degree a "slave hunt."

It is sufficient to compare these campaigns with the raids by African slave traders of recent times, whose main purpose was to capture the largest possible number of slaves. The Axumite troops acted differently. They first of all killed and only lastly took captives. The number of killed exceeds by far the number of the captured. Moreover, a significant part of those killed was made up of women and children. During the campaign into Afan, 503 men (evidently including juveniles) and 202 women were killed; 165 women and children were taken captive and only 40 men, and then [only] from the Ge'ez (?).[50] During the campaign on Kasu 602 men and 156 women and children—a total of 758 persons—were killed, not counting the multitude of those who drowned in the Nile or burned up in their homes.[51] A total of 629 persons were captured—415 women and 214 men (including juveniles and children of the male sex?). Here also the number of those killed exceeds the number captured.

That the total number of the killed and captured is given is very significant. This is the same as in modern war communiqués, where the "total enemy losses in human strength" figure. The result of the campaign for the author of the inscription was not primarily an enumeration of the spoils but a summary communiqué of the losses inflicted on the foe. The Axumites strove not so much to capture foes as to ravage, to destroy, and to frighten them. The driving of captives into slavery was subordinate to this purpose and had only secondary economic significance. This attests to the fact that the need for slaves was extremely limited among the Axumites. The custom of mass human sacrifices also indicates this. Dozens, even hundreds of captives were sacrificed to the gods instead of being turned into slaves. One of King Ezana II's inscriptions communicates concerning the sacrifice of 100 bulls and 50 captives to Mahrem the god of war.[52]

Little information has come down to us concerning the use of slave labor in ancient Axum. No doubt the king and noble Axumites used slaves as domestic servants and palace retinue.

Rufinus tells about the fate of Aedesius and Frumentius in Axum: "The king designated Aedesius as his wine steward. He [the king] entrusted to Frumentius, whose acuteness of mind and wisdom he immediately valued, his treasury and correspondence." Therefore the young men were greatly esteemed and the king loved them very much. "Dying, the king left his wife and young son as heirs to the throne, to the young men he granted complete freedom."[53] Nikephoros Kallistos expounds upon this episode more verbosely and colorfully.[54] The Ethiopian synaxarion life of Frumentius maintains that the king did not make Aedesius simply a slave but a "supervisor over the servants."[55] This only reflects the concept of the Ethiopians of the late Middle Ages when the life story about the first advancement of the royal slave was composed.

A picture of another slave who was in servitude to the Ethiopian king is painted by At Tabari. Alluding to Hisham ibn Muhammad al Kalbi and Ibn Ishaq, he tells about a slave who belonged to Abreha and had a great influence on him.[56] The medieval Ethiopian legend about the fall of the Axumite Kingdom (a story about one of the "miracles" of Yared, a legendary singer and composer) speaks of the fact that "his slave Merara"[57] became the successor of the last Axumite king. Most likely this Merara, whom historical tradition ascribes to the medieval Zagwe dynasty, was called a slave allegorically. But it is possible that the legend about the "slave" origin of some dynasties which had preserved paganism and had not been completely acclimated to the Christian-Ethiopian culture had a telling influence here. In a very late version of the legend about the founders of the Axumite Kingdom (the so-called *Kebra Nagast* of Lake Zwai) Ebn Hakim, son of Solomon, led into Ethiopia "three black slaves" (ሦስት ባርያት) of the Canaanite tribe. They received fiefs from him and ascended iron thrones while the thrones of the "Israelite" rulers were made of alabaster, gold, and silver.[58] At Tabari's expression in which he "compels" Abreha servilely to call himself and Ariat slaves of the Axumite king should not be taken literally. Abreha writes the nagashi: "Ariat was your slave (عبدك) and I am your slave."[59] Of course, this does not at all prove that the

Ethiopian rulers of Yemen were slaves of the Axumite king and it is even doubtful that Abreha would have referred to himself thus in a letter to the negus. In the Marib inscription he calls himself only '*azlī*—"vice-regent" (or vassal) of the Axumite king.[60] Possibly "the throne bearer" of the king of the Ge'ez, Abba Alke'o, mentioned in one of Ezana II's inscriptions, was a slave.[61] But also he could have been free.[62]

One source attests to the fact that the Ethiopians who settled in South Arabia had slaves. The inscription of the Sabaean kings Ilsharah Yahdib and Ya'zil Bayin mentions Habasha (Abyssinians) who turned up "far from their children and their slaves (*qnyhmw*)."[63] Evidently many Ethiopians in Arabia had slaves (or voluntary freedmen?).[64] However, it remains unknown whether these *qny* were slaves in the economic sense or only in the legal sense. In any event it is necessary to strictly distinguish legal "slavery" (i.e., personal dependence) from economic slavery.

The information preserved permits one to speak only about specifically domestic slavery in Axum. Nothing is known about other forms of slavery. Plantation slavery could not have been known to the Axumites; social and especially market relationships were not sufficiently developed in Axum. It is also impossible to speak of the use of slaves in mines or as oarsmen on galley ships. Also nothing is known about the use of slave labor in construction operations, which were carried out by whole communities, military detachments, or professional stonemasons. One can only assume that domestic slavery was the form of slavery known in ancient Axum.

One cannot doubt that wars were the main source of slavery in Axum. Nothing is known to us about other sources of slavery. In the Middle Ages, in Ethiopia, it was the practice for a creditor to sell into slavery a debtor or members of the debtor's family, likewise for a father to sell his children. It is possible that this custom, which had died out in the late Middle Ages, had appeared in the Axumite period. The turning of children —deserted or orphaned—into slaves was not known in medieval Ethiopia, nor is it probable that it occurred in ancient Axum.

Nothing is known about such a source of slavery as the enslavement of convicted criminals. In the concluding part of the Axumite inscriptions, in which their destroyers are threatened with exile and confiscation (or plundering) of all property, there is no threat of enslavement.[65]

Very little is known about the export of slaves. We know that slaves were sold for export from the Axumite Kingdom (strictly, from Adulis). One can only surmise about the possibility that they were sold in Axum itself. We can judge about the freeing of slaves from Rufinus' communication about Aedesius and Frumentius.

We can only guess at the legal position of slaves. In later periods slaves could occupy an extremely high position in society. In the Axumite period, tribal ties were stronger and royal authority weaker. Privileges of birth meant more and royal favor less. However, the example of Abreha, if he actually was a slave, indicates the possibility for fantastic elevation of a former slave. In Procopius Caesarensis' words, Abreha was the slave of a Byzantine merchant in Adulis.[66] Abreha entered Arabia together with the Ethiopian army, and as a result of a civil war, he became its ruler. He proclaimed himself the king of Himyar although he acknowledged the authority of the Axumite king over him.

The example of Abreha shows that the Axumites did not consider slavery an indelible stigma which forever kept a person devoid of full civil rights. Everything said about Abreha also pertains to Frumentius. It is true, the master of Frumentius was not some sort of foreign merchant but the Axumite king himself, and Frumentius acquired influence while still a slave. However, after he was freed from slavery and subsequently journeyed to Alexandria, Frumentius became the first bishop of Ethiopia. It must be pointed out, however, that in the period of his appointment as bishop Christianity was not yet the state religion of the country and the Axumite bishop (or metropolitan) could not enjoy that influence which he acquired later on. Nonetheless, the elevation of Frumentius is highly indicative of that position in which former slaves were found on the territory of the Axumite Kingdom.

The juxtaposition in the Sabaean inscription of "children and slaves" of the Ethiopians also indicates the benign quality of Axumite slavery. An analysis of the terms which signify slaves in the Ge'ez language leads us to the same conclusion. In Ethiopian inscriptions the word "slave" does not exist. It is met with only in book literature; those forms of it which date to the Axumite period are translations of Christian sacred books into the Ge'ez language. The translators (Axumites and the Graeco-Syrian missionaries who visited in Ethiopia) were obliged to find ancient Ethiopian equivalents of the concept of "slave," usually in the New and Old Testaments. The terms used by them evidently served for the designation of slaves in ancient Ethiopia. These are the following words:

ደቁቅ, *son, little boy*, and *slave* (from the root *dqq, to be minute, small*);
ወላድ, *son, young man*, and *slave* (from the root *wld, to bear, to be born*);
ገብር, *personally dependent, slave* (from the root *gbr, to do something* and *to fulfill an obligation*);
ቀጢን (compare the Arabic قطين , *inhabitants*), *household servants, man-servants, slaves*, and *bondwomen* (from the root *qtn, to be thin, frail*, and *to inhabit*).

To this it is necessary to add the later medieval term ባርያ, *by birth from the Baria people, slave* (it originates from an ethnonym).

These examples indicate that no distinction is made between blood sons, young boys, male youths, household servants, and slaves. Slaves probably were admitted into the Axumite army in a manner similar to later practice. Thus Abreha could have entered the Axumite army. Those interpreters (ተርጓሚት) who turned up in the army of Hadani Dan'el were possibly slaves. They served as intermediaries during the dealings of the Hadani with the inhabitants of one of the districts situated somewhere not far from Kassala, probably the Baria, who are mentioned in that same inscription.[67] At a later time such a practice was well known in Ethiopia. It is interesting to note that the ethnonym "Baria" became in the later Middle Ages one of the terms which signified a slave in general.

With a comparatively undeveloped slave-holding life style, the Axumites did not need a large number of slaves for satisfying their personal needs. Capture of slaves for sale probably had greater value since Axum carried on a significant foreign trade via Adulis. Pliny[68] speaks about the export of slaves from Adulis. "Ethiopian slaves" are authenticated in documents of the late Roman Empire originating from Egypt and other provinces and in Arabic sources of the VIII–X centuries A.D. Some of them could have been sold by Axumites. Even the Axumite kings, themselves, could have engaged in slave trade.

However, the dimensions of Axumite slave trade should not be exaggerated. Pseudo Arrian does not mention it at all, although he speaks in detail about the trading of other goods (via Adulis). He communicates only that from Malao—in addition to exotic goods—slaves were sometimes exported. Even in Egypt, which was traditionally supplied with African slaves, their number was not great during the Axumite period. Westerman counts a total of nine to ten mentions of black-skinned slaves in documents from Roman Egypt.[69] In the IV–VI centuries A.D., the period of the Axumite Kingdom's greatest development, there were somewhat more of them not only in Egypt but also in Constantinople. In connection with the conspiracy of Argyroprates in 563 A.D. with the purpose of killing Justinian, the Byzantine chronicles mention Ethiopian slaves called Hindus—a name usual for Ethiopians during that time in the Byzantine sources. These slaves were obliged to notify the people about the revolution which had taken place, which indicates their function and role in the life of the capital.[70] Early Muslim tradition maintains that the freedman who voluntarily served the prophet, called Salih ibn Adi (otherwise "Shukran," which means "Grateful" and is a typical slave name!), was a native of Abyssinia[71] (i.e., of the Axumite Kingdom). Among the prominent warriors of the young Muslim community were Africans: "Abyssinians"—Wahshi ("Wild"), the first muezzin of Islam, Bilāl, and many others. Among the Prophet's foes also were "Abyssinian" warriors, among whom in the famous battle near Uhud, Su'ab was especially distinguished.

In this period many Arab leaders of Hijaz had detachments of Ethiopian slaves. They were called "Abyssinians," "blacks," and "askari (soldiers)"

(عسكرى ; plural عساكرة) in distinction from indigenous Arab warriors. This word, probably of Ethiopian origin, subsequently entered the languages of many Muslim peoples with the meaning of "soldier." Pre-Islamic poets of Arabia glorified Ethiopian spear-throwers. Labid describes "Abyssinians" standing [and] leaning on their throwing spears and spears with broad blades. Antara called these spear-throwers أغراب العرب (ravens of the Arabs). Muhammad had a bodyguard of black warrior-slaves in Medina. They, by the way, entertained Ayesha, the wife of the Prophet, with their fencing. Conti-Rossini speculates that this was a dance dramatization. In Mecca, Ethiopian warriors constituted a self-governing community which was headed by a special "Lord of the Abyssinians" (سيّد الأحابيش).[72]

In the late period, all trade of the Axumite Kingdom with Egypt and the Mediterranean countries was sharply curtailed. But the border districts of Ethiopia maintained connections with the outside world and, having embraced Islam, continued to maintain and develop overseas trade.

Together with exotic goods, they exported black slaves. The main trading ports in this period were Dahlak, on the island of that same name, and also Zeila in Northern Somalia. A Chinese author of the IX century A.D., Tuan Chen-shi, speaks of the slave trade in this region. He writes that the inhabitants "of the country of Berbera have the custom of selling their own fellow countrymen in other countries, because they make far more on slaves sold in other countries than if they traded in them on the spot."[73] This can be explained not by an abundance of slaves which brought down the price on live goods but only by the insignificant demand for slave labor. Later, in the X–XI centuries A.D., Arab authors described in detail the dangers which awaited merchants at the shores of Berbera. However, the merchants feared being taken captive least of all. The local residents needed slaves for sale but Arab and Persian merchants did not buy fellow Muslims.

In the Axumite period the situation was exactly the same. Meropius and his fellow travelers were killed but not taken captive; only two young boys were spared. They were not sold but given to the king. Usually not slavery but death awaited foreign merchants who were captured by Ethiopian pirates. Diodorus tells of another similar kind of case (about the merchant Yambul and his fellow travelers whom the Ethiopians seized for sacrifice).[74]

All that is known to us about slavery in ancient Axum does not support the contention that the Axumite Kingdom was a slave-holding one. Slavery existed but did not create a predominant means of production. Slave trading, as a part of Axum's foreign trade, had greater significance.

The royal estate

Although all the information on slaves in Axum pertains to domestic slaves who belonged to the king, the sort of productive role they played in the royal establishment is not clear. The king undoubtedly had at his disposal property which would include the royal residence or palace, grain storehouses, and livestock. The herds were increased not only by natural growth but also by military spoils and royal tribute. The Adulis inscription tells how the king took away "property" from conquered tribes.[75] Cattle must have made up a significant part of this personal property. Ezana II's inscription speaks of the driving off of a large quantity of livestock by the king: cows, sheep, camels and "pack animals" (asses or mules?). In Afan, 31,957 cows and 827 "pack animals"[76] were seized. In Nubia the king seized 10,560 cows and 51,050 sheep.[77] In the Adulis inscription the king calls the spoils "his share,"[78] and in Ezana II's inscriptions captured livestock figure as "things which the Lord of the Heavens gave him."[79] It is clear that the lion's share of the spoils became the personal property of the king.

The Axumite king had at his disposal enormous herds. In the inscription concerning the resettlement of the six tribes of the Beja, Ezana I says that he gave their "kings" 25,140 cows. Moreover, he supplied the Beja with food and clothing.[80] Cosmas Indicopleustes tells that the Axumite king "from year to year" sent into the gold-bearing country of Sasu a trade caravan along with which they drove a multitude of bulls.[81] These bulls, evidently, were intended for provisioning of the caravan and were taken out of the royal herds. Along with the treasury, livestock constituted the principal wealth of the royal household. No wonder one of the ancient officials was called "ṣaḥāfē-lahm"—"clerk of cows" or "registrar of livestock." Such a title suggests that strict accounting existed in the royal household. Besides the ṣaḥāfē-lahm (among ancient officials) is mentioned an "accountant" or "observer of accounts."[82] Although original business documents have not been preserved, their traces are easily observed in the inscriptions of Ezana I and II. The following excerpts from three inscriptions undoubtedly retained the style of the household accounting documents:

" . . . And 503 men of Afan and 202 women were killed, a total of 705. Of those who accompanied the army there were taken captive: 40 men and 165 women and children, a total of 205. The spoils in cattle 31,957 and in pack animals 827. . . . "[83]

"Things which the Lord of the Heavens gave me: captives: 214 men, 415 women, a total of 629 captives. Killed: 602 men; killed, 156 women and children: a total of 758 killed. The total of killed and captured 1387. The spoils in cattle 10,560, in sheep 51,050."[84]

"They brought them to us together with their families and also three thousand one hundred and twelve—3112—cows and six thousand two hundred and twenty-four—6224—sheep and pack animals. And there was given to them meat and bread for food and beer and wine and well water for drink—all in a sufficient amount according to their number: (namely) six—6—kings with their people numbering four thousand four hundred—4400. They daily received twenty-two thousand—22,000—wheaten loaves and wine for four—4—months. . . . And we granted to the six—6—kings twenty-five thousand one hundred and forty—25,140—cows. . . . "[85]

The numerical strength of the six Beja tribes is given approximately, since to count them probably was considered impossible. But all the remaining numbers are startling in their scrupulousness. That each number was written in two ways—first in writing and then in figures—exactly as in monetary documents of the present time (in medieval Ethiopia they never wrote in that way) attracts attention. Only professional "business executives" and "accountants" could have introduced such a notation. The numbers are everywhere added correctly, summed up several times. All this can be explained only by strict calculation and constant accounting practiced in the royal household of Axum.

Evidently representatives of the Axumite nobility had their own large-scale households similar to the royal one, with large herds and stores of grains. To them belonged "villas" situated in Axum, Adulis, Matara, and other towns of the Axumite Kingdom.

The sole information about temple land holdings is contained in Ezana I's bilingual inscription, but only in the more complete Ethiopian texts. Here the transmitting of a land parcel[86] to Mahrem, the god-king of the Axumites, is spoken of. In the Ge'ez language the land parcel is designated by the terms ṣwn and bdḥ. In the Middle Ages these words did not signify any special categories of land. There is a communication about the fact that the Axumite kings, Asbeha and Gebre Meskal, gave land to the monasteries. Even their land deeds are cited, but all of them are spurious.[87] However, it is possible that there is a grain of truth in the tradition which ascribes to these kings the giving of land to the Christian churches.

Evidently the Axumite king was considered the supreme owner of all lands but it is not known to what extent he exercised this right. It is known that Ezana II gave a strip of land to the sanctuary of Mahrem. It is possible that this was a parcel from his own domain but it is also possible this land was taken from or bought from his subjects. In the concluding lines of Ezana II's inscriptions is contained the threat of land confiscation. Evidently, "the land of the Matlia" or "land of the BYRN" (or only part of it?) where Ezana I resettled the six Beja tribes actually was confiscated from some tribe or group of tribes.

It is not known if the king had a special land reserve at his disposal designated for his maintenance. Such a reserve actually existed in the Middle Ages, but it is not authenticated anywhere in the Axumite period. In my opinion it is highly probable that there were allotments of "royal land," which the Axumite peasants tilled and whose harvest went into the royal granaries. Boundary marker stones with inscriptions in the Ge'ez language, found in Axum and Matara, attest to the development of property rights.[88]

Tribute

The question of the methods of appropriation of surplus labor has paramount significance in determining the nature of economic relationships. In the Axumite Kingdom, surplus goods produced by conquered countries were appropriated by the kings in the form of tribute or of a primitive tax. Many sources attest to this. The Adulis inscription says that the conquered peoples were quickly assessed tribute. "Having been victorious in battles in which I personally participated and having subjugated all these peoples, . . . I granted to them their lands for a tax. But the majority of peoples submitted to me voluntarily and brought tribute. Having sent a war fleet, I conquered the kings of the Arrabites and Kinaidocolpitae who lived on the other shore of the [Red] Sea and commanded them to pay tribute for their land. . . . "[89] From the inscription it follows that the payment of tribute was a basic condition of land tenure among conquered populations. Evidently, any resistance to the payment of tribute resulted in their settlements being destroyed, their people driven into captivity, and their lands taken away for redistribution to Axumite colonists or their allies.

Procopius communicates that Ella Asbeha, "having gained a victory, killed many Omerites [Himyarites] and their king and placed over this people another king, an Omerite by birth named Esimitheus (Sumafa Ashwa), with the condition that he pay a yearly tax."[90] *The Martyrdom of Arethius* calls the Himyarites "payers of tribute to Ethiopia."[91] *The Book of the Himyarites* also communicates that Kaleb (Ella Asbeha) "assessed this country [Himyar] tax."[92] The inscriptions of Ezana II tell about the collection of tribute from subject peoples.[93] At the end of the Axumite period (middle of the IX century A.D.), Al Ya'kubi comments about taxes in the Axumite Kingdom: "The kings of the countries of Al Habasha (Abyssinia) are located under the authority of a great king, obligated to him and paying *haraj* (tax)."[94]

Of course the quantity of tribute varied greatly depending upon many conditions which are now impossible to establish. However, in all cases the tribute payment had certain common features: in principle, tribute was collected yearly; entire countries and districts were assessed tribute;

the payment of tribute by conquered peoples was a condition of their possession of their lands; the tribute was paid via the medium of local monarchs—kinglets. The princes of the Arabian possessions paid tribute through an intermediary—their closest sovereign, the Himyar king. In the period of Ethiopian dominion this was Sumafa Ashwa (Esimitheus), and later the Ethiopian usurpers. Probably the same thing happened with regard to coastal Ethiopian kinglets who were subject to the Adulis king, and with the kinglets of the separate tribes of the Beja. The Axumite king collected tribute from the kings of Adulis (Gabaza), Angabo, Aguezat, Walkait, Semen, and several others. And they, in turn, collected it from rulers of lesser rank and smaller districts. Thus a hierarchical system of tribute payment existed, which led to the enrichment of Axum at the expense of subject peoples. It also led to the consolidation of the authority of the more powerful kinglets over less powerful rulers, irrespective of whether they were formerly dependent or not. Thus tribute payment led to a strengthening of feudal relationships in Ethiopia.

In order to determine the role of tribute payment in the economic structure of Axum it is necessary to identify the basic economic goals pursued by the Axumite kings in connection with their subjugation of neighboring lands. We can exclude from among the economic goals "slave hunting," which could have prompted individual raids but not conquests for stable subjugation. I propose that it is possible to name three economic objectives that motivated the conquests: the guarantee of safety of trade routes, seizing of new lands for resettling surplus Axumite population, and assessment of tribute.

The first two goals were not fundamental during the period of the rise of the Axumite Kingdom. Tribute payment, therefore, was the main economic link which connected the peoples and the countries subject to Axum. It was the main economic incentive of the Axumite Kingdom. Yet the method of obtaining tribute was extremely primitive, being an expression of the simplicity and instability of the economic ties of Axum with the districts subject to it.

Historically the earliest method of collecting tribute was by means of personal visits by the king to the princes of subjugated lands. In Kievan Rus (the early Russian state) the yearly circuits of subject principalities and tribes, carried out by the supreme prince or his confidential agents (in the company of a military detachment) were of this kind. The subject communities were not obliged to deliver tribute to the residence of the prince but he himself, with a sufficiently strong force, appeared for the collection of tribute. By this method the prince achieved three goals at one time: he reminded the tribute payers of his might, fed (on the way) his bodyguard, and received valuable goods as tribute. In the event that the prince or his representatives were not able to appear for the collection of tribute, its receipt ceased and the dependence of the tribute payers on the suzerain lost its economic content. Thus personal collection of tribute by the king still very much resembled a military raid and not infrequently was accompanied by military operations, turning into a punitive expedition.

In the early Middle Ages, personal collection of tribute by the king existed in the peripheral countries of Europe (in Kievan Rus, Norway, Ireland, in the Holy Roman Empire of the time of Conrad II) and also in Oceania (on the islands of Yap, the Marshalls, Hawaii, Tahiti, etc.). Ethnographic literature on Africa reports it in no fewer than thirty countries, ranging historically from the Nubian pharaohs to Monomotapa (Empire of Zimbabwe) and geographically from the Indian Ocean shores (where the peripheral possessions of the state of Shambal were located) to Loango and Congo. It is also found in the peripheral possessions of the Oyo empire on the shores of the Atlantic.[95] In Northeastern Africa the practice of personal collection of tribute by the king was continued up to the XVI–XVII centuries A.D. Omar Dunka, the first Sennar sultan (1504–1533 A.D.), personally collected tribute. The Ethiopian neguses who were contemporaries of Omar collected tribute in exactly the same way. Usually vassal princes and vice-regents delivered the tribute to specified points through which the negus would pass, traveling over his possessions. Only the Emperor Galaudeuos (Claudius, 1508–1540 A.D.) "stopped the custom of his fathers to pass from place to place during his whole life up to the hour of non-transient calm and eternal assumption [i.e., his death]."[96]

When did this custom appear in Ethiopia? Did it already exist in the Axumite period? The Ethiopian legends which tell about the decline of the Axumite Kingdom give evidence about this: "In B'ela Nagashtat (The Wealth of Kings), ten generations of Axumite kings are spoken of who after the fall of the Axumite Kingdom, wandered from district to district, hiding in caves and clefts of the rocks."[97] If the image of the king who hid in the wilderness is connected with the ritual of his election to the throne[98] and with legendary tales, then the notion about the constantly wandering king possibly is connected with the custom of the personal collection of tribute by the king. Finally, the legend about one of the "miracles" of Yared says directly that the kings of late Axum traveled for the purpose of personal collection of tribute. The king Degnaizan (Degna Zhan in the text of the "List of Kings") "ruled Ethiopia by divine force and made the rounds of it from end to end."[99]

In just such expressions and in such a connection the Ethiopian sources of the late Middle Ages speak of the king's personal collection of tribute. It is possible to think that this is nothing more than an anachronism; that the author of the "miracles" of Yared projected an occurrence contemporary to him (the end of the XIV–XV centuries A.D.) into the Axumite period. However, one of the inscriptions of King Ezana II[100] evidently describes the personal collection of tribute by this king.

The Axumite king, in the company of an armed detachment, went about the country collecting gifts or tribute, renewing his authority over the tribes ("and he went out on a campaign in order to renew his kingdom"), and on the way feeding his bodyguard ("at each stop where he arrived he took provisions from the enemy of his country"). In another inscription, Ezana II says that in the country of the Angabo, the king of the Aguezat people who "brought gifts"[101] came to meet him.

Kaleb (Ella Asbeha) also says in his inscription that when he was in a certain district (the name of which is obliterated) the king and the "Aguezat peoples" appeared there "with their gifts," which consisted of many hundreds of head of livestock.[102]

It is significant that many tribes brought tribute not on their own territory but on a neighboring one. A similar practice existed also in the Middle Ages; medieval kings made the rounds of their possessions and the rulers subordinate to them came out to meet them at specified points lying on the path of the king's itinerary.

As the cited inscription states, the majority of the tribes was subjugated without armed resistance. Only the MTT [Matata] tribe paid tribute after a battle with the Axumites. Even tribes of remote Semen and Walkait brought tribute without battle. This would have been completely improbable if Ezana II had been for them a simple conqueror. Evidently all of these tribes, except the MTT [Matata], recognized his right to receive tribute. A stereotyped expression "he gave them laws, and they submitted" does not mean that they accepted these "laws" (or obligations) for the first time. The inscription itself says that Ezana II restored his authority over the tribes enumerated in the inscription. One of the main obligations of the conquered tribes was the recognition of the right of the Axumite king to receive gifts when he traveled on the tribe's territory as an honored guest. In order to exercise this right to the fullest extent, the king was obliged to regularly set out on the personal collection of tribute. Thus the right to gifts and food, connected with the custom of hospitality, took on a feudal content and was converted into a primitive tribute collection.

Evidently the obligation of *dergo* (or *durgo*), which was preserved in Ethiopia throughout the Middle Ages and into the recent past, was a remnant of such tribute collection. The tribute (dergo) was brought by local inhabitants to the monarch, to royal troops, to Ethiopian and foreign ambassadors, and to civil servants. In general, dergo was given to all individuals riding through subjugated lands to whom an emperor or prince had assigned the right to receive dergo. Dergo consisted of prepared food such as flat cakes [*injera* bread], oil, sauces, and drinks, and of small game and edibles. Sometimes this was supplemented by clothing, silver money, and pack animals.

We may speculate that the gifts (*gd*) which Ezana II received were virtually no different from medieval dergo. Probably the greater part of such gifts consisted of provisions both in the form of prepared food and in the form of small game and edibles. In the inscription (lines 18–20) it is said that Ezana II received provisions in those territories through which he passed.

Dergo was delivered in several ways. Inhabitants meeting the Axumite king upon his entry into their area delivered dergo daily (as long as the king was located on their territory). Later, at the demand of the Axumite king, they were obliged to deliver provisions for several days ahead, especially when the king set out on a campaign beyond the borders of the vassal lands. Moreover, their own king (and sometimes probably also the king of a neighboring vassal state) came to a meeting with the Axumite king ("the king of kings") bearing more valuable gifts: gold, ivory, handcrafted articles, and cattle. The size of such a gift could scarcely always have been precisely determined, but the gift could not have been too meager so as not to anger "the king of kings." The Axumite king could also demand pack animals, porters, and guides. Thus Ezana II's inscription about the punitive expedition against the Ge'ez says that the king received in the country of Atagau "camels and pack animals (asses or mules?) and men and women (as porters?) and provisions for twenty days." [103]

It is evident that dergo could be very great, especially in the context of Axumite military expeditions. Yet, even routinely, the king set out to personally collect tribute in the company of several hundreds or even thousands of people. In the cited inscription of Ezana II "he fed four of his armies." The tribes subject to Axum seem to have been obligated to supply with provisions not only the king himself and the force accompanying him but also royal representatives who were sent in his name to personally collect tribute; for example, his brothers. Any group of individuals sent by the king was eligible: embassies, trade caravans, tribes which were being resettled (and the detachments of Axumites who accompanied them), and foreign ambassadors who were traveling in the company of Axumite officials.

The above-cited inscription tells how Ezana II treated the Metine tribes mercifully. Having accepted their gifts, he gave them "provisions for the men and women" (evidently the Metine arrived in full force with women and children as this was done in similar instances later). The inscription has precisely this in view, saying that "*all* the people of the Metine arrived." It is not reasonable to assume that Ezana II ordered these provisions to be distributed from the royal storehouses. These storehouses could not have been located on the territory of the vassal kingdoms, since their allegiance had been lost during the period before the resumption of personal tribute collection. He therefore fed the Metine from the dergo brought to him the day before, perhaps by the Metine themselves.

It is also possible that Ezana II ordered that dergo be supplied to the Metine on the way while they were returning home. Therefore the story about the merciful treatment of the Metine had in view not so much Ezana II's generosity, which did not cost him much, but his authority over the tribes: upon one word from the king, they supplied the population of a whole district with provisions!

Ezana I intended to advertise such power by ordering the inscription about the resettlement of the Beja[104] to be composed in two languages using three alphabets. They were resettled in the company of Axumite troops, with large and small livestock (precisely enumerated in the inscription). The trek took four months. After this they were sent farther on into the Matlia district (probably modern-day Begemdir, i.e., the country of the Beja).

The inscription, in itself very brief, insistently emphasizes that en route the Beja were constantly supplied with food. When they set out on the way they were supplied "with meat and bread (or with poultry and grain) for food, and beer and wine and water for drink—all according to their number." On the road "they daily received 22,000 wheaten loaves and wine in the course of the four months while they were being brought" to Axum—five loaves per person. In Axum they were again supplied with food and clothing. When they were moved into the country of Matlia, the king ordered his subjects "to give them food again." It can be said that the comment about the accurate delivery of dergo occupies a primary place in the Greek text of the inscription. Probably while in Axum the Beja received provisions from the royal storehouses, but en route, undoubtedly, the local population supplied provisions to them. A total of 4400 people of the Beja were resettled. Together with the Axumite troops who accompanied them to Matlia, as many as five thousand persons were moved. The maintenance of such a mass of people placed an excessive burden on the shoulders of the population. Since the size of the dergo was not strictly determined it could have absorbed both surplus and locally required produce.

Personal tribute collection by the king was also burdensome to his royal bodyguard. The circuit of Northern Ethiopia for personal tribute collection by the king occupied no less than two or two-and-one-half months. Persons accompanying the king were, therefore, torn away from home for a long time.

Tribute from South Arabia, at least under Sumafa Ashwa and Abreha, was received by the Axumites in a consolidated form: the rulers of Himyar sent it. However, even here, evidently the Axumite kings on occasion did not relinquish the right of personal collection of tribute.

In sources which describe the actions of the Axumite kings in Yemen there are remarks on their personal collection of tribute. Thus in *The Life of St. Grigentius*, the king Ellesboam (Ella Asbeha) wandered about the cities of Himyar and consecrated churches. Everywhere he visited, the populace was enlisted in construction operations (i.e., labor conscription).[105] Did Ella Asbeha make the rounds of the cities out of piety alone? Or did he at the same time collect tribute? *The Book of the Himyarites* also speaks of the fact that the Ethiopian king made the rounds of the cities of Himyar.[106] It is most probable that the personal collection of tribute also took place.

The inscription from Safra,[107] which, according to paleographic data, can be dated to the beginning of the IV century A.D., gives new material about personal tribute collection by the king. The inscription, which contains the text of four laws (*'ḥgg*), speaks of some sort of Ethiopian king who visited the tribe and established a camp (if Drewes correctly interprets the terms and sense of lines 2–3, 5–6 [and] 23–24 of text A of the inscription under consideration). Text A, in my opinion, makes precise the size of the dergo given to the king (who is not directly named) and his people (*sbt*): "Here is what will be given to them if they camp (*zyhbm 'mr 'qm mqrt*)." On the first day the king's people get a first-class (?) sheep (*bg' zgb*); a sheep which has not lambed (or a barren sheep?), and honey or a cow and flour can be substituted for it. Besides that, the king's people receive wheat bread. On the second day, evidently, they are also entitled to an animal and bread (the distribution of the second day is not indicated in the inscription). On the third day of the sojourn in the tribe's territory the king receives a cow which has not calved (or a barren cow?) and one gabata[108] of honey wine (*tej*) (*ms*). If the king remains in camp longer his people get one qunna[109] of oil and flour. Beer is brought to them besides. The same is supplied them on the fifth and sixth days and beyond. The period of sojourn of the king on the tribe's territory and the numerical strength of his retinue are not limited by law.

It is interesting that dergo is interpreted as the king's share in the sacrificial meals. This is connected with the sacerdotal functions of the Ethiopian kings. It is possible that the personal collection of tribute was considered to be an *obligation* of the king; to visit lands of the tribes in order to maintain their fertility. For this "magic service" the king received the right of participation in the sacrificial meal. Later on, the kings began to use these sacrificial offerings widely (probably in the period of plowing) for feeding their retinues. The tribes were subject not only to the armed force of the king but also were in fear that the king might act so as to deprive their lands of fertility.

What rank of king does the Safra inscription speak of? This was scarcely the supreme ruler of the Axumite Kingdom. If this had been the case he would have been called the "king of Axum" or "the king of kings." Besides, the gifts which he received while collecting in person were *too* insignificant. Evidently the inscription speaks about the king of one of the regions of the Axumite Kingdom which were subject to Axum. Consequently, such kings also made the rounds of their lands personally collecting tribute. For them this personal tribute collecting was one of the main methods of taxation. Although the laws of Safra pertain to personal tribute collecting by the local king, they also throw light on personal tribute collecting of the Axumite king. It appears that the difference was merely in quantity.

Appropriation of sacrificial offerings

The inscription from Safra acquaints us not only with the personal collecting of tribute by the king and the bringing of gifts to him, but also with the right of the king and priest to receive a share during the offering of a sacrifice.

Text B of the inscription from Safra makes precise the quantity of sacrificed bread which was given to the king and to the priest. The text is headed "Laws about loaves which the king receives" ('*ḥgg zhbst zynš' ngš*).

The king receives 12 portions of bread[110] evidently brought for the sacrificial meal. The donor (*mqbl*) receives 9 portions (*dmr*) and the priest who carries out the sacrifice (*šw'*), 6 portions.

Text C says that during the dividing of a sacrificed cow the king receives one-half and the donor the other half and the hide. Drewes carefully studied the terminology of the inscription. He paid attention to the sacral character of the terms, to the general similarity of the texts (especially A, B and C), to the sacral laws about sacrifices among the ancient Jews, and also to the practice of modern-day Ethiopian peoples.

In the region of Serae, among the Tigrai, the leader has the right to receive the tongue and the "side" (almost half of the carcass) of an animal killed by the peasants on festive occasions. Such occasions would include community work, weddings, funerals, funeral feasts, St. John's Day, etc.[111] Among the Mensa, a pagan tribe of Eritrea, the leader receives the tongue and a shoulder blade (i.e., part of the carcass) from the so-called "cow of challenge"; of a sacrificed cow he receives only a shoulder blade.[112]

Among the Maria, another pagan tribe of Eritrea, an aristocrat has the right to specified parts of a carcass and whole animals killed by his "*tigre*" (bondsman). The *tigre* is obliged to give to his lord the tongue and the brisket of each cow killed by him, any barren cow, and wild honey found by him.[113] Among the Beni Amer of Northern Eritrea, a client gives to his master the brisket of each cow killed by him and any barren cow which turns up in his herd.[114]

The persons who conducted religious rites had similar privileges. Among the Mensa, the priest on a funeral holiday received a shoulder of a cow killed on the day of the death (the so-called "cow of the ants"), and also half of the carcass and the hide of a cow which was slaughtered for funeral feasts on the fortieth day after the death.[115] According to another communication, the priest received the shoulder of each cow which was slaughtered for funeral festivals and half the carcass and the hide from the "cow of the ants" and from the so-called "cow of the cords." In addition, from the cow slaughtered at the funeral banquets on the fortieth day after the death, the priest received the hind part, a side, and a fore leg.[116] The closest relatives of the deceased gave the cows.[117] It seems that similar rites exist also among other peoples of Northern Ethiopia.

Texts B and C of the inscription from Safra introduce us to the same circle of legal norms. It is reasonable to conjecture that the highly archaic obligations of modern-day peasants of Northern Ethiopia to the aristocracy (which are expressed in strictly specified offerings of sacrificial meat) have their origins in the Axumite period, and differ from them only in details. Moreover, it is reasonable to assume that in the Axumite period these practices must have had greater significance.

Text D of the inscription from Safra contains interesting information. Judging by the writing, it is somewhat younger than the other texts. When publishing it,[118] Drewes paid attention to its connection with offerings. I mistakenly saw in text D a decree about the variation of the make-up of the dergo.[119] Ryckmans supported, basically, the interpretation of Drewes but introduced important corrections into the translation and interpretation of the overall meaning.[120] A translation of the text according to Ryckmans follows:

"[1] Rules about gi [2] fts and clothing.
[3] This clothing of the bearer of [the gift]. And
[4] the giver of mon[5]ey and butter
[6] but not the giver of vegetable oil and
[7] the female giver of firewood."

The obligatory wearing of ritually cleansed clothing on the occasion of offering a gift of money and butter to a deity is being spoken of. A man who made a gift of vegetable oil and a woman who brought a gift of firewood could remain in ordinary or soiled clothing. It is difficult to say whether constant duties for the sanctuary, or voluntary gifts from time to time, were being spoken of. It is possible that both are meant. Firewood and vegetable oil probably constituted the obligatory part. Therefore it was possible to wear soiled clothing when bringing them. The collection of firewood was always the woman's job in Ethiopia. Aren't they speaking, in the case under consideration, about a hierodule, a temple priestess of a lower category? Perhaps she became a "bondwoman" of the deity and was obliged to bring him a gift of firewood? In any event, a male hierodule was obliged to bring vegetable oil. Other "slaves of god" had to sacrifice butter and money, but perhaps this was just the bringing of an offering from time to time. The obligatory deliveries of firewood, vegetable oil, and torches for the Axumite cathedral, during the Middle Ages, was the duty of the *dabtar*—a lower-status temple functionary.

The right to hunt elephants

In the *Bibliotheca* of Photius there is the following excerpt from the book of Nonnus about his embassy to Ethiopia: "On the road leading to Axum at the place called Aua, Nonnus and his fellow travelers saw an unusual phenomenon: this was a multitude of elephants, about five thousand. They were pastured on a broad field. None of the natives was allowed to come close to them nor to drive them from the pasture."[121]

First of all, the fact itself is startling: in the center of the Axumite Kingdom, in a densely populated agrarian country, an enormous herd of five thousand head of elephants was preserved. It is possible that by fault of the author, the copyist, or the person retelling the story, the number of elephants was exaggerated. But judging from context, a very large herd was being told about. Such herds were encountered in Africa before the spread of firearms, when periods of drought occurred. The elephant herd survived probably because the peasants were placed under the strictest ban on killing them. The remark of Nonnus that none of the natives dared to come close to the elephants confirms that this was actually so. Since much earlier times there was a high price and stable demand for ivory. If there had not been a ban on hunting in Northern Ethiopia there would not have been even a single elephant preserved in the Axumite period. Certainly there would no longer have been large-scale herds of these animals.

Pseudo Arrian comments that the greater part of the ivory entered Coloe (Matara) and Adulis from the districts located "beyond the Nile," i.e., to the south and southwest of the Tekezze-Atbara river system. Elephants were only rarely encountered on the seacoast in the environs of Adulis.[122] They may also not have been numerous in the plateau regions of Northern Ethiopia. And if after 300 years Nonnus saw here a herd of five thousand elephants, then this could only be because they were under the protection of royal authority. It is possible that King Ze Haqile, who was a contemporary of Pseudo Arrian, had forbidden the killing of elephants over the entire territory of the Axumite Kingdom. Perhaps in some districts, including Axum proper, such a ban had existed even earlier. Perhaps the deliveries of ivory from Northern Ethiopia to the markets of Coloe (Matara) and Adulis were insignificant, not only because here few elephants remained but also because hunting them was prohibited.

Probably the ban on hunting was applied only to the peasants. The Axumite king and his vassal kinglets were probably permitted to kill elephants. No wonder the titles "nagashi" and "negus" were connected with ritual hunting. The kings of Kaffa enjoyed the same privilege.

The privilege of hunting elephants permitted concentration of the ivory trade in the hands of the monarchs. Thus the royal privilege of elephant hunting had an economic significance; it supplied the king with a source of revenue.

In order to evaluate this essentially feudal privilege, it is necessary to imagine how heavy a burden it placed on the shoulders of the peasants. Elephants are migratory animals. The huge herd of elephants (if it was the sole one!) roamed over all of Northern Ethiopia, trampling peasant fields, demolishing huts, devouring the harvest and young plantings. The peasants were obliged to look on as the fruits of their labor perished, not even daring to come close to the elephants or to drive them from the pastures.

Trade

Axumite society lived primarily within a provincial economy. But to a certain extent trade relations were developed. The comparatively high level of craft activity in Axum presupposes a significant division of labor. Part of the handicraft articles could be converted into goods and sold in the local markets. The development of exchange found reflection in the language of the Axumites, which has a rich trade terminology. In Ge'ez one encounters verbs meaning "to exchange," "to sell," "to buy," "to travel for trade purposes," etc. In Axumite inscriptions the terms meaning "coin" [123] and "trade caravan" are preserved.[124]

Information about exporting from Ethiopia dates mainly to the very end of the Preaxumite period and to the beginning of the Axumite period. Such information has been preserved in Pliny the Elder (about the year 60 A.D.)[125] and *Periplus* (beginning of the III century A.D.).[126] Information which dates to the VI century A.D. can be found in Philostorgius, in Cosmas Indicopleustes, and in Nonnus.[127] All of these data can be presented in the form of a table (Table 2).

It is significant that in the list of exports neither handcrafted articles

Table 2. Axumite Exports

Pliny the Elder	Pseudo Arrian	Cosmas Indicopleustes	Nonnus and Philostorgius
		Gold	Gold dust
		Emeralds	
Obsidian	Obsidian		
Ivory	Ivory	Ivory	Ivory
Rhinoceros	Rhinoceros		
horn	horn		
Hippopotamus		Hippopotamus	
hide		teeth	
Tortoise			
shell			
Monkeys		Live animals	Live animals
Slaves		Aromatic	Aromatic
		substances	substances

nor products of agriculture or animal breeding (the primary occupations of the population of Axumite Ethiopia) are present.

In the V–VI centuries A.D. the Axumite Kingdom (via Adulis) carried on an extensive intermediary trade with Somali, Indian, East African, and South Arabian goods. But the list of export items from the country itself did not change. Pseudo Arrian tells of the nature of imported goods entering Ethiopia at the beginning of the Axumite period: "Into these places (into the possessions of the Axumite king, Ze Haqile or Zoskales) are brought crude, poor quality himatia made in Egypt for the barbarians, imitation colored abollas, linen bands hemmed on both sides, many kinds of articles made of transparent glass and murrhine vessels which were made in Diospolis (Thebes), brass . . . copper . . . iron. Besides these there were imported axes, poleaxes, knives, large round copper cups, a few denarii for foreigners living here, a little Laodicean (Syrian) and Italian wine, a little olive oil. And for the king, silver and gold vessels made in the local style and of outer garments abollas and kaunaks (burnooses), also not very costly, were imported. In the same way from the interior areas of Ariaca (Central India) they imported Indian iron and steel and Indian cotton fabric, particularly the wider (and coarser) fabrics, belts, 'skin' coats, and a few garments and cloth painted with lacquer."[128]

Some forms of handcrafted articles and agricultural products imported into Ethiopia were left out in this list. Thus, *Periplus* states that into Avalit and Berbera, on the very borders of the Axumite Kingdom, there was imported "a little tin," glass articles, tunics, "different cloth himatia in the barbarian taste," and dressed and dyed cloaks from the Roman

Empire. Also imported were agricultural products from Egypt: the juice of young Diospolis grapes, bread, wine, and from India sugar cane, grain (wheat, rice, bosmor), and sesame oil. One could add to these cinnamon of different kinds, and certain aromatic substances brought from India but considered as a local barbarian product.[129] Of these goods, at least tin, clothing, sugar cane, and aromatic resins would have had to be imported also into Adulis. Concerning the import of Indian and Somali goods into Ethiopia in the VI century A.D., Cosmas Indicopleustes relates: "The inhabitants of Berbera [received from somewhere] a multitude of spices; incense, cassia, sugar cane, and much more and they send all this by sea to Adulis [Eritrea], to Omeritia [South Arabia], into Inner India [Inner Arabia], and to Persia.[130] Indirect data indicate the importation of handcrafted articles from South Arabia. *Periplus* says nothing about the importation of Arabian goods into Ethiopia but describes in detail their importation into Azania. "There are imported into these [East African] markets, things primarily of local manufacture in Muza (Moha): spears, poleaxes, knives, awls, and different kinds of things made of glass. ... "[131] It would be strange if they had not been imported into nearby Ethiopia, which received similar goods from the Roman Empire and from India. Here it is necessary to add South Arabian fabrics, and clothing, for example, the famous Najran cloaks.

Excavations at Axum, Haoulti-Melazo, Adulis, and Tio yielded a number of metallic, ceramic, and glass items imported into Northern Ethiopia from South Arabia, Syria, Egypt, Meroe, and India between the I century B.C. and the beginning of the VII century A.D. Several fragments of a glass vessel from Roman or Byzantine Egypt were found in Axum in 1906.[132]

Excavations of the 1950s to the 1970s at Axum yielded a large number of finds of such a sort, primarily Mediterranean amphorae, ceramics imitative of Roman stamped pottery (*terra sigillata*), and glass flasks for ointments of Roman and Egyptian manufacture, etc.[133] The same such fragments and a scarab of a green glass substance without an inscription, probably of Roman time, were discovered at Adulis in 1907, and in 1962, also at Adulis, a Roman intaglio with the depiction of a lion (displayed in the archaeological museum at Addis Ababa).

In Axum in 1958 Byzantine bronze weights were found,[134] while among the archaeological finds at Adulis both Byzantine bronze scales and weights were discovered. As could be expected, Mediterranean and Theban amphorae are especially numerous here. At Matara, Mediterranean amphorae are also the most common type of articles of Byzantine-Egyptian manufacture. Moreover, fragments of a glass vase and an incomplete glass vessel of remarkable workmanship, a bronze Byzantine lamp and also two Byzantine gold crosses, three chains, a necklace of Roman silver coins of the II–III centuries A.D., and other objects were found in a late Axumite cache.[135] In Matara fragments of a glass vase were found. In Yeha beads of a glass paste were recovered.[136] In Tio, not far from Adulis, amphorae from Hellenic or Roman Egypt were discovered.[137] In Axum, in 1955–1958, fragments of glass and ceramic vessels from Roman or Byzantine Egypt were found, including a bluish goblet widening out in an upward direction, and large cylindrical amphorae with a brownish surface[138] (also produced in the Alexandria of Roman or Byzantine time, or possibly in Meroe). Similar cups were later found at Axum. In Havila Asserai, in 1954, four bronze cups from Meroe or Egypt of Hellenic or Roman times[139] were extracted from a cache. At Haoulti-Melazo, in 1959, excavations revealed two small figurines of blue faience which had openings for hanging.[140] They turned out to be amulets of the cults of Hathor and Ptah, probably of Meroitic manufacture. In Matara, in 1963, a Meroitic carnelian amulet depicting Harpocrates (the child Horus)[141] was found. Bruce saw and sketched in Axum in the XVIII century A.D. a stele depicting Horus with crocodiles, as well as a hieroglyphic inscription.[142] This monument is more reminiscent of the Meroitic stelae than of the Egyptian stelae proper. Among South Arabian articles discovered at Matara in 1965 there was a beautiful bronze lamp with the image of a ritual stag hunt.[143] In addition, four Sabaean coins were found in the region of Asmara.[144]

Indian articles were also uncovered. A stone stamp of the first centuries A.D. was found at Adulis in 1906.[145] And from Haoulti-Melazo several statuettes of molded fired clay are reported.[146] In the monastery of Debre Damo there were revealed several gold and silver coins of the Arab Caliphate (the earliest is dated 697 A.D. and the latest 934 A.D.) as well as silk fabrics: Coptic (VI–VIII centuries A.D.), Mesopotamian (VII–IX centuries A.D.), and Muslim Egypt (IX–XII centuries A.D.).[147]

The cited data about the importation of goods into the Axumite Kingdom can be presented in the form of a table (Table 3).

Besides, Cosmas Indicopleustes reports that Ethiopians (by which undoubtedly he means Axumites and the inhabitants of Adulis) received emeralds from the Beja and then sold them to India.[148] The emerald mines had passed into the hands of the Beja, who were under the hegemony of Axum at the beginning of the V century A.D. Yet long before this, the Adulis inhabitants could have participated in intermediary trade in precious stones mined in the lands of the Beja.

In Cosmas' time the make-up of Byzantine exports to Ethiopia evidently had changed in comparison with the time of Pseudo Arrian. Late in the IV century A.D. the Roman emperors issued a series of laws which prohibited the sale of many goods beyond the boundaries of the Empire.

Table 5. Goods imported into the Axumite Kingdom

Goods	From the Roman Empire	From Meroe	From India	From South Arabia	From Somalia
Iron, nonferrous metals and articles made of them	Iron, axes, poleaxes, knives, brass and copper, copper (and bronze) cups, scales and weights, lamps, tin	Iron, copper, bronze vessels	Iron and steel (and articles made of them)	(Spears, poleaxes, knives and awls), bronze coins, bronze vessels	
Articles of precious metals	Gold and silver vessels, decorations, crosses, denarii		Gold coins	Silver coins	
Glass and ceramic articles	Articles of transparent glass, murrhine, faience, and clay	Amphorae, ceramic statuettes	Artistic ceramics	Articles made of clay	
Fabrics and clothing	Coarse, poor quality himatia, linen bands, stoles, abollas, kaunaks (chitons, cloaks from Arsinoe), Coptic fabrics of the VI–VII centuries A.D.		Various Indian cotton fabrics and sindons made from them and materials (painted with lacquer) and kaunaks	(Fabrics?)	
Wine and sugar cane	Laodicean and Italian wine		Sugar cane		Indian cane sugar (re-exported)
Vegetable oils	Olive oil		Sesame oil		
Aromatic substances			Duaca, maceir	(Myrrh and incense)	Myrrh, incense (and gum)
Spices			Different kinds of cinnamon		Indian cinnamon (re-exported)

These laws remained in force during the course of the entire V century A.D. and into the beginning of the VI century A.D. It was forbidden to export weapons and metals (gold, iron, and copper) and also wine and oil.[149] This decree operated not only in relation to hostile countries but also in relation to friendly Ethiopia. (Procopius Caesarensis speaks about the ban under pain of death on selling of iron.[150]) All of this inevitably limited the trade of the Empire with Ethiopia. However, in many cases the ban could be breached with the agreement of the Roman-Byzantine authorities.

Probably some articles of import were intended primarily for foreigners who lived in the Axumite Kingdom. Evidently there were quite a few. Perhaps primarily for the Mediterranean residents, "a little olive oil" and also "a little Laodicean . . . and Italian wine" were imported.[151] However, wine could, in part, have been destined for the local aristocracy and also (from the middle of the IV century A.D.) for the needs of the Christian cult. The aristocracy acquired copper and bronze cups, glass articles, more expensive fabrics and clothing, aromatic substances, and sugar. Just as in neighboring South Arabia, aromatic substances evidently were used for cult purposes. Other goods were imported especially for the king. At the same time, some forms of goods—for example, cheap fabrics, glass beads, metal articles—were sold, at least in part, to ordinary consumers.

In the listing of the articles of export from the Axumite Kingdom we have seen that products of the peasant economy as well as those of craft specialists were entirely absent. Some of the exported goods (obsidian and tortoise shell) came from the seacoast. Other goods were brought from the interior. In the time of Pseudo Arrian the principal quantities of ivory and rhinoceros horn were brought into Adulis "from beyond the Nile" (i.e., from Tekezze-Atbara). Hippopotami lived only in the interior of the country, in the large rivers and lakes. The greater portion of exported products appear to have been obtained by the Axumites by means of military pillaging in the continental regions of Africa and also by means of trade with these same regions.[152] The most precious of the exported goods—gold—was obtained by the Axumites from Southwest Ethiopia (Cosmas Indicopleustes' land of Sasu). The Axumites gave in exchange cattle, bars of salt, iron,[153] and also probably fabrics and glass articles. Gold was obtained in part also as tribute and as military spoil.[154] Bracelets made by local smiths from imported brass, spears of imported iron, and other local metallic articles were also turned into trade goods.

Foreign merchants and local artisans had to buy, even if only in part, provisions from the peasants and aristocracy. Thus not only the cattle which were driven into Sasu but also agricultural products were converted into trade goods. Judging by the communication of *Periplus* and by indirect data, raw materials which were used by artisans and certain goods acquired by the peasants were imported into Axum. However, on the whole the Axumites' economy remained a subsistence-based one and market relationships had a limited sphere of operation. Trade developed not on the basis of production but because of military pillaging, tribute collection, and intermediary trade on land-sea routes.

The main bulk of Ethiopian goods was exchanged on the seacoast in the markets of Adulis and Avalit. However, foreign merchants traveled into the interior of the country, into the trading towns of the northern plateau. Enumerating the Ethiopian markets, *Periplus* calls the town of Coloe [Matara] the main ivory trading point. "From this town to [Axum], the capital of the so-called Axumites, lay a journey of five days. To Axum via the so-called [locality] of Kienion was taken all the ivory from that side of the Nile (Tekezze)." Since Pseudo Arrian described only the markets visited by Roman-Egyptian merchants, Axum and Coloe (Matara) undoubtedly belonged among them. In *Periplus*, Coloe (Matara) is called a city (πολις), while Adulis is called a village (χῶμη).[155]

Sources of the V–VI centuries A.D. attest that travelers from India and Byzantium constantly visited Axum. Evidently foreign merchants did not penetrate farther, and Cosmas Indocopleustes never was in the country of Sasu.[156] Trade with this country and with other interior territories of the continent right up to Meroe was monopolized by Axumites. In one of Ezana II's inscriptions, an Axumite trade caravan which was sent into Ethiopian Afan is mentioned. Indirect evidence of the land links of Axum with the Nile valley are preserved. Land trade brought to Axum considerable benefits. From Meroe they were able to bring back handcrafted articles and iron in bars [pig iron].

Sea trade was located mainly in the hands of foreign merchants, although the Ethiopians themselves conducted trade trips by sea to Arabia, India, Ceylon, and Egypt.

It is possible to judge the geographical limits of Axum's trade links by the goods which came into Ethiopia via Adulis. Laodicean wine came through the port of Laodicea (Latakia) from Asia Minor and Syria, Italian wine from south and central Italy. Pseudo Arrian mentions Indian iron, fabrics, and clothing imported into Ethiopia "from the interior localities of Ariaca" (i.e., from Central India). Adulis was thus connected with Italy, Asia Minor, Central India, and nearer countries. The export connections of Adulis stretched still farther. It is difficult even to indicate the geographic limits reached by goods of both Ethiopian and non-Ethiopian origin which were transported via Adulis. Ivory, gold, emeralds, and black slaves went to Central and East Asia, Asia Minor, and Europe. Spices and aromatic substances had a similarly wide distribution. Axumite goods have been certified in the Crimea, Spain, and China.

The activity of foreign merchants and Axumite merchants undoubtedly brought profit to the Axumite king and to the Adulis ruler.

Periplus says directly of certain goods that they were destined for the Axumite king. Evidently, at the beginning of the III century A.D., foreign merchants were obliged to make a gift to the king in proportion to their wealth. This was scarcely a firmly established tax; otherwise it would have consisted of a specified amount of ordinary goods. Instead, it consisted of costly gold and silver vessels, "not very costly" but also not "coarse and spurious" abollas and kaunaks. About 524 A.D. the Alexandrian patriarch sent a silver vessel to the Axumite king as a gift.[157]

During the heyday of Axum, regular duties may have been established. In Joannes Ephesius, whose work was preserved by Pseudo Dionysius, the Axumite king (Ella Asbeha) wrote the Himyarite king (Dhu Nuwas): "You have committed evil, killing Christians, Roman traders; you have curtailed trade and withheld the duties of my kingdom and other kingdoms."[158] Probably in the V–VI centuries A.D. trade duties in the amount of a specified portion of the goods brought were collected from foreign merchants. Joannes Ephesius may have been mistaken, however, in regarding the obligatory gifts as a genuine duty. Such income had considerable significance for the royal treasury, and the Axumite kings did not intend to refuse it. Not without reason the author of *Periplus*, who was a Graeco-Egyptian merchant, calls King Ze Haqile "miserly and self-interested."

It is reasonable to conjecture that Axumite kings directly participated in trade as this is reported for the Middle Ages.[159] Cosmas Indicopleustes describes caravans which the Axumite king sent to Sasu for gold.

"[Sasu] has many gold mines. From year to year the king of the Axumites, through the arhont of the Agau, sends his people there for gold. Many others with the same purpose go along with them so that altogether they comprise more than 500 persons. There they deliver bulls, salt, and iron. Upon arrival in that country they immediately arrange a camp (or make a stopping place) on that spot. Then having gathered a large amount of thorny brush they make a large fence and arrange themselves inside it. They kill bulls and over the thorny fence place salt, iron, and pieces of meat. Then the natives arrive, bringing with them gold in the form of pea-sized nuggets called *tankharas*, and place one, two, or more of them near a piece of meat or near salt or iron which they wish to acquire and go off some distance. The owner of the meat then arrives and takes the gold if he is satisfied with the price offered for the goods. After this the native who had made the offer draws near and carries off the meat, salt, or iron. If the owner of the goods is not satisfied with the amount of gold offered for his goods then he does not touch the gold and the native who had walked a little way off seeing that his gold is not taken either adds a few more pieces or takes his gold and leaves. Such is the custom of trading there since they speak another language and there is an extreme insufficiency of interpreters."[160]

The description of dumb bargaining between the Nubians and Roman-Byzantine merchants in Hierasycaminos on the southern border of Egypt dates to a somewhat earlier time.[161] The Nubian traders spread out (at an agreed upon place) goods which they had brought, including gold, ivory, and aromatic substances. The merchants who had come from Egypt also placed their goods opposite the Nubian goods in a quantity which was, in their opinion, equivalent to the value of the former. Elements of the legend of dumb bargaining clearly entered into Philostratus' description. We also find this legend in Herodotus but there it is confined to West Africa.[162]

It is supposed that the "dumb bargaining" was carried out at night and that the seller did not see the buyer. Cosmas Indicopleustes' words about the fact that the sellers (Axumites) "go off to some distance" (having placed the goods on the fence) should be compared with a similar detail of other stories about "dumb bargaining," where the sellers either go off to a distance of five days' journey or board a ship and sail off.

Such is the common legend invented in antiquity by merchants who did not wish to admit strangers to the secrets of trading with gold. Obviously, the Axumites transmitted the legend about "dumb bargaining" either to Cosmas himself or to his informants. But Cosmas was unable to completely believe it; therefore, he omitted the clearly improbable detail about "unseen" buyers and added the rationalistic argument about the insufficiency of interpreters.

But even in this form, Cosmas' report here and there causes perplexities. Why did the Axumites slaughter the bulls? Indeed it would have been simpler to sell them alive. After all, gold isn't copper (small change), which could not buy a whole bull, and the natives undoubtedly would have preferred a live cow to pieces of beef. And how did this meat not spoil during the prolonged "dumb bargaining," especially if the buyer refused to add gold and turned the meat back? Let us assume the most unfavorable case, since it shows all of the absurdity of Cosmas' version. Let us assume that the native refuses the meat and on the following day the Axumite adds a piece. The meat has hung on the fence all night, all of the following day, and part of the second night. Of course the meat had to be rotten. In Ethiopia people preferred fresh meat, preferably freshly killed. Only a few relatively backward tribes were less fastidious. What is known about the inhabitants of Sasu, however, suggests that as a people they had attained a rather high level of development. They mined gold, bought iron, and evidently knew how to process these metals. Indeed, the inhabitants of Sasu scarcely placed such a low value on gold that they exchanged it for pieces of meat. This is nothing more than the well-known motif of the trade Eldorado which is encountered in Herodotus (the Ethiopians of Nubia allegedly valued gold more cheaply than copper).

If the natives valued gold so low, would it not have been simpler for them, and indeed for the Axumites also, to exchange the virgin metal not for pieces of meat but for a live cow? The motif of the ignorance of the value of gold does not explain, wholly, the legendary detail with the pieces of meat. Indeed, for demonstrating this ignorance it would have been possible to leave out the slaughtering of the bulls and simply to report that for each bull the Sasu natives gave much gold.

In my article about Sasu[163] I wrote that the version about the slaughtering of bulls, the hanging of pieces of beef on the thorny fence, and the "dumb" trading of meat shows a genuine mocking by the Axumites (who used as food fresh meat—perhaps even raw, freshly killed) of the foreign merchant-seafarers who were used to eating meat which was preserved. But even this explanation is not sufficient. There is still another solution of the detail with the pieces of meat similar to the castle with the three secrets.

The Axumite informants of Cosmas were not so much the creators as the transmitters of the tale, which is a variant of a worldwide motif. In the middle of the I millennium B.C., and perhaps even earlier, a myth appeared about how virgin gold or precious stones were mined in some exotic inaccessible country. These riches were scattered in abundance in a valley guarded by eagles or griffins; sometimes among streams of fiery lava. Bold natives (Indians or Siberian Arimaspeans) drove bulls or sheep there, slaughtered them and threw pieces of meat into the valley to which the virgin metal stuck. The griffins (or eagles) seized the meat and rose upwards with it and the natives gathered the virgin metal or precious stones which were falling. An allusion to this legend is encountered in Aeschylus (*Prometheus Bound*), Herodotus (IV, 13), and later in Pliny (*Naturalis Historia*, VII, 2). All of these have as a source the ancient Greek poem *The Arimaspeans*, ascribed to Aristea, the son of Caistrobius from Proconnesus. The poem links the country of "griffins who guard gold" with the Altai. *The Miracles of India*, an Arabic composition of the IX century A.D., transfers its locale to Kashmir. However, there are versions that sometimes move it into Africa. At the juncture of the III–IV centuries A.D., Heliodorus mentioned a fantastic "team of griffins with reins of gold chains" (X, 26) whom the Axumites' neighbors, the Troglodytes, brought as a gift to the king of Meroe. The gold chains indicate the connection of the griffins with gold and the country of the Troglodytes is located in close proximity to Sasu.

It is entirely probable that caravans of Axumites going to Sasu drove herds of bulls with them, but the greater part of these undoubtedly went to members of the caravan for food. It is scarcely possible to speak of an organized and significant export of cattle.

In Cosmas' account the route from Axum to Sasu and back took all of six months. The trading continued only for five days—a detail emphasizing the difficulty of the undertaking. The caravan hurriedly returned to Axum in view of the approach of the rainy season. The duration of the season is exaggerated by a whole month: allegedly from the month of Epiphi (July) to the month of Thoth (September), whereas the season of heavy rains lasts only from August to September. This was done to make the difficulties of the journey frightening. Cosmas continues: "They (the Axumites) make the return journey armed to a man since among the inhabitants of that land there are those who threaten them and want to take away the gold [bartered for, in Sasu]." The dangers of the journey, although probable, are overemphasized. Cosmas was transmitting the biased tale of his informants. It is possible that he wanted to set out for Sasu with them and they spared no words in order to dissuade him from this undertaking.

In spite of the inaccuracy of Cosmas' information, it is possible to extract from his tale valuable details. Even if one considers that the numerical strength of the caravan (500 persons) is exaggerated, nevertheless some notion is created concerning the dimensions of trade with Sasu. The agents of the king made up the nucleus of the caravan but to them were added also other individuals, all undoubtedly Axumites. The main object of export from Sasu into Axum was gold in virgin form. The Axumites offered iron, salt, and cattle in exchange.

It is strange that Cosmas does not mention fabrics and other handcrafted articles. The inhabitants of Sasu would very likely have needed articles of glass, metal, and leather. Probably, in reality, trade in iron and salt was in the hands of Axumite merchants since it was prohibited to the Byzantines by their own government. Moreover, iron ingots, bars of salt, and cattle had a long tradition as units of monetary exchange in Ethiopia. The Axumite king and merchants could, according to their discretion, exchange or not exchange this local "currency" for money and goods of foreigners.

Evidently, also, the listing of goods delivered to Sasu was the product of a conscious literary creation, not by Cosmas of course, but by those who were interested in dissuading him from going on a trade expedition. Hence it is evident how carefully the Axumites guarded their monopoly on trade with Sasu.

Cosmas mentions a valuable detail on the organization of trade: a caravan to Sasu was sent "through the arhont of the Agau." In other words, the ruler of the district through which the caravan passed bore the responsibility for it. If the caravan was subjected to pillaging a severe punishment awaited the ruler. One of Ezana II's inscriptions tells how the Axumite king punished the inhabitants of Afan, who had pillaged and annihilated an Axumite trade caravan. A punitive expedition into this remote and comparatively poor country shows what significance trade had for the Axumite kings. What role trade interests played in the campaigns of the Axumites against Himyar is mentioned by Byzantine authors. Numerous materials which touch upon this question have been investigated in detail by N. V. Pigulevskaya.[164]

Only indirect data—the level of development of handicrafts and the presence of foreigners in the country—have been preserved concerning the internal trade of Northern Ethiopia in the Axumite period. The inscription from Safra gives the following equivalent costs: a grown (?) sheep = a sheep of some quality + some amount of honey = a cow + some quantity of flour. Honey was, of course, more valuable than flour, although the quantity of these products is not indicated. In the inscription, money (*'ld*)[165] is also mentioned but of what metal and of what origin is not indicated.

Avers: ΑΦΙΛΑC ᴜ ΒΑCΙΛΕΥC

Revers: ΑΣѠΜΙΤѠΝ ᴜ ΒΙCΙΔΙΜΗΛΗ

An Axumite coin minted in gold.

Money

At the beginning of the III century A.D. the Axumites still did not have their own coins. Silver money, "very little" at that, was imported. Pseudo Arrian emphasized that a certain number of gold and silver denarii were imported into Adulis and the Somali port of Malao, especially for the foreigners who were living there.[166] The sole Roman coins found so far on the territory of the Axumite Kingdom were in the necklace from Matara with fourteen Roman denarii of the II–III centuries A.D. Approximately at the same time in Debre Damo a large sum of Kushan coins turned up.

Perhaps, at the end of the II century A.D., Sabaean bronze coins also entered Axum. They were dated I–II centuries A.D. but were found in archaeological deposits of the IV–VIII centuries A.D.[167] Thus at the beginning of the III century A.D., the Axumites were already using foreign gold, silver, and bronze coins but only in limited quantities.

Side by side with the coins, more primitive forms of money were in use. Pseudo Arrian mentions the import into Adulis of bars of brass which were used "instead of coins." It is possible that bars of salt, iron ingots, and cattle served as money equivalents.

From the second half of the III century A.D., Axum began to mint its own coinage. The political significance of this step has been noted elsewhere. The introduction of its own coinage indicates the significance that market relationships had acquired in the Axumite Kingdom.

The Axumite gold coin constituted the basis of monetary circulation henceforth. Judging by the inscription from Safra it was called an "alado."[168] This gold coin, whose weight fluctuated, was usually coined in a single value. However, under Endubis, gold coins of two different values were issued. Coinage of gold and silver Axumite coins continued into the early VII century A.D. After King Gersem I it ceased, but copper money continued to be coined by Armah I, Hataz I, and Hataz II.

Copper and, in a considerably lesser amount, silver were in circulation as change. Anzani, in 1926, described 163 gold, 312 copper, and a total of 18 silver specimens among Axum coins.[169] Since then about 160 more Axumite silver coins[170] and about 1000 copper coins have been found.[171] However, if one takes into account that in contrast to copper and silver coins only a minimum number of gold coins have come down to us, and that all of them date to the period of the III–VII centuries A.D., then a clear predominance of gold was present in Axumite numismatics during its most spectacular epoch.

Coins were minted according to the Roman standard, which attests to the role of the Roman Empire in Axum's foreign trade. The weight of the gold coins of the first kings (of Endubis, of Aphilas, and in part of Ousanas) was from 2.40 to 2.75 g., which corresponds to the Roman semis (half a gold denarius) of the second half of the III century A.D. In the reign of Ousanas I the weight of the Axumite gold coin fell sharply to 1.70 g., and subsequently fluctuated from 1.70 to 2.19 g. Such a change of weight in the Axumite alado corresponds to the monetary reform of Emperor Constantine in 305–312 A.D. and subsequently to the weight fluctuations of Byzantine gold coins.[172]

The gold of Axumite coins is of extremely high purity. The silver content was of very low quality, sharply differing from the Roman. It seems that this is the same purity that Himyarite and other Arabian coins also had. The weight of silver money fluctuated greatly: from 1 to 3.3 g. There was a still more notable fluctuation in the weight of copper coins, but this was not so important since gold constituted the basis of Axum's monetary system. The relationship of the value of gold, silver, and copper money in the Axumite Kingdom is not known.

By the end of the VII century A.D., gold had almost completely disappeared from money coinage, although the silver and especially the bronze coins were minted to the end of the VIII century A.D. Axum had been cut off from sources of gold. The outward form of Late Axumite coins attests to the declines of monetary affairs. The foreign trade markets had fallen into a decline during the Late Axumite period. However, the caches of Omayyad and Abbassid coins of the end of the VII–X centuries A.D. at Debre Damo[173] speak of continued trade with the caliphate. In the Late Axumite period, newly issued coins were supplemented by old and foreign gold and silver coins.

Significantly, 90 percent of Axumite coins were found in Northern Ethiopia, the remaining ones were found primarily in South Arabia, and only a few of Ezana II's copper coins were found in Egypt. In India, Ceylon, Somalia, and East Africa not a single Axumite coin has been discovered, although Ptolemaic, Roman, Byzantine, Parthian, Sassanide and other coins were found. Roman-Byzantine authors, except Nonnus, connected with Arabic information say nothing of the export of gold from Ethiopia. Evidently only Arabia imported Axumite gold. Cosmas Indicopleustes also confirms this. The minting of its own gold coin may in part have been caused by the wish of the Axumite kings to monopolize the export of gold to South Arabia.

Urbanization and trade routes

In order to evaluate the significance of trade for the Axumite Kingdom it is necessary to define its role in the development of towns. The towns of Ethiopia appeared on sea and land trade routes beginning with the VI–V centuries B.C. The significance of some of these routes had evolved considerably by the end of the Preaxumite period.

Saba, Adulis, and Avalit—the main ports of Preaxumite and Axumite Ethiopia—arose at the intersections of sea and land trade routes. The sea route, from the ports of Egypt and Palestine along the Red Sea to the outlet into the Indian Ocean, was known and used since time immemorial. From the Bab el Mandeb Gulf it continued to the east by two branches: along the African coast to Cape Guardafui [Ras Asir, ancient Aromata], and along the Arabian coast into India and South Iran. At the beginning of the I century B.C., the length of time for sailing along the first of these routes was shortened significantly when Mediterranean sea captains learned to use the trade winds for sailing in the open ocean. By the II century B.C., both ocean routes which branched off from the Red Sea were continued far to the south and to the east—to Zanzibar and northern Viet Nam. The Red Sea coast of Ethiopia turned out to be in direct proximity to the most important sea routes. At the same time it was favorably situated also in relation to continental trade routes.

It is possible that Ptolemaic colonization (in the III century B.C.) had some sort of relationship to the initial rise of Adulis. At the beginning of the VI century A.D., Cosmas Indicopleustes found in Adulis a Greek inscription composed in the name of Ptolemy IV (222–205 B.C.) by some one of his subjects.[174]

Pliny considered runaway Egyptian slaves to be the founders of Adulis: it is possible that the popular etymologizing of the name Αδουλις (δοῦλος) played a role. In Pliny's time (i.e., by the middle of the I century A.D.) Adulis was the "greatest market of the Troglodytes and Ethiopians" and carried on a significant trade.[175]

Claudius Ptolemaeus knew Adulis and correctly enough (with an error common for southern points) defined its position by means of a system of coordinates.[176] Pseudo Arrian calls Adulis "a rather large village" (χώμη), but along with this indicates its growing significance in sea and land trade. The rise to prominence of Adulis is connected with the evolution of the Axumite Kingdom. From Adulis began a significant overland route from the Red Sea to the Nile Valley. From Adulis it led to the town of Coloe (Matara). According to the testimony of Pseudo Arrian, this segment of the route took three days. The following segment of the route, from Coloe to Axum, took five days. The entire route from Adulis to Axum comprised an eight-day journey.[177] Ironically, at the start of the XX century this route still took eight days to complete. Procopius Caesarensis and Photius, according to Nonnus, give larger figures; the former indicates that the route from Adulis to Axum took 12 days,[178] while the latter says 15 days.[179] Evidently these estimates are in error. Coloe (Matara) and Yeha, which had sprung up in the Preaxumite period, were intermediate stations on the route from Adulis to Axum.

From Axum, the caravan route into the Nile Valley went west to the shores of the Tekezze, then farther along the right bank of the river to the ford at Kemalke. Ezana II's troops were moved via this road in the conquest of Nubia. At the ford of Kemalke they were ferried across the Tekezze-Atbara and, continuing the journey to the west along the left bank of the Atbara, they came to the Nile (Sida). From here the Axumite detachments went separate ways upward and downward along the Nile.

An east-west route evidently began near Avalit. Parallel to it, but laid out farther to the south, were east-west routes from the ports of the Indian Ocean: Deiri, Opopi, Malao, and Rapti. Information about them is preserved by Ptolemaeus, Pseudo Arrian, and Cosmas Indicopleustes.

East-west caravan routes were much more numerous than the north-south ones, which had to compete with the Red Sea and Nile routes. Essentially only one land route is known which crossed the entire Nubian Desert and Ethiopia from north to south between the Red Sea and the Nile.

The Adulis inscription speaks definitely about the northern segment of this route: "I made the route from the localities of my kingdom to Egypt safe."[180] Both Cosmas Indicopleustes and Procopius Caesarensis knew the land route from Elephantine to Axum as a journey of days. According to Cosmas, it took 30 [days] travel;[181] according to Procopius, 30 [days] "for an easy (i.e., a good) walker."[182] According to *The Martyrdom of Arethius*, the Byzantine government wanted to send troops into Ethiopia for an alliance with the Axumites[183] via this route but renounced its intention. This route acquired great significance in the Middle Ages.[184] However, its role in the Axumite period should not be exaggerated. According to *Periplus* even the goods from Egyptian Thebes (glass and wine) arrived in Ethiopia by sea.[185] For Ethiopian trade the land route had second-degree or even third-degree significance in comparison with the Red Sea and Nile routes.

Evidently a northwest branch of the Axum-Adulis route existed. It proceeded from the region of Dunqulah, via the oases of Selem, Kufrah, and Jalu, to the shores of the Mediterranean Sea. The end points of this route were Cyrenaica to the north and the Ethiopian plateau to the south. The epistle of Synesius evidently mentions a trade colony of Axumites in the Jalu oasis.

From Axum to the south, the Axum-Adulis route also branched: the main road led through Atagau and Semen to Lake Tana and farther into Sasu. According to Cosmas Indicopleustes, the route from Axum to Sasu comprised a 50-day journey.[186] The number is very approximate. A minor branch of the route led south from Axum to Shoa and farther along the Rift Valley. A third branch of this route led into the region of the African Horn.

Thus Axum was at the junction of a series of caravan routes. This determined its position as an important center of long-distance trade. The trade significance of Axum is emphasized not only by the Roman-Byzantine merchants' visits to it but also by the commercial interests of the Axumite kings. To the south of Axum, in the interior regions of Africa, there were no large trade towns. This alone attests to the fact that Axum derived the principal benefits from trade on the caravan routes which passed through its possessions. Unfortunately, archaeological investigations of the towns of the Axumite Kingdom still do not permit one to compare their significance (in specific, limited segments of time). In many respects it is necessary to rely on scanty, frequently unclear and unreliable data of written sources. Pseudo Arrian knew Coloe (Matara) far better than

Axum, mainly owing to the greater closeness of Coloe to Adulis, where
he himself had visited. Moreover, in the presentation of Pseudo Arrian,
Coloe has greater trade significance than the "metropolis" of Axum. In
the VI century A.D., Nonnus called Axum "a very large town and seemingly
the capital of all Ethiopia." [187] At this time Axum occupied a far larger
area than any other Ethiopian town. Coloe (Matara) greatly lagged
behind it and only with difficulty endured competition from the capital
in long distance trade. Judging by excavations, Tokonda, Kohaito, Yeha,
and Manabiit were rather small towns, even smaller than Coloe in the
Axumite period.

It is difficult to evaluate the role of Ethiopian towns in internal or
local trade about which virtually nothing is known. Adulis and Coloe
(Matara) had an advantage over Axum in the exchange which had arisen
naturally between livestock breeders of the desert valleys and plateau
farmers, since both towns were located on the boundary between them.
Adulis had one additional advantage over Axum and Coloe (Matara)—
a coastal location. However, this advantage should not be exaggerated.
The town was laid out neither on the coast itself nor at the shortest distance
between the sea and the plateau. In this respect Preaxumite Saba and
modern-day Massawa were situated far more favorably than Adulis. Yet
its convenient geographical location created an opportunity for converting
Adulis into a significant trade town. This opportunity became an actuality,
however, not by virtue of geographic but by virtue of historic, economic,
and political reasons. The economic reasons involved the growth of trade
on the caravan routes through Coloe (Matara) and Axum, for which
Adulis was the closest outlet to the sea. Initially, Adulis was probably
singled out from among other coastal settlements because it was the center
of a small established state. Evidently an important local market was
located here.

However, the economic rise of Adulis would have been impossible if
within the country long-distance trade had not begun to be concentrated
on the routes that passed through Axum and Coloe (Matara). With the
formation of the Axumite Kingdom Adulis came under the special protection of Axumite kings, who converted the town into an "officially
established market." [188] By so doing, the Axumite kings attempted to
place the foreign trade of Ethiopia under their own control. Adulis was
obliged to pay feudal tribute after its subjugation to the Axumite kings.
But the benefits which Adulis accrued from its subjugation to Axum were
sufficiently great. The town grew, concentrating more and more trade
inside its own walls, at the expense of neighboring markets which were
falling into decay.

And the more broadly the authority of Axum was propagated, and the
more strictly the will of the Axumite king was fulfilled, the richer Adulis

grew. At first it arose at the expense of other Ethiopian ports; those which lay closest, subsequently more remote ones, and then the ports of South Arabia. Finally the Somali ports began to suffer from competition with Adulis. By the V–VI centuries A.D. their names die out of the trade-geographic descriptions. Adulis becomes a large-scale international port, a stopping point for ships bound for India, Ceylon, and Azania.

The ruins of Adulis occupy a large area comparable only to the area of Axum itself. Remains of three settlements which replaced each other in succession were discovered in Adulis: the comparatively small pre-Christian emporium ("a rather large village"—Pseudo Arrian); then the illustrious town of the IV–VI centuries A.D. (which Cosmas calls "the famous town of the Ethiopians"[189]); and finally a smaller, later town with an VIII century A.D. church. Here several Muslim graves were discovered which belonged to Arab merchants of the first centuries of Islam. Adulis, as a coastal trade center, was probably Christianized earlier than Axum. From the V century A.D. its Christians had their own bishop who served in the basilica. Many foreigners lived in Adulis, mainly merchants and seafarers.

The significance of Ethiopian towns as centers of handicraft production is less clear. While it is possible to speak of the construction, pottery, and jewelry crafts of Axum, Coloe (Matara), and Adulis, it has not been possible to precisely localize other crafts because of little archaeological study. Yet it is reasonable to suggest that not only long-distance trade but also local trade (the exchange of products of animal breeding, agri-culture, hunting, and household crafts) contributed to the evolution of towns.

On the other hand, political factors had an undoubted significance: the role of urban centers as the administrative focus of the territory which surrounded them. In this regard, of course, Axum, which was not only the center of its own region but also the capital of the entire Axumite realm, enjoyed an enormous advantage. The enormous riches which flowed into Axum, in the form of war spoils, tribute, forced labor, and trade profits, permitted the kings, the nobility, and the churches to under-take extensive construction and to attract skillful master craftsmen. The weakening of the urban nobility in connection with changes in the political situation and the decline of foreign trade must have quickly affected the fate of the artisans who served it. Even the brushwood gatherers in the neighboring mountains depended on the prosperity of the urban popu-lation.

The Christianization of Ethiopia strengthened the cultural and cult significance of the towns of the Axumite period. A church appeared in each town. Axum acquired the significance of the religious center of the country. In many cases the churches were built on the site of traditional sanctuaries, especially when those sanctuaries were located in Axumite towns. The most ancient monasteries in Ethiopia arose not in the "wildernesses" but close to populated points on the important caravan routes (in Axum, in Hagar-Najran, etc.).

Thus the towns of the Axumite Kingdom were centers of political, religious, and cultural life and also centers of long-distance trade. Moreover, churches and palaces which were built in the middle of the towns represented fortresses in which neighboring inhabitants were protected from hostile invasions. Economic and political reasons are closely intertwined in determining the fate of towns of the Axumite period.

Summary

The development of mercantile relationships in the Axumite Kingdom should not be exaggerated. The sphere of their operation was extended primarily over secondary branches of the economic system and affected agriculture very little. Basically the economy of Axum remained provincial. Small-scale subsistence production predominated. The peasantry was subject to an essentially feudal exploitation, the degree of which was still relatively small. They paid tribute or tax to the king and to the aristocracy, and participated in mass construction operations. The role of slave labor was not large and was limited to the household. Moreover, familial status of the domestic slave should be taken into consideration. Throughout the course of the Axumite era powerful remnants of a primitive (egalitarian) social structure were preserved. They were, however, probably stronger at the beginning of the period than at the end. We find that in Axum the formation of a class society was a prolonged process complicated by close and constant contact with egalitarian societies. This process was begun in the Preaxumite period and ended in the late Middle Ages, having ultimately led to the formation of a developed feudal society in Northern and Central Ethiopia. At the same time, the less-developed peoples of these and neighboring territories experienced the strongest influence from the direction of feudal Ethiopia.

IV

Political Organization
of the Axumite State

Historical development

In Axum, as in other early feudal societies, the first elements of a state organization developed in the course of the transformation of certain traditional institutions which had been inherited from an egalitarian social structure. The peoples' militia of tribal members was transformed into a feudal army. The institution of the tribal leader, the head of the people, its spokesman before real and imaginary forces, evolved into an early feudal monarchy.

Up until the IV–V centuries A.D. the state was in the process of formation; it was already carrying out its social functions but was still enmeshed by remnants of the primitive [egalitarian] social structure. This was true for all institutions of the Axumite state: the monarchy, the army, the officials. An analysis of social relationships in the Axumite Kingdom inevitably leads to the conclusion that a state organization was needed to keep subjugated people in a state of obedience, for the exploitation of the lower strata of the Axumite people themselves, for the repulsing of foes from new boundaries, for the extraction of trade profits and duties, and for maintaining the security and monopoly of trade routes.

During the time of the XIII–XIX dynasties of Egypt (XV–XIII centuries B.C.) there were tribal leaders in the country of Punt whom the Egyptians called kings and who possessed material attributes of their authority. In the Preaxumite period (V century B.C.–I century A.D.), the first states arose on the territory of Ethiopia. In the inscriptions there appears the word "king" (*mlk*); and depictions of the attributes of royal authority have been preserved. The traditional authority of the tribal leader, which personified and brought about the unity of the people, was being turned into the state institution of a monarchy. The process of turning the tribal leader into a monarch, which was begun in the Preaxumite period, was completed in the Axumite period.

The very residence of the Axumite king graphically demonstrates his power, authority, and inaccessibility to the people. The monarchy was the most important organ of the young Axumite state, the center around which

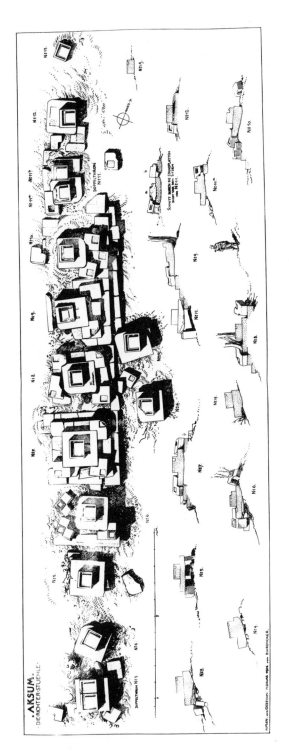

The stone thrones of Axum.

all elements of state organization were grouped and developed. Under monarchy we mean not only the person of the king himself (who was surrounded by a definite ritual, by ideas, by privileges, by authority and power) but also the whole assemblage of individuals who were provided with political authority by virtue of their closeness to the king. Here belong the mother of the Axumite king, his wives, brothers, kinsmen, courtiers, and confidential servants. The main (but not the sole!) representative of the monarchy was the Axumite king. He was, first of all, the military leader of the Axumites and the general of the Axumite militia. The greater part of Axumite campaigns known to us were carried out under the personal leadership of the king. The Axumite king, whose inscription Cosmas Indicopleustes copied, repeatedly speaks about his personal participation in campaigns.[1] Ezana II himself usually set out[2] on a campaign at the head of his troops. Only for the conquering of the rebelling Beja did Ezana I send troops under the command of his brothers.[3] Kings Gedara and Ella Asbeha sometimes personally led campaigns into Yemen, sometimes sent other individuals. Recently discovered inscriptions of Kaleb and Wazeb communicate that on campaigns these kings exercised supreme command, sending separate detachments on raids or heading them up at decisive moments. Two gold spears and a shield may have been the symbol of the military (and also the sacral) authority of the king.

At the same time the Axumite king was the supreme head of the Axumite people, their official representative before all real and imaginary forces. The king received foreign embassies. In intercourse with the gods he also came forward as the representative of the entire people. Gradually the king acquired unprecedented administrative authority. The will of the king was becoming the law, and was placed on the same footing with laws sanctified by custom. In the period of florescence of the Axumite Kingdom, the king began to intervene in matters of political succession in Axum's vassal possessions. In South Arabia, Ella Asbeha made Sumafa Ashwa of the Yazan family (which did not belong to the royal dynasty) the Himyarite king.[4] In Najran he named the son of Arethius the ethnarch, and introduced Ethiopian military colonies into Arabia.

Quite possibly Sumafa was connected with the Himyarite dynasty by marriage[5] but, if Ella Asbeha had so wished, more legal pretenders to the Himyar throne could have been found. Indeed, according to *The Book of the Himyarites* he sent 50 members of the Himyarite dynasty[6] into Ethiopia. Evidently the king could essentially "readjust" the traditional order. However, the king scarcely used the same authority on Axumites who had full rights. Nevertheless, by the end of the Axumite period, the former royal dynasties had completely disappeared from the territory of the Axumite Kingdom. Ultimately, the Axumite kings acquired such authority that they replaced vassal monarchs with their own deputies.

It would be incorrect, however, to represent the Axumite king, even in the florescent period of the Axumite Kingdom, in the form of a virtually absolute monarch. The governmental structure of Axum retained too many remnants of an egalitarian society for this to have been true. The development of feudal attitudes and feudal government organization, to the detriment of the tribal relationships, led at first to a consolidation of the king's authority over the tribes subject to him, but later (in the VIII–IX centuries A.D.) to the growth of feudal separatism and political splintering. The study of titles and privileges of the king and his officials permits one, to a certain extent, to trace the development of Axumite governmental structure and to understand many facts of Ethiopia's history.

The title of the king

The title "king of Axum" or "king of the Axumites" was the basic title of the Axumite kings in all periods. The latter form is usual in Greek (βασιλεὺς τῶν Αξουμειτῶν, βασιλευς τῶν Αξωμιτῶν) and Sabaean texts throughout the Axumite period. One also encounters in the Sabaean texts of all periods the name "king of the Abyssinians." And in Greek texts one sees "king of Ethiopia," but only in the comparatively late period (if we do not consider Ezana I's bilingual inscription, then the Axumite ruler was called the "king of Ethiopia" only in the V–VI centuries A.D.).

In the texts in the Ge'ez language (beginning with Gedara)[7] the Axumite king—in the shortest form—was called "the king of Axum" (properly "nagashi" of Axum). Undoubtedly, this form has the meaning of "king of the Axumites." And the Greek and Sabaean translations of the title are completely faithful: for the vassal rulers the title "negush" ("negus") was used.[8] The kinglets of the Beja, each of whom had on the average 600–700 subjects,[9] were also called in that manner. In the Greek text they were called kinglets (βασιλισχός) in distinction from king (βασιλεὺς) of Axum. The inscription from Anza, a small principality, was composed in the name of the king of the Angabo.[10] In three inscriptions (the Pseudo-Sabaean ones of Ezana II and Kaleb [Ella Asbeha]) the kings of the Aguezat who succeeded one another are mentioned in succession.[11] But probably the difference between nagashi and negush (negus) was not considered expecially serious.

Having attained unprecedented power, the Axumite kings tried to symbolize their new role with a new title. The subjugation of South Arabia permitted the Axumite kings to add to their former title the titles of the Himyarite kings: "[King] of Himer (Himyar) and Raydan and Saba and Salhen (the palace of the Sabaean kings)." In the VI century A.D. to this title was added the following part of the title of the Himyar kings: "(King) of the High Plateau and Yamanat and Tihamat and Hadramaut and all their Arabs." In that part of the royal title, right between *Raydan* and *Saba*, both Ethiopian texts of Ezana I's bilingual inscription introduce the name of the country of Habashat. In the Greek text of the bilingual inscription, this name is rendered as Ethiopia.[12] The Axumite Kingdom is designated by either of these words. The former (Habashat) is used among the Sabaeans, Himyarites, and Arabs, and the latter (Ethiopia) is used among the Greeks. However, in the case under consideration the region of the Red Sea coast of South Arabia named Habashat (a foothold of Axum's authority) is meant. Significantly, the expanded title with the mention of Habashat (or Ethiopia) is contained only in Ezana I's bilingual inscription, intended first of all for the foreign reader.

It is interesting to trace how the title of the head of the Axumite state became complicated over time. Gedara in his very brief inscription is called simply the "king of Axum." Later this original title designated the ruler on the Axumite coins. The Greek equivalent of this title—king of the Axumites (βασιλεὺς τῶν ᾽Αξωμειτῶν) also is typical of Axumite coins. In Sembruthes' inscription it is encountered only in a somewhat complicated form.

The unknown king who left the Greek inscription in Meroe calls himself only "king of the Axumites and Omerites (Himyarites)."[13] This is a brief designation of the African and Arabian possessions of Axum at that time. After the subjugation of Meroe, the royal title displayed the name Kasu (the Meroitic Kingdom). Evidently the conqueror of Meroe, a predecessor of Ezana I, assumed it just as he also assumed the name of the Beja and Siamo.

Ezana II's title is virtually no different from that of Ezana I. However, Ethiopia-Habashat does not figure in it.[14] The title of Kaleb (Ella Asbeha) is twice as extensive: "King of Axum and Himyar and Du Raydan and Saba and Salhen and the High Plateau and Yamanat and Tihamat and Hadramaut and all their Arabs and Beja and Noba and Kasu and Siamo and Darabat [and] ----t of the country of Asfai (?), slave of Christ, etc., etc."[15] His son Wazeb bore the title "King of Axum and Du Raydan and Saba and Salhen and Beja and Kasu and Siamo and Waitag (?), the slave of Christ, etc., etc."[16]

After the rise of an imperial Axumite Kingdom, its kings assumed a higher title—*nagasha nagasht* (ንጉሠ፡ ነገሥት, *king of kings*). It is encountered in all of the Ezana I and Ezana II inscriptions as the designation of their rank at the very end of the detailed royal title.[17] In the Sabaean inscriptions of Ezana I and II the construction ንጉሠ ፡ ነገሥት is translated as *mlk mlkn*; in the Greek inscription as βασιλεὺς βασιλέων.[18] The Greek inscription of King Sembruthes calls him the "king out of kings (βασιλεὺς ἐχ βασιλέων) of the Axumites."[19] Most likely this is an inaccurate translation of the title "king of kings." This title is not encountered again in the Axumite sources; however, it is authenticated in the Middle Ages and in modern times.[20]

The title "king of kings" had great ideological significance. In the first place, it indicated that the Axumite king occupied the same such position in respect to other subject rulers (kings) as they themselves occupied in respect to their subjects. In the second place, it demonstrated his superiority over the independent kings of neighboring countries. Only the Roman emperor (and later the emperor of the Eastern Roman Empire), the ruler of Iran, and the king of Northern India proved to be individuals of rank equal to him. In the third place, the title "king of kings" was highly reminiscent of the designation of a supreme deity or even of the sole god. This strengthened the sacral character of the royal authority and surrounded it with a still greater halo of divinity.

The florescence of the Axumite Kingdom began at the end of the II century A.D. By that time the title of "king of kings" was preserved as the highest title of the most powerful eastern monarchs (of Northern India, the Persian power, Armenia, Palmyra) with whom Axum was developing trade and other relations. Drewes[21] proposes that the title of "king of kings" was first assumed by Sembruthes after the Roman-Persian war of 296–297 A.D., in which the Axumites probably took part on the side of the Persians. However, this suggestion is scarcely well-founded. Axum, as we saw above, had entered into dealings with the states of the Near East and West Asia for several decades prior to 296 A.D. Nevertheless, it is entirely possible that Sembruthes was the first Axumite "king of kings." It would not be surprising, however, if it turned out as a result of future ethnohistoric research that one of Sembruthes' predecessors already had taken the title of "king of kings." This title put the Axumite king of the III century A.D. on a par with the most powerful rulers of the east.

The feminine equivalent of this title is *negeshta nagashtat*, "queen of queens" (known also in Sassanide Iran). Evidently only one woman in Ethiopia was thus called: the mother of the "king of kings" and after her the wife (or one of the wives?). The title of "queen of queens" was first authenticated only in the XVII century A.D. (by Almeida).[22] But it probably was inherited from the Axumite period, just as was the title "king of kings."

However, the title "king of Axum" remained the basic one even in the late period of the Axumite Kingdom. Probably the fact that former kings —vassals of the supreme king of Axum—disappeared facilitated the title's tenacity.

It is interesting to trace how this is reflected in the Greek sources. Philostorgius, who visited in Axum as a diplomat between 340 and 346 A.D., calls the Axumite king the "tyrant" (τύραννος, i.e., the monarch), but the king of the Himyarites, who was subject to him, the "ethnarch" ('εθναρχος, i.e., the tribal leader).[23] For Cosmas Indicopleustes (VI century A.D.) only one king (βασιλευς) exists. He calls the rulers of Adulis and Agau "arhonts."[24] His contemporary Nonnus (according to Joannes Malalae) calls the ruler of Axum the "king" (βασιλεὺς)[25] and those close to him he calls "members of the council, nobles-advisers" (συγχλητιχος). The same word usage is also encountered in Theophanes the Byzantine.[26] In Ezana II's inscription about the campaign into Nubia, and probably in Wazeb's inscription, some sort of noble personages from among non-Axumites are called "leaders" or "nobles" (masfan, plural masāfant).[27] This term was also known in the XIV century A.D. and later. Significantly all of the titles of feudal rulers of Northern and Central Ethiopia, authenticated in the XII–XIV centuries A.D. after the fall of the Axumite Kingdom, bore a typically "bureaucratic" character. These include hadani (nourisher, feeder, benefactor), aqābē sa'āt (observer of the hours), tsahafalam (ṣaḥāfē-lahm, registrar of cattle), makonnen (ruler), masafen (noble). They are clearly not of royal but of functionary origin.

Symbols of royal authority

The symbols of authority of Axumite kings can only be judged on the basis of extremely scanty data. These include depictions on coins, drawings in The Christian Topography of Cosmas Indicopleustes, descriptions of the reception of the Byzantine embassy by the Axumite king in Joannes Malalae's Chronographia, and a few archaeological materials.

On coins, Axumite kings are depicted with a fillet and (or) a crown on their heads. In their ears (or only in the right ear) an earring is shown. On their arms they wear bracelets and in their hands they hold one or two spears and a palm branch. These representations bear a markedly official character. It is possible, therefore, to propose that all the objects mentioned served as symbols of royal status. Ethnographic parallels, especially in Ethiopia and Eastern Sudan, confirm this notion. One of the Axumite stelae is decorated with a depiction of two spears.[28] On coins of the Late Axumite period the spear or palm branch in the hands of the king is replaced by a crook with a cross at the top. Other symbols of royal authority were the crown and the throne, depictions of which were preserved on late coins. Joannes Malalae tells also about the gold turban of Ella Asbeha.[29] Ethnographic parallels also confirm the significance of these objects as symbols of the royal authority.

The idolization of the king

The Axumite king was considered a son or direct descendant of the god Mahrem. Ezana (I and II) is called in the inscriptions "the son of Mahrem" or "the son of the unconquerable Mahrem."[30] The Greek inscription calls him "the son of the invincible god Ares,"[31] identifying the ancient Greek

Ares with the Axumite Mahrem. The king who left the Adulis inscription says: "All these peoples I conquered by the grace of my most great god Ares who fathered me. ... "[32] Yahveh spoke in precisely the same way to the king of Israel: "Thou art my son; this day have I begotten thee."[33] It is well known that religious themes of the Old Testament of the Bible were kindred to the religious themes of the ancient Semite-pagan peoples of Arabia and Ethiopia. South Arabian kings were also considered sons of the supreme tribal god. The *muqarrib* of Qataban was called "the first born (the first-born son) of the god Anbai."[34] And the king of Ausan was called "the son of the god, Vadd."[35]

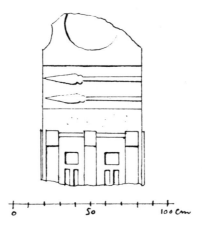

Upper part of an Axumite stele.

In medieval Ethiopia, and also in Janjero, a comparison of the king with the sun or a star was widespread. The king, the earthly incarnation of the heavenly gods, himself became a living god. Moreover, he eclipsed many heavenly gods who were merged into the single image of Mahrem. Since, the very image of Mahrem began to be conceived of as a reflection in the sky of the great king of kings, the mighty Axumite monarch, then the living king evidently also was merged with the image of the god. Perhaps upon dying, the Axumite king himself became Mahrem, and his son became the reigning son of Mahrem. It is, therefore, understandable that Ezana II had every reason to substitute in his title the name of his father (Ella Amida) for the name of Mahrem. Instead of the traditional slogan "son of Mahrem unconquerable by foes" he gives the expression "son of Ella Amida unconquerable by foes."[36] This was an attempt on his part to respond to his conversion to a monotheistic and Christian religion, by deleting mention of the name of Mahrem. But his "lord of the heavens" continued to be called "unconquerable by foes."[37] He does this despite the fact that the substitution mars the style of the inscription, bringing into it an intolerable repetition. Probably the name of Ella Amida remained the only possible substitute for the name of Mahrem. In the title of Kaleb (Ella Asbeha) and his son Wazeb the slogan "slave of Christ unconquerable by the foe" is encountered.[38]

It is unknown whether divine honors were rendered to the king during his life. After his death, his grave became the object of a cult. Burial vaults of Axumite kings were and are held sacred as religious monuments. In Christian medieval Ethiopia the king was surrounded by ritual and religious notions typical of idolized kings. It is possible that such notions already existed in the Axumite period, although not exactly in the same form as in the Middle Ages. The emperor Zara Yaqob introduced ritual obligatory for priestly kings and revived certain Axumite customs. The prohibition on approaching the monarch (*Brief Chronicles*[39]) dates to the times of Aizur,[40] one of the Axumite kings. This was done in order to protect ordinary people from the harmful power of the royal touch. Many features of this traditional ritual are connected with remnants of tribal structure in the dynastic customs of Axum. For example, one may see it in the custom of election of the king.

In the governmental structure of Axum undoubted vestiges of a tribal, egalitarian society are observable. They include remnants of a military democracy in the organization of the army, remains of a peoples' assembly, and a council of elders. At the same time, the Axumite monarchy was enmeshed by many remnants of intertribal relationships. To these belong the custom of the co-reigning of a king and a queen (who was the mother, sister, or daughter of the king), the special position of the king's brothers and his kinsmen, and the custom of electing the king by an oracle in the presence of the council of elders.

The position of the queen mother

The custom of the joint rule of a consanguineously related king and queen has extremely ancient roots. It is widespread throughout Africa. It was authenticated in ancient and medieval Nubia (in Napata and Meroe), in the Christian states, among the Shilluk and the peoples of South Gezira, and in Southwestern Ethiopia. The earliest information about the ruling of women in Axum is connected with legends about the origin of the Axumite Kingdom. They refer to an Ethiopian queen identified with the biblical queen of Sheba.

The most ancient and most popular of the legends of this cycle is contained in *Kebra Nagast*, where a surprising custom is told about which existed at a time when Ethiopia was supposedly still under the rule of the Jewish king Solomon (IX century B.C.). In those times "in the country of Ethiopia only a woman—a young girl who had not known [had relations with] men—could reign." Only Makeda, an Ethiopian queen, whom *Kebra Nagast* identifies with the queen of Sheba and with the Nubian *candace* [queen mother], changed this custom. She transmitted the throne to her son and decreed that "from now on in Ethiopia men will reign but women will not reign."[41] In the image of Makeda two historical personages appear to have been merged: the queen, mother of the first Ethiopian king David ibn Hakim (or Menelik I of the very late legends), and a young queen who was the sister and wife of a sacred king (who to avoid incest would not have been able to have children). *Kebra Nagast* presents Makeda as the sole ruler of the country. It is more likely, however, that ancient Ethiopian queens were *co-rulers* of the state, side by side with their sons and brothers (the kings of the legendary period). The story of Tyrranius Rufinus, who witnessed Axum at its height, definitely has in view the Axumite queen who ruled the country jointly with her son:

"Dying, the king [of Axum] *left as heirs to the throne his wife and young son.* To the youths (Aedesius and Frumentius) he granted full freedom. . . . However, the queen, not having more faithful friends in all the kingdom, urgently beseeched them to share with her the cares of ruling the country up to the time of the majority of her son. She especially asked Frumentius about this. . . . When the young child-king had grown up . . . the youths again returned to our (Roman) world, although the queen and her son repeatedly tried to keep them, asking them to stay."[42]

The queen was able to eclipse her co-ruler son only because he was very young. A grown and sufficiently energetic king was always the first personage in Axum. However, from Rufinus' tale it is evident that the authority of the queen-mother was retained while "the king was under age."

The title of the Ethiopian queen—*negeshta nagashtat*, "queen of queens"—is revealing. It can be compared with the title of Cleopatra, who was called the "queen of kings."[43] Possibly the Ethiopian formula of the title reflects the notion of ancient Axumites about the queen: that she was the sovereign of all the women of the kingdom. A similar conception is widespread among many African peoples.

The position of the king's brothers

Certain data indicate a special status for the Axumite king's brothers. Perhaps it involves the participation of an elder brother in the ruling of the state. The letter of the Roman emperor Constantius II is addressed not only to King Ezana I but also to his brother, She'azana. At the end of the letter, the emperor calls them simply "most honorable brothers," not singling out either of them and everywhere addressing both of them in the same way. The Alexandrine Monophysite bishop, Athanasius the Great, citing this letter, calls "Aizana" (Ezana I) and "Saizana" (She'azana) "most honorable brothers" and "sovereigns of Axum."[44] At the same time the official Axumite inscriptions were composed in the name of King Ezana I alone. She'azana, known to us from the letter, and also another brother—Hadefa—figure in one of these inscriptions. This is the famous three-language inscription about the resettlement of the Beja tribes bearing a decidedly official, international character. She'azana and Hadefa headed the Axumite forces in the campaign against the Beja.[45]

The king's brothers occupied a special position in Nubia, and also in the states of Southern Ethiopia. It is compelling to think that such an order also existed in ancient Axum. Possibly under its influence, the concept of the "brother kings" who ruled simultaneously in Ethiopia was built up. It is encountered in Constantius' letter and in Athanasius the Great's *Apologia*. The legend of the "brother kings," Abreha and Asbeha, "the baptizers of Ethiopia," is a final echo of it. Asbeha is the historical Ella Asbeha, an Axumite king of the early part of the VI century A.D. His name is well-known from Byzantine sources, Ethiopian legends, and Axumite inscriptions. Abreha is a contemporary of Ella Asbeha. He was a Yemenite king, an Ethiopian by birth, and a vassal of Axum.[46] He is known from Byzantine, Syrian, and Arabic sources.

The historic Abreha, however, was neither a brother nor a kinsman of Ella Asbeha. Late tradition made them brothers since they were contemporaries, occupied an approximately equal position, and because both were protectors of Christianity and spread it into Ethiopia and Arabia. Judging by everything, the legend of the "brother kings" was the creation of Syrian-Egyptian clergy. However, it is possible that it was created under the impression of actual facts; possibly the brothers (or one older brother of the king) played an important role in ruling the Axumite Kingdom. It is no wonder that (besides Abreha and Asbeha) some of the "Lists of Kings" name pairs of brother kings. Arfed and Amsi and Za Zigen and Za Rema are two such pairs. Strong and energetic kings in the heyday of the Axumite Kingdom possessed enormous authority, yet official etiquette placed the brother side by side with the Axumite king (in particular Ezana I).[47]

Our attention is drawn to the fact that all the campaigns of Axum which are known to us were carried out under the leadership either of the king himself or of his sons and brothers. The unknown king who left the Adulis inscription says about neighboring peoples that he conquered some by himself, while others were conquered by a chosen emissary, but precisely whom he does not say.[48] Ella Asbeha sent an expedition against Abreha under the leadership of an individual whom Procopius calls a kinsman of the king.[49] Perhaps this was an uncle on his father's side, the brother of the dead king. Joannes Malalae believed that Ella Asbeha placed a king "out of his family" over the Himyarites.[50] Joannes, as usual, confused both the fact itself and the king's name. But, perhaps a kinsman of the king actually was the vice-regent of Ella Asbeha or the leader of the Axumites in Himyar—perhaps the very same one Procopius speaks about.

Probably only a king, his son, or his brother (i.e., a person of corresponding rank: a future king, a brother of the reigning monarch, or his uncle—the brother of his predecessor) could lead the Axumite army. This rule may be a remnant of the ancient order of succession to the throne. It is well-known in dynastic customs of other states, especially African ones.

Order of succession to the throne

Ethiopian historical tradition maintains that in Axum the royal title and throne were inherited through the male line from father to son. The "Lists of Kings" give the characteristic formula of succession: "such a king fathered such [a king]." Only the brother-kings (Abreha and Asbeha, Arfed and Amsi, Za Zigen and Za Rema—of which supposedly the second in each pair succeeded the first) constitute an exception. Probably a childless king could be succeeded by his brother.

Byzantine sources speak of the transmission of the throne from father to son in Axum. Tyrranius Rufinus relates that Aedesius and Frumentius first served a certain Ethiopian king and then his minor son who had inherited the throne. *The Life of St. Grigentius* asserts that Ellesboam (Ella Asbeha) gave the throne to his son Atherphotam (?) and he himself withdrew to the high mountain of Ophar (the desert of Afar?). According to Muslim tradition, Ella Saham also voluntarily renounced the throne.[51] About the medieval king Lalibela, it is said that in old age he renounced the throne in favor of his son and became a hermit in the desert.[52] Most likely this is a pious fiction. But it cannot be ruled out that information about an actual custom underlies it. It is possible that in old age the Axumite kings were removed from the throne. In the pagan period they could even have been killed, whereas after the Christianization of Ethiopia aged kings became hermits. The significant duration of the reign of many kings would seem to testify against such an assumption. The Axumite king Sembruthes composed an inscription in the twenty-fourth year of his reign.[53] The author of the Adulis inscription composed it in the twenty-seventh year of his reign.[54] The "Lists of Kings" give still more prolonged reigns.

However, if the king came to the throne at the age of 13 to 25 and reigned 25 or 30 more years, then he would have attained advanced maturity but not old age. In Ethiopian literature the image of the aged king is entirely absent. It remains unclear whether the Axumite king had the right to occupy the throne into old age or whether the aged king was removed from the throne. However, upon ascending the throne the king was obliged to prove his strength and manliness in combat with wild animals, which evidently was considered a guarantee of the health and prosperity of the Axumite people.

Election of the king

In the chronicle of the Emperor Baeda Maryam (1468–1478 A.D.), a description is given of the rites which by tradition accompanied the ascending of the Axumite kings to the throne. Baeda Maryam, an in-significant figure, was the son of the famous Zara Yaqob (1434–1468 A.D.). For the first time in the later history of this country Zara Yaqob turned it into a centralized state. He grounded his reforms in an idealized notion about the Axumite Kingdom and the authority of Axumite kings, of whom he considered himself the heir and descendant. Zara Yaqob resumed the coronation of the emperors in Axum and tried to restore its archaic ritual, the founding of which is ascribed to the legendary Axumite king Gebre Meskal. When Emperor Baeda Maryam came to Axum for the coronation he found out about the old rite. Here is how the chronicle describes it: "And the king [Baeda Maryam] went into 'the house of vow-taking.' To him were led a buffalo and a lion according to the ancient custom in order that he strike them with his hand. But our King Baeda Maryam refused to strike them and ordered another to kill the buffalo but to let the lion live, as did his father [Zara Yaqob] in [that same] town of Axum when he carried out the rite of vow-taking."[55]

The emperor agreed to undergo the last rite—the taking of a second royal or throne name. Evidently the rite of vow-taking was considered not an additional rite, but rather a completion ceremony. A comparison with customs of the peoples of Southwestern Ethiopia make compre-hensible the significance of this archaic Axumite rite.[56] Evidently the Axumites of Zara Yaqob's and Baeda Maryam's time were trying, at the wish of these kings, to revive the custom of "election" of the king by wild animals.

"The house of vow-taking," as a place where the combat took place, resembles the special location where the sacred kings of Southwest Ethiopia kept their sacred animals, which were ferocious toward all strangers but obedient to them. There are reasons to assume that this custom existed in ancient Axum. When it was proposed that Zara Yaqob and Baeda Maryam fight with the lion it implied that the lions were kept in captivity according to the customs of ancient Axum. Lions kept in captivity are mentioned in one more place in Baeda Maryam's chronicle. This is where the emperor commands "the keepers of the lions" to set them on the bulls, again according to ancient Axumite custom.[57] Moreover, the comment of Cosmas Indicopleustes about the fact that he saw in the palace of the Axumite king giraffes and elephants[58] has been preserved, as well as those of Nonnus (in Joannes Malalae's transcription) about domesticated elephants.[59] The keeping of lions, leopards, and snakes in the royal palace was connected with the "election" of the king by wild animals.

If the "election" of the Axumite king by animals finds parallels in Southwestern Ethiopia, then the rite of vow-taking leads west and north-west from Axum into the zone of ancient Nubian civilization. The rite of vow-taking consisted of the emperor pulling out one of three small tablets with royal names marked on them (Gebre Meskal, David, and Kwast-antinos), taking the name thus chosen.[60]

Significantly, all three royal names belonged to legendary monarchs of the Axumite period: Gebre Meskal, to whom the establishment of the rite is attributed; David (he is also Menelik), the son of Solomon; and Kwastantinos (Constantine), whose reign according to Ethiopian tradition was especially prolonged.

No less significant is the circumstance that the selection took place in the presence of Axumite elders. As the chronicle writer emphasizes, participation in the rite of vow-taking was the privilege of 12 "lawyers" (ሊቃውንት ፡ አክሱም), the descendants of the Axumite tribal aristocracy. "And the king (Baeda Maryam) carried out the entire ceremony of vow-taking with only certain lawyers, without other people," whereas to other rites of the coronation were admitted not only the "lawyers" but also two or three of the king's attendants.[61] We may conjecture that the rite of vow-taking was a remnant of the actual election of the Axumite king by the council of elders, whose descendants were represented by the "lawyers." In such a case, the tablets with the royal names were originally intended not for one but for several candidates and it was not the pretender to the throne but the elders who performed the selection. The king of the Shilluk was chosen similarly, only special stones, not tablets, were used in the selection.[62] The king was elected by the council of elders with the participation of the people's assembly.[63] In ancient Nubia, the priests and elders elected the king with the formal participation of the people's assembly. Moreover, they called on the oracle and omens.[64]

In the states of Southwest Ethiopia, in Kaffa, Janjero, and others, the choice of the king was made by the council of elders. In contrast to the Sudan, here the people's assembly did not participate in the election of the king. Also the drawing of lots (which the "election" of the king by wild animals represented) was unknown. In Axum the people were com-pletely removed from participation in the rite.

Of course all this is nothing more than a theory whose hypothesis can be formulated in the following form: the legends about the Axumite kings preserved by medieval Ethiopian literature, in comparison with ethnographic material, permit one to propose that the kings of ancient Axum were elected by the council of elders and that the ritual of election was extremely close to the corresponding ritual among ancient and modern-day peoples of Northeast Africa.

It is difficult to present the real significance of the described customs in the social organization of Axum. There is no doubt that they were not an empty formality. Remnants of the tribal structure in dynastic customs bore, in themselves, the indelible stamp of an egalitarian infrastructure in competition with the new governmental order. They were essential "amendments" to the personal monarchical authority of the king. Limiting the monarchy, they slowed the development of a fully feudal state organization. The primary benefits of such a situation accrued not to the ordinary tribal membership but to the nobility: the king's mother, his brothers, kinsmen, and the elders. The tribal nobility acquired the means for influencing policy in the developing state.

The council of nobles

As was noted above, the election of the Axumite king occurred in the presence of the council of elders, or council of nobles. Many data compel one to propose that not only in early Axum but also during the florescence of the Axumite Kingdom the council of nobles was an influential organ of authority.

When Ella Asbeha occupied Himyar, a dual government was established in the country. Side by side with the indigenous administration and authority of the Himyarite king, an Axumite administration appeared. There are data which indicate that before Abreha usurped the authority, a council of nobles (who were the leaders of the colonists) headed it. *The Book of the Himyarites* mentions "noble Abyssinians" who were left with the Himyarite king by the Axumite king "in order to protect him from enemies."[65] They figure as some kind of entity, although they are not called a "council of nobles." *The Life of St. Grigentius* describes the council of nobles in more detail. In the capital of Himyar (Zafar) the king Ellesboam (Ella Asbeha) "summoned all of his megistans and satraps,[66] who constituted an assembly under the presidency of the most holy one [Bishop Grigentius]."[67] Bishop Grigentius headed the council of nobles only because the nagashi was located outside Himyar or because he intended to abandon it. Otherwise the council would have been obliged to sit under the presidency of the king.

In one of Ezana II's inscriptions there is a communication about the fact that during the campaign "the kings of the armies" (ንጉሥት ፡ ሰራዊት)[68] were convened by the king into a council. Littman proposed viewing them as the rulers of separate provinces. Some of the rulers bore (in medieval

and modern Abyssinia) the title of "negus" (ንጉሥ).[69] He also made
another proposition. Since among the names of the Axumite armies are
encountered the names of tribes (*Stammesnamen*), then the leaders of these
armies possibly were the kings or leaders of the tribes.[70] He translates
the expression ንጉሥ : ሰራዊት as *Fürsten der Truppen* (princes of the
armies).

It is entirely probable that the ancient Axumites organized the hierarchical units of the army along consanguineal lines, preserving the
integrity not only of families but also of tribes, and that the leaders of these
tribes were called kings (ንጉሥ). But there is not sufficient reason to
identify these supposed kings with "the kings of the armies" of Ezana II.
Furthermore, among the names of the armies there are no names of vassal
kingdoms, or "provinces" as Littman calls them. Therefore, the inscription
could only be speaking of kings of tribes or communities of the Axumite
Kingdom proper.

In the campaign, the kings of the armies evidently formed a council
under the Axumite king, or his representative—the supreme commander.
In the inscription of Alhan Nahfan II, his dealings with Gedara and
"the leaders of the expeditionary corps of Abyssinians"[71] are spoken of.
Evidently these were the same kings of the armies who, just as under
Ezana II, were summoned to the sitting of the council.

The council of Axumite military leaders, and nobles beyond the boundaries of Ethiopia, could only be a copy of the council in Axum itself.
Byzantine diplomats who visited the Axumite Kingdom knew about the
council's existence. Otherwise it would be incomprehensible why Joannes
Malalae, describing the reception of the Byzantine mission in Axum,
mentioned the council under the Axumite king. The Axumite king stood
in a huge chariot decorated with gold and drawn by four elephants. The
war spears and shields of his advisers and retinue and of the council surrounded him. In the make-up of the embassy to Alexandria the Axumite
king assigned "two of his advisers" (or "senators," συγχλητιχος).[72] Early
Muslim tradition recorded by authors of the VIII century A.D. and preserved in Tabari relates that the Kureishites, at the beginning of the VII
century A.D., sent an embassy with gifts "to the nagashi and his patricians
(بطارقته)."[73] However, the Axumite nagashi surrounded by the patricians
suspiciously resembled the Byzantine emperor Heraclius in those same
sources. Unfortunately, Axumite inscriptions do not mention either the
council of nobles or the court posts which could have been the privileges of
the council members. In addition to foreign sources, only the late legends
about the Axumite kings recorded in medieval Ethiopian books speak of
this.

The chronicle writer of Emperor Baeda Maryam relates that when the
emperor was in Axum a special stone was shown to him on which the ancient

kings sat in state in the council of the nobles. A second such stone was intended for the metropolitan. Twelve lawyers, descendants of the ancient Axumite nobility, were arranged on twelve stones to the right and to the left of the king and the metropolitan. "There were also other stones there" notes the chronicle writer.[74] In 1520 A.D. the Portuguese Alvares saw in Axum "12 stone easy-chairs" as well made from stone as if they had been made of wood; they were for "12 judges of the chief priest Joannes."[75] The stone thrones of Axum, investigated in detail by Daniel Krencker, were being spoken of. Alvares was also shown "the stone on which the bishop sat."[76] However, the legend itself, which depicts the Axumite king surrounded by the council of elders, interests us. It is possible that it dates to Early Axumite times.

Kebra Nagast contains another legend. According to this work, the biblical king Solomon sent to Ethiopia his son by an Ethiopian queen. Together with him he sent the first-born sons of his people, who also became the founders of the Axumite Kingdom. Here they occupied the same position that their fathers did in Israel. In *Kebra Nagast* a session of what may possibly be the council of nobles is described. It mentions the speeches of its members, the pooling of resources, by which they arranged for the acquisition of a *tabot* whereupon each member brought 10 double drachmas apiece with a total of 140 double drachmas being collected. This suggests that the council of nobles consisted of 14 members. However, enumerating all members of the council, *Kebra Nagast* mentions 18 persons not counting the king.[77] Of the 18 names of posts, at least nine are clearly of foreign or medieval Ethiopian origin. But two posts—*hadani* and *ṣaḥāfē-lahm*—were probably retained from the Axumite period. The authority was in due course usurped by the hadani after having turned the king into an honored but weak-willed figure.[78]

Possibly among the first offices to be included in the council of nobles two additional ancient posts are concealed: the *afa negush* and the *aqabe heg. Afa negush* literally means "the mouth of the king." He is mentioned for the first time under Zara Yaqob, but could have existed even earlier. In *Kebra Nagast*, the Archdeacon Elmeyas is said to have become "the mouths of god" and the "observer of law" (*aqabe heg*), i.e., "the observer of Zion" ("the ark of the covenant"), and "the mouths of the king" (*afa negush*). Elmeyas and the high priest Azaryas were the closest advisers of King David ibn Hakim (otherwise Menelik I). He never undertook anything without their advice. They were also intermediaries between the king and his subjects.[79] These two nobles and also "all the powerful of Israel" (members of the council of nobles) were "similar not to servants but to the father and teacher" of the Axumite king.[80]

Of course the clergymen (the authors of *Kebra Nagast*) were trying to present these two extremely influential nobles of Axum as supreme church officials. But in order to explain their influence it was necessary to endow at least one of them with the posts of *afa negush* and *aqabe heg*. Possibly the authors of *Kebra Nagast* simply substituted the priests for two other members of the council of nobles, namely the first two most influential ones who were also connected with the most ancient tradition. Probably the *aqabe heg* and *afa negush* existed under the Axumite kings and were members of the council of nobles.

The connection of the title "*aqabe heg*" with the term by which other members of the council of nobles were designated—"*ba'ala heg*" (lawyers) is undoubted. The memory of the high position which the *aqabe heg* occupied in the Axumite Kingdom was preserved into the Middle Ages. In the synaxarion *Life of Abba Salama* it is said of Frumentius that he was the *aqabe heg* of Axum—the closest adviser and helper of the king.[81] Perhaps in remembrance of the Axumite *aqabe heg*, Zara Yaqob elevated the *aqabe sa'at* of Hayq ሐይቅ (or of Lake Haik, according to Buxton), who probably was considered his successor. Moreover, the service of the *aqabe sa'at* under a sacred king bore a ritual character.[82] Perhaps we see reflected in this the legends about the customs of the Axumite period which Zara Yaqob tried to revive. But what kind of ritual functions the *aqabe heg* fulfilled cannot be determined. It cannot be ruled out that, as a ritual functionary, the *aqabe heg* was simply confused with the *afa negush*.

The post of *afa negush* was not linked with the post of *aqabe heg* by accident. The *aqabe heg* (observer of the law) was connected with the judiciary functions of the king, and the *afa negush* in the late Middle Ages was turned into the supreme judge. At the beginning of this century, when the Ethiopian cabinet of ministers was officially established, the *afa negush* became the minister of justice or, more precisely, was placed on equal footing with the minister of justice of contemporary governments. But back in the extremely ancient period he fulfilled purely ritualistic functions under the king whose "mouths" he was. Evidently the *afa negush* was a "linguist" through whom the sacred king of Axum addressed other persons. It is no wonder that Azaryas and Elmeyas in *Kebra Nagast* are intermediaries between the king (who lived in strict solitude) and his subjects. Probably the Axumite king was not able to directly address an interlocutor without his "linguist"—the *afa negush*. Later on such a "linguist" appeared under the prince (*makonnen*) of Tigre (the nuclear territory of the Axumite Kingdom) and under the *nebura-ed* of Axum (Father Superior of the Axumite church). Both of them to a greater or lesser degree pretended to the authority of the ancient Axumite kings and rivaled the first Solomonides (the kings of the Shoan "Solomonic" dynasty).

What did the Axumite council of nobles represent in themselves? In the legend about the twelve "lawyers," who together with the Axumite king sat in state (on stones under an ancient tree), this meeting is pictured as the ancient council of elders, the heads of the most noble families of Axum. In *Kebra Nagast* this is a council of the feudal nobles who occupied the court posts. The so-called *Kebra Nagast of Lake Zwai*[83] represents the utmost degeneration of the legend.

In documents of the VI century A.D., two titles of Ethiopian military leaders are encountered. The leaders of the Axumites in Zafar in 518 A.D. were called B'B'WT.[84] These are the words ኣበ: ኣበዊት (father of fathers) of the Ge'ez language. Abreha calls himself in the inscriptions (in the Sabaean language) *Rmhys Zbymn* (the latter word has the variant *Zybmn* and others).[85] Drewes interprets this as "spear of the right hand,"[86] which is by no means indisputable. What the significance of these titles was and what role their bearers played in the Axumite council of nobles remains unknown.

Evidently side by side with the council of elders or council of nobles there existed in Axum still another organ of collective authority—the people's assembly. Probably it represented a gathering of free Axumites or warriors. An analysis of the composition and organization of the Axumite army leads to a similar impression.

The army

In three inscriptions of the Axumite king Ezana II (V century A.D.) there are mentioned military detachments (*sarwe*; plural, *sarawit*) of the Axumite Kingdom: Sabarat, Serae, Damawa, Dakuen, Laken, Hara, Metine, Mahaza, Falha, Halen. Modern translators of the inscriptions call these detachments armies or corps (Littmann, *Truppe, Truppen*;[87] Budge, army, armies;[88] Conti-Rossini, *serué, corpi di milizia*;[89] Kammerer, *la colonne, les colonnes*;[90] Doresse, *les troupes*,[91] etc.). A detailed analysis of even those few data which have been preserved concerning these armies permits one not only to understand their actual character but also to learn about Axum's social structure.

Among the names of these detachments, the names of peoples and countries subject to Axum are not encountered except for the dubious case of the army of the Metine. Evidently the armies of King Ezana II represented the army of the Axumite Kingdom proper, without its external possessions. It is possible that in some cases auxiliary detachments of subject tribes accompanied the Axumite army. The names of some of his "armies" are cited in Kaleb's [Ella Asbeha's] Axum inscription. Among them are Hara, Dakuen, and Falha.[92] Hara, Damawa, Sabarat, Hadefan, and Sabaha are also mentioned in Wazeb's inscription.[93] At the same time the names of "armies" of the subject Kushite tribes—Atagau, Gabala, Agau, Azabo, and perhaps Ma'at—are encountered in Kaleb's inscription.[94] In Wazeb's inscription the Agau militia is named also under the listing of "armies."[95] The king whose inscription Cosmas Indicopleustes copied says that he "ordered the peoples" of Ραύσων (Rausoi) and Σωλατέ (Solate) to guard the seacoasts.[96] However, when enumerating the subjugated peoples and the duties imposed on them he does not once say that they were obligated to help him in campaigns. In the very beginning of the inscription he declares "Having commanded the peoples closest to my kingdom to preserve the peace I bravely made war and subdued in battles the following peoples. . . ."[97] Among the conquered peoples even the Ge'ez, Agame, and Aua (tribes of modern-day Tigre) turned up. Hence the peoples closest to his kingdom lived in *direct proximity* to Axum. And even they were not obliged to participate in Axumite campaigns but were only obliged "to keep the peace" during military operations. In battles with the Sabaeans in Tihama both Abyssinians and local tribes subject to them and also the Beja[98] participated. In the Marib inscription of Abreha, his armies— "Abyssinian and Himyarite"—are mentioned.[99] Although Ethiopians who had settled in Arabia are being spoken of and not Axumites proper, the Beja would have had to be sent to Arabia at the order of the Axumite king.

The author of *The Martyrdom of Arethius* maintains that Ella Asbeha ordered against the Himyarites not only his armies proper but also the "Ethiopians-barbarians" subject to him. However, the difficulties of the route to the seacoast through the waterless deserts and mountain passes killed off the majority of them.[100] It must be taken into account that the campaign of 525 A.D. was one of the largest-scale undertakings of Axum, and fully comparable to the wars at the end of the II and beginning of the III centuries A.D. Probably only Axumite armies proper usually participated in campaigns.

If one compares the estimated numerical strength of the people of Axum with the numerical strength of Axum's armed forces, then it turns out that the Axum army represented a militia of all people enjoying full rights who had attained a certain age. Just as any militia, it would have had to be built on a territorial basis. Evidently, the names of Ezana II's armies correspond to the names of the territorial units into which the Axumite region was divided (without the self-governing regions subject to Axum).

Attempts have been made to find a translation for the names of the armies and the ethnic names of the kings, but they have not been very successful. Halevy tried to explain the ethnic name of Ezana I and II, Be'ese Halen, as "Helleneophile"; Conti-Rossini tried to explain the ethnic name "*Bi'si (Be'ese) Dimele*" from the Arabic root دمل . He translates it as "conciliator," "peace maker."[101] In notes to a new translation of the Axum inscriptions, Littmann proposes a translation of the words "Army of Daken" (*Truppe Daken*) as "Army of the Elephant." This designation he compares with the Hausa word *giwa* ([elephant,] by which a shock detachment, i.e., a detachment of royal bodyguards, is called).[102] The translation of the word "Daken" (or Dakuen) as "elephant" is stretching things. It is understandable why on the coins the words *"Be'ese Daken," "Be'ese Halen,"* and *"Be'ese Dimele,"* being written with Greek letters, remained without translations into the Greek. Moreover, the names of the remaining armies and the ethnic names are untranslatable. Doresse proposes that the armies represented the militias of the large tribes.[103] This does not contradict our view, although it sounds imprecise. The names of the Axumite armies find analogies among the ethnonyms of the Ethiopian-Nubian zones. Moreover, the majority of these names belong to the most widespread ones.[104] This indicates a connection between the armies and small districts from which they were drawn and the family-tribal groups of ancient Axum.

The ethnic titles of the kings in Ezana II's inscriptions and on ancient Axumite coins, which coincide with the names of some armies, attest to the same thing. In his inscriptions, Ezana II is called "Ezana son of Ella Amida of the ethnos (·በእሲP) Halen";[105] Ezana I is also called a man of the ethnos Halen (·በእሲ : ሐለን). The word ·በእሲ (man) designated the belonging to an ethnic or territorial group. We do not know of a case when such a form would designate the belonging to some sort of dynasty. Therefore, to translate the expression in question as "of the family of Halen," "of the dynasty of Halen," would be inappropriate. በእሲP : ሐለን is the unique personal title or ethnic name of Ezana. The Greek inscriptions on his coins contain this name in the form Βισι 'Αλήν or Βισι 'Αλένε.[106] The names Ezana I and Ezana II, whose ethnic character causes no doubts, coincide with the name of one of the armies—Halen. The name of another army—Dakuen—coincides with the ethnic name of another Axumite king, Endubis (Ενδύβις). On his coins, Endubis is called Βισι Δαχύ (Bi'si Daku) or Βισι Δαχύν (Bi'si Dakun).[107] This once again indicates the connection of the names of Ezana II's armies with the ethnonyms of ancient Axum. Moreover, the very terminology of the inscriptions identifies Ezana II's armies with territorial-ethnic subdivisions of the Axumite peoples. In the inscription about the campaign into Nubia, Ezana II, side by side with ሰራዊትP (my armies) uses አሕዛቡP (my peoples) as a synonym.[108] In the inscriptions about the personal collection of tribute, Ezana II speaks about the Metine peoples,[109] who in another inscription are called the "army of the Metine" (ሰርዌ : ምጢኖ).[110] The Adulis inscription also mentions "the peoples 'Αννινέ (Annine) and Μετινέ (Metine)."[111] In Wazeb's inscription, the words ሰራዊት and አሕዛብ are used as synonyms.[112] In Kaleb's inscriptions a similar meaning for the term አሕዛብ is encountered.[113] In Sabaean inscriptions of the time of Alhan Nahfan II and Ilsharah Yahdib II, the Axumite detachments are called by the Ethiopian term *'aḥzāb* (*'ḥzb ḥbšt*, *'ḥzb ḥbšn*),[114] similarly to the way their king is called by the Ethiopian term *nagashi*. The military detachments of Axum are also called "camps" (*'dwr 'ksmn, 'dyrm*).¹¹⁵ There is even the expression "princes (*'qwl*) and leaders (*'qdm*) and communities (or peoples—*'š'b*) of Abyssinians (*'ḥbšt*)."¹¹⁶ Consequently each of the armies of Ezana II, Kaleb, Wazeb, Gedara, and Asbeha was at the same time "a people." It is thus possible to understand that the army represented a militia of all able-bodied males who enjoyed full (?) rights of one of the tribes into which the Axumite Kingdom was originally divided. In such an instance the names of the armies coincided with the names of the tribes.

A meeting of all the Axumite armies may have represented the national assembly of Axum.¹¹⁷ Such meetings of warriors (according to their tribal communities) were summoned probably only for the declaration of the royal will (and the will of the council of elders). It is not very probable that in the period of the Axumite Kingdom's maximum development the people's assembly played an independent role. However, the fact that Axumite kings did communicate personally about the assembly of all their armies indicates that they attached considerable significance to it. The author of the Adulis inscription erected his victory throne after the campaign "during an assembly of all his forces." Ezana II, in the inscription about personal collection of tribute, tells about a meeting of all his armies on the eve of the campaign. In another of Ezana II's inscriptions, the meeting of Axumite armies during a campaign beyond the borders of Axumite territory, in the locality of Makaro, is spoken of. In a third inscription, about the campaign on Afan, Ezana II tells about a meeting of Axumite armies on the eve of a campaign in the locality of Alaha.¹¹⁸ In all instances known to us, the Axumite armed force gathered before a campaign, during a campaign, or directly after it, and always either at the borders of Axumite territory or beyond its boundaries. There is no information at all about a meeting of the armed force in the capital of Axum. But this does not mean that it did not occur.

The mottoes on Axumite coins speak of the significance of popular opinion (and probably also of its spokesman—the people's assembly). Mottoes on coins and the declarative sentences in Ezana II's late inscriptions, which were similar to them, proclaim the king's concern about the happiness of his peoples, his country, or his town. This is not boastful self-glorification but rather demagoguery: the king clearly was striving for the good will of the people. Consequently the people (probably in the person of the people's assembly) took some sort of part, albeit only symbolic, in the resolution of governmental affairs.

The fact that demagogic inscriptions on Axumite coins replaced the more ancient inscriptions of the pagan period which featured the ethnic name demands attention. The mottoes of early coins consist of the king's name, an indication of his royal dignity—*Basileus Axomiton* (βασιλεύς

Aξωμιτῶν) or *nagaśa* (*neguśa*) *Axum* (ንጉሠ : አክሱም) —and his ethnic name. Mottoes of later coins consist of the king's name, an indication of his royal dignity, and a demagogic slogan.

Thus the demagogic slogan on later coins replaces the ethnic name on early coins. It can, therefore, be proposed that the demagogic expression is, to a certain extent, equivalent in its significance to the ethnic name. If the demagogic motto indicates a formal "democracy of the people" (independent of its true content), then the ethnic name quite possibly speaks of some sort of authority or privileged position of that ethnos whose name the king took. It is natural to suppose that the king took the ethnic name not arbitrarily but under a system strictly defined by tradition, and that the privileged position of the ethnos did not depend on the king's kindness, but rather that the king himself was obliged to adopt the ethnic title in the name of the privileged ethnos.

All investigators (except Turayev) think that the ethnic name is nothing other than the name of a family or a dynasty. However, this opinion does not explain the fact that *all* of the Axumite kings had different ethnic names. Ezana I and II were called by the name of the ethnos of Halen (compare to "Army of Halen"). Endubis was called by the name of the ethnos of Dakuen (compare to "Army of Dakuen"). Kaleb (Ella Asbeha) was called by the name of the ethnos of Lazan, Wazeb by the name of the ethnos of Hadefan (compare to "Army of Hadefan" in his armed forces). Aphilas was called by the name of the ethnos of Dimele. Ousanas I was called by the name of the ethnos of Gisene. Wazeba I was called by the name of the ethnos of Zagali. And Eon was called by the name of the ethnos of Anaaf. Yet it would be improbable that they would all have belonged to different dynasties. We know nothing about the armies of Dimele, Gisene, and Zagali, but they probably existed just as did the armies of Halen and Dakuen. In any event, in the inscriptions of the Preaxumite period the ethnonym ZGLY is encountered.[119]

In Kaleb's Axum inscription there is mentioned a certain " 'Afar, man (*b's l-*) of Hara and Dakuen."[120] Perhaps this is the "negus" of the corresponding "armies"? For the "ethnic name" the use of the particle la- instead of the usual *status constructus* is rare.

Evidently the Axumite armies and the tribal communities from which they came had a privileged position (and, perhaps, also authority). And the Axumite king, at some period or another, became the representative of the privileged "army." This is reminiscent of the Order of Galla (Oromo) and of some other peoples of Ethiopia (the Conso, for example).[121]

It is interesting that the ethnic name Be'ese Azal was borne by Ethiopian kings of the XIII–XIV centuries A.D., Lalibela and Amda Seyon. As Turayev correctly indicates, this shows that the ethnic name in no way signifies a dynasty since according to Ethiopian tradition, Lalibela and

Amda Seyon belonged to different dynasties.[122] It is interesting that these two kings, who ruled one hundred years apart, had identical ethnic names. Probably this was caused by the "necrosis" of the title in the late epoch.

The frequency of mention of armies in Ezana II's inscriptions varies. In inscriptions about the campaign on Afan, three armies are named: Mahaza, Hara, and Dakuen. In the inscription about the campaign against Aguezat and Angabo, seven armies are listed: Mahaza, Hara, Metine (twice each), Daken (Dakuen), Laken, Falha, and Serae (once each). In inscriptions on the campaign into Nubia, seven armies are listed: Serae and Falha (twice each), Hara, Mahaza, Halen, Sabarat, Damawa (once each).[123] In all three inscriptions the Mahaza army is mentioned four times, Hara three times, Daken, Metine, and Falha each two times, Sabarat, Laken, Halen, and Damawa once each. The armies are named only when the king dispatched them but not when he himself led them into a campaign.[124] Obviously, therefore, the Halen army is mentioned only once. It is natural to assume that the king more frequently sent on independent raids the militias of those communities which were least connected with Axum and had the largest number of troops. The Metine army evidently was such a militia. The first mention of the Metine is contained in the Adulis inscription. The king speaks of his war with the "peoples" Ἀννινέ (Annine) and Μετινέ (Metine) who lived in the steep mountains somewhere neighboring on Axum.[125] Evidently these Μετινέ were the Metine of Ezana II's inscription. In Ezana II's inscription about personal collection of tribute, he relates that when he "arrived in the land of the HMS" (Hamasien?) to him "appeared all of the people of the Metine"; the king "gave them laws and they submitted to him and he allowed them to go away to their land."[126] However, in the inscription about the campaign on Aguezat and Angabo, Ezana II dispatched the Metine army together with other Axumite armies.[127] In the Adulis inscription, the Μετινέ (Metine) are represented as a strong and numerous people.[128] Evidently under Ezana II this people was included in the make-up of the Axumite Kingdom and the new statute "of the Metine peoples" was formed by those "laws" which Ezana II had given them. In the inscription it is not said that the Metine paid tribute like the other subjugated peoples. On the other hand, just as did the indigenous Axumites, they took part in Ezana II's campaigns. It is significant that although the Metine army is named in only one inscription it is mentioned there twice. The king was especially ready to dispatch the Metine on independent raids. Evidently the Metine army was the least Axumite of all of Ezana II's armies. The poor state of preservation and still uncompleted deciphering of the inscriptions of Kaleb and Wazeb do not permit them as yet to be fully analyzed. However, it is possible to note that Wazeb also sent on a raid the "army" of Hadefan, whose "ethnic name" he bore, as part of the make-up of the most numerous corps of his army.

In spite of the fragmentary and unclear information it is possible to observe in the governmental structure of the Axumite Kingdom undoubted traces of a military democracy. A people's militia of Axumites constructed on a territorial-tribal basis, a people's assembly, or assembly of warriors according to their tribes, the rotation of the privileged position of tribal communities (which prevented the hegemony of a privileged group), the well known attention of the king and council of elders to popular opinion— all of these represented remnants of a military democracy.

The royal bodyguard

It is not known whether Ezana II had at his disposal, in addition to the people's militia, his own personal detachments. It is true that one of his armies bore the name of Hara. The king's retinue or bodyguard, as opposed to other armies (ሰራዊት) which were assembled on a territorial basis, was, in the Middle Ages, called exactly the same thing (ሐራ) or almost the same (ሃራ). Thus, The Life of Aaron Mankerava mentions the "meeting of the retinue (or bodyguard) and the army (ጉባኤ ፡ ሃራ ፡ ወሰራዊት)."[129] However, there is no such contrast in Ezana II's inscriptions. Moreover, the "Army of Hara" (ሰርዌ ፡ ሐራ)[130] is spoken of, which would have been stylistically inadmissible if the word Hara were not a proper name but represented a term for designating the royal retinue. What is more, it is virtually impossible that the king would have sent his own bodyguard on independent raids instead of keeping it constantly located near his person. Moreover, in Ezana II's inscriptions it is said three times that the king sent into raids "the army of Hara." He sent only the army of Mahaza more frequently. Consequently, the "army of Hara" was not a royal bodyguard but represented one of the detachments of the people's militia.

During a campaign against the rebellious Aguezat and Hasat, King Kaleb also sent the "army" of Hara just as other "armies" on raids against the enemy. However, in Wazeb's inscription, it is possible that the Hara are contrasted to other detachments, i.e., to the militias of Axum and the subject peoples. However, the deciphering of this place in the inscription is doubtful.[131]

Probably, nevertheless, the Axumite king had a detachment of body-guards. It is difficult to imagine that the powerful Axumite king would not have had his own guard. Perhaps, it was precisely the tribal community of Hara which was obliged to supply the king with a specified number of bodyguards. In such a case, as a consequence, the royal bodyguard which developed out of this guard began to be called by the term hara. Kebra Nagast transmits the notion of the Axumite king surrounded by body-guards.[132] Joannes Malalae describes the Axumite king surrounded by his "council" or court: these Ethiopians standing around the king were armed with spears and shields; they were singing or playing musical instru-ments.[133] Probably bodyguards and musicians, as well as nobles, were to be found before the person of the king. Moreover, many other servants, free men, slaves, Axumites, and foreigners certainly surrounded the king. During campaigns they could constitute an armed retinue or bodyguard of the king. Exactly in the same way, in the Middle Ages, a king's close relatives, retainers, courtiers, servants, pages, slaves, etc., constituted the armed retinue of the king.

The people's militia and military colonies of Axumites constituted the primary military force of the Axumite state. The privileged position of these tribes in relation to vassal communities created a vivid contrast. This contrast increased with the growth of the Axumite power. It is possible that property and rights differentiations inside the Axumite Kingdom (about which virtually nothing is known) led to a narrowing of the circle of individuals who participated in military campaigns. Thus, the militia was converted into an army which constituted a part of the governmental organization.

The population of the subject tribal communities could probably, in some instances, participate in military actions (as in the case of Abreha, or his contemporaries the Axumite kings Kaleb and Wazeb). But enlisting it frequently to make attacks on neighboring countries was avoided (let us recall the failure of the project of enlisting the Ethiopian-barbarians by Ella Asbeha in a campaign on Himyar). Evidently there were two reasons: the weakness of the central authority and the fear of the Axumites to develop the war capability of their subjects.

Thus in Axum at its height an army appeared which was composed of the armed retinue of the king and privileged communities of military colonists. It became the germ of the feudal army of the Ethiopian Middle Ages which existed with few changes up to the Second World War.

Besides the bodyguard the king had civil servants and court servants. Historically only one such servant is known—Frumentius, who according to Rufinus' testimony headed the royal "exchequer and correspondence." Apparently there was no narrowly specialized civil-service apparatus. It has been shown that Frumentius was a royal slave; slaves wholly dependent on the king became his court agents or his stewards. Probably they managed not only the revenue accounting but also collection of taxes and correspondence with foreign and vassal kings.

A royal civil service devoted to the monarchs and not connected with the tribal and lineage organization represented a qualitatively new unit of authority. It made up one of the important institutions of the feudal state which was taking shape.

The courts

One can only conjecture how justice was administered in Axum. Evidently "the king of kings," "kings" of separate tribes, and heads of lineages and of families possessed the right to judge free Axumites. They scarcely made judicial decisions by themselves, without the participation of the elders or some other counselors of corresponding rank. It is not without reason that the Axumite council of elders is called the council of "lawyers" (በዐለ : ሕግ). Probably the "lawyers" under the presidency of the king constituted the highest judicial organ. It was possibly during the Axumite period that the post of *aqabe heg* (ዐቃቤ : ሕግ—observer of the law) and *afa negush* appeared.

Although the first code of written laws appeared in Ethiopia much later, the necessity for precisely fixed legislation already existed in the Axumite period. It was evoked by the development of social stratification. The first laws treat property relationships—property and distribution. The sole records of ancient Ethiopian law discovered up to the present are the four "laws" in the inscription from Safra. They date approximately to the first half of the III century A.D. The laws (carved in stone) were made for general review; in the case of an argument it was easy to appeal to them. The fixing of the standards of dergo was in the interests of tribal members. It tended to restrain the growth of exploitation of small producers on the part of the monarchy, which was growing stronger. The written laws of Safra, therefore, express a certain compromise between the evolving early feudal monarchy and the peasant community. Significantly, not the king but the tribe itself, in the person of its "lawyers" in whose name evidently the laws were composed, emerged officially as the lawgiver.

The formulation of the laws permits one to imagine the order of their adoption. The laws (except the sacral law about the offering of sacrifices, text B) have the headings "Rules (*tzkr*) about feeding [during] the stay [of the king on the territory of the tribe]."[134] "Rules about gifts and clothing," "Laws about bread which the king will receive." The word "laws" (*'hgg*) emphasizes the legislative nature of the text. In two instances, for imparting a legislative force to the text directly before it (text A) or directly after it (text C) there is added the word *hg*—[this is] the law! The texts themselves are extremely laconic. Evidently they were solemnly proclaimed by the author (or authors) in the presence of the entire nation according to a traditional formula. Moreover, the word ሕግ (plural, እሕጋግ) before or after the proclaimed text imparted to it a legislative force. Thus the laws of Safra were validated in the tradition of customary law. The principles of common law are reflected in prohibitory formulas of the Axumite inscriptions, which are simultaneously formulas of punishment and condemnation (see Table 4).

In spite of the rearrangement of certain words, the formula in general is stable. In the spirit of the principles of customary law ("an eye for an eye," "a tooth for a tooth"), the nature of the crime and of the punishment are designated by the same words. According to tradition, "the condemnation-punishment" has to be in the singular, although the plural is required by

Table 4. Prohibitory Formulas on Inscriptions

	l'mb if	*z* some body	*'msn l'b (')n wnql wnšt* defaces and [anew] inscribes and moves and overthrows	*ly [mt]* —he will die	*[w]zmd wwld* and family, and children	. . . . he will be exiled?	*'m b[ḥ]r* from the land	
DAE, IV, No. 6, 7, 21–23	if	some body	defaces and [anew] inscribes and moves and overthrows	—he will die	and family, and children	he will be exiled?	from the land	
DAE, IV, No. 10, 26–28	አእመ if	ሀ some body	ዘቀለ : ወይሠለ : overthrows his [throne] and moves it	ወእቴ፥ he	ወብሒስሡ. : ወሀምዱ. : and his land and his family	ለይኒኅቀል : ወይኒትሠሡት : will be moved and overthrown	አስበሐሕ ሡ. : from his land	
DAE, IV, No. 11, 50–51	አእመ if	ሀ some body	ሠቀለ : ወዘሠሁት moves his [throne] and overthrows it	ወእቴ : he	ወሀምዱ. : and his family	ይUUረ[ጽ] : ወይኒትሠሡአ : will be eradicated and moved	አስበሐሕ ሡ. : from the land	eradicated

the meaning. In the inscription *DAE*, IV, No. 11, an innovation is clearly apparent; instead of the verb .ჶሠⵏ in the second part of the formula, the verb .ჶሠረ፞ (he will die) is used, and moreover it is used twice. This persistent repetition of a threatening and significant word produces a powerful impression.

Littmann in *DAE*, IV, No. 11, restored the last syllable of the word .ჶሠረ[ℱ] as ℱ, similar to the last word of the formula. The verb, therefore, acquires a plural number [form]. In my opinion, here, just as in the following word, a singular had to be used according to tradition. In the word .ჶሠረℱⵏ the tradition is broken already by both the repetition of the verb and its novelty. The verb assumed, against tradition, the plural number required by the meaning. The word ጵ· በሕC is translated in two ways: "from the land" and "from the country." The two translations do not, in essence, contradict one another, imparting to the formula of condemnation-punishment an expanded meaning. The word in the fifth column of each of the Ethiopian texts of the bilingual inscription (*DAE*, IV, No. 6, 7, 22) is read as *l-y[mt]* ("he will die!"). The word .ჶሠረℱ in *DAE*, IV, No. 11, evidently corresponds to *l-ymt*, (*ymtm* of *DAE*, IV, No. 6 and 7) alluding to one or another form of violent or "magic" death. What do we have here? The threat of the death penalty for the criminal himself, his children (*wld*), and his relatives (or members of the family *zmd*)? But why then is the death penalty invariably connected with the driving of the criminal from the land (or his exile from the country)?

This seeming contradiction can be explained in the following way: The criminal and his relatives were placed outside the law; they were deprived of land, exiled from Axum, and all who encountered them had the right to kill them. However, such a nonpunishable killing of a criminal cannot be completely identified with the death penalty carried out by the organs of governmental authority.

The Ethiopian texts of the bilingual inscription contain, moreover, an alternative to the prohibitory formula. It is an encouraging formula: "That one who honors this, let him be blessed."[135]

The punishments enumerated in the condemnation-punishment formula evidently coincided with the actual measure of punishment. Declaring a man outside the law, which was accompanied by the threat of death; exiling him with all his family, and his close (or even more distant) relatives; and confiscating all property, was probably the supreme measure of punishment which an Axumite could undergo.

In one of Ezana II's inscriptions another punishment is mentioned which was not so severe as it was disgraceful. Significantly, only foreigners were subjected to it. Ezana II ordered Abba Alke'o, the king of the Aguezat, stripped naked.[136] In their turn, the Nubians stripped bare the envoys of

Ezana II.[137] Exactly in the same way, in the XIV century A.D., King Amda Seyon ordered the disgracing of Phillip of Debre Libanos. He was brought to the king bound, and was stripped before the whole court, the troops, and the royal wives. Moreover, the king said "You ought to be ashamed of yourself, monk!"[138] Such a "penalty by shaming" was applied in the XV–XVI centuries A.D.[139] In all cases it was applied to noble, official, or illustrious persons for whom it was especially degrading.

Information is preserved about one more form of punishment: keeping in chains, something not unlike prison confinement. In Ezana II's inscription about the campaign on Aguezat it is said that the prisoners were "chained."[140] In Matara were discovered two separate burial places of people in iron fetters. Anfray, who discovered them, is inclined to consider the buried persons as prisoners.[141] In medieval and modern Ethiopia prisoners and criminals sometimes are subjected to long imprisonment in chains. Moreover, nobles, in particular vassal kings, were chained in pairs with their slaves. The slave looked after his lord and at the same time hindered him from running away. Evidently a similar lot also befell Abba Alke'o, the king of Aguezat who was chained with his throne bearer, sent to Axum, and imprisoned in Ezana II's palace. Abba Alke'o was not an Axumite. Perhaps keeping in chains was applied only to foreign prisoners. It could have been supplemented by subsequent conversion into slavery. This was the punishment for mutiny against the Axumite king.

In spite of fragmentary and incomplete information, the absence of any comment on [capital] punishment and tortures in sources of the Axumite period is scarcely accidental. Sources of medieval Ethiopia, and of the neighboring Himyarite Kingdom, are literally overflowing with them. Even in Himyar, where capital punishment was undoubtedly practiced, the Axumite king did not execute anyone, although he threatened with death apostates who in the course of a year did not return to Christianity.[142] This omission by the sources cannot be explained by their biased nature. Indeed, they comment about pillagings and murders inflicted by Ethiopians. Probably the Axumite governmental system simply had not developed, by the VI century A.D., such judicial sanctions as tortures, corporal punishment, mutilation, and the death penalty.

However, killing of a criminal (which was not punishable under the law) could not be distinguished, in essence, from public [capital] punishment if he was brought as a sacrifice to the gods. The sources, however, speak only about bringing foreign captives as a sacrifice to Mahrem.

Thus the judicial authority and legal norms of Axum display a complex combination of the traits of incipient stratification with traits of an egalitarian social structure. Moreover, even extremely archaic elements, for example, the principles of customary law, come to serve the early feudal state.

Vassal kingdoms

The lands beyond the borders of the Axumite Kingdom proper represent "external" vassal possessions of Axum. All the territory of the Axumite power was divided into a series of kingdoms and tribal unions; the first and most powerful of them was Axum.

Initially it was the kingdoms or principalities of Northern Ethiopia (which surrounded Axum) which belonged to the category of vassal states. Subsequently, the state and tribal unions of South Arabia, of Nubia, of the Nubian and Danakil deserts, and of Central and Northwestern Ethiopia were added.

In Ezana I and II's inscriptions are enumerated the following "kingdoms" and groups of tribes:

A. *Northern Ethiopia*—Axum, Aguezat, Angabo, Gabaza (Adulis).

B. *Northeastern Africa*—Kasu (Meroe), Beja, Siamo, Afan, Semen, Walkait (?), Baria, Hasat, Mangurto.

C. *South Arabia*—Himyar (together with Saba, Du Raydan and Salhen).

In the V–VI centuries A.D. the following lands emerged as isolated possessions of the Axumite kings:

A. *Extra-Ethiopian*—the Himyarite Kingdom, Northern Nubia, the country of the Beja.

B. *Ethiopian plateau*—the country of the Agau near Lake Tana; Siamo, Aguezat, Hasat, Asfai (?), Waital (or Waitag) in the southeast; and Adulis (it is possible to assume that Semen and Baria were then autonomous).

On the territory of Ethiopia itself, Epiphanius distinguishes Axumites, Adulites, and Siamo (Taiano). The first two are set off from the last. Cosmas speaks of the country of "Adulia" and about the "arhont" of Adulis, who was subordinate to the Axumite king.[143] He also mentions the "arhont" of the Agau, also dependent on Axum. Joannes Malalae distinguishes in the Axumite Kingdom a "king" and "arhonts of the provinces."[144] Finally, in Halevy's opinion, Pseudo Dionysius mentions the Adulis king who warred with the king of Axum.

Of course, the authority of the Axumite king over vassal kings was not everywhere identical. It remained weakest in the "external" possessions and in the remote border regions. The insufficiency of sources does not permit one to establish to what degree Nubia, the country of the Beja, and the Danakil desert were dependent on Axum. It is easier to evaluate such dependency with respect to South Arabia. In reality, the authority of Axum in the Himyarite Kingdom depended on the actual relationship of the forces of these two states. It grew especially in the years when South

Arabia was occupied by Axumite troops and it completely vanished in the reign of Dhu-Nuwas. The Himyarite kings who acknowledged the authority of Axum had their own vassals and entire dependent kingdoms. Thus the Kindite Kingdom in Central Arabia was under the influence and authority of Himyar, even in the period of the greatest dependence of this latter country on Axum (in the reign of Sumafa Ashwa). The borders of the Kindite, Lakhmide, and Ghassanide kingdoms formed the furthest boundary of Axumite political influence. Beyond it, the zones of influence of Iran and Byzantium began.

The rule "the vassal of my vassal is not my vassal," which presupposes a higher development of feudal juridical norms, scarcely existed in Axum. However, the Axumite kings did not directly interfere in the affairs of the Kindites; the kings of Himyar did this.

The legends recorded in the VIII century A.D. by Ibn Hisham, and preserved by At Tabari, possibly speak about some kind of special privileges of the Himyarite king in relation to his subjects. Dhu-Nuwas allegedly made a multitude of keys to the treasure houses of Yemen and gave them to the Ethiopians, saying: "Here are money and lands for you, but leave me the people and posterity."[145] It is possible to interpret this legend as an echo of the juridical norms which stipulated that the Axumite king, as conqueror, was considered the owner of the land, but that the people who inhabited it (except the Ethiopian colonists) remained subject only to the Himyarite king himself and only via him were subject to Axum. This legendary episode, however, is not reliable historical evidence.

The Himyarite Kingdom paid tribute to Axum irregularly. The Himyarites were obliged to render assistance to the Axumites in their campaigns against other kingdoms and tribes, but probably only on the territory of Arabia. In this respect they were looked upon more as allies than as reservists. However, the information of the sources is too scanty to speak more definitely. Syrian sources and the example of Sumafa Ashwa show that the Axumite king could raise to the Himyarite throne persons who pleased him. It is, however, not known whether such an act was legal from the point of view of Axumite and Himyaritic customs.

Even in the period of the greatest influence of Axum in Arabia, the Himyarite kings received foreign embassies as independent sovereigns. Such was the case under Sumafa Ashwa, under Ma'adikarib and Abreha, and during the reign of Ezana I. Abreha numbers the Axumite embassy in first place among other embassies.[146] The inscription terminologically distinguishes: (1) the embassy of the Axumite king; (2) the missions of the great powers, Byzantium and Iran; and (3) representatives of the North Arabian kings. Yet Abreha calls himself a "vassal" (? 'azlī)[147] of the Axumite king. Possibly this is an official term for designating vassal sovereigns on the territory of the Axumite power.

Of course, the ruler of Adulis or of Siamo could not enjoy such actual independence as Abreha. But their rights and obligations were probably identical. In Ethiopia itself, the "arhont" of the frontier mountain Agau, an ethnically homogeneous population to which he had tribal affinity, felt himself more independent than the "arhont" of Adulis, a port city with an ethnically mixed population, organically linked with Axumite politics.

By the end of the Axumite period, the "kingdoms" of Northern Ethiopia vanished, completely absorbed by Axum. At the same time, all external possessions were separated from it. The system of vassal states seemingly had disintegrated. However, in reality, it was preserved in a new form as a system of hereditary feudal possessions. Cerulli[148] correctly noted this. With the liquidation of the former monarchies, and the replacement of vassal kings by vice-regents/nobles, the juridical basis of local separatism was shaken. But this does not mean that separatism itself—inherent to the feudal structure—vanished. As the Axumite Kingdom evolved it achieved continually greater political unity. The period of Axum's decline was marked by a growth of feudal separatism and anarchy, only partly restrained by ideological factors—that is, by traditions of Axumite unity, feudal ethics, Christian religion, and consciousness of common danger in the struggle against external and internal foes.

Summary

The combination of remnants of the primitive social structure with elements of a feudal governmental system was characteristic of the whole governmental structure of Axum. Subsequent development of the Ethiopian political infrastructure represented an intensification and enrichment of the latter at the expense of the former. It is clearly evident in a comparison of the political structure of Axum with that of medieval Ethiopia.

The Axumite governmental system was able to arise and develop only under specific local conditions. That is: (1) when the embryonic feudal relationships were interwoven with elements of the lineage-tribal, slave-holding, and mercantile relationships; (2) when the rather small nation of the Axumites conquered a series of countries, part civilized, part "barbarian"; (3) when the African sacred monarchy headed up an enormous power which included the territories of Northern Somalia, Eastern Sudan, and South Arabia; and (4) when the process of the formation of a class society and state proceeded with accelerated rates unprecedented in Puntian and Preaxumite Ethiopia.

The separate elements of ritual, royal titles, and some attributes of the royal authority reached Axum from more developed states, especially South Arabia, Meroe, and Egypt. But as a legal historical entity, the Axumite political system could develop only in Northern Ethiopia. In the Late Axumite period, when at the boundaries of the country the Arab world power arose and cut off Ethiopia and Nubia from other civilized countries, the characteristic traits of the traditional Axumite political system took on the hue of a still greater originality. The autochthonic origin of the traits is emphasized still more by the fact that they, in essence, are not at all connected with Christianity. At the same time, the Axumite political system was unable to exert a great influence on the formation of political institutions in the countries neighboring it. Some had their own ancient political system. Others, like Northern Somalia, Eastern Ethiopia, and Beja, still had not set out on the path of complex political development. As far as the territories of the central and southern parts of the Ethiopian plateau are concerned, they lay beyond the borders of the Axumite expansion and came under North Ethiopian influence only later, after the downfall of the Axumite Kingdom. Only the lands of Agau and Siamo (between Lake Tana and Lake Haik) constituted an exception. However, the local African roots of the Axumite civilization gave to its governmental system a resemblance and kinship with the governmental systems of other African countries.

Those very same characteristic traits—the presence of remnants of the primitive social structure, the growing elements of class inequality and constraint, and the adaptation to the African environment—are exhibited by Axumite ideology, the other principal component of the structure of ancient Ethiopian society.

V

Ideology

The ideology of Axumite society has been as little investigated as all of the other aspects of its internal life. In this part of the book we will investigate such forms of ideology as religion, political ideas, rights and morality, and literature and art. The last two areas will be touched upon only to the extent that they are forms of ideology.

Pagan gods

Magic tales and legends from the most ancient North Ethiopian religious beliefs are preserved in medieval literature and modern folklore. Especially popular is the legend about the monstrous serpent who, in time immemorial, reigned in the north of Ethiopia.

Astarte—the embodiment of the planet Venus, the deity of fertility and love—was one of the supreme gods of ancient Ethiopian, South Arabian, and other Semitic peoples. Among the Babylonians the name Astarte was Ishtar; among the Canaanites it was Ashtarath; in Qataban it was Ashtar; and among the Sabaeans it was Astar. In Ethiopia it was pronounced as Astar, closest to the Hellenized form. Just as among the Southern Arabs, and also among the Canaanites of Ugarit, Astar was represented among the Ethiopians in the form of a man—not as a woman, as among the Northern Semites.

The cult of Astar is authenticated by many inscriptions of the Preaxumite period.[1] As the inscriptions of Ezana I and Ezana II show,[2] the cult of Astar flourished in Axum from the middle of the IV century to the second half of the V century A.D., a period in which monotheistic religions were spreading. What is more, the Ethiopian translation of *Ecclesiastes* calls the Biblical-Christian God Astar.[3] This attests not only to the relatively early dating of the translation but also to the significance of Astar in the Axumite pantheon.

In Preaxumite Ethiopia, Almouqah (Iliumkuh), the tribal god of Saba, was also held sacred. The Sabaeans called themselves *wld 'lmqh*—"sons of Almouqah." The cult of Almouqah was undoubtedly brought into Ethiopia by Sabaean colonists. Besides the inscriptions of the Preaxumite period, an inscription of the Axumite king GDR, on a bronze staff from

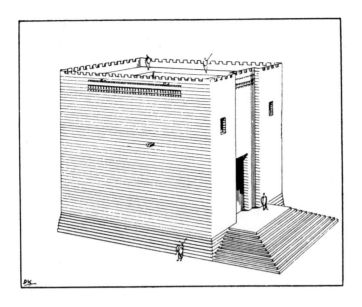

The South Arabian Preaxumite temple at Yeha.

Havila Asserai (Asbi Dera), was dedicated to Almouqah. Sanctuaries of Almouqah were located in Asbi Dera and Melazo. In one inscription the god (or goddess?) 'RG (Arg, Ereg?) is also mentioned. This deity is unknown to the other sources.

Some personages of the ancient Ethiopian astral pantheon proved to be unusually tenacious. Littmann investigated the astral myths of Northern Ethiopia, using documents preserved at the beginning of this century. Astrological myths of the Mensa and other tribes of Tigre go back to ancient times[4] and preceded not only the Christianization of Axum but also the decline of the astral cults. The moon is revered as a god by all the Mensa, both Muslims and Christians. During an eclipse of the moon they say that the moon is dying. At this time no one lies down to sleep. Journeys are interrupted. All pray for god to have mercy, to spare the moon. As soon as the eclipse ends people begin to rejoice wildly, celebrating "the recovery" of the moon. There is a belief that after a lunar eclipse some prominent person must die.

It is thought that the young moon brings success. During the appearance of a new moon the Mensa say "Arro (or Helial) has recovered." During the new moon [phase] magic rites are performed.[5] Conti-Rossini proved that the Ethiopian deity Gad, with whose cult medieval "saints" struggled, was none other than the moon god.[6] Conti-Rossini also connects the worship of the toro antelope, which is witnessed in modern Ethiopia, with the cult of the moon. Maria Höfner proposes comparing the traces of the cult of the toro antelope with the cult of the stone ram, which is a characteristic of South Arabian religions.[7]

Maria Höfner connects the famous stelae of Axum with the cult of the dead. The name of the stelae—Haoulti, known from the inscriptions from Matara[8] and Anza,[9]—she derives from the root ḥwl, "to go around in a circle" (compare the Arabic حول).[10] This inscription from Matara, which tells about the dedication of works "to the fathers" of the tribal members, evidently attests to the cult of ancestors, traces of which were also preserved in the Middle Ages. Thus the cult of the dead, to whom the funeral stelae were erected, merged with the cult of ancestors. Dishes and other objects of everyday life found in the burial places attest to a belief in a life beyond the grave. Possibly in the religion of Preaxumite and Axumite Ethiopia, just as in other Semitic countries (Canaan, North and South Arabia), there existed a developed cult of "the lords of the mountains," which later merged with the images of Christian "saints."

On the site of the Debre Damo monastery there was evidently a mountain sanctuary in antiquity. On the site of the Debre Libanos monastery (Livan mountain) there was also probably a sanctuary of Mata, "the lord of Debre Mata" (the lord of Mata mountain), as the patron saint of the monastery was called in medieval documents. Here the name Mata is understood as the second name of St. Libanos (Livanius), the mythical founder of the monastery. Probably Almouqah and Erg were also "lords" of mountain sanctuaries ("mountain places").

During the Preaxumite period in Northern Ethiopia and South Arabia a single religion, pantheistic in nature, was established. A trinity of supreme gods—the embodiment of heavenly bodies—headed the pantheon. In the victory inscriptions of the Axumite kings (of the pagan period) a great god and a triad of gods always figure. It is easy to trace this according to the inscriptions when they are put in table form (see Table 5).

As is evident from the table, the triad figures only in two of the seven pagan inscriptions. It recedes into second place before the personage of the supreme god. Moreover, the composition of the triad does not coincide in the inscriptions. In the Adulis inscription, Zeus, Ares, and Poseidon constitute the triad.[11] In Ezana II's inscription about the campaign on Afan, Astar, Beher, and Medr compose the triad.[12] In the "Sabaean" text of the bilingual inscription of Ezana I, Astar, Beher, and Mahrem constitute the triad.[13] And in the "Ethiopian" text, Astar, Medr and Mahrem compose the triad.[14] It is difficult to say which Axumite deity is concealed under the name of Zeus. Maria Höfner proposes that it is Astar.[15] Ares is Mahrem. Poseidon is the god of the sea and sea trade, to whom the

Table 5. Axumite Pagan Gods

	Inscription in the Greek Language					Inscription in the Ge'ez Language			
Adulis	*From Abba Penteleon*	*From Meroe*	*Bilingual of Ezana I*	*Bilingual of Ezana II*		*DAE, IV, No. 8*	*DAE, IV, No. 9*	*DAE, IV, No. 10*	*DAE, IV, No. 17*
". . . By the mercy of my supreme god Ares",	"to Ares the invincible [god] of the Axumites"	Ares	Ares	"Invincible Mahrem [Ares]"		The king—son of Mahrem	The king—son of Mahrem	The king—son of Mahrem invincible for [to] the foe	
". . .A sacrifice to Zeus, Ares, and Poseidon"				"Astar, Mahrem, Beher [Medr]"				Offering of sacrifice to Mahrem	
								Dedication of a throne to Astar, Beher, and Medr	Astar and Medr

A South Arabian Preaxumite incense burner
of carved stone.

king brought sacrifice "for those sailing on the sea."[16] Probably the
inscription calls some sort of local deity Poseidon. Perhaps this was the
protector of Adulis and a god of the Icthyophagi.

Agatharchides the Kindite, as early as the II century B.C., communicated
that the eastern extremity of Somalia "is called Poseidonia because
Ariston who was sent by Ptolemy for the investigation of the Arabian
seacoast dedicated there (in Somalia) an altar to the god Poseidon."
Even if there actually was an altar dedicated to Poseidon by Ariston,
this still does not mean that he introduced the cult of Poseidon into Somalia.
Most likely, naming the country Poseidonia indicates a spread of the cult
of Poseidon into this area by the time of the arrival of the Greeks. The
legendary tale about Yambul and his fellow travelers who fell captive
to the Ethiopians (the Icthyophagi of Somalia) attests to this. The Ethiopians wanted "to bring captives as a sacrifice," having dispatched them in
a boat into the open sea.[17] Judging by everything, the natives brought
this sacrifice to the sea god, who could easily have been identified with
the Greek Poseidon. A cult of the sea god could scarcely have flourished
in landlocked Axum, which lay in the interior of the Ethiopian plateau.
Attempts to find him in the form of Beher are not appropriate. Thus, at
least one member of the Adulis triad is of local and not Axumite origin.

On the other hand, in Ezana II's inscription about the campaign on Afan and in the Ethiopian texts of the bilingual inscription of Ezana I, all members of the divine triad are undoubtedly Axumite gods. Astar emerges in first place and this is not accidental. After him come Beher and Medr. The word *beher* (·ΠdьC) means, in the Ge'ez language, simply "country" or "land." The word *medr* (?.ꞁ·C) is used in this same sense. According to the investigation of Vycichl, the word *beher* signified cultivated land and *medr* land in general.[18] There were attempts to identify Beher with the sea because of the consonance with the Arabic جر (*bahr*),[19] but they were supported by no kind of proofs and do not at all explain the facts. Thus Nielsen's scheme of the Ethiopian triad of gods, which, in his opinion, embodies primary elements and corresponds to the Babylonian triad Anu-Bel-Ea (Sky-Earth-Sea),[20] does not hold up.

Of the South Arabian astral triad, the Axumite triad preserved only Astar. But even he, evidently, received a new name. The gods of the Moon and Sun slipped out of the triad; their symbols—depictions of the sun and the moon—passed over to Mahrem.

Judging by the term *Egzi'abḥēr* ("the god Beher" or "the lord of the Earth"—the name of the deity among Ethiopian Christians), Beher was a male deity. *Medr* is a word which in its ordinary meaning was of feminine gender and signified a female deity. Medr is reminiscent of the goddess-mother of the agricultural cults.

Mahrem (forbidden) emerged in the role of the heavenly god of the Axumites. Probably he also had another name which it was forbidden to pronounce. Did it perhaps coincide with one of the names of the lunar deity? Mahrem is reminiscent in many ways of the Semitic moon god. The sun-moon symbols are depicted on the stelae from Axum, Matara, and Anza, and on coins of the pagan kings of Axum. They probably pertain to Mahrem—the dynastic and tribal god of the Axumites. In Ezana I's bilingual inscription, the Mahrem of the Ethiopian text[21] is called Ares in the Greek text.[22] All the Greek inscriptions of the Axumite kings[23] (except Sembruthes' inscription, where the name of the god is absent) give the name Ares. As is well known, the Athenian Ares is considered the god of war. In the inscriptions of Ezana I and Ezana II, in Ethiopian, Mahrem, as the god of war, is called "invincible to the foe."[24] In the Greek text of the bilingual inscription[25] of Ezana II and in the Greek inscription from Abba Penteleon,[26] Ares is also called "invincible." In the Adulis inscription the king calls Ares "his greatest god" who bestows victory on him.[27] In the Greek inscription of the Axumite king from Meroe, the victory of the Axumites is also attributed to the grace of Ares.[28] As a tribal parent-god in the inscription from Abba Penteleon, Ares is called the "god of the Axumites."[29] As a dynastic god, the kings called Ares-Mahrem "their greatest god" (in the Adulis inscription), and the god who gave birth to the king (in the inscriptions of Ezana I and Ezana II).[30] Thus Ares-Mahrem was: first, the god of heaven; second, the tribal god of the Axumites; third, the invincible god of war; fourth, the forefather and parent [father] of the king, the founder of the royal family (whereupon, each king was considered the earthly incarnation of Mahrem); and fifth, Mahrem was considered a god-king. The kings of Axum dedicated victory thrones to him in the capital and in Adulis.

Mahrem—the god of war and of the monarchy—clearly prevailed over the agricultural triad similarly to the way in which the sky prevails over the earth and a sacred monarch prevails over the people. At the same time, in the person of Mahrem, war took the upper hand over peaceful work, acquiring an unprecedented significance in the social life of Axum. It became an affair more honorable and welcome to god than peasant labor, which was sanctified by the precepts of the ancestors. In the religion of early Axum, therefore, characteristic traits of an ideology of class inequality are evident. This is the ideology of an evolving feudal society. It sanctified and morally elevated pillaging, military force, and the continually growing centralized authority of the king.

Under such socio-historical conditions, the religious-ideological system of the Axumites was very susceptible to influences from the direction of the more developed systems of the ancient civilizations which already existed at that time in the subtropical zone.

One of these was Mithraism, which was born in Central Asia and reformed in Iran. As is known, Mithraism exerted a notable influence on Christianity. The temples of Mithra were built not only in Syria and other eastern provinces of the Roman Empire but even in Rome itself. Everywhere that the Roman legionnaires penetrated they brought the cult of Mithra. In the east, Mithraism exerted an influence on the religion of the Dards and other peoples of Northwestern India and also, according to the research of L. N. Gumilev, on the peoples of Tibet and Mongolia.[31] There is a definite resemblance between the invincible war-sun Mithra or Mihra and the invincible sun-moon Mahrem. This question, however, is in need of a special investigation.

The influence of ancient Greek religion on the religion of the Axumites shows up only in the identification of Mahrem with Ares in the Greek inscriptions of the Axumite kings. Procopius Caesarensis and *Odoiporai apo Edem* (*Itineraries from Eden*)[32] mention "Hellenic beliefs" of the Axumites and Beja but this, according to the terminology of that time, meant simply "pagan cults."[33]

Numerous Egyptians by birth brought to Axum the ancient Egyptian religion in its very latest forms. Bruce, who visited Axum in the XVIII century A.D., observed here a marble sculpture of Horus provided with a hieroglyphic inscription.[34] Judged by Bruce's drawing, this sculpture dates to the Hellenic or Roman period and was made in Egypt proper.[35] It was probably intended for cult needs of the Egyptian trade colony. Separate elements of the Egyptian religion were able to penetrate into the milieu of the local population. In Adulis (excavations of Paribeni, 1907) a glass scarab was revealed.[36] The time of its fabrication is not known but probably it was synchronous with the statue of Horus. During the 1959 excavations at Haoulti-Melazo, two blue faience figurines were discovered. These are Meroitic amulets of Hathor and Ptah, probably of Roman time.[37] The Meroitic amulet of the infant Horus found during the excavations at Matara,[38] and also the stele with the Egyptian-Meroitic sacred symbol of life (the ankh ♀) discovered at Axum in 1972 approximately 200 meters north of the gigantic stelae,[39] date to this same epoch. In the medieval Ethiopian *Lives of the saints*, worship of Horus and Serapis is mentioned, but this, evidently, is a literary reminiscence. The sacral functions of the Axumite kings and their idolization were mentioned earlier.

Animal and human sacrifice

The Axumites brought sacrifices to their gods. Evidently, live sacrifices constituted the major part of propitiatory offerings. Even today, Ethiopian Christians, Muslims, Falasha Jews, Kemants, and "pagans" offer live sacrifices. The Amhara, Tigrai, Galla, Danakil, Agau, and peoples of South and Southwest Ethiopia carry out the sacrifice of a goat (more rarely of a sheep) during the entry (more precisely the carrying in) of a bride into the home of the betrothed and of a newborn child into the paternal home. The sacrifice of a bull (*querbān—qurbān* of the ancient Arabs) is carried out among the Tigrai and Tigre as a memorial (*tazkar*) seven years after the death of a relative. Polera[40] showed that the *tazkar* in essence represents an expiatory rite very close to the corresponding rite among the ancient Jews. Probably this is a common Semitic custom which had entered Ethiopia and Palestine from Arabia, together with the Semite-pagan emigrés. The Gurage sacrifice a cow, goat, or sheep before a collective tilling of barren banana plantings. By this sacrifice they try to guarantee the protection of the plantings from insects. Erotic dances are performed during the sacrifice and indicate a connection with fertility rites. Half of the sacrificial meat is eaten by the participants of the sacrifice in the evening immediately after the sacrifice is made; the other half of the meat is eaten on the next day.

In some cases preference for a barren cow as an object of sacrifice is displayed. Possibly the age-old practicality of the peasants plays its role here, reinforced by sacral motives. The sacrifice of a barren cow is noted among the Tigrean Akkele Guzai (in Eritrea).[41] Among the Baria, they bring into the house the killed barren cow as a funeral sacrifice.[42] In the

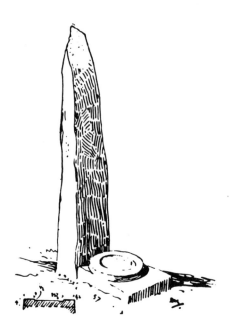

Stele with altar, Yeha.

inscription from Safra also, according to Drewes' interpretation, a barren cow and a barren sheep figure.[43]

One of Ezana II's inscriptions speaks of sacrificing 100 bulls at one time to Mahrem.[44] The inscription from Safra also is connected with the sacrifice of a cow and contains, in the opinion of Drewes, a series of special terms which relate to the ritual of slaughter.[45] In particular, the priest-slaughterer (*sĕwāʿi*) figures here.[46] Inscriptions from Preaxumite Ethiopia[47] speak of the slaughter of a cow; the legend about the serpent-king also tells about the sacrifice of goats.

Judging by the inscriptions from Safra, sacrifices of products of agriculture and apiculture were also made. However, it is not known whether aromatic substances were burned to the Axumite gods, but this form of offering is quite probable.

Even in the Preaxumite period a statue of an animal was being substituted for the live sacrifice. Bronze and stone statuettes of sacrificed bulls, rams, goats, camels, and wild animals have come down to us, and also depictions of stone [mountain] rams, bulls, and gazelles with dedicatory inscriptions engraved on stone. All of them are of Preaxumite and Early Axumite date. The bronze statuette of the bull from Zeban Kutur has an inscription which speaks of the dedication of a young bull (lgʿ) to Astar "here and there."[48]

Text D of the Safra inscription leads us into a circle of rites and ideas connected with sacrificial offerings. A gift consisting of money and butter was brought by a person in ritually clean clothing. For bringing firewood and vegetable oil clean clothing was not obligatory. Ryckmans, who explained the text, found analogies among the ancient Jews (Genesis 35:2, II Kings 10:22, II Kings 22:14) and also among the Sabaeans (penitential code published by I. Yu. Krachkovsky[49] and later by G. Ryckmans[50]) and also identified it with the Muslim custom of wearing *ihram* during hadj.[51]

The incipient social stratification of Early Axum is reflected in Axum religion by the custom of offering human sacrifices. In the Adulis inscription, the offering of sacrifices is only mentioned but precisely what kinds are not stated.[52] In Ezana II's inscription about the campaign on Afan a sacrifice to Mahrem is indicated—100 bulls and 50 captives.[53] In the legends about the serpent-king, human sacrifices are mentioned. Sacrifices were brought, possibly, to the pedestals of the stelae which were shaped in the form of altars. The blood flowed into depressions cut in the form of cups.

In South Arabia, only animal hecatombs are known but not human ones. Human hecatombs probably are an African feature introduced into the Axumite religion, although ancient Semites, for example, the Phoenicians, knew human sacrificial offerings.

Representations of Meroitic kings personally bringing sacrifices of people and animals are preserved. Heliodorus describes in detail the offering of sacrifice to the Meroitic gods: four horses, four bulls and twelve captives; six young men [youths] and six young girls [maidens].[54] In all cases known to us, as Heliodorus emphasizes, sacrifices involved foreign captives.

The offering of human sacrifices to the sun god among the Beja is well-known.[55] Human sacrifices to Poseidon among the ancient inhabitants of Berbera were spoken of earlier (the story of Yambul). In the Middle Ages, ritual sacrifice offerings (of members of the family proper) took place from time to time among Ethiopian Christians in the extreme northwest of the country. *The Book of Light/Maṣhafa Berhân*) of King Zara Yaqob and *The Life of Takla-Hawaryat*[56] tell about them. Finally, even at the very end of the XIX century A.D., human sacrifices were practiced by the kings of Kaffa, Janjero, and the states of the Ometos. Here, not captive foreigners but local inhabitants were offered as sacrifice. One way or another, the custom of human sacrifice was propagated in Northeastern Africa. Significantly, the Axumite kings offered human sacrifices (and also their sculptural substitutes) only to the god Mahrem.

In Axum, sacrificial offerings must have frightened the conquered and exploited. At the same time they presented a pleasurable spectacle for the residents of Axum. The propagation of Christianity led to the disappearance of this custom from the official religious sphere. It was, however, preserved up to the late Middle Ages in secret ritual practice.

Monotheism

During the reign of Ezana I the religion of the Axumites underwent change. Foreign monotheistic cults took root in Axum and in its African possessions. These cults were represented by the Christianity of various sects and by Judaism. These included Monophysites from Egypt, Syria, Constantinople, and South Arabia; Orthodox from Byzantium and Himyar (such as Bishop Grigentius); and also Nestorians. Thus, in Ethiopia Cosmas met residents of Socotra who professed Nestorianism. Side by side with Christianity, Judaism entered the Axumite Kingdom. Its bearers probably were Jewish merchants from Palestine, Egypt, and Arabia. By the beginning of the VI century A.D., Judaism had spread widely in Axum's Asiatic possessions. Subsequently the Falasha adopted Judaism. Halévy suggested that Jews were resettled in Semen by Ella Asbeha after 525 A.D.[57] It is possible that there were also Jews among the Axumites. An archaic Axumite inscription has been preserved with the name of a certain Yehudi (*yhd*),[58] who could have been a Jew. Interesting, but extremely unreliable, information is provided by one of the *Brief Chronicles* which relates that prior to the baptism of Axum under Ella Asbeha "some (Ethiopians) believed in Arwe, others were Jews." "In those times there still was no Turk (Muslim)," the *Chronicle*[59] adds.

The significance of the Jewish religion in Axum should not, however, be exaggerated. Yet it is difficult to find an author who would not speak about the so-called Judaic features of Ethiopian Christianity.[60] Here belong circumcision, the honoring of Saturday, and even dancing in churches— similar to the ritual dancing of King David. But not one of these customs can be traced to a direct borrowing from the Jews. Circumcision of boys was widespread in the ancient Near East and also in Northeastern and Eastern Africa, from Egypt to Zululand. The honoring of Saturday was introduced into Ethiopia in the XV century A.D., not under the direct influence of the Jews but on the basis of Christian dogmas. Moreover, Saturday was not so strictly celebrated as Sunday. As far as dances during divine services are concerned, this was an ancient and widespread practice in churches of the Near East, and it probably entered Ethiopian Christianity from local pagan cults. Therefore, the influence of Judaism on Ethiopian Christianity should be understood to have involved a sharing of common ideological frameworks but not specific ceremonial rites.

The ideas of monotheism entered Axum not only from the Near East but also from Asia. The first Indians appeared on Ethiopia's shores in the Preaxumite period. Probably the Indian colony on the island of Socotra arose then, the name of which, by the way, is of Indian origin. In the III century A.D., Indians who lived in Axum maintained constant connections with their homeland. At the end of the Preaxumite period, an ocean route from Egypt and the Mediterranean to India and the Far East was established. Adulis was one of the main stops on this route. In Adulis and later also in Axum there appeared Indian, Ceylonese, and Socotran merchants, accompanied no doubt by learned travelers: Brahmins, Jainists, and Buddhist monks. Traces of Indian influence are visible in the religious architecture of Axum, but the evidence does not appear conclusive. Ethiopian monks wore special robes (*haiyawa*) made of three pieces of cloth and decorated in a yellow color. They are strikingly similar to the clothing of Buddhist monks of Ceylon and Southeast Asia.

Under the influence of Near Eastern and Asiatic monotheistic religions, the religious consciousness of the Ethiopians changed. As more foreigners came to Ethiopia and settled within its borders, more and more Ethiopians became followers of foreign religions. We have seen that the Christianization of the Axumite Kingdom proceeded over the course of a prolonged period of time—more than two centuries. In this same period the very strongest penetration of other monotheistic religions into Ethiopia was occurring: Judaism, Buddhism, Manicheanism, and also the indefinite monotheism of Arabia. In the course of the III and IV centuries A.D., foreign monotheistic religions, local agricultural cults, and the "official" cult of Mahrem more or less peacefully co-existed on the territory of the Axumite Kingdom.

Other cults, connected with the practice of witchcraft, were also bound to exist. All of these religions mutually influenced each other. Traces of them can be detected in the medieval and modern religious beliefs of the Ethiopians. The relative vitality of the cult of Mahrem was the result of its official political role. The vitality of the agricultural cults, on the other hand, can be explained by the deep roots they had put forth in the religious consciousness of the peasants. The agricultural cults, therefore, affected the monotheistic religions little by little. The official cult of Mahrem, supported artificially, was not so universal and profound. It retained its official form but gradually acquired a monotheistic content.

Simultaneously with these developments, Axum witnessed the rise of its own distinctive monotheistic religion. It was, in many respects, similar to the indefinite monotheistic faith of South and West Arabia which arose under the influence of those same foreign monotheistic religions and which existed from the IV century A.D. to the time of Muhammad.[61] Having arisen almost simultaneously in both countries, the indefinite monotheism of Arabia supported the monotheism of Ethiopia and vice versa. This is noticeable in the religious terminology of the Axumite inscriptions.

Only two such inscriptions have been preserved. One of these is the well known "Christian" inscription of Ezana II (about the campaign into Nubia). All the authors except Turayev and Littmann call it "Christian."

Turayev recognized that the inscription was monotheistic but found it difficult to consider it Christian.[62] Littmann at first unconditionally proclaimed the inscription Christian[63] but subsequently showed the connection of its ideas and designations with the cult of Mahrem[64] and also of Astar.[65]

Only one almighty and universal deity figures in the inscription. Similar to the works of Christian literature, this inscription of Ezana II is begun with its dedication to a god, whereas in all pagan inscriptions first come the name and title of the king. Similar to the Christian god, the god of the inscription is a *triune god*. He is called by three different terms: "The Lord of All," "The Lord of the Heavens," and "The Lord of the Earth" (for "Earth" both the words Beher and Medr are used). All three names undoubtedly designate one and the same personage—the sole, universal god. Thus the term "Lord of All" (ግዘአ ፡ ቡኩሉ) was used as a stylistic substitute for the term "Lord of the Heavens" (እግዚአ ፡ ሰማይ). In another instance the god is called "The Lord of the Heavens and Earth" (እግዚአ ፡ ሰማይ ፡ ወለምድር). He is that one who rules in "Heaven and on Earth" (ምድር).

The primary designation of the god in this inscription is "The Lord of the Heavens" (እግዚአ ፡ ሰማይ). He is called by that title at the very beginning in the introductory formula and then seven times more. Two times the god is called "The Lord of the Earth" (እግዚአ ፡ ብሔር, እግዚአ ፡ ምድር) and once "The Lord of All." "The Lord of All" appears after an extensive philosophical definition: "By the strength of the Lord of the Heavens who made me the sovereign, who is to everyone Eternity, who is perfect, who reigns, who is invincible to the foe. . . . By the strength of the Lord of All I waged war." The terms "Lord of the Heavens" and "Lord of Earth" are used in one and the same sense[66] but the composer of the inscription clearly prefers addressing the god as "The Lord of the Heavens." "The Lord of Earth" and "The Lord of the Heavens" frightens and conquers the foe and "The Lord of the Heavens" gives the king spoils of war. Probably these two designations were preliminarily connected with two different cults; the designation "The Lord of the Heavens" was connected with the more official one. This could only have been the cult of Mahrem merged with the cult of Astar. "The Lord of Earth" or the "god Beher" and the "god (goddess) Medr" is clearly connected with the merged cult of Beher-Medr. In such an instance, the inscription about the campaign into Nubia reflects the ultimate merging of Mahrem, Astar, and Beher-Medr under the influence of the ideas of Christianity. Let us recall that the brief Greek version of the inscription concerning the campaign into Nubia is entirely Christian and monotheistic. In it, in place of the "God of the Heavens," the "God of Earth," and the "God of All" figures the Trinity, Jesus Christ (also called "His [God's] son" and simply "Christ"), and God.

These terms are stylistically interchangeable in the inscription just as the three terms for designating God in its Ethiopian version.[67] In the inscriptions of Kaleb and Wazeb the place of the "god Mahrem unconquered by the foe" is occupied by Christ "unconquerable by the foe," to whom the specific functions of the war[like] god of the Axumites were transferred.

Evidently also other Ethiopian deities merged with the concept of a single god who became polymorphic, since each deity was represented by its own personification. But the chief gods composed a triad or, more precisely, several triads: The Sun, the Moon, and Venus; Zeus, Ares, and Poseidon; Mahrem, Beher, and Medr. These triads blended with each other and merged into the image of a universal god. Moreover, the universal god became a *triune god* similar to the god of Christian dogmatics. This facilitated the acceptance of Christianity. Undoubtedly the notion of a *triune god* appeared in Axum as the natural product of a conceptual familiarity with local deity triads. But the explicit formulation and inculcation of this idea arose only under the influence of the preaching of Christianity.

The last inscription of Ezana II is considered the sole memorial of Axumite indefinite monotheism. However, a recently discovered inscription from Wadi Menih reveals these same religious notions. It says, "I, Abreha, a native of Axum [or the proper name Takla Axum, literally meaning "plant of Axum"]. And I remained here. I arrived [by the strength] of the Lord of the High Heavens with my son."[68] The expression "[by the strength] of the Lord of the High Heavens" almost precisely repeats the phraseology of Ezana II's inscription. It is significant that the author of the inscription from Wadi Menih bears the Judaeo-Christian name of Abreha. He could have been a Jew or a Christian. This was an Axumite who had turned to one of the monotheistic religions but his monotheism was just as indefinite as in Ezana II's inscription.

Possibly the church at Ouchatei Golo near Axum belonged to this cult. It is dated to the Christian period (middle of the VI to VIII centuries A.D.) but is clearly not Christian. Judging by the large basalt font and "holy of holies" attached from the east,[69] ablution and secrecy played a prominent role in the ritual.

The religious terminology of South Arabian indefinite monotheism found its way into the Christian inscriptions of Axum, as illustrated by Wazeb's inscription. Arabic Christianity probably played the role of intermediary. In it "God the Father" was called by the term "Rahman." This was true regardless of sect. A similar practice could be observed among Jews, Hanifites, and later among the Muslims. In Wazeb's inscription we find the expression *bmḫmr rḥmnn* ("by the grace of Rahman"), which was borrowed from the ancient South Arabian language.

In the final analysis, this indefinite monotheistic religion became a preparatory stage for full Christianization. But since the propagation of

Christianity in Northern Ethiopia took at least 200 years, this preparatory stage was extremely prolonged. It represented a period of the coexistence and syncretism of old pagan beliefs, foreign monotheistic cults, and indefinite monotheistic religion. This period began in the middle of the IV century A.D. and continued at least up to the reign of Kaleb (Ella Asbeha) in the VI century A.D. The Christian necropolis at Kohaito arose sometime during the V or at the beginning of the VI century A.D. Evidently in the VI century A.D. the pagan temples of Axum, Adulis, and Yeha were converted (or rebuilt) into churches.

The religious policy of Ezana II and of Ella Asbeha and his successors bore a decidedly Christian character. In the Greek inscription of Ezana II first appear the "eucharistic" Christian formulae similar to the mottoes of the Axumite coins of the VI century A.D. This inscription, for the first time in Ethiopia, calls the Axumite king "the slave of Christ" (δοῦλος Χριστοῦ), long before the Byzantine emperor at the beginning of the VII century A.D. introduced the name "slave of God" into his title. In inscriptions of Kaleb and Wazeb we find that same formula in the form of *gbr krsts* (*gäbrä Krĕstos*). On coins of later Axumite kings we also find pious-military formulae: On Ioel's coins the motto "Christ [is] with us!" (*Krsts msln*) appeared. On the coins of Gersem I "Christ will conquer!" (or "conquers") appeared. On the coins of Mahadayas there appeared "Who conquers with the cross" (*z-b-mw-b-msql*).[70] The crown and scepter of the king were decorated with a cross. On coins the king was depicted with three crosses, each of which was a little smaller than his face. But concerning the persecution of the Heterodox in the VI century A.D. and in the Late Axumite period nothing is known. Muslim tradition speaks of the sojourn in the Axumite Kingdom of Muslims persecuted in Mecca. As indicated above, the church of the VI–VIII centuries A.D. at Ouchatei Golo was clearly non-Christian.

Here and there within the kingdom's territory, especially south of the rivers Mareb and Tekezze, the majority of the population remained non-Christian. Even today, Jewish and Kemant (a semi-Christian cult) communities flourish in this area. In Ethiopian Christianity itself (in its ideas, mythology, and ritual practices) are preserved a multitude of pre-Christian pagan elements. The old pagan myths about the earth mother, about Mahrem, about Almouqah, Venus (Astar), and "the lords of the mountains" continued to live under the new guise of Mary, God the Father, Christ, "Saint" Za Manthas Kedus, the God of the Holy Spirit [the Holy Ghost], "sainted" founders of monasteries, etc. During the Axumite period these pagan elements in Ethiopian Christianity were still stronger than in the Middle Ages.

The four churches of the Axumite period reconstructed from pagan temples, and the churches of Enda Cerqos, each have three cult locations: the altar, a treasury (diaconicon), and a baptistry where the rite of christening was carried out. Excavations at Matara discovered three churches of the VI–VIII centuries A.D. One of them, which is very small, has been rebuilt two or three times. Another one very much resembles a chapel over a burial vault and constituted part of a domestic architecture complex. The third is a village basilica with three major rooms and a baptistry with an aqueduct.[71] In the churches of the VIII century A.D. the baptistries are absent. Evidently christening (as in modern-day Ethiopia) was beginning to be conducted in the rivers. S. A. Kaufman notes the simplicity and severity of the appointments of the Axumite baptistries. However, the altars, the diaconica, and the windows of the churches both in the Axumite period and later were luxuriously decorated.

Unfortunately, information about the folk-religious beliefs of ancient Axum has not been preserved. However, well-developed Ethiopian folk ritual, well-known in the Middle Ages, undoubtedly played an important role in the religious life of Axum, as it does in Ethiopia today. It was sometimes conducted in opposition to official cults. Yet some folk ritual and folk beliefs were adopted by the official religion (Christianity), thereby depriving them of their traditional conceptual framework.

The development of religion in the Axumite Kingdom was a complex process which operated not only under the influence of spontaneous factors (economic and social development, social inequality, mutual interaction with religions of other peoples, etc.) but also under the influence of conscious governmental policy. The development of religion in the Axumite period led to the establishment of perhaps more complete unity of religious ideas throughout the territory under Axumite control. The territory consisted of six main regions: Northern Ethiopia, the Danakil desert, portions of Somalia, the country of the Beja, Nubia, and South Arabia. Axumite rulers strove to unite all of these regions under their hegemony not only by means of political and economic institutions but also by spreading a common religious ideology. At first the indefinite monotheism which was acceptable alike to Christians, Jews, local monotheists of Arabia, Ethiopia, and Nubia was such an ideology. Then, partly perhaps as a consequence of protracted struggle between Jews and Christians (in South Arabia and also, probably, in Ethiopia), Christianity became the official ideology of Axum. The Axumite kings strove to propagate it in all countries subject to them. In South Arabia they used military force and judicial repressions for the implanting of Christianity. In Nubia and the country of the Beja, Christianity was propagated not only from Egypt but also from Ethiopia. The testimony of Joannes Ephesius about a group of Christian-Axumites in Alva on the eve of its complete conversion to Christianity has been cited above. In the words of Al Hamdani, in the IX century A.D. the Nubians and the Beja called Allah (the sole god) by the name Behir[72] (a variant of Az Zabehir[73]); this is an extremely accurate transmission of the Ethiopian

Beher (Egzi'abḥēr), the name of the deity of the earth and of the Christian God. In the VI century A.D. Nubia was Christianized. The tribes of the desert plains, however, remained pagan although their religion also experienced the influence of Christianity. Beginning with the reign of Ezana II, and especially of Kaleb, religion began to play an increasingly greater role in the ideology and politics of Axum. The isolation of Ethiopia and Nubia (as a result of the Muslim conquest of Palestine and Egypt) led to the utmost growth of the significance of Christianity in the ideology of the Axumite society, and of religious ideology in the entire life of the country.

However, both in the Early and Late Axumite periods, religion was not the entire ideology. Side by side with it there existed political, legal, and moral ideas often virtually independent of the religious ones, especially in the earlier period.

Political ideology

One can only conjecture about the political ideas propagated in Axumite society on the basis of common notions about its social and governmental structure. These ideas did not remain unchanged over the expanse of the Axumite Kingdom's thousand-year history. However, to trace their development is virtually impossible. Ideas about the divine origin of royal authority and the idolization of the Axumite king were discussed earlier. The idea of the divine selection of the Axumite king, to whom the sole universal god provided a special protection, emerged during the reign of Ezana II. This idea was bound to be strengthened in subsequent centuries in connection with the spread of monotheistic religions and especially of Christianity.

With the strengthening of the monarchy, ideas of customary law (which represented remnants of a military democracy in the consciousness of the people) died out. The rejection by the kings of the official ethnic name was possibly connected with the decline of these ideas. The demagogic slogans that replaced ethnic names on the coins bore a clearly declarative character. On the coins of Ezana II's successors appears the Greek motto Τοúτο 'αρεσῃ τῇ χώρα: "In order that [this] be pleasing to the country." [74] The king clearly was striving for popularity among the people. The stability of the demagogic slogan was scarcely accidental; it reflected the stability of the official doctrine. Its first traces can be observed in late inscriptions of Ezana II—in the Ethiopian and Sabaean texts of the bilingual one, and in the "monotheistic" inscription where the king reflects concern about the fame of his town (or country) and is concerned that there be "no burdens" on his people.

On some of Kaleb's coins the motto " Τουτο 'αρεσῃ τῇ χώρα " or the analogous Ethiopian motto "z-'dl l-hgr" ("indeed this is pleasing to the town")[75] is preserved. But later it dies out, being replaced by the pious formula "Θεου 'ευ χαριστια" ("in thanksgiving to God"). Kaleb now thanks the God who gave him authority and no longer recalls his obligations to the people. This pious slogan is repeated by coins of the closest successors of Kaleb.

Variations are observed later. Coins of Esbael are in general devoid of "demagogic" and "pious" slogans. On Eon's coins the ethnic name is revived. On Wazena's coins there is the demagogic slogan "*l-'ḥzb ydll*"[76] ("with absence of the weak"). "In order that [this] be pleasing to the peoples." The "peoples" of Axum proper are meant. On Ioel's and Gersem I's coins, pious slogans appear: "*Krsts msln*" ("Christ [be] with us!") and "*Krsts ym*'" ("Christ conquers!"). Later, on the coins of Israel and Hataz I there appears the motto: *'bkḥ z-bŝ hbg* (or *hbl?*).[77] But on the coins of the kings of the VIII century A.D., Armah II and Hataz II, appear new demagogic slogans: on the coins of Armah—*fŝḥ l-ykn, l-'ḥzb* ("So that there be joy to the peoples"), *fŝḥ w-slm l-'hzb* ("joy and peace to the peoples"); and on the coins of Hataz—*ŝhl l-'ḥzb* ("good will [or grace] to the peoples!").[78] There appears to be some kind of ideological movement which evidently is a reflection of a political struggle. There is no direct evidence for this. One can speak only about a struggle of two trends in official Axumite ideology: the monarchical idea connected with Christian unitarianism, and the "demagogic," which is based on local traditions.

Laws and morals

Extremely little information is preserved concerning the law and legal procedures of ancient Axum. No code of written laws remains from the Axumite period. Indeed, it probably did not even exist. The first collection of legal standards appeared in the XVII century A.D. This is the well-known *Fehta Nagast* (*The Legislation of the Kings*) compiled on the basis of Coptic-Christian law in application to Ethiopian conditions. In this respect, the *Fehta Nagast* is reminiscent of *The Laws of the Omerites* (Himyarites), compiled in the VI century A.D. for the inhabitants of South Arabia on the basis of Christian-Byzantine standards, but taking into account local conditions.[79] They scarcely had a serious application in Himyar or, for that matter, in neighboring Ethiopia. However, in church practices of the Axumite Kingdom after its Christianization, Roman-Byzantine legal standards would have had to be applied for the first time. They could have been obligatory for Roman subjects who lived in Axum and Adulis and, to a far lesser degree, for Christianized natives. Jewish, Indian, and Ceylonese merchants evidently used their own religious law when they had dealings with their own fellow countrymen and co-religionists. It is no accident that early Muslim tradition extols the tolerance of the Axumite kings of the beginning of the VII century A.D.

At the end of the Axumite period, emigrés from Arabia introduced into the coastal regions of Ethiopia Muslim religion and Muslim law. In Islam, legal standards were contained in the religious literature itself, beginning with the Koran. In Christianity this is not so. Therefore the influence of Christianity on Ethiopian law was never especially strong even after the appearance of the *Fehta Nagast*. In the Axumite Kingdom, standards of customary law prevailed which were reflected in the prohibitory formulae of inscriptions of Ezana I, Ezana II, Kaleb, and Wazeb. These were spoken of earlier.

Of all the forms of ideology the ethical is the least ascertainable. It is especially difficult to reconstruct moral standards of Axumite society since neither original sacred books nor any kind of extensive artistic literature was left behind. Nothing has remained except a few inscriptions. Incidentally, penitential inscriptions are almost completely absent among these. It is possible to assume that in the period in which Axum flourished morals played an important role in the upholding of the authority of the monarchs and of other aristocratic personages. At least Ezana II was very concerned about imparting a high moral aspect to his image in the inscriptions. He strove to show himself as a just, magnanimous king who cared first of all about the welfare of his people.

He asserts that all of his raids were provoked by a hostile party and that he himself was only protecting traditional order and justice in relationships among peoples. The arrest of the Nubian leaders is explained by the fact that they were suspected of espionage. The arrest of the Afan *alite* is explained by his responsibility for the annihilation of an Axumite caravan. The king of the Aguezat was arrested when his "perfidy" was discovered. This characteristic also fits the inscriptions of Kaleb, Wazeb, and Ezana I. Evidently the standards of feudal morality were reflected in inscriptions of the Axumite kings.

That little which is known about political ideas, laws, and morals in the Axumite Kingdom attests to significant remnants of egalitarian political forms, and to a lack of the development of non-economic constraints on Axumites. These traits are revealed also in the other forms of Axumite ideology: literature and art.

Literature and art

I have devoted a special article to Axumite literature[80] which there is no point in repeating here. The development of Ethiopian literature up to the beginning of the late Middle Ages proceeded mainly in the framework of oral, popular, and professional creative work. Right up to the XIV–XVI centuries A.D., written literature played a secondary role. In the Preaxumite and Axumite periods it was represented only by epigraphic genres, the flowering of which dates to the IV–VI centuries A.D. After the propagation of Christianity, a rather small book literature intended for church needs appeared which, on the whole, was translated from the Greek. The Axumites and the tribes of the Preaxumite period did not have artistic or historico-mythological books; a well-developed oral literature substituted for them completely. Historical legends and religious myths were carefully preserved in the memories of many generations. Singer-reciters and peoples' poets knew an enormous quantity of verses and were able to improvise in the framework of traditional genres. A significant part of all of this folklore, plus the sung-spoken creative work, was the property of the entire population. The most powerful remnants of the primitive social structure—i.e., the presence of the familial-tribal divisions and traditions, the presence of the communal life style, and the weakness of class distinctions—all contributed to the dominance of oral literature.

A written language existed but served mainly for the sacral and business needs. Together with this (in the Preaxumite but more especially in the Axumite epoch) there gradually developed a written literature of an epigraphic sort. However, the translation of Christian books from the Greek, and the development of individualistic monasticism, created objective prerequisites for the emergence of a book literature. The conservative force of earlier social traditions had a telling effect on the fact that these prerequisites were not taken advantage of in the Axumite period. Only the appearance of victory inscriptions and feudal epic "stories"[81] attest to the development of class inequalities in Axumite literature.

In the Axumite period, Ethiopian representational art and architecture flourished. An excellent essay by Kaufman,[82] written by this experienced art critic and architect on the basis of extensive factual material, is devoted to their investigation. Here the development of Axumite art from its sources up to the monuments of the XIV–XV centuries A.D. is traced in detail from the viewpoint of aesthetics and technology. While examining Axumite art from an ideological viewpoint it is not out of place to repeat the thought which I enunciated elsewhere[83] about the natural development of gigantism in Axumite art.

Preaxumite art does not know either gigantic buildings nor colossal statues. Only during the Axumite period do we have the creation of the palace complex of Ta'akha Mariam, the 33.5-meter stele and other huge obelisks on a 114-meter base, the 5-meter bronze statue, etc. The trend toward gigantism, or gigantomania, reflected the tastes of the Axumite monarchy and fulfilled its ideological function—to inspire reverential trepidation before the grandeur and force of the sovereigns of these monuments. The relative wealth and overseas connections of the trade towns of Adulis and Coloe (Matara), the striving of their inhabitants toward comfort and ease, is reflected in the houses and necropoli at these sites. In Axum itself the contrast is striking between the palaces, churches, and royal

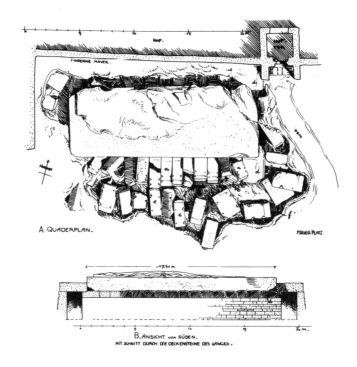

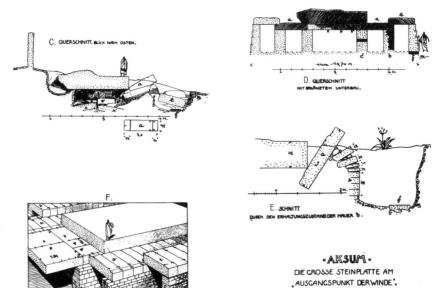

A. QUADERPLAN.

HOF.

EISERNE MAUER.

FREIER PLATZ

B. ANSICHT VON SÜDEN.
MIT SCHNITT DURCH DIE DECKENSTEINE DES GANGES.

C. QUERSCHNITT. BLICK NACH OSTEN.

D. QUERSCHNITT
MIT ERGÄNZTEM UNTERBAU.

etwa 10,70 M.

E. SCHNITT
DURCH DEN ERHALTUNGSZUSTAND DER MAUER b.

F.

QUERSCHNITT. REKONSTRUKTION.

·AKSUM·
DIE GROSSE STEINPLATTE AM
„AUSGANGSPUNKT DER WINDE".
AUFGEN. u. GEZ 1906 VON D. KRENCKER.

The Nefas Mawcha, Axum.

necropoli on the one hand and the wretched little houses of the common people on the other hand.

Music, singing, and dancing became the servants of the monarchy and the church. Singers and musicians practiced their art at royal receptions, as Joannes Malalae relates.[84] The appearance of the king before the people was accompanied by the dancing of women. The chronicle of the Emperor Zara Yaqob, who revived the ancient Axumite rites, asserts thus "When our king Zara Yaqob arrived in the land of Axum in order to carry out the whole rite of coronation, as his fathers the [Aksumite] kings did, all the people of the city and the monarchs in great joy met him—and many women performed a dance continuously according to their ancient order. During his entry into the walls of [Axum] the *makonnen* of Tigre and the *nebura-ed* of Axum stood to the right and to the left waving olive branches since such was their custom, therefore the *makonnen* of Tigre was called 'the observer of flies.'"[85] Undoubtedly, before us is a very ancient rite evidently correctly dated to the Axumite epoch.

We know that in the Ethiopian church singing, music, and even dances play a very large role. Local tradition dates the appearance of music, singing, and dances during divine services to the Axumite epoch. According to Ethiopian tradition, the inventor or reformer of Ethiopian church singing and the creator of the Ethiopian scale was Yared, a native Axumite who is considered a contemporary of one of the Late Axumite kings (Gebre Meskal).[86] All of this, to one degree or another, attests to the ancient integration of divine ritual with art.

Appendix. Sources on the History of Axum

The history and culture of the Axumite Kingdom (II–IX centuries A.D.)—
one of the greatest states of ancient and medieval Africa—have been given
little scholarly attention. Because of the paucity of epigraphic sources and
scanty archaeological effort, writings of foreign authors scattered fragmen-
tarily in manuscripts in the Greek, Latin, Syrian, Arabic, Coptic, and other
languages remain virtually the main sources on Axumite history. Proper
chronicles and other manuscripts probably did not exist among the
Axumites (with the exception of translations of Christian religious texts
into the Ge'ez language).

Probably the basic part of the preserved manuscripts has already been
published and in this area there is no reason to anticipate a large number
of new finds (*The Book of the Himyarites* in the 1920s and *The Chapters* of Mani
at the end of the 1930s and in recent time one of the two *Letters* of Simeon
Betharsham were the latest finds). On the other hand, new inscriptions
are being discovered continuously and the number of finds is growing with
the scope of archaeological operations. Unexcavated sites of Ethiopia, the
Sudan, and countries of the Arabian peninsula certainly conceal many as
yet undiscovered inscriptions, which will provide broad and relatively
reliable material on Axum's history.

The number of discovered written sources has already grown so much,
however, that the time has come to classify them and to provide a summary
review.

All sources are divided, according to their origin, into local or foreign
ones. All local sources are composed in the Ge'ez or Greek languages.

Sources can be divided into nine groups on the basis of content: (1)
epigraphic memorials, (2) diplomatic documents, (3) legislative acts, (4)
apologetical and polemical works, (5) chronicle writings, (6) itineraries,
(7) scientific-geographical works, (8) cult and hagiological literature, and
(9) artistic literary works.

The authenticity of written sources is determined by their origin, by
their belonging to one or another of the enumerated groups, by the time
of their appearance, and by their authorship.

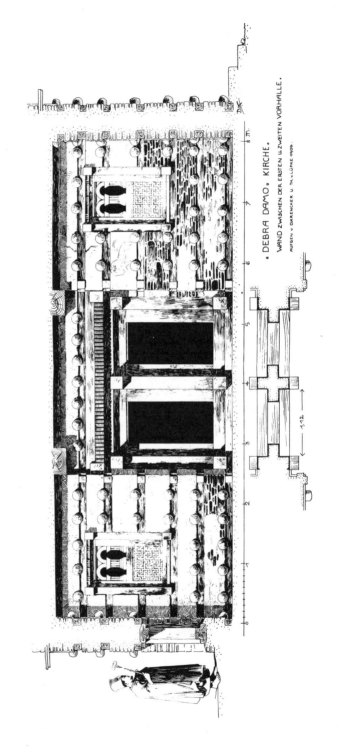

. DEBRA DAMO . KIRCHE .

WAND ZWISCHEN DER ERSTEN U. ZWEITEN VORHALLE .

AUFGEN. v. DARENCKER U. TH. v. LÜPKE 1906.

An interior wall of the church of Debre Damo.

Epigraphic memorials

As a rule the most authentic and valuable (albeit tendentious)˙ are the epigraphic sources, including inscriptions on coins of the Axumite kings. These are divided into four basic categories: (1) official inscriptions in the Ge'ez language, (2) official inscriptions of the Axumite kings in the Greek language, (3) private inscriptions of local origin and also inscriptions of foreigners who turned up in Ethiopia, and (4) Sabaean inscriptions from South Arabia which mention Ethiopians and the Axumite Kingdom. All of the inscriptions on coins belong to the first two groups.

The Ethiopian and Greek inscriptions of the Axumite kings have special importance: those of the unknown kings of the III–IV centuries A.D., Sembruthes (III–IV centuries A.D. [?]), Ezana I (IV century A.D.), Ezana II (V century A.D. [?]), Wazeb (VI century A.D.), and Kaleb (Ella Asbeha) (VI century A.D.). Of Ethiopian inscriptions alone no less than ten have been preserved, including the Ge'ez-language texts of the Ge'ez-Greek bilingual inscriptions of Ezana I and Ezana II. They are carved on the Axum stelae and also the Marib (Yemen) stelae. As a whole these ten epigraphic sources exceed in volume all of the remaining inscriptions in the Ge'ez language of the I–XVI centuries A.D. taken together. The five Greek inscriptions of the Axumite kings (including the two texts of the bilingual) complete this category of sources. They are, however, inferior to the Ethiopian royal inscriptions in their significance since it is precisely the latter which contain the most valuable information on history, geography, socio-economic and governmental structure, ideology, and the culture of the Axumite state.

First Jacques Ryckmans[1] and then Franz Altheim and Ruth Stiehl[2] and finally Janos Harmatta[3] and Jacqueline Pirenne came to the conclusion that "Ezana's inscriptions," just as the coins of this king, in reality belong to two or even three different rulers. Franz Altheim and Ruth Stiehl maintained that in the inscription of Ezana (II) concerning the campaign into Sudan there are Monophysite formulae of the confession of the faith and therefore it should be dated to the V century A.D. Harmatta has accepted this conclusion. Jacqueline Pirenne went still farther. First of all, she agreed to recognize Ezana I, who is mentioned as the addressee in the letter of Emperor Constantius II (337–361 A.D.), as the author only of the bilingual inscription about the resettlement of the six tribes of the Beja. Further, Pirenne—reading the first letter of the royal name as ጸ (Ṣ) or Θ (Th)—considers not Ezana but Tazena, who ruled at the end of the V century A.D. or during the VI century A.D., to be the author of three other inscriptions, including two pagan ones and a Christian one. Still another inscription whose author is considered to be Ezana she ascribes to a king of the beginning of the V century A.D. named Mḥdys[4] (Mahadayas?). Moreover, this French investigator considers that still another king named Ezana ruled in Axum in the middle of the VI century A.D.[5]

Beginning in 1960–1961, Pirenne radically revised the chronology of the Red Sea countries of the end of antiquity and the early Middle Ages.[6] Extreme difficulties lie on this path of Axumite study. First of all, because of the paucity of material, chronology on the basis of paleography is absent, although Pirenne, in particular, has made a series of valuable observations on Ethiopian paleography. Secondly, there is no generally accepted chronology based on numismatic data. The old chronology of Arturo Anzani[7] was recently revised by his compatriot F. Vaccaro,[8] the best expert on Axumite coins; moreover, J. Pirenne has proposed a series of additional corrections. In the third place, Axumite annal writings are absent and information contained in some versions of the lists of Axumite kings is extremely unreliable. Fourthly, sources different in nature—inscriptions, coins, communication of foreign authors, lists of kings—give a multitude of royal names. No doubt in some cases one person bore more than one of these names while in other cases the same name was given to several different persons. However, strictly speaking, at the present time, we are not in a position to say with certainty how many Axumite kings bore the name of Ezana or Kaleb or Armah or Gersem, etc. Almost every historian and numismatist has a somewhat different opinion on this score. More than any of the other researchers, J. Pirenne considered several kings as having the same name.[9]

In our opinion the most reliable criteria for establishing the time and authorship of the Axumite inscriptions remains their internal content, including the titling of kings, in comparison with data of numismatics and narrative sources.

Applying these criteria to Ezana's inscriptions, we see that all of the inscriptions have a series of common traits, namely:

1. The name of the king, and in the majority of inscriptions except the bilingual one ($DAE\ 4+6+7$) the name of his father—Ella Amida.
2. The "ethnic name" of the king.
3. The language, with the exception of insignificant peculiarities in the bilingual one ($DAE\ 4+6+7$).
4. The social, political and religious terms, and the system formed by them, with the exception of small distinctions in the bilingual ones which will be discussed below.
5. The idea of the Ge'ez-Greek bilingual inscription with three texts, the first of which is Greek, the second in the Ge'ez language with Himyarite script, and the third in the same language with Ethiopian script.

Moreover, the bilingual inscription ($DAE\ 4+6+7$) has a series of additional distinctions, of which the following are the most important:

1. The name of king Ezana is given without the name of his father.
2. In the concluding part of the title is added the name of the country of the

Habashat ("Ethiopia" in the Greek text), which is absent in all of the other Axumite inscriptions.

It should be noted that in the inscriptions of Kaleb (Ella Asbeha) we find more differences from the basic group of Ezana's inscriptions than from the bilingual inscription (*DAE* 4 + 6 + 7). But, in spite of the fact that the differences are far fewer than the traits of similarity, we must recognize that the title of the author of the bilingual (*DAE* 4 + 6 + 7) differs from the title of Ezana, son of Ella Amida. Evidently the author of this inscription is that Ezana to whom the letter of Emperor Constantius was addressed while Ezana, son of Ella Amida (Ezana II), is one of his later successors.

The bilingual inscription (*DAE* 4 + 6 + 7) of Ezana I tells about the resettlement of six tribes of the Beja from the northern to the southern boundaries of the Axumite Kingdom. It is carved on a large granite stele, in contrast to the inscriptions of Ezana II, which are engraved on limestone slabs. The Greek text occupies one side of the stele and the other is occupied by the two parallel texts in the Ge'ez language—one in Himyarite script, the other in the archaic Ethiopian consonantal alphabet.

The earliest of Ezana II's inscriptions is the one about personal collection of tribute (*DAE* 8), composed in the Ge'ez language with Himyarite script, which tells about the resumption of making the regular rounds of his possessions by the king. The next inscription (*DAE* 9) is about the campaign of the Axumites against the vassal principality of Aguezat, located probably in the foothills of present-day Eritrea. This inscription, like two later ones, is composed in the already reformed vocalized Ethiopian script. The inscription reckoned to be the third one (*DAE* 10) speaks about the campaign against the country of Afan, probably in Eastern Ethiopia near the boundaries of present-day Somalia. The fourth and largest inscription (*DAE* 11) tells about the campaign of Axumites into Kasu (Nubia). In contrast to all of the earlier pagan inscriptions, this inscription is monotheistic (while its recently discovered Greek version is Christian). Here, in addition to information about Axum, is contained extremely valuable information about Eastern Sudan.

The inscriptions of Ezana I and Ezana II were discovered in the last century and early entered into scientific use. Salt discovered the Greek text of Ezana I's bilingual inscription in 1805 and copied and published it. In 1835 Rüppel copied one of the Ethiopian texts of this bilingual inscription and two inscriptions of Ezana II. Theodore Bent and D. H. Müller again published these inscriptions.

Even at that time, the authorship of some of Ezana II's inscriptions was being debated. They were ascribed to Ella Amida, Hezana, and Tazena. Later, at the beginning of this century, Enno Littmann after several vacillations chose not to identify as their author the specific historic personage, the Axumite king Ezana [I], contemporary of Constantius II.

A rather broad scientific literature devoted to the inscriptions existed by the beginning of this century. In 1913 all five inscriptions were published by Enno Littmann with a commentary and German translation.[10] Littmann's publication eliminated errors of previous copies, added the second Ge'ez text of the bilingual inscription, and gave an improved translation. In 1948 Littmann once again prepared the three latest inscriptions for print, having corrected the translation in accordance with Nöldeke's observations[11] and having somewhat revised the commentary. This publication came out in 1950.[12]

In 1969 three more limestone stelae with four royal inscriptions were discovered in Axum: one Greek and three in the Ge'ez language with Himyarite script. Two of them on one stele proved to be the "pseudo-Sabaean" (in the Ge'ez language but with Himyarite script) and the Greek versions of Ezana II's inscription about the campaign into Nubia, the Ethiopian text of which is known as inscription *DAE* 11. Thus the latter proved to be part of a bilingual inscription of the same type as Ezana I's bilingual one. French Ethiopists who investigated the new stelae even advanced this hypothesis: Are not all of Ezana's other inscriptions similar bilingual ones? Or, perhaps, in general are not all of the large royal inscriptions of Axum bilingual ones with three parallel texts?

The "pseudo-Sabaean" text of the inscription about the campaign into Nubia has badly deteriorated and lends itself poorly to deciphering and restoration.[13] On the other hand, the Greek text is exceptionally well preserved and permits one conclusively to revise the chronology of inscriptions of Ezana I/Ezana II. While the religious terminology of the Ethiopian text is directly monotheistic, in the Greek text it is Christian, even Monophysite.[14]

The third inscription, composed in the name of Kaleb (Ella Asbeha), the well-known Axumite king of the VI century A.D., tells about his war with the rebellious principalities and tribes of Aguezat and Hasat[15] (about which the inscriptions of Ezana II also communicate, while later Arabic geographic sources communicate about Hasat or Al Has).

The fourth inscription belongs to Ella Asbeha's son Wazeb. It tells of his military operations in the interior of Ethiopia[16] against the principality WYTL (or WYTG). Unfortunately this inscription—one of the largest Ethiopian inscriptions in general—lends itself poorly to interpretation. In Axumite inscriptions we find a multitude of words which are not duplicated in the texts of literature in the Ge'ez language. The late Soviet Semitologist V. P. Starinin was correct when he said to the author of these lines that the living Ge'ez language has come down to us very incompletely.

The following peculiarities are characteristic of royal inscriptions of the epoch of Axum's ascendancy: (1) the inclusion of a relatively large amount of text with information both necessary and superfluous; (2) two languages and three systems of writing, whereas the remaining Axumite inscriptions are composed only in the Ge'ez with one script—the Ethiopian consonantal and later the Ethiopian vocalized script.

In 1947 still another of Kaleb's inscriptions was found by the Egyptian archaeologist Fakhry in Marib (Yemen). It was published in 1963 by the well-known Egyptian philologist Murad Kamil[17] and then for a second time with several corrections by André Caquot.[18] The vocalized inscription, which is very poorly preserved, tells about a campaign on ships and about military victories, and quotes the Psalter. Evidently the campaign of Ella Asbeha into Himyar in 525 A.D. is being spoken of. Consequently, this Axumite king is the author of the inscription.

The three inscriptions of the Hadani Dan'el which date to the very end of the Axumite period (IX century A.D. to the beginning of the XI century A.D.) constitute another group of official Ethiopian inscriptions in the Ge'ez language. They are engraved on one of the stone dedicatory thrones of Axum.

The throne and the inscriptions which cover it were first described by Salt and later published by Littmann in reports of the Axum expedition.[19] These inscriptions are of great interest not only for the history of late Axum but also for earlier periods. One of the inscriptions, as has been shown in a special article, is a work of epic literature reworked in the form of a victory inscription.[20] It is very important for the history of epic literature in general and literature of the Axumite period in particular.

The unvocalized inscription from Matara was discovered as early as 1895. First published by Conti-Rossini in 1896,[21] it was left partly untranslated by him. Littmann again published it in 1913 and provided the following translation:

> The 'GZ [people of 'Agaz?] raised
> this stele for the sake of its fathers
> and built a canal (?) from Aua-
> Alapho and from ṢBL.[22]

In 1945 Ullendorff gave a new interpretation to the inscription. He translated the last two lines as "[the Agaz people] subjugated the young and strong men of Aua-Alapho and ṢBL."[23] Finally, in 1962, Drewes gave a third and most probable interpretation. He translated the controversial lines in the following way: the stele "was transported by his ['GZ] friends from Subla and Aua-Ilpha." Moreover, the two last names proved to be old names of Baraknaha and Gunarguna, known for their ancient churches.[24] The inscription should be dated according to its paleographic peculiarities to the middle of the second half of the IV century A.D.[25]

During the Italian occupation of Ethiopia an inscription in the Ge'ez language on an ancient obelisk from Anza was discovered by chance and published by Conti-Rossini in 1942.[26] No more than four or five inscriptions were discovered in Ethiopia during this period in spite of the presence in the country of thousands of educated Europeans who had penetrated into formerly inaccessible places. The inscription from Anza was composed in the name of the king of the Angabo people and is important for the study of the social structure of ancient Ethiopia. Conti-Rossini and Cerulli date it to the II century A.D.[27] However, in our opinion it is far younger than Gedara's inscription from Asbi Dera and somewhat older than the inscriptions of the first half of the IV century A.D. Accordingly, this inscription from Anza dates to the end of the III century A.D. or to the first half of the IV century A.D.

In 1954, in a sanctuary at Havila Asserai, a bronze votive object was found with an inscription in Ge'ez.[28] Drewes read it as "GDR, king of Axum, seized control of the passages (?) of 'RG and LMQ." [29] However, in 1957 Jamme gave a new far more valid translation: "GDR, king of Axum, submitted before (the gods) 'RG and Ilmaque (LMQ)." [30] Both investigators date the inscription on the votive object to the end of the II century A.D. However, as the result of the very newest discoveries, the date should be moved to the middle of the III century A.D.

In May 1955 at Safra, close to the village of Kohaito known for its remarkable dam, a stone was discovered with an extensive Ge'ez inscription. The inscription, consisting of four texts of a legislative nature, contains exceptionally important material about social relationships and law in the Axumite Kingdom. It was not published until 1962.[31] According to the form of the letters, virtually identical to that of the letters of the Ethiopian text of Ezana I's bilingual inscription, this unvocalized inscription should be dated to the IV century A.D.[32]

Finally, the mottoes of Axumite coins constitute a special group of official inscriptions in the Ge'ez language. The Axumite kings of the end of the III century A.D. to the middle of the IV century A.D. minted coins with legends in Greek.

Also, no less than six royal inscriptions of Axum in the Greek language have been preserved, including the two Greek texts of the bilingual inscriptions of Ezana I and Ezana II. The longest of the Axumite inscriptions in Greek has not been preserved in the original but was copied by Cosmas Indicopleustes at the beginning of the VI century A.D. and included in the text of his *Christian Topography*.[33] This inscription on the famous Adulis monument contains information of exceptional value. Its essential shortcoming is the omission of the name of the person who dedicated it, which makes it difficult to identify with one of the well-known Axumite kings. Dillmann identifies it with Ze Haqile.[34] Drouin was inclined to consider the person who dedicated it to be King Ella Awda (or Za Ella Awda),[35] known only from the "Lists of Kings." Glaser at first (in 1890) thought that the inscription was left not by an Axumite but by a Himyarite king, but under the influence of criticism retracted this hypothesis and acknowledged the author of the Adulis inscription to be an Axumite king who ruled after Ze Haqile.[36] At present, thanks to the investigations of J. Pirenne[37] and A. Drewes,[38] the inscription can be attributed to the Axumite king Sembruthes and dated to the beginning of the IV century A.D.

Another Greek inscription of four short lines gives the name of the person who dedicated it: Sembruthes or Sembrythes (Σεμβρυϑης). It was discovered and copied by Sundström[39] in 1903. Then Littmann[40] again published it. This inscription dates to the beginning of the IV century A.D. Perhaps it is only three years younger than the Adulis inscription. Because of the place in which it was found it is known as the inscription from Deqe Mehari.

The third inscription composed in Greek has also come down to us without the name of the king who dedicated it. It was discovered in Abba Penteleon by the German Axum expedition and published by Littmann in his report.[41] The inscription which mentions a campaign of the Axumites into "a country along that side of the sea" dates to the III century A.D. or to the beginning of the IV century A.D. It is badly damaged, yet has great value and contains information on the politics and religion of Axum.

The fourth Greek inscription of an Axumite king was found beyond the borders of Ethiopia in Meroe. Sayce discovered and published it in 1909.[42] It also is badly damaged and does not contain the name of the person who dedicated it; only his title has been preserved. The inscription, which tells about a campaign of the Axumites into Sudan, dates to the beginning of the IV century A.D. and holds great interest for the investigation of the political history as well as the religion of Axum.

Finally, the Greek texts of the bilingual inscriptions and the Greek legends on the Axumite coins round out the category of official Axumite inscriptions in the Greek language.

In addition to official inscriptions, a certain number of private inscriptions have been preserved. They belong both to natives of the Axumite Kingdom and to foreigners who were located there. All of the private inscriptions are composed in the Ge'ez language, with the exception of the brief dedicatory inscription from Abba Penteleon which is composed in Greek. Judging by the names, it belongs to emancipated Roman slaves of the epoch of the Antonines. The inscription was discovered by the German Axum expedition in 1906 and published by Littmann.[43] This expedition also discovered two more private inscriptions composed in the Ge'ez language in Axum: the inscription of stonemasons on one of the stone building blocks and the inscription of a certain Yehudi (Iudi).[44] The first inscription is vocalized and dates to the V–VII centuries A.D. The second is unvocalized and dates to the end of the III century A.D. or to the middle of the IV century A.D. In the V–VII centuries A.D. a vocalized inscription in Ge'ez of a certain "Davit (David) the Egyptian" was left, which was discovered by Bruce in Axum as early as the XVIII century A.D. and rediscovered later by Salt and Bent. It also was published by Littmann.[45]

The inscription on the stone font from Axum, which was discovered long before the remaining unvocalized inscriptions, dates to an earlier time. Rüppel discovered and copied it in 1832 or 1833.[46] After seven years the inscription was again copied by Theophile Lefebvre.[47] Dillmann did not give the first translation of it until 1878: "The stone which Ahlal made in order to wash himself."[48] In 1911 Littmann gave a new interpretation of the text: "The bowl which was made by Ahlal for the place of worship."[49]

Later, in 1962, Drewes proposed a new translation. Considering the last word of the inscription $mst'zl$ to be a proper name, he corrected Littmann's[50] translation accordingly. No one was satisfied with Drewes' translation. G. Ryckmans pointed out that the word $mst'zl$ ($masta'zil$) had in the Christian period a connection with liturgical dances in the churches.[51] In any event this was some kind of cult term connected with temple ritual. Judging by the script the inscription dates to the end of the III century A.D.[52]

The next unvocalized inscription of six lines was discovered in 1906 by F. L. Griffith on one of the pyramids in Meroe (A. 19). This inscription, which was also published by Lepsius,[53] has not yet been completely deciphered. The reading of separate groups of words was established by Littmann.[54] After the Second World War, Laming-Macadam discovered and published one more extremely archaic Ethiopian inscription—unvocalized—of three lines, on the northern outside wall of Temple T at Kawa. Rabin[55] tried to translate it but his translation is not indisputable. Just as do the above named authors, I consider both Ethiopian inscriptions from Nubia to be private ones.

Still another unvocalized private inscription in Ge'ez was found on the eve of the Second World War in Egypt at Wadi Menih on the ancient caravan road to Berenika. It was not interpreted and published until 1954 by Littmann.[56] The inscription, which mentions the "God of the Heavens," is especially interesting for judging the religious concepts of the Axumites; according to its content, style, and paleography it should be dated to the middle of the IV century A.D.

Three private vocalized inscriptions in the Ge'ez language date to the VI–VII centuries A.D. They are of emphatically Christian content and are embellished with crosses. The first of them, a tombstone inscription from the church at Ham, was discovered by Monneret de Villard and published by him in 1940.[57] It gives the name of the Axumite king Ella Sahel and a series of facts on the culture of Christian Axum. Another inscription of four lines was found by Conti-Rossini on Mt. Edith.[58] A third inscription from

Saro (Akkele Guzai region) was published by Drewes in 1962.[59] The historical value of these latter inscriptions is not great. They are interesting by virtue of their containing quotations from Christian books. Moreover, the inscription from Saro bears a social coloration. Judging by paleography, the inscription from Ham is somewhat older. The inscription from Saro is younger and the inscription from Mt. Edith is still younger. In the first of these inscriptions the words are separated by a vertical line as in Ezana's inscriptions. In the inscription from Mt. Edith the words are separated by a colon, as in the inscription of Hadani Dan'el and in the medieval books. In the inscription from Saro both forms of separations are used but the colon predominates.

In recent times two of the earliest inscriptions in Ge'ez have been discovered.[60] Both of them are on bronze statuettes of bulls offered as sacrifices. The inscriptions are read from right to left and in general do not have word separators. The tracing of the letters is extremely archaic. The statuettes and the inscription are scarcely older than the beginning of the III century A.D.

Among the comparatively recently discovered inscriptions in the Ge'ez language three are of special interest. One of them, which according to the tracing of the letters is dated to the same time as the inscription from Anza, is carved on a large undressed stone in the town of Axum itself. It consists of the word *dawal*, "territory boundary," and two proper names plus auxiliary particles. Evidently this inscription is on a boundary-marker stone.[61] Two other inscriptions came from Matara. One of them is probably also a boundary marker. The content of the other is unexplained. The peculiarity of this inscription is the designation of the number "one hundred" by its initial letter ፭ (in Ge'ez "one hundred" is ፼ችት; compare with the Amharic መቶ and Arabic مِئَة); the number of letters ፭ written one after another corresponds to the number of hundreds of objects—most likely head of cattle.[62] The hundreds in the recently discovered inscription of King Wazeb, son of Ella Asbeha, are designated in the same way.

Even the extremely brief inscriptions of the Axumite period can be of interest to the historian, paleographer, and linguist. Inscriptions on intact vessels and graffiti on crocks from Matara are such.[63] Speaking of inscriptions on vessels, I must mention one more on an Axumite alabaster lamp found in South Arabia; however, this epigraphic document is known to me only from a photograph.[64] A late Himyarite inscription from Sehuf Emni in Eritrea, unique for Ethiopia of Axumite time, which has attracted undeservedly little attention of epigraphists-philologists, is of interest.

In addition to epigraphic sources of Ethiopian origin or those found on Ethiopian territory, the Himyarite-Sabaean inscriptions are important for the history of Axum. They permit the study of a civilization which was territorially and chronologically close, and the investigation of the politics of a state which maintained various links with Axum. Many inscriptions were left by individuals who were either political opponents or allies of the Axumite kings. Some of the inscriptions directly mention Axumites and events of their history.

The following inscriptions from South Arabia in the Sabaean language which were published prior to the Second World War have the utmost significance for the history of Axum: (1) The inscription of the Himyarite prince Alhan Nahfan, which mentions the Axumite king Gedara; this inscription was published in 1920[65] in a photograph and as yet there is neither a transcription nor a detailed analysis of it.[66] (2) The inscription of the Hamdanite prince Abikarib Yuhaskir and his brothers, published in a photograph[67] and translated into French by Conti-Rossini.[68] (3) The inscription of the Hamdanite princes Rabsams Yazid and Yakbayyam Ya'zil, published in a photograph along with the two previous ones[69] and translated into French by Conti-Rossini.[70]

A series of new inscriptions was discovered in the 1940s as a result of Egyptian expeditions to Yemen and Saudi Arabia by Kh. Y. Nami, A. Fakhry, and H. Philby (an Englishman who embraced Islam). Nami published a series of Himyarite inscriptions of the III–IV centuries A.D.,[71] among which four are of interest also for the history of Axum (especially Nami 26, Nami 43, and Nami 72 + 73 + 71). Fakhry not only discovered new Sabaean and Himyarite inscriptions, but also made improved copies of the previously known ones.[72] A series of Fakhry's inscriptions, repeated in subsequent publications, are extremely important for the history of Axum. Philby also discovered new inscriptions.[73]

In 1951–1952 a multitude of Himyarite inscriptions of the II–IV centuries A.D. were discovered in the south of Saudi Arabia and Yemen by G. Ryckmans' expedition. He later published them. Geukens discovered several more inscriptions of which two—Geukens 3 and 7—contain information important for the history of Axum; Jamme published them.[74]

Almost all of Ryckmans' inscriptions are interesting for the history of Axum since they were left by contemporaries and neighbors who were sometimes political opponents, sometimes allies of the Axumite kings. Three inscriptions of the end of the II–III centuries A.D.[75]—Ry, 533,[76] Ry, 535, and Ry, 539[77]—mention Axumites and are of interest for the history of Ethiopia. Around the second of these a whole controversy flared up as a result of which the chronology of Axumite and Sabaean-Himyarite history was revised.

Finally, an American expedition at the beginning of the 1950s discovered a new series of inscriptions in Marib, the capital of the Sabaeans. Especially important for the history of Axum are Ja, 574–577, 585, 631, 635, 639 and several others.[78]

All of these inscriptions contain important, even unique, data which permit us to make more precise the chronology of Axumite history and certain features of the social and political structure of the Axumites. They are especially valuable by virtue of the fact that they essentially supplement information about military operations which the Axumites carried out in South Arabia and give a notion about the Arabian possessions of Axum. All of the enumerated inscriptions and also the inscription of the Adulis monument can be dated to the middle of the III century A.D. or to the beginning of the IV century A.D.

One other group of Himyarite inscriptions, especially important for the history of Axum, dates to the first half of the VI century A.D. They were composed by local kings and princes: Marsa'ilan Yanuf, Ma'adikarib, Yusuf As'ar Masruk Dhu-Nuwas, Sharakh'il Yakbul, Sumafa Ashwa, Abreha, and others. The most important inscriptions of this group are the following: (1) the inscription from Husn al Gurab, known since 1834,[79] to which numerous pieces of literature are devoted; (2) the Marib inscription of Abreha, which has been repeatedly published—even with a Russian translation (*CIH*, 541);[80] (3) the inscription of Sumafa Ashwa from the Istanbul museum (*RES*, 3904), known since 1927–1928 and also repeatedly issued;[81] (4) one more inscription of Abreha published by G. Ryckmans; (5) a third inscription of Abreha discovered in Yemen by the American expedition and published by A. Jamme (*Ja*, 546); (6–8) three inscriptions of King Yusuf Dhu-Nuwas which speak of events of the years 517–518 A.D. Two of these were published in 1953 by G. Ryckmans (*Ry*, 507; *Ry*, 508) and the third was published in 1962 by A. Jamme (*Ja*, 1028).[82] In addition to the enumerated ones, other Sabaean-Himyarite inscriptions have well-known significance for the history of Ethiopia although they do not mention Axum and the Ethiopians.

Diplomatic documents

Official diplomatic documents constitute a special category of written sources. Letters sent and received by Axumite and Himyarite kings belong to this category. None of them are preserved in the original but are included in full, or in short excerpts, in chronicle and religious-polemic works.

The letter of the Roman emperor Constantius II (337–361 A.D.) to the Axumite king Ezana I, which was written about 356 A.D., is preserved in its entirety. The text of the letter is quoted by Athanasius the Great in his *Apology to the Emperor Constantius*.[83] The authenticity of the text is un-doubted. Athanasius included it in a letter addressed to Constantius himself. Despite the fact that the *Apology* was directed against the emperor, the text of the letter does not display any sort of traces of hostile editing. The letter reached Athanasius in the original or as a copy probably via his friends at the Axumite court.

The text of the letter of the Byzantine emperor Justinian to the Axumite king Ella Asbeha has been preserved in excerpts quoted from memory by the ambassador himself in his memoirs. This ambassador was most likely either Julian or Nonnus. Excerpts from this composition along with bits of the letter turned up in Joannes Malalae's *Chronographia*,[84] and also in the *Chronographia* of Theophanes the Byzantine (who calls the ambassador Julian).[85]

Other diplomatic letters have been preserved only in very free paraphrases. The letter of the Himyarite king Dhu-Nuwas (Yusuf) to the Lakhmide king Al Munzir III has come down to us in the exposition of persons hostile to both kings. These individuals (Avraam, the father of Nonnus; Simeon, the bishop of Beth Arsham who was the author of the two *Letters* about the Himyarite martyrs; Sargis or Georgis, the bishop of Rusaphius, who probably was the author of *The Book of the Himyarites*) personally were present during the reading of Dhu-Nuwas' letter to Al Munzir III. The existence of the letter is known from several sources: the *Letters of Simeon Betharsham*, *The Book of the Himyarites*, *The Martyrdom of Arethius*, and others. However, its text is preserved only in the *Letters* and sources dependent on it. The following three works are meant: (1) the Monophysite chronicle of Joannes Ephesius (John of Asia, John of Amida), who was the pupil of Simeon Betharsham (Joannes included one of the *Letters* in his own work); (2) the chronicle of Pseudo Dionysius Tel Mahr, who rewrote the *Letter* from Joannes' chronicle; (3) the chronicle of Zaharios Miytilenios, who briefly set forth the same *Letter*.

With each new rewriting of Simeon's *Letter* it was subjected to new distortions. The text of the letter cited in the *Letters* cannot be considered as genuine: it compromises Dhu-Nuwas and glorifies his enemies. Simeon himself notes in the first of the *Letters* that "the king of the Himyarites did not write all of this in his letter."[86] If the fact of the existence of the letter does not provoke doubt, then its content is transmitted by Simeon at least tendentiously. It is possible to propose that Simeon not only included in the text of the letter sentences which did not exist in it but at the same time did not fully transmit its content. However, in spite of the distortion in the *Letters*, a little of the genuine content of the letter was preserved.

This cannot be said of the preserved texts of letters which the Axumite king Ella Saham and the Muslim Prophet Muhammad supposedly exchanged. The Axumite king in his letter speaks with the tongue of a pious Muslim. The text of both letters has been preserved in the *History of Prophets and Kings* which At Tabari wrote, based on works of Arabic sources of the VIII–IX centuries A.D.[87] and also in a comparatively late Arabic composition *Sirat al Halibiia*. In 1938 there was found in Damascus a parchment with a letter of Muhammad to the Axum nagashi. Such parchments with letters of the prophet to the rulers of Iran and Egypt were published in the last century and in recent years; the argument about their authenticity continues to the present time. The publisher of the document, D. M. Dunlop, and specialists from the British museum including the famous Arabist Margolis, recognized the parchment from Damascus as an article from the last century.[88] Actually this is a well-preserved brown parchment of correct rectangular shape with a text written with correct Cufic script, which is virtually no different from the version of the "letter of the Prophet" cited in *Sirat al Halibiia* (even the obvious errors coincide). However, in the argument about the possibility of using the "letters of Muhammad" (in the versions which have come down to us) as a historical source we must not forget the famous remark of Mark Bloch about the fact that at the height of the Middle Ages many documents were prepared simply to replace lost ones and not with the purpose of deliberate falsification. Arab historians quoting the texts of the "letters of the Prophet" first of all followed the oral tradition and the Koran; therefore one cannot speak of any kind of precise transmission of documents. But the very fact of the correspondence between Muhammad and the Axumite king is entirely probable. The content of the letters is not known.

Legislative acts

Legislative acts constitute another category of official documents. Of local Ethiopian legislation only the recently discovered inscription from Safra has been preserved. Roman codices of the emperors Theodosius and Justinian give some information useful for the history of Axum. The Axumites are even mentioned in Theodosius' codex. Certain articles of the Roman codices concern trade of the empire with "barbarians," including inhabitants of the Axumite Kingdom. *The Laws of the Himyarites*, whose compilation is ascribed to the Himyarite bishop Grigentius, are also of interest.[89] These "laws" were left as the fruit of a purely literary creation and had no sort of practical application. However, they contain some information about the Himyarite Kingdom in the period of Abreha's reign.

Apologetical and polemical works

The Laws of the Himyarites is a source which overlaps both the category of legislative acts and the category of literary-polemical works. They are memorials of publicism of the time and possess all of the virtues and shortcomings of publicism. The literary-polemical works of the IV–VI centuries A.D. are of interest for the history of Axum. One of them, *Apology to Emperor Constantius*, was directed against the Arians. Three others were directed against the South Arabian Jews. All of these works are important for an analysis of the political situation in which the Axumites operated, upholding the independence of their state and subjugating neighboring countries to it.

Apology to Emperor Constantius[90] was written by the Alexandrine bishop Athanasius the Great in 357–358 A.D. (between February 24, 357 A.D. and October 2, 358 A.D.).[91] In it is contained information about the first Axumite bishop Frumentius and about the letters sent by Constantius II to the king of Axum. The text of one of the letters is included in the *Apology*.

The Axumites are mentioned in a letter of Synesius of Cyrene written about 410 A.D., not long before Synesius occupied the post of bishop of Ptolemais in Cyrenaica.[92] He tells of the struggle of the Christians with the barbarians (or Berbers) in the south of Cyrenaica—in the Jalu oasis, in the opinion of investigators of Synesius (for instance, Schwartz).[93] Based on Synesius' text, Caquot and Leclant have advanced the highly likely hypothesis that a rather numerous colony of Axumites with their own Christian clergymen is referred to. They could have gotten there via Nubia and the oases of Selim and Kufrah along the ancient caravan route.[94]

Four literary-polemical works date to the time of the persecution of the Himyarite Christians under Dhu-Nuwas: two *Letters* to Simeon, Archimandrite of Gabula (Jabala), written by Simeon Betharsham;[95] the *Epistle to the Najranians* of Jacob of Serug; and the verses of Joannes Psaltes. Simeon Betharsham's *Letters* were written in Syrian, the first one at the very end of February 519 A.D. and the second one, which was recently discovered, in July of 519 A.D.[96] They emerge simultaneously as propagandistic appeals, historical memoirs, and plans of concrete political actions. As sources they are highly subjective but provide interesting traits of the historic situation of that time when all of the Monophysite East looked to Kaleb, the Axumite nagashi, with hope.

The *Epistle to the Najranians* by Jacob of Serug was also written in Syria and in the Syrian language. It is an exhortation to the Najran inhabitants in their calamities. In the beginning of the letter Jacob speaks of the tribulations which befell the Najranians in such a way that one is permitted to think that these tribulations were still going on. Jacob died at the end of November, 521 A.D.,[97] consequently, the *Epistle to the Najranians* was written between the end of 518 A.D., when the news of the siege of Najran reached Jacob of Serug, and the autumn of 521 A.D.

The verse of Joannes Psaltes of Beth Autonius was written in Greek almost simultaneously with Simeon's *Letters*. During the life of the author, who died in 538 A.D., the verse was translated into the Syrian language by Paul of Edessa.[98] In 675 A.D. the translation was collated with the Greek original and corrected by Jacob of Edessa. It is this version which has been preserved up to the present while the Greek original and the preliminary translation have been lost.[99]

The two *Letters* of Simeon, the *Epistle* of Jacob of Serug, and the verse of Joannes Psaltes and its Syrian translation show what sort of response the Najran killings evoked in Syria and other Christian countries. The correlation of the politics of Axum and other powers with Christian social opinion becomes clear: in the period when Christianity was the sole world religion, it amounted to world social opinion.

The Book of the Himyarites also is devoted to events in Himyar in the beginning of the VI century A.D. It was written in Syria in the Syrian tongue soon after Dhu-Nuwas' overthrow by the Ethiopians and the return of King Kaleb [Ella Asbeha] to Axum. It is possible that the author of the book was Sargis (or Georgis) Rusaphius. King Abreha is not mentioned in *The Book of the Himyarites*, consequently it appeared between 526 and 535 A.D. This work stands at the boundary of the literary-polemical, chronicle-historical, and hagiological genres. It is advantageously distinguished from the hagiological monuments by its realism, its tendency toward exactness, and an almost complete absence of the legendary element. *The Book of the Himyarites* is one of the most valuable narrative sources on the history of Axum. It was first published in 1924 by the Swedish orientalist Møberg[100] and still has not been sufficiently investigated.[101]

One more composition of the polemical genre dates to the rule of Abreha—*Debate with the Jew Ebran*—ascribed to the Himyarite bishop Grigentius.[102] It was composed in Byzantium in the second half of the VI century A.D. but transmits an atmosphere of a sharp ideological struggle between Christians and Jews of South Arabia. The *Debate* is closely linked with *The Laws of the Himyarites* and *The Life of St. Grigentius*, representing together with them the orthodox trend in historical tradition. An Old Slavic translation of the *Debate* also exists, which was executed in the XVI century A.D.

Chronicle writings

Historical chronicles—Roman, Byzantine, Syrian, and Arabic—constitute the next group of narrative sources. Evidently the Axumites themselves did not have historical books and chronicles.

The most ancient of this group of sources is *The History of Divine Aurelian*, written in Latin in the IV century A.D. in the reign of Diocletian or Constantine, but on the basis of III century A.D. sources.[103] Its author was Flavius Vopiscus the Syracusan. *The History* makes up part of a collective work of historians of the IV century A.D., *Scriptores historiae Augustae*. Herein is mentioned a group of Axumites, Beja, and southern Arabs who arrived in Rome in 274 A.D. with Aurelian and who took part in his triumphal procession.[104] Vopiscus commits a pair of obvious anachronisms: his description of the triumphal procession evokes bewilderment but was probably made on the basis of authentic sources although supplemented with additional personal fantasies of the author or editor of *Scriptores*.

The Byzantine chronicle writings communicate significantly more information about Axum. Their information pertains basically to the first to third decades of the VI century A.D. Of them the most valuable is Procopius Caesarensis' *History of the wars of the Romans with the Persians, Goths and Vandals*. Procopius was a famous historian during the reign of Justinian. Procopius devoted two chapters of his book (XIX and XX) to a description of the Axumite Kingdom, the Beja, the Himyarites, the wars of the Axumites with the Himyarites, and diplomatic relations of Byzantium with them and with others.[105] Chapter XIX interrupts the course of the story about the historic events of chapters XVIII and XX and is an historic and geographic reference. In chapter XX Procopius describes events in South Arabia in 517–547 A.D.: the campaigns of the Axumites and the embassy of the Byzantines there. Procopius' information is detailed, frequently unique, and generally reliable since it was obtained at firsthand. One of his informants was Julian, the Byzantine ambassador to Axum and South Arabia. Procopius was the secretary of the famous Belisarius and found himself in the very thick of political events of a leading world power. This gives special value to his communications.

At the beginning of the second book of the work, Procopius mentions "Summus, the brother of Julian, who not long before had been sent as an ambassador to the Ethiopians and Himyarites."[106] This was "not long" before the events of 540 A.D., since the embassy of Julian took place evidently in 531 A.D. Probably, as Pigulevskaya proposes, in the case being considered Procopius simply ignored the chronology of events.

In chapter three of the second book of his work, Procopius tells about a remarkable episode. In 539 A.D. an Armenian embassy was visiting in the residence of the Persian ruler Khosru Noshirwan. In a speech addressed to the supreme head of the Sassanide power, the Armenians tried to evoke uneasiness in him by reason of the successes of Byzantine diplomacy in Axum and Himyar. They pointed to the alliance of the emperor Justinian with these two states: "Had he not concluded an alliance with the Ethiopian kingdoms about which the Romans had not formerly heard? He had already seized lands of the Omerites [Himyarites] and the Red Sea."[107] Of course, the Armenian ambassadors were consciously exaggerating the influence of Byzantium in Ethiopia and South Arabia; nevertheless, their knowledge of the affairs of the region under discussion is extremely significant.

The views of Procopius on the policy of Ethiopia and Himyar merit attention. He connects it with economic conditions: the desire to seize fertile lands, the trade policy of Byzantium and Iran, the activity of Jewish and Persian merchants, and also the Byzantine-Iranian conflict. With all of their one-sidedness and subjectiveness, Procopius' views are based on actual facts.

Nonnus' composition is another extremely valuable source. Nonnus, of Syrian origin, was a hereditary Byzantine diplomat. His father Avraam son of Euporos (or Avraam bar Euporos of *The Book of the Himyarites*) was present in Al Hir at the court of Al Munzir III when the letter of Dhu-Nuwas addressed to this ruler was read out. Nonnus himself later, probably after 531 A.D., personally visited Ethiopia on behalf of Emperor Justinian and obtained an audience with King Ella Asbeha. In his composition Nonnus tells of the journey to Axum and of the political events which brought about this journey. Unfortunately, Nonnus' book has been preserved only in a few fragments in Joannes Malalae,[108] Photius,[109] and Theophanes the Byzantine.[110] Except for Photius none of them named their source and Theophanes even confuses the embassy of Nonnus with the later embassy of Julian. However, part of the description of the Byzantine embassy in Joannes Malalae (who in turn served as a source for Theophanes) is given in the first person; this means that it is borrowed from the ambassador himself. The name of the Himyarites in Joannes Malalae is given in two forms: the form usual for Greek authors Ὁμηρῖται and the extremely rare form Ἀμηρῖται (the latter form is even used for the name of the Amhara). The form Ἀμηρῖται is encountered precisely in those parts of Joannes Malalae's composition which are borrowed from the ambassador's book. However, in Photius, in the paraphrasing of Nonnus' book, the Himyarites are also called Ἀμηρῖται.[111]

There is still one more striking coincidence: the Byzantine ambassador in Joannes Malalae describes the turban on the Axumite king's head and calls it Φακιόλιν; this description does not appear in Photius but the remark has been preserved that "the ancients called the turban (Φακιόλιν) a bean."[112] It is possible to add one more fact: judging by the excerpts in Photius, Nonnus was interested in elephants. The Axumite king's chariot to which elephants are harnessed is described in the excerpt in Joannes Malalae. Therefore the assumption of Mordtmann, which was further developed by Pigulevskaya, that Joannes Malalae used Nonnus' composition (along with other sources) is highly possible.

Nonnus introduces interesting information about Ethiopia and the trading of the Byzantines with it, a paraphrase of a letter sent by Justinian to Ella Asbeha and a description of the reception of the Byzantine ambassador by the Axumite king. The last mention of the Red Sea Icthyophagi, whom he personally observed, belongs to Nonnus.

Information about VI century A.D. Axum occurs also in works of later

Byzantine authors. The *Chronographia* of Joannes Malalae (VI century A.D.) has already been mentioned. It is primarily an abridged and vulgarized version of Joannes Antiochus' *Chronographia*, which was composed in Greek and has not come down to us in its entirety. Joannes Malalae also used Nonnus' work. He merges the Ethiopian-Himyarite wars of 517–525 A.D. into one and mistakenly dates the wars to the reign of Justinian, who did not come to the throne until 527 A.D. On the other hand, he correctly dates Nonnus' embassy to the reign of Justinian.

The third *Chronographia* which mentions VI century A.D. Ethiopia belongs to the pen of Theophanes the Confessor or the Byzantine[113] (end of the VIII century A.D. or beginning of the IX century A.D.). The text of Theophanes which has come down to us is greatly tainted.[114] It contains all of Joannes Malalae's information but the description of the Ethiopian-Himyarite wars is given in somewhat more detail. Joannes Malalae served as the main but not the sole source of Theophanes. A comparison of the corresponding texts of Joannes Malalae, Theophanes the Byzantine, and the Syrian church historian Joannes Ephesius shows that the description of the Ethiopian-Himyarite war, its causes and consequences, were taken by them from one and the same source, probably the *Chronographia* of Joannes Antiochus. Thus, Joannes Ephesius (preserved by Pseudo Dionysius Tel Mahr) relates the following: On the eve of the campaign of Ethiopian troops on Himyar "it so happened that there was a war between the Indian king Aksundon (or Ksenodon) and another king of 'Inner India,' Aidug (or Aidog), who was a pagan." The latter emerged from the war as the victor, accepted Christianity, and carried out a campaign against the Jewish king Dhu Nuwas (Dimnos, Damian, Damianos) who had been killing and pillaging Byzantine merchant Christians. Before he advanced against Dhu-Nuwas, Aidug wrote to him: "You did wrong when you killed Roman trader-Christians; you curtailed trade and delayed duties of my kingdom and other kingdoms. Especially you have damaged my kingdom."[115]

Joannes Malalae gives elements of extremely similar information (in spite of the difference of the languages); moreover, both the description of events and their succession and also proper names and terms coincide. At the base of his tale lay at least two sources, one of which—an account of the Byzantine embassy of 627–631 A.D.—calls the king of the Axumites Ella Asbeha while the others call him Anda(s). A comparison of the texts shows that the second source is the same one that Joannes Ephesius used, probably Joannes Antiochus' *Chronographia*.

Joannes Malalae dates the reign of Andas to the VI century A.D.: "At that time when the most holy emperor Justinian ruled, the Persian ruler was Kavadh Darasten the son of Firuz; the ruler of Rome was Alaric, a descendant of Valmeriac; King Childeric ruled Africa—a descendant of

Genseric; over the Indians or Aukcomites ruled Andas who had adopted Christianity; and over the Iberians ruled Zamanaz."[116] But since Justinian and Kavadh I ruled contemporaneously in 527–531 A.D., the reign of Anda(s) would have to be dated to that time. Furthermore, the sole war of the Axumites in Himyar in this time segment was undoubtedly the victorious campaign of 525 A.D. in which the Byzantine fleet also participated (to which, by the way, Theophanes the Byzantine alluded).[117]

Evidently, this Andas is that same personage whom Joannes Ephesius calls Aidug or Aidog. In the work of Theophanes the Byzantine the same name is encountered in the forms of Adad, Adab, Areta, etc. Theophanes does not mention the city of Axum. He calls the Byzantine ambassador Julian. He has borrowed a series of details (even possibly the ambassador's name) from Procopius' *History*. Other [errors] undoubtedly were evoked by an inaccurate comprehension of the source—Joannes Malalae's *Chronographia*. Joannes Malalae in general does not call the ambassador by name. Perhaps some sort of information had come down to Theophanes about events in Arabia in the "year of the elephant." Perhaps even the chronological confusion is in part explained by this. The embassy (of Julian or Nonnus), which was constituted in the reign of Justinian, is dated by Theophanes to 571 A.D. in the reign of Justin II (in the original [Malalae] it is dated to 564 A.D., or 6064 "since the creation of the world").

Both Joannes Malalae and Theophanes the Byzantine also mention important events of Axumite history such as the official Christianization of the country and, possibly, the Axumite-Iranian war. Moreover, at least the first of these events is dated to the reign of Andas-Andad in Axum and Dhu-Nuwas (Dimnos-Damion) in Himyar. Theophanes dates it to 535 A.D. (i.e., with an eight-year correction 543 A.D.). But according to inscription *CIH* 541, at that time King Ella Uzena occupied the Axumite throne and Abreha ruled in Himyar. Both were Christians. In that year the Byzantine embassy, which the same inscription mentions, visited Himyar and probably also Axum.

Thus the authors of the *Chronographias*, like Joannes Ephesius, are clearly not in harmony with the chronology. Nevertheless, some scholars are striving to find a place for the mysterious Andas or Aidug in the history of Axum, having identified him with some individual who had existed more authentically. J. Halévy has advanced an extremely astute proposition: the name Aidug could have been formed as a result of an error of the Syrian copyist from the name "Adul," Adulis, while "Aksundon" could have come from "Aksumiton," "Aksumites" (genitive case in Greek).[118] N. V. Pigulevskaya accepted this restoration of Joannes Ephesius' text, which was undoubtedly tainted in the part under consideration.[119] Janos Harmatta proposed identifying Andas or Andad, king of the Axumites, with Ella Amida and Sembruthes (Sembrythes). It is known that the former was the son of Ezana II and the latter was the author of a brief Greek inscription possibly of the III–IV centuries A.D. The opponent of Andas—the Jewish king of the Himyarites, Dimnos—Harmatta identifies not with Dhu-Nuwas but with Dhu-Maahir of the list of kings of Himyar in the works of Arab authors of the IX–X centuries A.D.[120] J. Pirenne also identifies Andas with Ella Amida and the latter with King Wazeba (Ouazebas) known from coins which, according to their type, can be dated to the second half of the V century A.D. On the other hand, she considers Aidug a predecessor of Andas. She prefers to read this name as Aidog and identifies it with the name Ella Adog (variants are El Adob, Seladoba, etc.) of the lists of Axumite kings.[121] But nonetheless Joannes Ephesius is clearly speaking about those same events that Joannes Malalae and Theophanes the Byzantine are speaking of!

First of all we must state that not only is the text of Joannes Ephesius tainted but also that both Joannes Malalae and Theophanes the Byzantine set forth highly inaccurately the source common to them. Evidently in that source (in the *Chronographia* of Joannes Antiochus?) there already occurred a confusing of the history of the Christianization of the Axumites with the history of the Ethiopian-Himyarite wars which is inexplicable to us.

Since the story about naming Joannes, who was the *prosmonarios* of the church of St. Joannes in Alexandria, as bishop of Axum (which is told by Joannes Malalae and Theophanes and also by *The Martyrdom of Arethius*), evidently is based upon actual fact, no doubt at that time the king of Axum, Ella Asbeha, actually sent a delegation to Egypt to invite the bishop to the country. But this was not the first bishop of Axum, since the king of that time was not the first Christian ruler of that country. However, having found out about the naming of bishop Joannes, the provincial cleric Joannes Antiochus connected this event with conversations about the fact that the Axumites, it turns out, were also Christians and decided that the Christianization of the distant "Indian" people had only just happened. In short he, in ignorance, connected two different events. This could easily have taken place in the provincial surroundings in the east of the Byzantine empire in the period when the king of the Axumites received widespread fame in connection with the annihilation of the Christians in Himyar and his role as protector of Christians from the Judaeo-Himyarites. Before this, many did not even know that the Axumites had long ago adopted Christianity. Such ignorance was also characteristic of medieval Europeans. With what tardiness did the news about the acceptance of Christianity by the Slavic peoples and the Lithuanians reach the provincial cleric-chronicle writers! Even in the XI century A.D. in Chartres, Bishop Fulbert was ineffably surprised at receiving gifts for his church from Knute the Great, the king of Denmark and England, since he considered him a pagan.

With such a high probability of misrepresentations it is not profitable to attempt to determine what real names are concealed behind Aidug-Andas or the king of the Himyarites "of the Angane family." All the hypotheses one could wish for are possible.

The pages of Joannes Ephesius' chronicle, written in the Syrian language, correspond to the texts of Joannes Malalae and Theophanes the Byzantine. This portion of Joannes Ephesius' chronicle has been preserved only in the third part of a later Syrian chronicle of Pseudo Dionysius.[122] Evidently Joannes Ephesius, like Joannes Malalae and Theophanes, depended in his description of the Ethiopian-Himyarite wars on Joannes Antiochus. Moreover, Joannes Ephesius and the authors who repeated him preserved one of the *Epistles* of Simeon Betharsham about the Himyarites.

Joannes Ephesius preserved unique information about the Byzantine policy in Nubia. This information relates to the period when Empress Theodora was still alive, i.e., prior to 548 A.D.[123] Joannes tells about the embassies of Justinian and Theodora to Nubia, about the activities in Nubia of the Byzantine missionaries Julian, Theodore, and Longin, and about the interrelationships of local states—Nobados (Northern Nubia), Mukurra, Alwa, and the northern Beja.

Joannes Ephesius in a number of other valuable documents quotes excerpts from letters of Longin and the kings of the Nubian states. In Longin's letter to the Alexandrine Patriarch Theodore, the Axumites (Axymites) are mentioned. Longin communicates about the Christianization of the king, the nobility, the royal family, and the common inhabitants of Alwa. Then he adds: "But also to some of the Axumites who had fallen into Julian's error [heresy] they said: 'Christ suffered intolerable suffering but not in the mortal body,' we imparted the rightness of the faith and demanded of them a written renunciation of this heresy."[124]

It is possible the name of the Axumites got into the letter by mistake instead of the Nobados Nubians, the companions of Longin in Alwa. Indeed, it was precisely among them that the Monophysite missionary Julian, who was sent by Theodora, operated. He should not be confused with his namesake, the ambassador to Ethiopia. However, it is not ruled out that the real Axumites were meant, those encountered by Longin in Southern Nubia in direct proximity to his country. In such an event Longin's letter could throw some light also on the relationship of the most southerly of the Nubian states to Axum over two or more centuries after the death of King Ezana I.

The *History* of Joannes Ephesius, the first Syrian church historian, exerted an enormous influence on all of his literary heirs. Among them the greatest is the Syrian historian of the XIII century A.D., Barhebraeus (or Bar Hebroyo; in Arabic Abu-l-Faraj). In his chronicle there is curious information about the appearance of Christians in Ethiopia as early as the time

of Emperor Constantine the Great (who died in 337 A.D.),[125] possibly
having in view the activities of Frumentius and Aedesius.

Important communications about the Axumite Kingdom in the works
of the first church historians date to the middle of the IV century A.D.
Tyrranius Rufinus about 401 A.D. concluded his *Historia ecclesiastica*, which
was a Latin translation and continuation of Eusebius' Greek work. Rufinus
was a person who merited trust and his *Historia* is a reliable source. He
was well educated and lived in the east of the empire in Alexandria and
Jerusalem, from whence he made a journey through Egypt, Syria, and
Mesopotamia.

In his book, Rufinus introduces a story about the activity of Frumentius
and Aedesius, the organizers of the first Christian communities in Ethiopia.
In passing he communicates some information about the country which
relates to the fate of the heroes of the story. Rufinus emphasizes that he
heard the history of Frumentius and Aedesius "from Aedesius Tyrus himself." Rufinus could have become acquainted with Aedesius in Tyre. In
Alexandria, Rufinus was on friendly terms with Athanasius the Great and
his circle, i.e., with people who knew Frumentius personally. Therefore,
there can be no doubt that he received his information firsthand. It is true,
as Bolotov indicated, that the chronological and geographical coordinates
of Rufinus' story are confused, "but fact itself is faithfully transmitted by
Rufinus."[126] Up to the present not a single investigator has doubted the
trustworthiness of the basic information which Rufinus communicates. It
is possible, over and above the geographical and chronological confusion,
to accuse him of tendentious exaggeration of Frumentius' authority and
the successes of Christian propaganda; but in this Rufinus' informants can
be at fault. All of the historico-political and social conditions of the tale
are completely authentic.

The history of Frumentius and Aedesius is encountered in a later and
verbose retelling in Nikephoros Kallistos, a Byzantine writer of the XIV
century A.D.[127] This work is also called *Historia ecclesiastica*. Besides Rufinus'
book, other sources for the tale about Frumentius and Aedesius were
scarcely at the disposal of Nikephoros. All the discrepancies must be
attributed to the fantasy and style of Nikephoros. Moreover, Rufinus' tale
was borrowed by authors of church-historical writings, by the "church
fathers"—Socrates, Sozomen, and Theodoret.[128]

Frumentius and Aedesius were canonized in the Orthodox, the (Roman)
Catholic, and the Copto-Ethiopian churches. In connection with this, there
appeared "lives" of Frumentius in the Latin, Greek, Coptic, Arabic, and
Ge'ez languages. In the Ethiopian version, Frumentius is identified with
Abba Salama and Aedesius with Sidrak. Their activity is dated to the
reign of the legendary Axumite kings—Ella Alada, Ella Asguagua, Abreha,
and Asbeha. Moreover, a series of cultural life-style details is communicated

which oral tradition could have preserved from the Axumite period. In this lies the basic value of the Ethiopian version.

Information about the Axumite Kingdom and its neighbors is contained in still another *Historia ecclesiastica* which belongs to the pen of Philostorgius, a Greek author of the V century A.D. His work was finished between 425 A.D. and 433 A.D. Philostorgius knew of the events of 425 A.D. but he does not mention the Constantinople fire of 433 A.D. This composition has been preserved only in excerpts, the greater part of them included in Photius' *Bibliotheca*.[129] The preserved fragments contain valuable information about the Roman embassy of Theophilus Indusius to Ethiopia and Himyar in the reign of Ezana I, about the propagation of Christianity in South Arabia, about trade and trade routes of the Red Sea countries; however, this information can be gathered only indirectly, from such passages as those which describe the wild animals exported from Africa and the route of the Roman embassy. Philostorgius communicates interesting information about Syrians of South India and Socotra, who lived, according to his testimony, right up to the boundaries of the Axumite Kingdom.

In many respects *The Book of the Himyarites*, which was spoken of above, approaches the chronicle genre. Syrian sources, including *The Book of the Himyarites*, underlay the information about the Ethiopians and Himyarites of the VI century A.D. which is communicated by a certain Arabo-Christian chronicle, the so-called *Chronicle of Seert* composed in medieval Syria in the Arabic language.[130] In a paraphrasing it preserved parts of *The Book of the Himyarites* which had vanished.

Arab-Muslim historians—Muhammad al Kalbi, his son Hisham, Ibn Ishaq, Al Hamdani, At Tabari, Al Mas'udi, Ibn Khaldun, Al Baladsori, Ad Dinawari, Abu'l Fida, and others—transmit another tradition. In contrast to the Roman-Byzantine and Syrian sources, not one of the enumerated Arab authors was a contemporary of the events which he described. However, in their works they used oral and written sources close in time to or even contemporary with those events. Arab historical works communicate many facts of the political and social life of the Axumite Kingdom in the VI century A.D. and also of the end of the period of florescence and of the period of late Axum—the VII–IX centuries A.D. Information from Arabic sources about events of the VI century A.D. is frequently contradictory. The sources abound with legendary details, inaccuracies, etc. However, their value should not be underestimated. A. G. Loundine is completely correct when he says: "With the appearance of new epigraphic material the presence of a well-informed South Arabian tradition continues to be further confirmed. Some information which had earlier been considered legendary has been confirmed and in a series of cases even the reasons for the errors of the Arabic sources have been successfully clarified."[131]

Unfortunately the works of the earliest Arabic sources (VII century A.D.) have not come down to us; however, they were probably used by the later authors. In the VIII century A.D. and beginning of the IX century A.D. the Arab historian-traditionalists were creating [their works], which included their individual versions of *Life of the Messenger of God* (i.e., Muhammad): Ibn Ishaq (died about 767–769 A.D.), Muhammad Ibn as Sa'ib al Kalbi (died in 757–758 A.D.), and his son Hisham (died about 820 A.D.). Their compositions have been preserved in quotations in At Tabari (838–923 A.D.).

At Tabari, of Iranian origin, lived and wrote in Iraq. His enormous work *History of the Prophets and Kings* (والملوك تأريخ الرسل) was written on the basis of Arab oral and especially written sources.[132] At Tabari preserved information of the VIII-century-A.D. historians about events in the Himyarite Kingdom, about the Ethiopian dynasty in South Arabia, about its overthrow by the Persians, about the dealings of the Meccan Kureishites and the first caliphs with the Axumite Kingdom. He also mentions the Ethiopians and Beja who were his contemporaries. The information communicated by At Tabari is exceptionally valuable. It is all the more strange that with the exception of two rather small excerpts it was not included in the Soviet publication *Arabic Sources of the VII–X centuries*.[133]

The works of Al Hamdani (died 945 A.D.) are of great, independent interest. Al Hasan ibn Ahmed al Hamdani descended from the ancient South Arabian tribe of Hamdanites. A great Yemen patriot and very important expert on local history and also the history and geography of the rest of Arabia, he knew the Sabaean language and writing. His works use the richest and most reliable local tradition and also tales of travelers or seafarers about foreign countries including Ethiopia. Al-Hamdani also makes use of epigraphics (Sabaean-Himyarite) and archaeology, since he regularly describes historic monuments. His major work, the *Book of the Crown* (كتاب الاكليل), is preserved in its entirety but is scattered over various libraries of the world. Unfortunately, Book VI, the most interesting volume for the history of Axum, which describes the period from the ascending of the throne by Dhu-Nuwas up to Islam, has not as yet been published.[134]

Al Baladsori (Ahmed Ibn Yahya ibn Djabir al Baladsori, died in 892 or 893 A.D.), who was of Iranian origin, is well known as the author of two basic works: a collection of Arab genealogies, *The Book of Noble Genealogies* (كتاب انساب الاشراف)[135] and *The Book of Conquest of Countries* (كتاب فتوح السبلدان).[136] The first of them contains an enormous quantity of biographies and simply names of persons, including those of persons connected with the history of the Axumite and Himyarite Kingdoms. The second tells about the conquests of the first caliphs.

In the works of other Arab historians—Abu Muhammad Abdallah ad Dinawari (otherwise known as Ibn Qutayba) (828–889 A.D.), also of Iranian origin and the author of numerous and varied works; Al Mas'udi, who is called the "Arabian Herodotus" (died 956 A.D.); and the great Maghribian Ibn Khaldun—it is possible to find interesting details about events in Himyar of the VI century A.D. In the works of Al Fazari, Al Mas'udi, Al Ya'kubi, and other Arabian geographers of the VIII–X centuries A.D., data are found about late Axum. However, the works of the latter authors belong to the geographic literature.

Itineraries

In ancient geographic literature we find valuable materials on the history of the Axumite Kingdom. Most of all they are contained in the geographic works of a practical nature, in peripluses and itineraries. In the periplus of Agatharchides the Kindite (II century B.C.) there is a description of the coastal tribes and towns of Ethiopia and of several relatively backward peoples of the interior parts of the continent. Agatharchides' periplus is preserved only in a paraphrasing in Diodorus Siculus and in Strabo. These authors and also Artemidorus, whose lost work was written according to the materials of Agatharchides and then used by Strabo and Diodorus, added to Agatharchides' facts a series of other ones. These authors, especially Strabo, write a little about the trade routes of Northeast Africa. However, not one of them says a word about the towns of the Ethiopian plateau, or about the peoples of the developed North Ethiopian civilization.

The first information about them is contained in *Periplus of the Erythrean Sea*, which was the work of an unknown author. This remarkable work was ascribed to Arrian, the author of *Indica*. Therefore the author of this *Periplus* is called Pseudo Arrian. [This is the *Periplus* frequently cited in this book and listed in the Bibliography at the entry Pseudo Arrian.] Judging by the language and the content of the memorial, its author was a Greek-speaking Egyptian merchant who lived in the period of Roman domination in Egypt. More precise dating of *Periplus* is possible by reference to the political situation described in it and by the historical personages mentioned. However, in this effort complications arise, the solving of which is extremely difficult. It is necessary to know precisely: (1) the political situation on the African continent, (2) the political situation on the Arabian peninsula, (3) the political situation in Iran, India, and Ceylon, and (4) to identify the names of the Axumite, South Arabian, Indian, and Ceylon rulers mentioned in *Periplus*, and the years of their reigns. Up to now these problems have not really been solved. In an excellent article, Jacqueline Pirenne,[137] whose work played a decisive role in the refinement of the chronology of ancient South Arabia, pointed out the main shortcomings of the former dating of *Periplus*. Pirenne proposes and substantiates the dating of this major historical resource to the beginning of the III century B.C.

The majority of historians have accepted the new dating but some have expressed doubts and have even resolutely objected to it. These include A. Jamme (*1957 BSAOS,*) ; A. Dihle (1965) and W. Raunig (1970).

In a recently published investigation of M. Rodinson, the opinion is argued in detail that the *Periplus of The Erythrean Sea* could have been written in the broad time segment between the beginning of the II century A.D. and the beginning of the III century A.D. (M. Rodinson, 1974/1975; 1975/1976).

Periplus communicates very valuable facts about the trade of the Axumite Kingdom and the Somali Berbers with the Roman Empire, India, and Arabia, describes the trade route from Axum and Northwest Ethiopia to the shore of the Red Sea, and gives information on the Ethiopian king Zoskales in whom it is not difficult to recognize Ze Haqile, who is mentioned in the "Lists of Kings" of Axum. Aside from Ptolemaeus, the author of *Periplus* is the first to mention Axumites and their capital or "metropolis." [138] The undoubted merits of *Periplus* are the precision of the factual material, the soberness of the judgments, and the detailed nature of facts which relate to the sphere of trade activity.

These traits bring *Periplus* together with *The Complete Description of the World and Its Peoples*, a unique "economic-geographic encyclopedia" of the late Roman empire. This monumental work was written about 350 A.D., as is evident from the events mentioned in it.[139] In form *Description* belongs to the very same genre of periploses and itineraries as the above-mentioned works. It was composed in Latin. Two versions of *Description* have been preserved: the earlier version A, which is set apart by its poor Latin, and B, which is a highly literate version. The author of *Description* was a Syrian, possibly a merchant. He gives a vivid and naive picture of the trading prosperity of Syria and its towns, of Egypt and of Alexandria—i.e., of those parts of the Roman empire with which the Axumite Kingdom was most closely linked. The first paragraphs of *Description* speak of the countries and peoples of the east, beyond the boundaries of the Roman empire. This part of the *Description* (§1–20) is extremely close to the so-called *Itineraries from Paradisiacal Eden up to the Romans*. Probably it is a translation of one of such itineraries, most likely from the Greek language. The first paragraphs contain information about the route from Adulis to India and about the possessions of the Roman Empire, about the ivory trade, about the Axumite Kingdom and Ethiopian-Himyarite relations (§18), and also about the trade of the Somali Berbers with Alexandrine Egypt.

Judging from its content, *Itineraries from Paradisiacal Eden up to the Romans* already existed in the IV century A.D. Several texts of it which are close to each other have been preserved, and also a Georgian translation or more precisely a recension.[140] One of the Greek texts was published in 1910 by Klotz;[141] the other—based on the manuscript of the Public Library in Leningrad—was published by N. V. Pigulevskaya.[142] The *Itineraries* describe the sea route from the Axumite Kingdom to North and South India and to Ceylon and indicate the duration of the voyage. Moreover, the religious affiliation of the Axumites is indicated.[143]

Scientific-geographical works

The scientific-geographic literature in Greek, Latin, and Arabic contains valuable information about the Axumite Kingdom. In Latin there is only one source of this category: the *Natural History* of Pliny the Elder.[144] It is a compilation of Greek works which existed by the middle of the I century A.D. As a scholar-investigator Pliny does not rank high. Nevertheless, in *Natural History* for the first time the town of Adulis is named and the make-up of exports from Ethiopia is enumerated in detail. Pliny says nothing about the Axumite Kingdom; for him Adulis was "the greatest market of the Troglodytes."

In a classical work of ancient Greek geography, Claudius Ptolemaeus' *Geography* (II century A.D.),[145] the Axumites and peoples who neighbored them are mentioned. Ptolemaeus still knows nothing about the very prominent role of the Axumites in Ethiopia. His *Geography* also describes the sea route from Egypt to India and East Africa which passed along the shores of Ethiopia. He names the towns of Adulis and Meroe and gives their geographical coordinates. Ptolemaeus communicates much that is interesting about the Somali Berbers and East Africa. A large part of this information was borrowed by him from a lost work of Marinus of Tyre (beginning of II century A.D.). The work of Marinus of Tyre, transmitted by Ptolemaeus, is close in time with the *Periplus of the Erythrean Sea*.

The *Geography* of an unknown VIII century A.D. author, the so-called Ravenna Anonym, for the major part goes back to Ptolemaeus and Marinus. The author gives some information on the geography of northern and western Ethiopia in the period of florescence of the Axumite Kingdom. However, some of the information of Ravenna Anonym clearly dates to the ancient epoch. He divides all of the territory south of the Sahara known to him in Africa into three parts: Axumite Ethiopia, the Ethiopia of Candace (i.e., of the Meroite queen-mother who bore that title), and the Ethiopia of the Troglodytes (the country of the Beja). The very terminology —Candace and Troglodytes—indicates sources from antiquity.

The first Armenian geography, *Ashkharatsuits* (beginning of the VII century A.D.), whose authorship remains unestablished, mentions Axumites, Beja, and "Ethiopia" under which Nilotic Nubia is implied (the Nile flows through this country from the country of the Axumites). This information about Africa (with the exception of the late glosses) was obtained by the Armenian geographer from the widely known work of Claudius Ptolemaeus.[146]

Ptolemaeus' *Geography* served as a model and to a significant degree as a factual basis for Arabic works on mathematical geography. Two authors —Muhammad ibn Musa al Khwarizmi[147] (first half of the IX century A.D.) and Suhraba[148] (second half of the X century A.D.)—name Adulis (ادولی) and indicate its coordinates.[149] Moreover, they knew the Nubian towns. Al Mas'udi also mentions Adulis.

The Christian Topography of Cosma Indicoplou (or Cosmas Indicopleustes)[150] stands by itself among scientific-geographic sources. Cosmas obtained his nickname because of bygone journies to India which were unusual for a monk and highly attractive for monastic surroundings. A Hellenized Egyptian from a port town, he had evidently in his youth been a merchant and had made trade voyages to Ethiopia, India, and Ceylon. The *Christian Topography* was written by Cosmas after becoming a monk, probably at the Sinai monastery around 550 A.D. He mentions two solar eclipses: February 6 and August 17, 547 A.D.[151] He had visited in Ethiopia "25 years prior to the present days," i.e., before writing the book.[152] Cosmas' work pretends to high accuracy and objectivity but in this respect it is a giant step backwards in comparison with the works of Marinus and Ptolemaeus and his successors. The primary value of *The Christian Topography* lies in its digressions from the basic account, wherein Cosmas gives recollections of the countries he visited. He visited in Adulis and Axum, and he visited the palace of the Axumite king and described it in detail. He also described the Adulis monument and copied its inscription. Probably Cosmas did not come across this monument by chance. He writes that King Ella Asbeha ordered the "arhont" of Adulis to deliver to him (evidently to Axum) the Adulis monument. Perhaps the "arhont" suggested that Cosmas or his fellow traveler translate the Greek inscriptions on the monument which he was being forced to send to the king. Cosmas writes about the propagation of Christianity in Axum "and in all of the country around it," about the trade of the Axumites and the inhabitants of Berbera with South Arabia, Persia, the island of Socotra, Northern India, Ceylon, the Eastern Roman Empire, and also with the Beja and the gold-bearing country of Sasu. There is information in Cosmas' work about Northwest Ethiopia, Somalia, and East Africa. For the main part, this information has the value of being the live and direct impression of an eyewitness. But sometimes Cosmas is mistaken. Thus, indicating the time of his visit in Ethiopia, Cosmas says, "When I was in those places, 25 years before the present days, at the beginning of the reign of Justin, the Roman emperor, the Axumite king of that time, Ellatsbaa ('Ελλατζβάας) [i.e., Ella Asbeha], was making ready to go to war against the Omirites

[Himyarites]."[153] The name of Ella Asbeha was transmitted exceptionally accurately in Greek. But his campaign against the Himyarites in 525 A.D. had to be at the end rather than at the beginning of the reign of "Justin, the Roman emperor," i.e., Justin the Elder or the First (518–527 A.D.). However, two circumstances must be taken into account. First, Cosmas, traveling beyond the borders of the Roman empire, could have found out about Justin's ascending to the throne after a great time lapse. Second, all of the Near East was expecting an Ethiopian-Himyarite war immediately after 518 A.D. and King Ella Asbeha "was making ready to go to war against the Himyarites," evidently right after his ascent to the throne. Consequently Cosmas' mistake is not so great and is entirely pardonable. He knew the Ge'ez language to some extent. Sometimes Cosmas took on faith the yarns of the Axumites and Ceylonese. At times he joined his own fantasies to them, but always with the very best motives as a "scientific" geographer. Some traits relate the *Christian Topography* to the religious literature but it is first of all a geographic work.

Cosmas Indicopleustes also wrote one more book, which has been lost, in which he described the universe "on that side of the ocean (i.e., the Mediterranean), these and all the southern regions from Alexandria to the Southern Ocean," i.e., the entire African continent![154] Numerous other works of Cosmas which could have contained information about Axum and Ethiopia have also been lost.

Cult and hagiological literature

Works of cult and hagiographic literature belong to the category of religious written sources proper. Information about Ethiopia is contained in ancient Egyptian cult hymns and in the Old Testament. In early Christian literature such information is entirely absent, although information about the Meroitic Kingdom can be found in it.

The Christian treatise of Epiphanius, written soon after 394 A.D., contains an interesting communication. Four versions of the treatise have been preserved; the most complete is in Latin.[155] The Georgian and Armenian exist in large excerpts and the Coptic in fragments.[156] Epiphanius enumerates the people who dwelt on the shores of the Red Sea and along the sea route to Ceylon: Himyarites with Adulites (inhabitants of Adulis), Beja and Berbers, Teyano (or Taijano), i.e., Siamo, Socotrans, Ceylonese, etc. By Epiphanius' list it is possible to gain some notion about the stops which the Roman ships made on the route to India and Adulis.

The events of the VI century A.D. found reflection in Byzantine hagiographical works: *The Martyrdom of Arethius* and *The Life of [St.] Grigentius, the Omerite Bishop*, i.e., the Himyarite bishop. The former is of special importance. As N. V. Pigulevskaya proved, *The Martyrdom of Arethius* is connected with reliable and fresh oral information received from Himyarite refugees in Al Hir, the capital of the Arab-Lakhmides.[157] Written in Greek in the first half of the VI century A.D., *The Martyrdom* was subsequently translated into the Arabic, Armenian, Georgian, and Ge'ez languages. The time of the composing of *The Martyrdom of Arethius* is between 535 A.D. and 545 A.D.

This work contains a very large quantity of historical facts which pertain to the political history of Himyar and Axum and to the social attitudes and governmental structure of these countries. Sometimes they are given in the form of historico-geographical references but more often can be extracted from the text of the story itself. Primarily, *The Martyrdom of Arethius* describes events in South Arabia in the years 517–526 A.D. The Najran killings of the autumn of 518 A.D., the personal "martyrdom" of "Saint" Arethius (Ḥaris) and his fellow citizens for the Christian faith, occupy a central position in the narrative. *The Book of the Himyarites* tells of this in more detail. There is a series of factual errors in *The Martyrdom*, the origin of which is entirely understandable. The author knew the Red Sea countries only by hearsay and because of certain personal qualities misunderstood specific details. However, certain errors are in need of special explanation. Studying the different versions of *The Martyrdom of Arethius*, Irfân Shahîd and M. van Esbroeck uncovered a whole series of strange chronological incongruities in the description of events of the years 524–525 A.D. in Alexandria, Axum, and Himyar.[158] Two campaigns of the Ethiopians into South Arabia in 517 A.D. and 525 A.D. are confused. The date of Ella Asbeha's campaign is given incorrectly: October 835 according to the Antioch Seleucidian chronology, i.e., 522 A.D. The coastal fortifications of Dhu-Nuwas are turned into chains stretched between the Arabian and African shores and a series of geographic inaccuracies creeps in. Judging by the method of dating used, the author of *The Martyrdom* was an inhabitant of Antioch and reflected the views of local circles. He is also connected with governmental circles and interests. Therefore, along with Procopius Caesarensis' *History*, *The Martyrdom* is one of the main sources on Byzantine politics in the Red Sea countries in the period of the Ethiopian-Himyarite wars.

N. V. Pigulevskaya gives the following characterization of *The Martyrdom of Arethius*: "With the considerable dependence of *The Martyrdom of Arethius* on *The Book of the Himyarites* there are, however, no bases to attribute the information of a reference nature to the unpreserved parts of Cosmas Indicopleustes, [Joannes] Malalae, and Procopius Caesarensis, who represent a secular and historical stream in the materials about Arabia and Ethiopia which they had at their disposal in Byzantium."[159] In other words, one should not speak about direct borrowing but rather about common oral sources. "The preface of *The Martyrdom of Arethius*," continues N. V. Pigulevskaya, "contains details of an historic nature which permit one to provide a more profound analysis of the facts. In it should also be noted the acquaintance with the official Byzantine policy and the striving to maintain its prestige."[160] This conclusion of N. V. Pigulevskaya is corroborated with convincing examples.[161] Thus the value of *The Martyrdom* for the history of the Axumite Kingdom is great.

Carpantier published the Greek text of [*The Martyrdom*] with a Latin translation and commentary in 1861.[162] In 1899 Pereira published, in addition to the Greek, the Arabic and Ethiopian versions, having supplied them with an excellent analysis and translation into the Portuguese language.[163]

The Martyrdom of Arethius, which was composed in Syria, uses Syrian materials (communications of Syrians who had visited in Ethiopia and Arabia, who had heard the Himyarite refugees in Al Hir) and remains within the limits of the Syrian-Monophysite tradition. The Orthodox faction vied with the Monophysite faction in the church, in politics, and in literature. "The tendency of the Melkites (Orthodox believers whom the Byzantine government protected) to occupy a firm position in Arabian towns"[164] engendered the Orthodox trend in literature on Christian Himyar. This trend is connected with the name of Grigentius, the Himyarite bishop who held to Orthodoxy and enjoyed the protection of both the Byzantine government and the Himyarite king Abreha. Two works are attributed to Grigentius—*The Laws of the Himyarites and Debate with the Jew Ebran*, which were spoken of earlier. *The Life of* [*St.*] *Grigentius* tells about his activity, at first within the boundaries of the empire and later in Ethiopia and South Arabia.

The Life of [*St.*] *Grigentius, the Omerite Bishop* (i.e., Himyarite Bishop) was published with a Russian translation and analyzed in detail by A. Vasiliev.[165] It is full of legendary details, factual distortions, and inaccuracies characteristic of hagiographic works; but the basis of the monument is historical and many interesting facts are faithfully transmitted. *The Life of* [*St.*] *Grigentius* can be used, although with great caution, for investigating the social relationships and customs of Himyar, of the Ethiopians in Arabia, and of the Axumite Kingdom of the VI century A.D.

Slavic origins are attributed to Grigentius. He was supposedly a Slav from Mezia (Bulgaria and Romania). Perhaps, therefore, the brief versions of his *Life* were popular in the Slavic Orthodox countries.

The cult and hagiological literature includes the synaxarion lives of Kaleb, Arethius, and the legendary "seven saints"; Abba Salama, Abba Harima, Abba Penteleon, and other Syrian and Egyptian missionaries, the Christian "enlighteners" of the Axum Kingdom. They were composed in the late Middle Ages, partly on the basis of Arabic translations of Greek hagiographic monuments and partly on the basis of local legends. Here belongs *The Life of Yared*, the legendary singer and composer, and several other Ethiopian literary monuments. They basically reflect local legendary tradition.

"Ethiopia" or the Axumite Kingdom as one of the great states of world history is mentioned in *The Revelation* of Pseudo Methodius, written in the second half of the VII century to the VIII century. Here we find a curious genealogical legend extolling the Axumite nagashi (V. Istrin, pp. 17, 20).

The Axumite Kingdom is mentioned in *The Chapters* of Mani, the founder of the Manicheism (216–276 A.D.). It is true that only the Coptic translation of *The Chapters*[166] has been preserved. If the Manicheistic tradition in the case under consideration actually goes back to the III century A.D. and is not a later insertion, then this place in *The Chapters* is one of the first mentions of the flourishing of Axum.

The Koran mentions the Mecca campaign of King Abreha, whose whole life was connected with the history of Axum. It would be possible to relate the numerous versions of *The Life of the Messenger of God* to the Muslim church-historical and hagiographic literature; however, these have already been examined above. Unfortunately, information about Ethiopia and other African countries has not been revealed in Indian sources—either in epigraphic ones or in works of the religious cult literature.

Artistic literary works

The works of artistic literature—the historical novels of the end of the Roman Empire—constitute the final category of written sources on the history of Axum.

One of them, the *Aethiopica* (Αἰθιοπικὰ) of Heliodorus, is devoted to the story of two lovers—a Greek youth and an Ethiopian woman, i.e., the Meroitic ruler's daughter. The Meroitic Kingdom in the period of its ascendency and Egypt seized by the Persians (VI–V centuries B.C.) are the historical and geographical background of the novel. Written works of Greek authors, both those preserved to our times and those which have not turned up, from Herodotus to contemporaries of Heliodorus, served primarily as the novel's source of historico-geographic information. Perhaps Heliodorus was not the real name of the author but his pseudonym. In any event he calls himself "Heliodorus the son of Theodosius the Phoenician of the family of Helios from Emesa."[167] The novel was written at the juncture of the III–IV centuries A.D. Along with anachronisms and the legendary element in the novel are preserved extracts from extremely valuable sources. The description of the Meroitic Kingdom and the sources of the Nile and also of a series of African peoples have enormous value. In the novel there is also described the congratulatory embassy of Axumites in Meroe—transparently reminiscent of a similar embassy in Rome in 274 A.D. It is possible that Heliodorus used one of the descriptions of Aurelian's triumphant procession. Apart from the source of his information, Heliodorus' novel is one of the first sources which mentions Axumites. The novel has been translated into many languages, including Russian, in which it has been published three times.

Information on the Axumite Kingdom is contained in the novel of Pseudo Callisthenius about Alexander of Macedonia. This novel enjoyed enormous popularity in the Hellenistic and Roman periods and in the Middle Ages, and was translated into many languages, including Arabic and Ge'ez. Information about Axum is contained in the treatise "About India and the Brahmins," which is included in the text of the novel. It is considered that the treatise was borrowed from *Historia Lausiaca*, composed by Palladius about 420 A.D.[168] Whoever the author of the treatise was, the information communicated by him is basically reliable and attests to a personal acquaintance with India, Ceylon, and Ethiopia. In his own words, he visited India together with Moise, the bishop of Adulis. The author visited Adulis, Axum, and the Cape of the Aromats in Somalia. He speaks about individual Byzantine-Egyptian and Indian travelers in the Axumite Kingdom and about Axumite merchants in Ceylon, and gives some other information on Ethiopia. In addition to the Greek versions of the novel, the early Latin translation, in which the treatise "About India and the Brahmins" was preserved in the most complete form, is of great value.

The early Latin translation was done by a certain Julius Valerius Alexander Polemon about whom nothing else is known. The abundance of vulgar Latin forms[169] is striking. The translation can be dated to the V (not earlier than the end of the IV) century A.D. In the middle of the X century A.D. still another Latin translation of the novel about Alexander appeared, which belongs to the pen of Leo the Neapolitan. This translation in all respects is inferior to the earlier one.[170] In addition to the Latin, the novel about Alexander was also translated into the Syrian, Armenian, and Arabic languages. There is also an Ethiopian translation, not directly from the Greek but from the Arabic translation.

Legendary traditions based on hundreds of years of oral tradition border on the written sources. In addition to the above mentioned hagiographic sources, this legendary tradition is preserved in *Kebra Nagast*, an Ethiopian work composed in Egypt in the Coptic language then translated into the Arabic language (no later than the XIII century) and from the Arabic into the Ge'ez language between 1314 and 1322 A.D. and in the medieval Ethiopian chronicles.

Recently Irfân Shahîd proposed and successfully substantiated a hypothesis according to which the Coptic work which was the basis of *Kebra Nagast* was written at the beginning of the VII century or even more likely in the middle or second half of the VI century (Shahîd, 1976, pp. 133–178).

Moreover, elements of onomastics and toponymics of the Axumite period are contained in one place in the *Legend of the Campaign of 'Amda Seyon* (XIV century A.D.).[171] Here belong the numerous "Lists of Kings" of Axum not recorded until the XIV–XVI centuries A.D. A multitude of works beginning with the first publication of the "Lists" in the Ethiopian grammar of Mariano Vittorio in 1552[172] and ending with the newest articles[173] have been devoted to their study. Drouin's[174] and Conti-Rossini's[175] studies are of special value. In the "Lists," names of Axumite kings are encountered which are also known to us from other sources. This alone already speaks of the historical nature of the "Lists." They comprise about 10 percent of the names of the "Lists." However, the majority of the names are distorted, the chronological order of their succession is confused, and the years of the reign are nearly always unreliable. Nevertheless, "The Lists of Kings of Axum" must be enlisted for historic studies.

Also, the "deed of the Axumite kings Ella Abreha and Asbeha" [sic!] to the Axumite cathedral is a conscious falsification which used the ancient historical legends.[176] The historic element in the "deed" is so insignificant that it can be virtually ignored in the appraisal of this "document" as a historic source. The listing in the "deed" of rather small districts and communities situated around Axum is interesting for historical geography. The historical legend of *Kebra Nagast of Lake Zwai*,[177] which is based on information of the late Middle Ages, is of still lesser interest. For the history of Axum, several Arabian legends recorded in the VIII–IX centuries A.D. can also be enlisted. Philby[178] recently undertook an attempt to give a historical interpretation to them, in our opinion unsuccessfully.

In our opinion, in the study of history of African countries prior to the last two centuries—when the number, pithiness, and reliability of sources grew sharply—one must not neglect even grains of useful information no matter how uncoordinated and unreliable they might be. Axumite historiography is a clear example of how the sum total of uncoordinated, in all respects heterogeneous sources in which elements of information are sown as grains, present as a whole to the investigator significant material for the re-creation of historic truth.

Abbreviations of Titles of Publications and Collections

ACISE	*Atti del Convegno Internazionale di studi etiopici*, Rome, 1959.
AE	*Annales d'Ethiopie*, Addis Ababa-Paris.
AEC	African Ethnographic Collection, Leningrad.
Aeg	*Aegyptus*, Rome.
An	*Antiquity*, Oxford.
APAW	*Abhandlungen der K. Preussische Akademie den Wissenschaften zu Berlin*, Phil.-hist. Klasse.
Ar	*Archaeologia*, Oxford.
BA	*Byzantine Annals*, St. Petersburg-Moscow.
BH	*The Book of the Himyarites*, ed. by Axel Møberg, Lund, 1924.
BO	*Bibliotheca Orientalis*, Leiden.
Bol	*Il Bolletino*, Asmara, Ethiopia, vol. I, 1953.
BSGI	*Bolletino della R. Società Geografica Italiana*, Rome.
BSOAS	*Bulletin of the School of Oriental and African Studies*, Washington.
CEA	*Cahier d'études africaines*, Paris.
CIH	*Corpus inscriptionum semiticarum ab Academia Inscriptionum et Litterarum humaniorum conditum atque digestum. Pars quarta. Inscriptiones himyariticas et sabaeas contiens*, I–III, Paris, 1889–1929.
CSCO	*Corpus Scriptores Christianorum Orientalium*, Paris.
DAE	*Deutsche Aksum-Expedition*, Berlin, 1913.
EI	*Encyclopédie de l'Islam*, Paris.
ES	*Ethiopian Studies*, Manchester, 1963.
FF	*Forschungen und Fortschritte*, Berlin.
Ja	A. Jamme, *Sabaean inscriptions from Maḥram Bilqîs (Mârib)* = A. Jamme, 1962. This abbreviation is employed when citing inscriptions by number, as "*Ja*, 576."
JA	*Journal Asiatique*, Paris.
JAH	*Journal of African History*, Cambridge.
JRAS	*Journal of the Royal Asiatic Society of Great Britain and Ireland*, London.
Kush	*Kush*, Khartoum.
MA	*Martyrium sancti Arethae et sociorum in civitate Negran, Acta sanctorum*, octobris, t. X, Brussels, 1861.
MAH	*Messenger of Ancient History*, Moscow.
Man	*Man*, London.
Mus	*Le Muséon*, Louvain.
Nāmī	نمي
NCh	*Numismatic Chronicle*, London.
PAA	*Peoples of Asia and Africa*, Moscow.
PC	*Palestinian Collection*, Leningrad.

PO	*Patrologia Orientalis*, Paris.
RA	*Revue Archéologique*, Paris.
RaSE	*Rassegna di studi etiopici*, Rome.
RES	*Répertoire d'épigraphie sémitique*, Paris.
RINSA	*Rivista Italiana di numismatica e scienze affini*, Rome.
RN	*Revue numismatique*, Paris.
RRAL	*Rendiconti della Reale Accademia dei Lincei*, Rome.
RS	*Revue sémitique*, Paris.
RSE	*Rivista degli studi etiopici*, Rome.
RSO	*Rivista di studi orientali*, Rome.
Ry	G. Ryckmans, *Inscriptions sud-arabes*. Employed when citing inscriptions by number, as "*Ry*, 535."
SMSR	*Studi e materiali di storia delle religioni*, Rome.
SNR	*Sudan Notes and Reports*, Khartoum.
TEI	*The Encyclopedia of Islam*, London.
ZA.	*Zeitschrift für Assyriologie*, Weimar-Berlin-Strassburg.
ZDMG	*Zeitschrift der Deutschen Morgenländischen Gesselschaft*, Leipzig.

Notes

I. The Political History of Axum

1. [E. O. Winstedt], pp. 72, 73.
2. K. Mannert, Bd. I, S. 140.
3. Diodorus, III, 43; ed. Oldfather, v. II, p. 171.
4. Strabo, XVI, 4, 18; p. 777 in the Mishchenk Russian-language translation.
5. R. Hennig, v. I, p. 289. [in Russian]
6. T. Mommsen, 1949, *History of Rome*, p. 544.
7. Diodorus, II, 55; ed. Oldfather.
8. Tyrranius Rufinus, *Historia ecclesiastica*, X, pp. 9, 10 (cited according to R. Hennig, 1961, v. II, p. 25. [in Russian])
9. Pseudo Arrian, §4, p. 265 (henceforth this reference will be called simply *Periplus*). [Yu. Kobishchanov follows the Russian translation of S. P. Kondratiev; an English version by W. H. Schoff (London, 1912) is available.]
10. [E. O. Winstedt], p. 76.
11. *Periplus*, §20, p. 270; §23, p. 270.
12. Ibid., §24, p. 271.
13. T. Mommsen, 1949, p. 544.
14. J. Lesquier, p. 34.
15. A. J. Drewes, 1962, pp. 102–106.
16. Ernesta Cerulli, 1960, *Punti di vista*, p. 16.
17. Pliny, VI, 172; ed. D. Detlefsen, 267; ed. B. H. Rackham.
18. In the opinion of historian-geographer A. Herrmann, Ptolemaeus concluded his work about 170 A.D. and gathered the information no earlier than 150 A.D.
19. Claudius Ptolemaeus, IV, pt. I, 7, 10; ed. Mullerus, 1879.
20. Claudius Ptolemaeus, IV, pt. I, 7, 5; ed. Mullerus, 1879.
21. H. von Wissmann, 1957, SS. 317, 322; H. von Wissmann, *Zur Geschichte*, 1964, S. 65–69; H. von Wissmann, *Himyar*, 1964, p. 472.
22. A. Dillmann, 1878, S. 200, 202, 203.
23. M. E. Drouin, p. 155.
24. E. Glaser, 1891, S. 202–212.
25. J. Pirenne, 1956, pp. 180, 181.
26. A. J. Drewes, 1962, p. 106.
27. H. von Wissmann, *Himyar*, 1964, pp. 472, 480.
28. The Greek language was still preserved for a long time in inscriptions on coins.
29. [E. O. Winstedt], pp. 74, 77.
30. B. A. Turayev, 1914, *Ancient East*, p. 248. [in Russian]
31. See Yu. M. Kobishchanov, 1964, *The gold-bearing country of Sasu*. [in Russian]
32. E. Glaser, 1891, S. 992 (cited according to A. J. Drewes, 1962, p. 104, note 1).
33. A. Kammerer, 1926, *Essai*, p. 59, note 1.
34. L. P. Kirwan, 1960, p. 172.

35. *Periplus*, §2, p. 265.
36. [E. O. Winstedt], p. 76.
37. *DAE*, IV, no. 2, S. 3.
38. *DAE*, IV, no. 3, S. 3.
39. C. Conti-Rossini, *Les listes*, 1909, p. 292.
40. *DAE*, IV, S. 3.
41. C. Conti-Rossini, 1919, p. 239, nota 1.
42. A. J. Drewes, 1962, pp. 106, 107.
43. See H. von Wissmann, *Himyar*, 1964, pp. 475, 476.
44. J. Pirenne, 1969, pp. 303–311; A. G. Loundine, 1974, pp. 95–103.
45. According to the new chronology of Loundine and J. Ryckmans (see A. Loundine et J. Ryckmans).
46. A. J. Drewes, 1960, p. 107.
47. J. Pirenne, 1956, p. 179; A. J. Drewes, 1962, pp. 87, 88. Ricci alone (L. Ricci, 1958, p. 457, nota 15) decisively objected against the identification. Drewes recognizes it as undoubted (A. J. Drewes, 1962, p. 107).
48. *CIH*, 308, 11; *Nāmī* 72 + 73 + 71, 2.
49. *Ja*, 631, 15, 21; 577, 3, 10; *Ja*, 577, 10.
50. *Ja*, 631, 13.
51. C. Conti-Rossini, *Les listes*, 1909, pp. 227, 286. There are also the similar names Agdur [and] Agdar (ibid., pp. 271, 280).
52. A. Caquot et A. J. Drewes, pp. 32–38; A. J. Drewes, 1956, p. 181.
53. A. Jamme, *Ethiopia*, 1957, p. 79.
54. Ibid.
55. J. Pirenne, 1956; A. J. Drewes, 1960, p. 104.
56. A. Loundine et J. Ryckmans, p. 411.
57. *CIH*, 350, 7; J. Bent, pp. 247, 248; C. Conti-Rossini, 1921, pp. 10–35.
58. Nāmī, 72 + 73 + 71; A. Jamme, 1962, p. 292; H. von Wissmann, *Himyar*, 1964, pp. 469–470, note 104, 105.
59. H. von Wissmann, *Himyar*, 1964, p. 471.
60. *CIH*, 155, A. Jamme, 1962, p. 294; H. von Wissmann, *Himyar*, 1964, p. 471.
61. *CIH*, 308, 308 bis.
62. A. Jamme, 1962, p. 294.
63. Conti-Rossini (1921, p. 14) proposed that Gedara did not head up military operations in Arabia, but entrusted command to his generals; these latter Conti-Rossini calls "chiefs of the fortresses" and Drewes [calls them] "chiefs of the fortified spots," translating the term *mṣr* of inscription *CIH* 308, 12 as "fortified spot, fortress." However, Jamme translates *mṣr* as "expeditionary corps" (A. Jamme, *Ethiopia*, 1957, p. 80). Jamme's opinion that the mention of Gedara in the inscription together with "chiefs of the expeditionary corps" attests to his personal participation in the military operations is the most likely.
64. Jamme speaks only of four campaigns (A. Jamme, 1962, p. 295) but lists five (ibid., p. 300).
65. C. Conti-Rossini, 1921, p. 14.
66. *Ry*, 533, 21, 22.
67. A. Jamme, 1962, p. 302.
68. *Ja*, 633.
69. A. Jamme, 1962, p. 135.
70. H. von Wissmann und M. Höfner, S. 119, note 3.
71. A. Jamme, 1962, p. 135.
72. *Ja*, 631.

NOTES 287

73. A. Jamme, 1962, p. 303.
74. H. von Wissmann, *Himyar*, 1964, pp. 473, 474.
75. A. Jamme, *Ethiopia*, 1957, p. 80; A. Jamme, 1962, p. 303.
76. A. J. Drewes, 1960, p. 102, note 3; H. von Wissmann, *Himyar*, 1964, p. 476, note 123.
77. A. Dillman, *Lexicon*, 1865, col. 885–887. Compare Yu. M. Kobishchanov, *Communications*, 1962, p. 40.
78. A. Jamme, 1962, p. 302; H. von Wissmann, *Himyar*, 1964, p. 475.
79. A. Loundine et J. Ryckmans, p. 411.
80. *Ja*, 635.
81. H. von Wissmann, *Himyar*, 1964, p. 474.
82. Ibid.
83. *CIH*, 314+954.
84. A. Loundine et J. Ryckmans, p. 411.
85. *Ja*, 576 (*Ry*, 535) 11.
86. H. von Wissmann, *Himyar*, 1964, p. 476.
87. A. Jamme, 1962, p. 316.
88. *Ja*, 575, 4; *Ja*, 574, 10.
89. *Ja*, 576, 11 and following; 577, 5 and following; *Ja*, 576, 1–2; 577, 8–12.
90. H. von Wissmann, *Himyar*, 1964, p. 477. Inscriptions *Ja*, 577, 3, 6 and 585, 14–15 mention *GRMT wld ngšyn*—now "Garamat son of the nagashi," now "Garami subjects of the nagashi"—but judging by context more likely the first is correct. Moreover, some sort of "Abyssinians of Sabcalum" are spoken of (*Ja*, 577, 12), probably the name of a community.
91. The English traveler Salt at the beginning of the XIX century first identified Ζωσκάλης with Ze Haqile (H. Salt, *A Voyage to Abyssinia* . . .). Wissmann proposed that under this name was concealed not an Axumite king but a "coastal" (*za-sahlē*) ruler, but in later works he retreated from this hypothesis. [For a discussion of the Ethiopian "Lists of Kings," see C. Conti-Rossini, 1909.]
92. J. Pirenne, 1961, *Une problème-clef*; A. Loundine et J. Ryckmans.
93. H. von Wissmann, *Himyar*, 1964, p. 480.
94. *Periplus*, §5–6, pp. 265, 266.
95. *Periplus*, §2, pp. 264, 265.
96. Other shortcomings are the poor acquaintance with the situation in districts remote from the sea; in Saba (as opposed to Himyar), in Axum, and in the Ethiopian plateau (as opposed to Adulis), etc.
97. Bent first directed attention to the former (J. Bent, p. 176).
98. *DAE*, IV, S. 8, no. 5.
99. F. Anfray et G. Annequin, 1965, p. 68.
100. A. Mordini, 1960, *Gli aurei Kushāna*, p. 253.
101. C. Schmidt, Bd. I, Kephalaiz LXXVII. Doresse suggests reading "Nile" instead of ϭⲓⲛⲉⲱⲥ ⲛⲉⲓⲗⲉⲱⲥ (1957, *L'Ethiopie et l'Arabie*, p. 57, note 28; 1957, *L'empire du Prêtre-Jean*, vol. I, p. 119). Caquot and Leclant resolutely rejected this strange hypothesis (A. Caquot et J. Leclant, 1959, p. 117, note 3). From a general historical viewpoint this is unlikely.
102. *Periplus*, §6, p. 266.
103. H. de Contenson, 1959, p. 8, pl. XIV; p. 12, pl. XIV c; A. Gaudio, pp. 4, 5. A total of four or five Sabaean-Himyarite coins was found: two in Eritrea (Vaccaro collection in Asmara) and two or three in Axum.
104. T. Mommsen, 1949, p. 506.
105. [A. I. Dovatur], 1957, *Scriptores*, XXVI; Flavius Vopiscus the Syracusan,

XXXIII, 4, p. 235.

106. Flavius Vopiscus the Syracusan, XII, 10, p. 237.

107. C. Conti-Rossini, *Storia*, 1928, p. 124.

108. Heliodorus, IX, 19, pp. 462, 463. [An English translation (Thomas Underdowne, 1587) entitled *An Aethiopian Romance* was republished in the 1920s by E. P. Dutton & Co. (New York) and George Routledge & Sons (London). In this English version, the incident quoted above can be found in the Tenth Book, at p. 310.]

109. A. F. Arkell, 1955, p. 169.

110. A. H. Sayce, pp. 189, 190.

111. L. P. Kirwan, 1957, p. 37.

112. R. Lepsius, S. 13; *DAE*, I, S. 50; M. F. Laming-Macadam, v. I, pp. 111–118.

113. H. St. J. Philby, 1950, pp. 268 ff.

114. A. J. Drewes, 1962, p. 107.

115. *DAE*, VII, no. 1–2; *DAE*, VI, no. 1–2; *DAE*, IV, no. 1–5.

116. *DAE*, IV, no. 4, 6, 7.

117. *DAE*, IV, no. 4, 26.

118. *DAE*, IV, no. 6, 15; no. 7, 15. The differences in the text lie mainly in the writing and orthography and partly in the vocabulary.

119. Cited according to N. V. Pigulevskaya, 1946, pp. 35, 36. [in Russian]

120. Ibid., p. 122.

121. F. Altheim and R. Stiehl, 1961, *Ezana*, S. 245; F. Altheim, S. 168–174, 181–184.

122. *DAE*, IV, no. 6, 26; no. 7, 26.

123. *DAE*, IV, no. 4, 30–31; no. 6, 18–19; no. 17, 18–19.

124. *DAE*, II, SS. 44–45, fig. 81, 82.

125. Tertullian (*Ad Nationes*, II, 18) named Ethiopia among the countries where Christian communities existed. However, his "Ethiopia" is the Meroitic Kingdom according to the terminology of that time. Tertullian's information is clearly based on the apocryphal legend about the adoption of Christianity by the eunuch of the Meroitic queen Candace. Barhebraeus maintained that in Constantine's time Christianity was propagated in all of Egypt, Ethiopia (Habšah), and Nubia (Nubah) (Abbeloos and Lamy, 1877, v. I, p. 54). However, there is nothing to prove the validity of this information. Perhaps Barhebraeus confused Constantine with Constantius?

126. G. Sapeto, p. 396; A. Dillmann, 1950, p. 34.

127. Cited according to R. Hennig, 1961, v. II, pp. 25–26. [in Russian]

128. V. V. Bolotov, 1907, pp. 267–269. [in Russian]

129. Sergew Hable-Sellassie, in the report "Church and State in the Aksumite Period" read at the III International Conference of Ethiopists in Addis Ababa, turned his attention to the following fact: the Emperor Constantius, in his letter, addressed Ezana [I] as if he were the actual head of the Ethiopian church.

130. V. V. Bolotov, 1907, p. 270. [in Russian]

131. [J. P. Migne], v. 25, p. 631; R. Hennig, 1961, v. II, p. 30. [in Russian]

132. *DAE*, IV, no. 6, 3; no. 7, 3.

133. *DAE*, IV, no. 4, 9.

134. Text: see [J. P. Migne], 1961, t. 25, p. 635; C. Conti-Rossi, 1928, *Storia*, p. 149; R. Hennig, 1961, v. II, pp. 29, 30 [in Russian]; J. Doresse, 1957, *L'empire*, v. I, pp. 151–153; V. V. Bolotov, 1907, pp. 267–269. [in Russian]

135. [J. Bidez], 3_4, p. 92; N. V. Pigulevskaya, 1951, pp. 72, 74, 75. [in Russian]

136. A. Klotz, S. 608–610; N. V. Pigulevskaya, 1951, pp. 408–410. [in Russian] [Also see Vasiliev, 1936.]

137. [O. Günther], p. 749.

138. [E. O. Winstedt], pp. 72, 119, 365.

139. *BH*, p. 14b, CX.

140. E. Littmann, 1954, *On the old Ethiopic inscriptions*, pp. 119, 123.

141. A. Caquot et J. Leclant, 1959, p. 174.

142. [J. P. Migne], t. 66, cot. 1501.

143. Cited according to A. Caquot et J. Leclant, 1959, p. 114.

144. A. Caquot et J. Leclant, 1959, pp. 173–177.

145. B. Priaulx, pp. 277, 278. Priaulx thinks that the Greek version of Pseudo Callisthenes' treatise is tainted since according to Pliny the Troglodytes lived in the Adulis region and not near the cape of the Aromats. This is a misunderstanding. First, Pliny is not so much an authority on geography that referring to him is a sufficient basis for refuting Pseudo Callisthenes. Second, authors of antiquity called different African peoples, including the inhabitants of modern Somalia, Troglodytes. [Also see Mullerus, 1846.]

146. E. Schwartz; E. Honigmann.

147. A. E. W. Budge, 1928, *A History of Ethiopia*, p. 15.

148. *DAE*, IV, no. 4, 19.

149. [J. B. Chabot], t. II, pp. 54, 55; N. V. Pigulevskaya, 1951, p. 269. [in Russian]

150. [L. Dindorff], p. 433.

151. [J. Bidez], $3_5 3_6$, p. 35; N. V. Pigulevskaya, 1951, pp. 78, 79. [in Russian]

152. [E. O. Winstedt], pp. 69–72, 119, 322, 324, 325.

153. Ibid., p. 72.

154. [L. Dindorff], p. 458.

155. *MA*, p. 747. [Hereafter in this text, *The Martyrdom of Arethius*.]

156. N. V. Pigulevskaya, 1951, pp. 299–302. [in Russian]

157. [S. Destunis], 1876, I, 19, 100, p. 251.

158. V. V. Bolotov, 1907, p. 272. [in Russian]

159. Olympiodorus, 37. See Skrzhinskaya, p. 230. [in Russian]

160. *DAE*, IV, no. 8, 5–6.

161. In the inscription of Gorseot (the king of Napata), there is mention of the Matata people somewhere in Southeast Nubia (see A. E. Budge, 1912, pp. 128, 129). The phrase quoted is from *DAE*, IV, no. 8, 21–24.

162. *DAE*, IV, no. 9.

163. *DAE*, IV, no. 10; E. Littmann, 1950, II, SS. 110–114.

164. P. L. Shinnie, 1957, pp. 82–85.

165. L. P. Kirwan, 1957, pp. 37–39.

166. K. Mikhalovsky, 1967. [in Russian]

167. A. E. Budge, 1928, *A History*, pp. 114–115.

168. Compare U. Monneret de Villard, 1938, *Storia*, p. 25.

169. In the original (*DAE*, IV, no. 11, 9–10) ውሕለ[ፆ፡ሀ]፡ብሽ: ፋይ፡ሕ : ፀብሽ literally "war against black and red ones." Drewes (A. J. Drewes, 1962, p. 98, note 2) sees in this expression an idiom with the meaning of "war against everyone." Compare the Arabic حرب الاحمر والاسود with this same meaning. The expression "black and red ones" in the sense of "all peoples" is noted by him in Sabaean inscriptions from South Arabia and in an inscription in the Sabaean language from Ethiopia. In Ezana II's recently discovered Greek inscription (lines 24–25) it is also mentioned that the Noba attacked the Mangarto (Mangruto), Hasa,

Bareotai (Baria), and Atiabitai (Atiab) after which these tribes called on Ezana for protection (F. Anfray, A. Caquot, P. Nautin). The direct reference to the appeal of these tribes to the Axumite king who evidently was considered their suzerain and protector is especially interesting. The Atiabitai or Atiab are encountered only in this inscription and nothing further is known about them. The Baria up to this time lived in the inter-river Tekezze and Gasha. The Hasa or Has lived south of Suwakin. The first mention, after Ezana II's inscription, of the Has (in the form of Al Hasa) is contained in a work of an Arabic geographer of the X century A.D., Ibn Hawqal. In publications of Kubbel and Matveev, just as in their predecessors' publications, instead of الخاصة a somewhat distorted spelling is given (1960, pp. 41, 58).

170. Kirwan proposes that Ezana II himself destroyed the Meroitic temples in Jebel Barkala, Sanama, and Kawa (L. P. Kirwan, 1957, p. 40). Ezana II himself says that his troops destroyed the temples and smashed the statues of the gods. It stands to reason that these temples and sculptures had to be preserved from Meroitic times. Hence it is possible to advance a conclusion about the nature of relations which were built up between the Noba and the Meroites. Littman thought that one of the Ethiopian inscriptions in Meroe was composed by a soldier of Ezana II (*DAE*, I, 50). Actually it is approximately synchronous to Ezana II's reign, but neither the king nor his campaign is mentioned in the inscription. In general the Axum inscriptions from Nubia are in need of additional study.

171. Up to now this expression has been translated literally.

172. *DAE*, IV, no. 11, 48.

173. *DAE*, IV, no. 8, 9.

174. *DAE*, X.

175. B. A. Turayev, 1914, *History of the Ancient East*, pp. 354, 355. [in Russian]

176. E. Littmann, 1950, II, SS. 126, 127.

177. J. Doresse, 1957, *L'empire*, v. I, p. 151.

178. E. Littmann, 1950, II, SS. 126, 127.

179. F. Anfray, A. Caquot, et P. Nautin.

180. The most ancient of the published monotheistic inscriptions found in South Arabia dates to 384 A.D. (see J.M. Solà Solé, pp. 197–206). However, only part of the already discovered South Arabian inscriptions have been published. And how many of them still have not been discovered? The majority of the vaguely monotheistic inscriptions from South Arabia date to the V–VI centuries A.D. Nevertheless, it is possible to propose that "vague monotheism" was born in South Arabia approximately in the middle of the IV century A.D.

181. H. Müller, 1894.

182. R. Lepsius, 1852, S. 52; W. Jones, v. IV, pp. 1–17.

183. A. Grohmann, 1915, SS. 57–58.

184. G. Sevak, p. 46. [in Russian]

185. D. A. Olderogge, pp. 761–765.

186. [J. B. Chabot], t. II, p. 58; A. G. Loundine, 1961, p. 22.

187. I. Guidi, 1881, p. 14.

188. A. G. Loundine, 1961, pp. 21–23. [in Russian]

189. Ibid., p. 32. [The Russian text hereafter identified this man by various of these names, which have been edited herein to identify him consistently as Dhu-Nuwas.]

190. [J. P. Chabot], t. II, p. 55; N. V. Pigulevskaya, 1951, p. 270 [in Russian]; see also [L. Dindorff], p. 433; Theophanes (ed. De Boor), p. 244.

191. *BH*, p. 3b, CI.

192. *MA*, p. 722.
193. *BH*, p. 3, CI. F. Altheim and Ruth Stiehl (1969, S. 301–304) read this name as Hayawaha.
194. C. Conti-Rossini, 1909, *Les listes*, p. 292.
195. *BH*, pp. CI, CV.
196. A. G. Loundine, 1961, p. 34. [in Russian]
197. *BH*, p. CV, tells of the church burning. For the *Chronicle of Seert*, see A. Scher, *Histoire nestorienne*.
198. Irfân Shahîd, pp. 241–250.
199. *BH*, p. CXXXIV.
200. *BH*, p. CV.
201. J. W. Hirshenberg, p. 334, note 25; N. V. Pigulevskaya, 1951, p. 282. [in Russian]
202. I. Guidi, 1889, SS. 409–412.
203. [E. O. Winstedt], p. 119.
204. *Ry*, 507, 4–5; 508, 4; *Ja*, 1028, 3–4.
205. *MA*, pp. 728a, 734.
206. *BH*, pp. VII-VIII.
207. *MA*, p. 742.
208. Irfân Shahîd, pp. 241–250.
209. I. Guidi, 1881; N. V. Pigulevskaya, 1951, p. 232 [in Russian]; Irfân Shahîd, pp. 241–250; P. Devos, p. 109.
210. Schröter, SS. 360–399; N. V. Pigulevskaya, 1951, p. 277. [in Russian]
211. Schröter, SS. 400–405; Pigulevskaya, p. 277. [in Russian]
212. R. Schneider, 1974, pp. 771–777.
213. [E. O. Winstedt], p. 319.
214. *BH*, p. IX.
215. *MA*, p. 731; [L. Dindorff], p. 458; Theophanes, ed. De Boor, p. 245.
216. The following sources call him Ella Asbeha (or Ella Asbaha with greater or lesser distortion): the inscription of Sumafa' Ashwa' (*RES*, 3904, 6), "The Lists of Kings," Cosmas Indicopleustes, *The Martyrdom of Arethius*, *The Life of Saint Grigentius*, Procopius and sources dependent on him, Nonnus, and Joannes Malalae. The Christian-Biblical name of Kaleb is given by the "Lists of Kings" by coins and by *The Book of the Himyarites*. An inscription recently discovered in Axum gives both names: Kaleb and Ella Asbeha.

In Sumafa' Ashwa's inscription Ella Asbeha is called 'L'BḤH with the omission of the letter *ṣ*. The final H appeared, as in Arabic, completely regularly; if the author of the inscription had not so carefully copied the Ethiopian pronunciation, but had "Sabaeanized" the name of Ella Asbeha, then it would have received a final *t*.

Cosmos Indicopleustes, of all the foreign authors, most accurately transcribed the name of Ella Asbeha. He calls him Ellatsbaa[s] (Ελλατξβάας). If we consider that by means of the Greek language it is impossible to render the Semitic sound *X* and that the emphatic *ṣ* already in the Axumite period had, evidently, changed into the ejective affricate *ts* and that an initial *'a* most often merged with the *a* of the preceding word, then the unusual precision of the rendering of the Ethiopian name by the Greek has no equal. Judging by Cosmas' transcription and that of other foreign authors, the king's name was pronounced Ella Asbaha and only later acquired the modern form of Ella Asbeha. In this form it found its way into the "Lists of Kings" and also into later Ethiopian writings. Here we preserve the traditional Ethiopian spelling of the name. Ella Asbeha or Ella Asbaha in the Ge'ez language means "he who makes the day break" (compare the Arabic صباح "morning").

217. [L. Dindorff], p. 458.

218. *BH*, p. 55, CXXXIX.

219. Up to the present the Ethiopian church has remained Monophysitic.

220. *MA*, p. 743.

221. N. V. Pigulevskaya, 1951, p. 298. [in Russian]

222. *Ry*, 515.

223. A. G. Loundine, 1961, pp. 45–48. [in Russian]

224. *MA*, p. 747.

225. Ella Asbeha's imperfect inscription mentions "his port" (ⸯⲤⲓ⸱), ship (ⲇⲃⸯⲤ) and the division of "peoples" of the king, probably, into two landings (Murad Kamil, p. 11). A. G. Loundine (1961, pp. 49, 121) proposes that the fleet carried out two trips. Loundine loses sight of the impossibility for ships of that time to sail against the northwest monsoons; ships would not have been able to return to Ethiopia in order to make a second landing.

226. *BH*, p. 6a, CIII. Møberg, the investigator of *The Book of the Himyarites*, contrasting this source with *The Martyrdom of Arethius*, first reached the conclusion about the simultaneous landing in two places (*BH*, p. XXXV).

227. *CIH*, 621, 8–9.

228. *CIH*, 621, 9.

229. Tabari, ser. I, pp. 928, 929.

230. *MA*, p. 755; *BH*, pp. 45a, 46b, CXXXIV–CXXXV.

231. Tabari, ser. I, pp. 928, 930.

232. *MA*, p. 775.

233. *BH*, p. 54a, CXIII; *MA*, p. 757, A. Vasiliev, pp. 33–36. [in Russian]

234. A. Caquot, 1965.

235. In the chronicles of Joannes Malalae and Theophanes the Byzantine, is this event not confused with the baptism of the Axumites where the pagan king Andas (or Adad) makes a vow to baptize [Axum] in the event of a victory over the Jewish king of Himyar?

236. *RES*, 3904, 4; [S. Destunis], 1876, I, 20, 104, p. 274; *BH*, p. 54a–55b, CXIII–CXL.

237. *BH*, p. CXLII. In *The Life of Saint Grigentius*, 36 months are mistakenly mentioned. [See Vasiliev, 1907.]

238. *RES*, 3904, 3; A. G. Loundine, 1961, pp. 54, 55. [in Russian]

239. *BH*, p. CXIII.

240. *RES*, 3904, 7. It is interesting that the word '*akabe* is encountered in compound titles of medieval Ethiopian nobles: '*akabe-heg*, '*akabe-sa'at*, and others.

241. Rubin (1960) proposes an earlier date, 526–527. (See N. V. Pigulevskaya, 1964, *The policy*, pp. 76, 77. [in Russian])

242. [S. Destunis], 1876, I, 20, p. 280; II, 10.

243. Compare N. V. Pigulevskaya, 1964, *The policy*, p. 84. [in Russian]

244. [S. Destunis], 1876, I, 20, p. 281.

245. [S. Destunis], 1861, pp. 483–485.

246. [L. Dindorff], pp. 456–458.

247. [S. Destunis], 1861, p. 484.

248. Theophanes, pp. 244, 245.

249. Many modern investigators repeat the error of Theophanes and Joannes Malalae. The notes of Nonnus (quoted in Joannes Malalae and Theophanes) were first ascribed to Julian. When Mordtmann (J. H. Mordtmann, 1881, S. 702)

proved Nonnus' authorship, Fell (W. Fell, *Die Christenverfolgung*) tried to dispute his conclusion, maintaining that Julian also would have been able to leave a book about his embassy to Ethiopia. Smith recently proposed that Julian and Nonnus were in one and the same embassy (S. Smith, pp. 449, 450), and Kawar (J. Kawar, SS. 61, 63) proposed the following explanation: Julian and Nonnus were in a single embassy but Julian acted in Ethiopia and Nonnus in Arabia and then came to Julian with an account. However, N. V. Pigulevskaya pointed out the lack of substantiation and the artificiality of similar explanations: Julian and Nonnus had independent assignments and were invested with plenary powers. Why would they have had to meet in Ethiopia? (N. V. Pigulevskaya, 1964, *The policy*, pp. 76, 82. [in Russian])

250. John of Ephesus, 1923, p. 140.

251. [S. Destunis], 1876, I, 20, pp. 274, 275, 281.

252. Tabari, ser. I, p. 931; [V. Guirgass], pp. 43, 44; "*Kitāb ul-aiwâl, gāni li-Abial-Faraj 'Alī al-Isfahāni*," Bulaq 1285, pp. 69–72; A. G. Loundine, 1961, pp. 61–62. [in Russian]

253. [S. Destunis], 1876, I, 20, p. 275.

254. Tabari, ser. I, p. 934.

255. A. G. Loundine, 1954, part 11.

256. A. G. Loundine, 1961, p. 122. [in Russian] Let us recall that the Bishop Grigentius was Orthodox; consequently under Abreha, the Himyarite church was headed by an Orthodox bishop.

257. *RY*, 506. The Hanifites and Jews, Christians, and other monotheists of Arabia called God "Rahman." This term was adopted by Islam as an epithet for Allah and, as shown by a recently discovered inscription of Wazeb (the son of Ella Asbeha), was used by Ethiopian Christians of the mid-VI century A.D.

258. [S. Destunis], 1876, I, 20, p. 275.

259. Tabari, ser. I, p. 931.

260. A. G. Loundine, 1954, pp. 5–6. [in Russian] Loundine translates the term '*azlī* as "deputy."

261. Ibid.

262. A. Vasiliev, p. 66. [in Russian]

263. A. G. Loundine, 1954, pp. 5–6. [in Russian]

264. A. J. Drewes, 1962, pp. 108–111.

265. C. Conti-Rossini, 1928, *Storia*, p. 210.

266. Enrico Cerulli, 1956, p. 26.

267. A. E. Budge, 1928, *A History*, v. I, pp. 114–115.

268. John of Ephesus, *Lives of the Eastern Saints*, 1926, p. 222.

269. C. Conti-Rossini, 1897, *Note etiopiche*, I, pp. 1–2; C. Conti-Rossini, 1928, *Storia d'Etiopia*, p. 266; L. E. Kubbel and V. V. Matveev, 1965, pp. 92–98. [in Russian]

270. L. E. Kubbel and V. V. Matveev, 1948, p. 242. [in Russian]

271. A. G. Loundine, 1961, pp. 86–89. [in Russian]

272. Tabari, ser. I, p. 957.

273. Ibid., pp. 1181–1185, 1189–1198, 1560–1570.

274. C. Conti-Rossini, 1909, *Les listes*, pp. 292, 294, 318.

275. Tabari, p. 1640 and following.

276. V. V. Barthold, 1925, *The Koran*, pp. 108, 110.

277. Tabari, ser. I, p. 1181.

278. Conti-Rossini, 1928, *Storia d'Etiopia*, pp. 203, 204.

279. A. Vasiliev, p. 36. [in Russian]

280. *MA*, p. 758; Tabari, ser. I, p. 1570.

281. Schneider, 1974, pp. 777–786.

282. A. G. Loundine, 1954, p. 5.

283. [S. Destunis], 1876, I, 20, p. 275.

284. C. Conti-Rossini, 1909, *Les listes*, pp. 271, 280.

285. Ibid., pp. 293, 294.

286. U. Monneret de Villard, 1940, p. 61; D. Buxton, 1949, pl. 83; E. Cerulli, 1956, *Storia*, p. 22.

287. Tabari, ser. I, p. 1889.

288. C. Conti-Rossini, 1928, *Storia d'Etiopia*, p. 212.

289. Tabari, ser. I, pp. 2595, 2613.

290. C. Conti-Rossini, 1928, *Storia d'Etiopia*, p. 214; U. Monneret de Villard, 1948, pp. 175–180.

291. C. Conti-Rossini, 1928, *Storia d'Etiopia*, p. 268.

292. P. Margolin, 1881, pp. 6, 7, 12–15, 18, 36, 37, and following [in Russian]; C. Conti-Rossini, 1925, *Leggende*, pp. 104–120.

293. L. E. Kubbel and V. V. Matveev, 1965, p. 110. [in Russian]

294. L. E. Kubbel and V. V. Matveev, 1960, pp. 38, 40. [in Russian]

295. V. Minorsky, 1937, pp. 164, 165, 473, 474.

296. *DAE*, IV, no. 14, SS. 46, 47.

297. The kings of the medieval "usurper" dynasty of Zagwe (C. Conti-Rossini, 1901, p. 12; Enrico Cerulli, 1943, pp. 274–276) which had come to replace the Axumite kings and also the rulers of certain Ethiopian lands of the XIV century A.D. bore this same title. Possibly, during the heyday of the Axumite Kingdom the title "hadani" belonged to a noble so close to the king that it proved extremely easy for him to usurp the authority. Usually the word hadani (ሐዳኒ) is translated as "protector," "nourisher." It comes from the root *ḥdn*—"to feed," "to breast feed," "to nourish," "to embrace." The Ethiopian ሐዳኒ in form corresponds precisely to the Arabic حاضن (benefactor) and حاضنة (wet nurse) and the semantics of the fundamental meanings of this root coincide in both languages. Therefore I would construe the word *hadani* as "feeder" (see Yu. M. Kobishchanov, 1962, *Legend*; Yu. M. Kobishchanov, 1964). Probably the king of the Axumites, like other sacred kings, was [ritually] unable to touch food with his hands. A special noble, i.e., a hadani (feeder), fed him, placing the food in the king's mouth. The post of the royal "feeder" inevitably became extremely honored in proportion to the degree of the consolidation of the monarchy and the idolization of the king.

298. C. Conti-Rossini, 1928, *Storia d'Etiopia*, pp. 303 ff.

II. Economic Resources

1. Tabari, ser. I, p. 927.

2. *MA*, p. 747.

3. See N. V. Pigulevskaya, 1951, p. 300. [in Russian]

4. *BH*, p. 45a, CV. In the Himyarite inscriptions (*Ry*, 507, 4) the annihilation of 309 Ethiopians is mentioned. Probably only the first group was meant. The remaining 280 men were burned in a church.

5. *MA*, pp. 722, 723.

6. [S. Destunis], 1876, I, 20, 107, p. 275.

7. Schneider, 1974, pp. 770, 776.

8. C. Conti-Rossini, 1942, pp. 21–28; A. J. Drewes, 1962, pp. 65–67, pl. XXII.

9. *DAE*, IV, no. 4, 19–21; no. 6, 7–10; no. 7, 7–10.

10. A. J. Drewes, 1962, pp. 49 et suiv.
11. *DAE*, IV, no. 7, 9; no. 6, 9; no. 4, 19.
12. B. A. Turayev, 1902, p. 103 and following; Yu. M. Kobishchanov, 1964, *Early information*, p. 6 [in Russian]; Yu. M. Kobishchanov, 1964, *Les données*, pp. 9, 10. [in Russian]
13. C. Mullerus, 1851, IV, p. 179; [S. Destunis], 1861, p. 487.
14. [E. O. Winstedt], p. 71.
15. C. Mullerus, 1851, IV, p. 179; [S. Destunis], 1861, p. 487.
16. L. I. Prasolov, pp. 371, 373 [in Russian]; F. Simoons, 1960, pp. 64, 65.
17. N. I. Vavilov, pp. 3, 13, 23, 24, 209, 210, etc. [in Russian]
18. R. Portères, p. 207. Portères traces the name of the plant to the ancient Egyptian word *t'eff* (wheat). However, in ancient Egypt t'eff itself was unknown. Instead, millet (*Eragrostis pilosa* P.B., which is related to it) was cultivated there, as it is even today in Nubia.
19. Ibid., p. 204.
20. *DAE*, IV, no. 4, 17; no. 6, 12; no. 7, 13.
21. [E. O. Winstedt], p. 119.
22. Job, 39: 9. [In the King James version the beast is a unicorn.]
23. P. Graziosi, pp. 61–70; A. Mordini, 1941, pp. 54–60; W. Stiehler, S. 263; J. Leclant et A. Miquel, p. 107, pl. L, b.
24. B. A. Turayev, 1902, p. 140. [in Russian]
25. V. Franchini, 1957, pp. 1–12; V. Franchini, 1964, pp. 97–102.
26. V. Franchini, 1959, p. 287; F. Anfray, 1967, pp. 44–45.
27. [E. O. Winstedt], p. 71.
28. Only in the XIV century A.D. do there appear numerous references to horses in Ethiopia.
29. The opinion even exists that the domestication of the one-humped camel occurred in the first millennium B.C. near the northern boundaries of Ethiopia.
30. C. Conti-Rossini, 1903, p. 181.
31. L. E. Kubbel and V. V. Matveev, 1960, pp. 26, 29. [in Russian]
32. *DAE*, IV, no. 9, 7.
33. *DAE*, 11, 24, SS. 42–46.
34. Schneider, 1974, pp. 771, 776.
35. *DAE*, IV, no. 11, 24.
36. A. J. Drewes, 1962, p. 45.
37. Strabo, XVI, I, §17; pp. 792, 793 in the Mishchenk Russian version.
38. L. E. Kubbel and V. V. Matveev, 1960, pp. 26, 29. [in Russian]
39. *DAE*, IV, no. 10, 21, 22.
40. *DAE*, IV, no. 11, 43, 44.
41. Schneider, 1974, pp. 771, 776.
42. Ibid., pp. 778, 785.
43. *DAE*, IV, no. 12, 7, 8, 19, 20, 32, 33; no. 13, 10, 11, 14–16.
44. *DAE*, IV, no. 10, 30.
45. *DAE*, IV, no. 4, 28, 13, 14; no. 6, 16, 17, 7, 8; no. 7, 17, 7, 8.
46. A. J. Drewes, 1962, p. 60, notes.
47. [L. Dindorff], p. 457.
48. *Periplus*, §6, p. 266.
49. T. Mommsen, 1949, p. 511.
50. [E. O. Winstedt], p. 71.
51. A. Lukas, p. 624.
52. G. Tringali, p. 150.

53. Pliny, VI, 29, I, ed. Detlefsen.

54. *Periplus*, §5, p. 246.

55. F. Anfray, 1963, *La première campagne*, p. 105, pl. CXI, b.

56. H. de Contenson, 1963, *Les fouilles à Haoulti en 1959*, p. 48, pl. XLIX, b.

57. [E. O. Winstedt], p. 324.

58. C. Conti-Rossini, 1928, *Storia*, tav. LIX, No. 191; Tringali, p. 151.

59. [S. Destunis], 1876, I, 102, p. 252; *Periplus*, §6, p. 266.

60. *Periplus*, §5–7, pp. 266–267.

61. H. de Contenson, 1959, *Les fouilles à Axoum en 1957*, p. 12, pl. XIV, a–b.

62. J. Leclant et A. Miquel, 1959, *Reconnaissances*, pl. LVIII, a.

63. H. de Contenson, 1963, *Les fouilles à Haoulti en 1959*, pp. 44, 49, pl. XLII, b, 1–3; LIII, a.

64. F. Anfray, 1963, *Une campagne*, p. 176, pl. CLII, h–k, CLIII, b, c, CLIV, a–h.

65. H. de Contenson, 1959, *Les fouilles à Axoum en 1957*, p. 28.

66. H. de Contenson, 1963, *Les fouilles à Haoulti en 1959*, p. 44, pl. XLII, b, 2; F. Anfray, 1963, *Une campagne*, pp. 176, 181, 184, 185, 196, pl. CLI, d–k.

67. *DAE*, II, S. 204, fig. 427, no. 85.

68. F. Anfray, 1963, *Une campagne*, pp. 187, 188, pl. CLII, a–c.

69. H. de Contenson, 1959, *Les fouilles à Axoum en 1957*, pl. XIX, 6, 7.

70. F. Anfray et Guy Annequin, 1965, pp. 59, 67, pl. LXVIII: F. Anfray, 1967, pp. 34–42.

71. H. de Contenson (1963, *Les fouilles à Haoulti en 1959*, p. 48) distinguishes "blackish" and "greenish" patinas.

72. F. Anfray, 1963, *Une campagne*, pp. 179, 181, 182, 184, pl. CL, a, b; F. Anfray, 1963, *La première campagne*, p. 102; F. Anfray et G. Annequin, 1965, p. 59, pl. LXVIII; F. Anfray, 1967, p. 42.

73. C. Conti-Rossini, 1928, *Storia*, tav. LIX, no. 191.

74. H. de Contenson, 1963, *Les fouilles à Haoulti en 1959*, p. 48, pl. XLIX, b.

75. F. Anfray, 1963, *Une campagne*, pp. 176, 181, 186, pl. CLVI, a.

76. A. Mordini, 1960, *Gli aurei*, pp. 252, 253.

77. [E. O. Winstedt], pp. 318, 319, 320.

78. [L. Dindorff], p. 457.

79. *DAE*, IV, no. 4, 23–31; no. 18, 19, no. 7, 18, 19.

80. *DAE*, II, SS. 44, 45, fig. 81, 82.

81. R. Paribeni; *DAE*, II, SS. 199, 200; C. Conti-Rossini, 1928, *Storia*, tav. LVII, pp. 179–181; J. Leclant, 1959, pp. 3–24, pl. III–XII; A. Caquot et J. Leclant, 1956, pp. 226–228; H. de Contenson, 1959, *Les fouilles à Axoum en 1957*, pp. 25–34, pl. XIII–XX, XVII; H. de Contenson, 1959, *Aperçus*, pp. 101–106; F. Anfray, *La première campagne*, 1963, pp. 102, 103, pl. CVII.

82. F. Anfray did a great deal for the study of Ethiopian ceramics of the Axumite period. However, this area of archaeological investigations has only begun to be developed systematically. See: F. Anfray, 1968, pp. 1–74; F. Anfray, 1965, pp. 217–222; F. Anfray, 1972, SS. 60–76. Anfray's investigations now permit us to delineate several types of ceramic vessel of the Early and Late Axumite periods and also of two Preaxumite periods and several local variants typical for Axum, Adulis, and Matara.

83. F. Anfray, 1974, p. 767, pl. VI, fig. 1–2.

84. Their photographs: *AE*, v. III, 1959, pl. III, IV, IV bis, XV, XVI, XVII.

85. H. de Contenson, 1963, *Les fouilles à Haoulti en 1959*, p. 44, pl. XLII, a, XXXVII, b, c.

86. H. de Contenson, 1959, *Les fouilles à Axoum en 1957*, p. 31, pl. XIX, 8. In

Haoulti clay models of houses of the Preaxumite epoch were found.
87. H. de Contenson, 1963, *Les fouilles à Axoum en 1958*, p. 12.
88. [E. O. Winstedt], p. 318.
89. U. Monneret de Villard, 1935, *Aksum*, appendix.
90. *DAE*, II, SS. 70–75; fig. 153, 157.
91. H. de Contenson, 1959, *Aperçus*, pp. 101–106.
92. *DAE*, II, SS. 107–110, fig. 245–247, SS. 110–112, fig. 248, 249, SS. 112–119, fig. 250–260.
93. F. Anfray, 1972, pp. 63 s.
94. Ibid., p. 63.
95. R. Sundström, in E. Littmann, Preliminary Report, pp. 171–182; R. Paribeni; F. Anfray, 1974, pp. 749–753.
96. F. Anfray, 1963, *La première campagne*, pp. 87–169; F. Anfray et G. Annequin, pp. 49–68; F. Anfray, 1974, pp. 754–759.

III. The Socio-Economic System
1. For example, Enrico Cerulli, 1960, p. 8.
2. The Axumite Kingdom, *Soviet Historical Encyclopedia*, v. I, p. 311; 1961. [in Russian]
3. For the author's views on these questions see Yu. M. Kobishchanov, *Africa*, 1974. [in Russian]
4. *Ja*, 575, 5–6.
5. *DAE*, IV, no. 6, 23; no. 7, 23; no. 10, 26–29; no. 11, 50–51.
6. *DAE*, IV, no. 10, 26–29; see also *DAE*, IV, no. 11, 50–51.
7. Schneider, 1974, pp. 772, 777, 779, 786.
8. *Ja*, 575, 6.
9. *DAE*, IV, no. 8, 7–8.
10. *DAE*, IV, no. 9, 5–6.
11. *DAE*, IV, no. 8, 26–27, 10–11.
12. *DAE*, IV, no. 11, 37–48.
13. A. Kammerer, 1926, *Essai*, pp. 168–170; A. Anzani, 1926, pp. 87–89, 92.
14. Schneider, 1974, pp. 771, 774.
15. André Caquot, 1965, pp. 223–228.
16. Schneider, 1974, pp. 778, 780, 781, 783, 785.
17. *DAE*, IV, no. 12, 34.
18. *DAE*, IV, no. 13, 5.
19. *DAE*, IV, no. 11, 37, 38.
20. A. Kammerer, 1926, *Essai*, pp. 168–170; A. Anzani, 1926, pp. 87–99.
21. A. G. Loundine, 1961, pp. 93–110. [in Russian]
22. A. G. Loundine, 1954, p. 9. [in Russian]
23. [S. Destunis], 1876, 1, 20, 106, p. 275.
24. A. G. Loundine, 1961, p. 97, etc. [in Russian] See my review on this work: Kobishchanov, 1962, "Review," pp. 231–232. [in Russian]
25. [S. Strelcyn], pp. 98–99, 113–114, 158.
26. *Ja*, 577, 5; A. Jamme, 1962, pp. 77–78.
27. J. T. Bent, p. 195.
28. [E. O. Winstedt], p. 72.
29. A. J. Drewes, 1962, pp. 67–68; *DAE*, IV, S. 61, no. 34.
30. A. J. Drewes, 1962, pp. 65–67; C. Conti-Rossini, 1942, pp. 21–28.

31. [E. O. Winstedt], p. 77.
32. *CIH*, IV, pp. 415–420; A. G. Loundine, 1954, p. 10. [in Russian]
33. [A. Vasiliev], 1907, pp. 63–64. [in Russian]
34. *DAE*, IV, S. 52, no. 21.
35. [E. O. Winstedt], p. 74.
36. A. H. Sayce, pp. 189–190.
37. *DAE*, IV, no. 9, 9–12, 19–20.
38. *DAE*, IV, no. 10, 9–20.
39. *DAE*, IV, no. 9, 6–8.
40. *DAE*, IV, no. 11, 16–43.
41. Schneider, 1974, pp. 771, 775, 775.
42. Ibid., pp. 778, 784, 785.
43. Tabari, ser. I, pp. 927–938. [in Russian]
44. *BH*, p. 56a, CXIII.
45. Murad Kamil, *An Ethiopic inscription found at Mareb:* ዐዞዐፀ : ዐበሳበፖ "and they took him into captivity and robbed him."
46. *RES*, 3904, 8.
47. *DAE*, IV, no. 12, 34.
48. *DAE*, IV, no. 13, 17–18.
49. *DAE*, IV, no. 14.
50. *DAE*, IV, no. 10, 17–20.
51. *DAE*, IV, no. 11, 18, 21–22, 32–33, 40–41, 42–43.
52. *DAE*, IV, no. 10, 30.
53. Tyrranius Rufinus, *Historia ecclesiastica*, lib. X, cap. 9–10 (cited according to R. Hennig, 1961, v. II, p. 25). [in Russian]
54. Nikephoros Kallistos, *Historia ecclesiastica*, lib. VIII, cap. 35 (cited according to R. Hennig, 1961, v. II, p. 25). [in Russian]
55. G. Sapeto, pp. 395–397; A. Dillmann, 1950, pp. 33–35.
56. Tabari, ser. I, pp. 930–933. [in Russian]
57. B. A. Turayev, 1905, p. 4. [in Russian]
58. C. Mondon-Vidailhet, pp. 261–264.
59. Tabari, ser. I, p. 931.
60. A. G. Loundine translates '*azlī* as "vice-regent" (A. G. Loundine, 1954 [in Russian]); however, the terms '*qb* and *ẖlf* are used in Sabaean in this sense.
61. *DAE*, IV, no. 9, 12.
62. Free "throne bearers" who possessed conditional holdings and who developed them by their labor are known in medieval and modern Ethiopia. In particular they are mentioned in Bruce's book.
63. *Ja*, 575, 5.
64. The meaning of the term remains unclear.
65. *DAE*, IV, no. 6, 21–26; no. 7, 21–25.
66. [S. Destunis], 1876, I, 20, 106, p. 275.
67. *DAE*, IV, no. 12, 14–15, 18, 19, 27.
68. Pliny, IV, 29, 174; [Detlefsen], p. 267. As early as the beginning of the XV century b.c. slaves were exported from this region. The inscriptions in the temple of Deir el Bahri, describing an expedition sent into the country of Punt by Queen Hatshepsut, mention the loading onto Egyptian ships of "inhabitants [i.e., slaves] with their children." In the inscription of Thutmose III (the husband and successor of Hatshepsut), on a stone stele in the Paris museum, is listed "the tribute which was brought to the pharaoh from the land of Punt," which includes "36 black slaves and bondwomen."

69. Periplus, §13, p. 268. See A. Vallon, 1941, p. 597; also see W. Westerman's appendix to A. Vallon's book.

70. See N. V. Pigulevskaya, 1946, pp. 150–151. [in Russian]

71. Tabari, ser. I, p. 1778. [in Russian]

72. C. Conti-Rossini, 1928, *Storia*, pp. 204–206; H. Lammens, pp. 425–482.

73. Cited according to Ya. M. Svet, p. 130. [in Russian]

74. Diodorus, II, 55. The story about Yambul is a romantic tale, but its information about pirates is an element of historical realism in this literary work.

75. [E. O. Winstedt], p. 74.

76. *DAE*, IV, no. 10, 21–22.

77. *DAE*, IV, no. 11, 43–44.

78. [E. O. Winstedt], p. 74.

79. *DAE*, IV, no. 11, 40–45.

80. *DAE*, IV, no. 4, 22–28; no. 6, 12–16.

81. [E. O. Winstedt], pp. 70–71.

82. [S. Strelcyn], p. 107.

83. *DAE*, IV, no. 10, 17–22.

84. *DAE*, IV, no. 11, 40–43.

85. *DAE*, IV, no. 4, 12–22. Compare with the above cited passages from the inscriptions of Kaleb [Ella Asbeha] and Wazeb.

86. *DAE*, IV, no. 6, 25–26; no. 7, 26.

87. C. Conti-Rossini, 1895, pp. 4, 5; C. Conti-Rossini, 1901, no. 1–5, etc. Only Turayev objected against the indisputable arguments of Conti-Rossini concerning the falseness of the land deeds.

88. A. J. Drewes et R. Schneider, pp. 96–102.

89. [E. O. Winstedt], p. 75.

90. [S. Destunis], 1876, I, 20, 105, p. 274.

91. *MA*, p. 722.

92. *BH*, p. 56a, CXIII.

93. *DAE*, IV, no. 8, SS. 18–24; no. 9, SS. 24, 25.

94. L. E. Kubbel and V. V. Matveev, 1960, p. 38 (Arabic text).

95. Yu. M. Kobishchanov, 1972, pp. 65–78. [in Russian]

96. B. A. Turayev, 1936, p. 143. [in Russian]

97. B. A. Turayev, 1901, p. 168. [in Russian]

98. Yu. M. Kobishchanov, 1963, *The election*, p. 143. [in Russian]

99. B. A. Turayev, 1905, p. 2. [in Russian]

100. *DAE*, IV, no. 8.

101. *DAE*, IV, no. 9, 6.

102. Schneider, 1974, pp. 771, 775.

103. *DAE*, IV, no. 9, 7–8, 23, 24. There it is also said that in a certain country, where Ezana's troops where located, "they brought water" for his people.

104. *DAE*, IV, no. 4, 6, 7.

105. A. Vasiliev, 1907, p. 64. [in Russian]

106. *BH*, p. CXI.

107. A. J. Drewes, 1962, no. 73, A–D, pp. 30–64.

108. A *gabata* in modern Ethiopia is: (1) a large clay vessel; (2) a measure of liquid and dry substances.

109. A *qunna* in modern Ethiopia is a measure of liquid and dry substances equal to a quarter or an eighth of a gabata.

110. With vocalization of *'šr wkl't* as ꭐꭐꮯ : ꮤ'ꭰꭰꮲꭴ : . With vocalization as ꭟꭐꮮ : ꮤ'ꭰꭰꮲꭴ ("twenty-two"), the number is not divisible by three like

the two following numbers, whereas in a sacred text it is natural to expect the numbers three, six, nine, twelve.

111. C. Conti-Rossini et L. Ricci, pp. 206, 199, nota 2; A. J. Drewes, 1962, pp. 63, 51.

112. [Maria Höfner], 1959, §29(9) : A. J. Drewes, 1962, p. 61.

113. W. Munziger, 1864, S. 237; C. Conti-Rossini, 1929, p. 713; A. J. Drewes, 1962, p. 63; [René Henri], p. 6.

114. W. Munziger, 1864, S. 312; C. Conti-Rossini, 1929, p. 726.

115. K. G. Rodén, p. 252, A. J. Drewes, 1962, p. 61.

116. [Maria Höfner], 1959, §29(9) : A. J. Drewes, 1962, p. 61.

117. K. G. Rodén, p. 61.

118. A. J. Drewes, 1962, pp. 53, 54.

119. Yu. M. Kobishchanov, 1963, *Social relationships*, p. 144. [in Russian]

120. G. Ryckmans, 1962, pp. 246–266; [R. Henri], p. 5.

121. C. Mullerus, 1851, p. 179; [S. Destunis], 1861, p. 486.

122. *Periplus*, §4, p. 265.

123. A. J. Drewes, 1962, pp. 32, 44, 53.

124. *DAE*, IV, no. 10, 7.

125. Pliny, VI, 29, I, VI, 29, 173, 174; XXXVI, 196.

126. *Periplus*, §3–7, pp. 264–267.

127. [E. O. Winstedt], pp. 69, 70–71, 320, 322, 324, 325. Photius, *Bibliotheca*, 3, p. 2; C. Mullerus, 1851, p. 178.

128. *Periplus*, §6, p. 24 (Schoff).

129. *Periplus*, §7, 8, p. 25 (Schoff).

130. [E. O. Winstedt], p. 69.

131. *Periplus*, §17, p. 269.

132. *DAE*, II, SS. 221–225.

133. F. Anfray, 1972, p. 62.

134. H. de Contenson, 1963, *Les fouilles à Axoum en 1958*, p. 12, pl. XX.

135. F. Anfray et G. Annequin, pp. 68–70, fig. 12; F. Anfray, 1967, p. 73; F. Anfray, 1974, p. 752, pl. II, fig. 2.

136. F. Anfray, *La première campagne*, p. 105; F. Anfray, 1963, *Une campagne*, pp. 177, 185, pl. CLVI, b, CLV, b.

137. J. Leclant, 1956, p. 34, note 3.

138. A. Caquot et J. Leclant, 1956, p. 288; H. de Contenson, 1959, *Les fouilles à Axoum en 1957*, p. 31; H. de Contenson, 1963, *Les fouilles à Axoum en 1958*, pp. 11–12, pl. XIII, b–c, XX.

139. A. Caquot et J. Leclant, 1956, pp. 226–234; A. Caquot et A. J. Drewes, pp. 17–41; J. Doresse, 1960, pp. 411–434.

140. H. de Contenson, 1963, *Les fouilles à Haoulti en 1959*, p. 43.

141. J. Leclant, 1965, *AE*, VI, pp. 86–87, pl. LXVII, 1.

142. J. Bruce, vol. II, chap. III; U. Monneret de Villard, 1948, p. 133; B. Van de Walle, 1953, pp. 238–247; L. P. Kirwan, 1960, p. 173, note 25.

143. F. Anfray, 1967, p. 46 s.

144. F. Vaccaro, 1953, *Monete sudarabici*, pp. 6–7; A. Gaudio, pp. 4–5; H. de Contenson, *Les fouilles à Axoum en 1958*, p. 8, pl. XIVe, p. 12, pl. XIVc.

145. R. Paribeni, fig. 49; C. Conti-Rossini, 1928, *Storia*, tav. LIX, no. 188.

146. H. de Contenson, 1963, *Les fouilles à Haoulti en 1959*, pp. 45–46, pl. XLVII–XLVIII, a–c.

147. D. Matthews and A. Mordini, pp. 50–54; A. Mordini, 1960, *I tessili*, pp. 229–248.

148. [E. O. Winstedt], p. 324.

149. *Codex Justinianus*, 4, 41, 1–2, pp. 178, 179.

150. [S. Destunis], 1876, I, 19, 102, p. 252.

151. *Periplus*, §6, p. 24 (Schoff).

152. *Periplus*, §4, p. 265.

153. [E. O. Winstedt], pp. 70, 71.

154. Compare *DAE*, IV, no. 11, 27.

155. *Periplus*, §4, p. 265. Pseudo Arrian clearly had not been to Coloe and had only heard about this city while he was in Axum.

156. See Yu. M. Kobishchanov, 1964, *The gold-bearing country*, pp. 96, 97. [in Russian]

157. *MA*, p. 743.

158. [J. B. Chabot], t. II, p. 55; N. V. Pigulevskaya, 1951, p. 270. [in Russian] We find a similar expression in the chronicles of Joannes Malalae and Theophanes the Byzantine.

159. Thus in *Kebra Nagast* we read: "[The Ethiopian queen] had great wealth, splendid clothing, servants and merchants; they traded for her on the sea and on land in the Indias and in Aswan" (S. Strelcyn, p. 70). "Merchants visited King Solomon and took from him gold and silver, giving him that which he needed" (ibid.). In the Ethiopian chronicles of the XIV–XVIII centuries, the organization of government trade is described with virtually the same expressions. "Royal merchants," who were headed by a "chief of merchants," were dispatched beyond the borders of the Empire; or foreign merchants (Armenians, Arabs, etc.) visited the royal court and sold to the head of the Ethiopian government goods which he needed, receiving primarily gold in exchange.

160. [E. O. Winstedt]. pp. 70, 71.

161. Philostratus, VI, 2, p. 136.

162. Herodotus, t. I, IV, 196.

163. Yu. M. Kobishchanov, 1964, *The gold-bearing country*, p. 103. [in Russian]

164. N. V. Pigulevskaya, 1951. [in Russian]

165. A. J. Drewes, 1962, pp. 32, 44, 53, 54; D 4–5.

166. *Periplus*, §6, 8, pp. 266, 267. In M. M. Khvostov's opinion (p. 170) *Periplus* by "foreigners" means "Greek merchants located in Adulis and in other trade cities of the Axumite Kingdom." Most likely he had in view foreign merchants from India, Ceylon, and South Arabia, since they were "foreigners" for Pseudo Arrian.

167. H. de Contenson, 1963, *Les fouilles à Axoum en 1958*, p. 8, pl. XIV, e.

168. A. J. Drewes, 1962, no. 73–D, 4.

169. A. Anzani, 1926.

170. A. Anzani, 1941; W. L. Clark; A. Mordini, 1959; F. Vaccaro, 1967; M. B. Hornung, 1973, V. XXXVII, pp. 64–68. The work of the Ethiopian numismatist Kinfu Kidane, published in 1968 at Addis Ababa in Amharic, should also be noted. Between 1966 and 1970, according to M. B. Hornung's observations, "several dozens of gold, approximately two dozen of silver, and no less than one hundred copper Axumite coins passed through the hands of traders in Addis Ababa (Hornung, p. 65). According to information obtained by us in Addis Ababa in 1966, a similar number of gold and silver Axumite coins was acquired by collectors in the preceding five years. Thus the number of Axumite coins discovered as a result of excavations should be multiplied by two in order to obtain the total number of finds of recent years.

171. D. Matthews and A. Mordini, p. 51; H. de Contenson, 1959, *Les fouilles*

à Axoum en 1957, p. 32; H. de Contenson, 1961, *Les fouilles à Ouchatei Gulo*, p. 5; H. de Contenson, 1961, *Trouvailles*, p. 16; H. de Contenson, 1963, *Les fouilles à Axoum en 1958*, pp. 5–8, pl. XIV, d, f, g; F. Anfray et G. Annequin, pp. 57–58, 64, 72; F. Anfray, 1967, p. 42 s.

172. A. Anzani, 1926, p. 14.

173. A. Mordini, *Gli aurei Kushāna*, 1960, p. 253; D. Matthews and A. Mordini, pp. 50–51.

174. [E. O. Winstedt], pp. 72, 73.

175. Pliny, VI, 172.

176. Claudius Ptolemaeus, IV, 7, 2; ed. Mullerus, 1879.

177. *Periplus*, §4, p. 265.

178. [S. Destunis], 1876, I, 19, 101, p. 251.

179. [C. Mullerus], 1851, p. 179. [S. Destunis], 1861, p. 486.

180. [E. O. Winstedt], p. 75.

181. Ibid., p. 69.

182. [S. Destunis], 1876, I, 19, 102, p. 256.

183. *MA*, p. 743.

184. Yu. M. Kobishchanov, 1962, *Communications*, pp. 36–38. [in Russian]

185. *Periplus*, §6, 7, pp. 266, 267.

186. [E. O. Winstedt], p. 70. F. Anfray thinks that in the Axumite period there were three actual cities (Axum, Adulis, and Matara), three towns or *villes* (Tokonda, Kohaito, and Gulo Makeda), and several dozen settlements of smaller size (villages). Approximately half of the villages and five out of six of the urban settlements (except Axum itself) were located to the east of Eritrea on the route from Adulis to the heart of the northern Ethiopian plateau (F. Anfray, 1974, p. 747 s.).

187. C. Mullerus, 1851, p. 179. [S. Destunis], 1861, p. 486.

188. Compare *Periplus*, §4, p. 265; Pseudo Arrian mentions Ichthyophagi, who brought tortoise shell for sale "into this small trade town."

189. [E. O. Winstedt], p. 72.

IV. Political Organization of the Axumite State

1. [E. O. Winstedt], pp. 74–77.

2. *DAE*, IV, no. 8, 9, 10, 11.

3. *DAE*, IV, no. 4, 6, 7.

4. A. Vasiliev, 1907, pp. 63, 64. [in Russian]

5. A. G. Loundine, 1961, p. 53.

6. BH, p. 56, a, CXLII.

7. A. Caquot et A. J. Drewes, p. 32.

8. The titles "nagashi" and "negush" come from the root *ngs* (variant *ngš*), a series of meanings of which in Semitic languages is connected with ritual hunting, sacrifice, ritual profanation. It is possible that the very titles "nagashi" and "negush" are connected with the priestly functions of the king.

9. *DAE*, IV, no. 4, 18–19; no. 6, 7–8.

10. C. Conti-Rossini, 1942; A. J. Drewes, 1962, pp. 55–57.

11. King SWSWT (Sawsawat?) in *DAE*, 8, 7–8; king Abba-Alke'o in *DAE*, 9, 9–12; "king of Aguezat" (anonymous) in Kaleb's [Ella Asbaha's] inscription from Axum (lines 29–30), R. Schneider, 1974, p. 771.

12. *DAE*, IV, no. 4, 3; no. 6, 1; no. 7, 1.

13. A. H. Sayce (line 1 of the inscription).

14. *DAE*, IV, no. 8, 1–4; no. 9, 1–3; no. 10, 2–4; no. 11, 2–4.

15. Schneider, 1974, pp. 771, 773.

16. Ibid., pp. 777–778, 780.

17. *DAE*, IV, no. 9, 3; no. 10, 4; no. 7, 3; no. 11, 4; and also no. 8, 4.

18. *DAE*, IV, no. 6, 2; *DAE*, IV, no. 4, 5.

19. *DAE*, IV, no. 3, 1–2. This expression has been interpreted as "one of the kings" or "king, son of a king" (the last version was recently proposed by Professor P. Petridis of Addis Ababa).

20. Up to 1974 the Ethiopian emperors were called by this title.

21. A. J. Drewes, p. 105.

22. Manuel d'Almeida, *Historia Aethiopica*, I, 6 (cited according to W. Vycichl, 1957, *Le titre*, p. 201).

23. Philostorgius, *Historia ecclesiastica*, 3_4, p. 34. N. V. Pigulevskaya directed attention to this (1951, p. 75).

24. [E. O. Winstedt], pp. 71, 72.

25. [L. Dindorff], pp. 457–458.

26. Theophanes, pp. 244–245.

27. *DAE*, IV, no. 11, 25–27; Schneider, 1974, pp. 778, 781.

28. *DAE*, II, S. 28, Fig. 53.

29. [L. Dindorff], p. 457.

30. *DAE*, IV, no. 8, 4; *DAE*, IV, no. 9, 4; no. 10, 5; no. 6, 2, 3; no. 7, 2, 3.

31. *DAE*, IV, no. 4, 5, 6.

32. [E. O. Winstedt], p. 77.

33. Psalms 2:7.

34. *RES*, 3540 and 3883.

35. *RES*, 3902, no. 137; 3884, 1–3.

36. *DAE*, IV, no. 11, 4.

37. *DAE*, IV, no. 11, 6.

38. Schneider, 1974, pp. 771, 773, 777–778, 780. In the XII–XIV centuries A.D. the Ethiopian kings called themselves "monarchs by the power of Christ unconquered by foes." As B. A. Turayev indicated, this is a clear Christianization of the Axum title.

39. The *Brief Chronicles* are to be distinguished from the great royal chronicles of the Ethiopian kings of the XV–XVI and XIX–XX centuries. The former are brief compilations extending from the Creation to the XVIII (or in some variants to the end of the XIX) century. The authors of the *Brief Chronicles* were ṣaḥāfē-te'ezāz (registrars of orders) and lesser clerks or scribes of the staff of the ṣaḥāfē-te'ezāz. See Basset, 1881; A. Caquot, 1957, *Les chroniques*; C. Conti-Rossini, 1893; C. Conti-Rossini, 1899 (wherein the concept *Brief Chronicles* was established); C. Conti-Rossini, 1940; C. Foti, 1941; I. Guidi, 1893; I. Guidi, 1926; V. M. Platonov, 1966; B. A. Turayev, 1906, *Ethiopian manuscripts*; B. A. Turayev, 1910. [the last three references in Russian]

40. R. Basset, pp. 411, 412; A. Caquot, 1957, *La royauté*.

41. [S. Strelcyn], pp. 87, 88.

42. Tyrranius Rufinus, *Historia ecclesiastica*, X, 9–10 (cited according to P. Hennig, 1961, v. I, p. 25 [in Russian]).

43. [L. Dindorff], p. 199.

44. J. P. Migne, t. 25, pp. 631–638.

45. *DAE*, IV, no. 4, 6, 7; *MAB*, II, SS. 98–109.

46. V. V. Bolotov first advanced this idea (1907, v. II, p. 273). [in Russian]

47. The peculiarities of the epistolary style do not exclude the interpretation

of the expression "most honorable brothers" in Constantius' letter as "my brothers" (such an interpretation was recently proposed by Professor Ruth Stiehl. Also, individuals not related to him [the king] could bear the title "brother of the king."

48. [E. O. Winstedt], p. 77.
49. [S. Destunis], I, 20, p. 275.
50. [L. Dindorff], p. 457.
51. Tabari, ser. I, p. 1570.
52. B. A. Turayev, 1902, p. 71. [in Russian]
53. DAE, IV, no. 3, 3.
54. [E. O. Winstedt], p. 77.
55. J. Perruchon, 1893, p. 145; B. A. Turayev, 1936, pp. 88, 89. [in Russian]
56. See Yu. M. Kobishchanov, 1963, The election, pp. 141, 142. [in Russian]
57. J. Perruchon, 1893, p. 175; B. A. Turayev, 1936, p. 104. [in Russian]
58. [E. O. Winstedt], p. 319.
59. [L. Dindorff], p. 458.
60. J. Perruchon, 1893, p. 145; B. A. Turayev, 1936, p. 88. [in Russian]
61. J. Perruchon, 1893, p. 145; B. A. Turayev, 1936, pp. 89, 103, 104. [in Russian]
62. W. Hofmayr, S. 145.
63. E. Evans-Pritchard, p. 23.
64. I. S. Katsnelson, 1960. [in Russian]
65. BH, p. 56a, CXLII.
66. Of course this is only an attempt, via comparison with Persian models, to somehow designate the position and authority of the Ethiopian nobles.
67. A. Vasiliev, 1907, p. 66. [in Russian]
68. DAE, IV, no. 9, 13.
69. DAE, IV, S. 26.
70. Ibid.
71. CIH, 308, 12.
72. [L. Dindorff], p. 434.
73. Tabari, ser. I, p. 1189.
74. B. A. Turayev, 1936, p. 69. [in Russian]
75. U. Monneret de Villard, 1935, Aksum, appendix.
76. DAE, II, SS. 45–49, 51–69.
77. [S. Strelcyn], pp. 107, 108, 112, 113.
78. Concerning the post of ṣaḥāfē-lahm see Yu. M. Kobishchanov, 1963, Social relationships, p. 135. [in Russian]
79. [S. Strelcyn], p. 114.
80. Ibid., pp. 146, 147.
81. G. Sapeto, p. 396; A. Dillmann, 1950, p. 33.
82. B. A. Turayev, 1936, p. 59, etc. [in Russian]
83. C. Mondon-Vidailhet, pp. 259–268.
84. BH, p. CV.
85. A. J. Drewes, 1962, pp. 108–111.
86. CIH, 541; Ry, 506; Ja, 546.
87. DAE, IV, SS. 25, 29, 34.
88. A. E. Budge, 1928, A History, v. I, pp. 247, 248, 256, 257.
89. C. Conti-Rossini, 1928, Storia, p. 134.
90. A. Kammerer, 1926, Essai, pp. 90, 91.
91. J. Doresse, 1957, L'empire, v. I, pp. 144, 147.
92. Schneider, 1974, pp. 771, 774.

93. Ibid., pp. 778, 781, 783.

94. Ibid., pp. 771, 774.

95. Ibid., pp. 771, 784.

96. [E. O. Winstedt], p. 75.

97. Ibid., p. 74.

98. *Ja*, 574, 576, 577, 631, 21 (see pp. 27–28).

99. A. G. Loundine, 1954, pp. 25–26, 75. [in Russian]

100. *MA*, p. 747.

101. C. Conti-Rossini, 1927, p. 178.

102. E. Littmann, 1950, S. 113.

103. J. Doresse, 1957, *L'empire*, v. I, pp. 144, 145.

104. See Yu. M. Kobishchanov, 1962, *The "armies,"* pp. 96, 97. [in Russian]

105. *DAE*, IV, no. 8, 1; no. 9, 1; no. 10, 1–2; no. 11, 2.

106. A. Kammerer, 1926, *Essai sur l'histoire*, pp. 157–159.

107. B. A. Turayev, 1901, *Two Axumite coins*, pp. 44–49 [in Russian]; *DAE*, I, S. 47; A. Kammerer, 1926, *Essai sur l'histoire*, p. 157.

108. *DAE*, IV, no. 11, 37.

109. *DAE*, IV, no. 8, 13.

110. *DAE*, IV, no. 9, 15, 25.

111. [E. O. Winstedt], p. 75.

112. Schneider, 1974, pp. 778, 781, 783–784, 785.

113. Ibid., pp. 771, 774; A. Caquot, 1965.

114. *CIH*, 314, 14, 17; *CIH*, 350, 11; *Ja*, 574, 5; 577, 3, 10; 585, 15–16. The publisher of two late inscriptions, Jamme (A. Jamme, 1962, pp. 61, 78, 79, 92) translates the word '*ḥzb* as "bands" (fighting bands); in Arabic the word حزب , plural أحزاب, can actually have such a meaning, but in the Sabaean language the word '*sḏ* is usually used to mean "bands."

115. *Ja*, 574, 7; 577, 4.

116. Kh. Y. Nāmī, 72 + 73 + 71, 2. Wissmann suggests that the South Arabian tribes subject to the Ethiopians are meant (H. von Wissmann, 1964, *Himyar*, p. 471).

117. In the neighboring kingdom of Meroe the meeting of the troops also represented a people's assembly; here it even took part in the election of the king. For more details see I. S. Katsnelson, 1949, pp. 73–81; I. S. Katsnelson, 1960. [in Russian]

118. *DAE*, IV, no. 8, 20; no. 9, 32; no. 10, 11–13.

119. A. J. Drewes, 1962, no. 6, 13, pp. 11, 28.

120. Schneider, 1974, pp. 771, 774; A. Caquot, 1965, pp. 225–228.

121. H. Wohlenberg und A. E. Jensen, *Im Lande des Gada*, 1936, SS. 196–201, 335–378; A. E. Jensen, 1941, SS. 84 usw; A. E. Jensen, 1942, pp. 217–259; Ernesta Cerulli, pp. 57, 59 ff.; A. Leggese, pp. 11–14; C. R. Hallpike, pp. 184–188.

122. C. Conti-Rossini, 1901; B. A. Turayev, *Carlo Rossini*, 1904, p. 66. [in Russian]

123. *DAE*, IV, no. 10, 9–10; no. 9, 13, 15, 21, 24, 25, 27, 34; no. 11, 30, 34, 35.

124. Thus, in his inscription on personal collection of tribute Ezana II simply mentions "four of his armies" (*DAE*, IV, no. 8, 18).

125. [E. O. Winstedt], p. 75.

126. *DAE*, IV, no. 8, 13–15.

127. *DAE*, IV, no. 9, 15, 25.

128. [E. O. Winstedt], p. 75.

129. B. A. Turayev, 1902, p. 139. [in Russian]

130. *DAE*, IV, no. 9, 25–26; no. 10, 9–11; no. 11, 29–34.

131. Schneider, 1974, pp. 771, 774, 778, 783–784.
132. [S. Strelcyn], p. 115.
133. [L. Dindorff], p. 457.
134. As V. P. Starinin so kindly pointed out to me, the word used here ሰበት (written in the unvocalized form as ሰበት, *sbt*) comes from a well-known Semitic root with the meaning "to stay, to be located." Thus my interpretation is "stay-(ing)" (in the time of the regular circuit). In A. J. Drewes (1962, pp. 31, 35) it is translated "royal cortege" but he is not convinced of the translation's correctness.
135. *DAE*, IV, no. 6, 23–24; no. 7, 23–24.
136. *DAE*, IV, no. 9, 11.
137. *DAE*, IV, no. 11, 11.
138. B. A. Turayev, 1902, pp. 402, 403. [in Russian]
139. The chronicle of Emperor Baeda Maryam (1468–1478 A.D.) tells how privileged troops of this emperor, having committed a tactical blunder through presumptuousness, suffered a defeat. Many of them perished or fell into captivity. "The king was furious at those who survived. . . . " "For this he punished them having placed the lungs of an ass and a bull near their noses and near their shaming places, according to ancient custom. Whereupon they stood naked. And thus they remained in the house of his kingdom not being forgiven for 10 days" (B. A. Turayev, 1936, pp. 92–93 [in Russian]). This custom—of placing criminals or captives naked in the sun and mocking them—also existed in neighboring Sudan, as sources of the VI and XIII centuries A.D. attest.
140. *DAE*, no. 10, 10–12.
141. F. Anfray, 1963, *La première campagne*, p. 102.
142. *BH*, p. CXXXIX.
143. [E. O. Winstedt], pp. 70, 72, 365.
144. [L. Dindorff], pp. 457, 458.
145. Tabari, ser. I, p. 930, pts. 2–6.
146. A. G. Loundine, 1954, sec. 88. [in Russian]
147. J. Ryckmans proposed the reading *'tly mlkn*, and the translation "His majesty the king" (see A. F. L. Beeston, *Abreha*, p. 102). However, besides the arbitrary substitution of letters, the new reading is not justified by the context.
148. Enrico Cerulli, 1960, pp. 5–8.

V. Ideology

1. *DAE*, IV, S. 57; no. 27, 1; A. J. Drewes, 1962, no. 68, 69, 70, pp. 26–27, pl. VI, XX.
2. *DAE*, IV, no. 10, 25; no. 6, 20; no. 7, 21.
3. Enrico Cerulli, 1956, p. 24.
4. E. Littmann, 1908, *Sternensagen*, SS. 298–319.
5. Ibid.; M. Höfner, 1962, SS. 560, 561.
6. C. Conti-Rossini, 1928, *Gad e il dio Luna*, p. 53. Gad is also the name of a well-known god of Palmyra.
7. M. Höfner, 1962, SS. 553 usw.
8. *DAE*, I, no. 34; A. J. Drewes, 1962, p. 67.
9. A. J. Drewes, 1962, p. 65.
10. Clusters of stelae are called Haoulti in Northern Ethiopia.
11. [E. O. Winstedt], p. 77.
12. Cited according to R. Hennig, 1961, v. I, p. 250. [in Russian]
13. [E. O. Winstedt], p. 77.

14. *DAE*, IV, no. 10, 25–26.
15. M. Höfner, 1962, SS. 555–567.
16. *DAE*, IV, no. 6, 20–21; no. 7, 21.
17. Diodorus, II, 55; ed. Oldfather, v. II, p. 51; ed. Becker, v. I, pp. 257–259.
18. W. Vycichl, 1957, *Egzi'abḥēr "Dieu,"* pp. 249–250.
19. D. Nielsen, 1912, S. 589 sq.; M. Höfner, 1960, SS. 435–445.
20. D. Nielsen, 1912, S. 592.
21. *DAE*, IV, no. 7, 2, 18, 21, 26; no. 6, 2, 18, 26.
22. *DAE*, IV, no. 4, 6, 29.
23. [E. O. Winstedt], p. 77; A. H. Sayce, 2; *DAE*, IV, no. 1, 7; no. 4, 6, 29.
24. *DAE*, IV, no. 6, 2–3; no. 7, 3–4; no. 9, 4; no. 10, 5.
25. *DAE*, IV, no. 4, 6, 29.
26. *DAE*, IV, no. 1, 8.
27. [E. O. Winstedt], p. 77.
28. A. H. Sayce, 2.
29. *DAE*, IV, no. 11, 2.
30. *DAE*, IV, no. 10, 30; more often the king is called the son of Mahrem (*DAE*, IV, no. 8, 4; no. 9, 10, 5; no. 6, 2; no. 7, 2).
31. L. N. Gumilev, 1968, pp. 31–38; B. I. Kuznetsov and L. N. Gumilev, 1970, pp. 72–90; L. N. Gumilev, 1970, pp. 279–301; L. N. Gumilev, 1975, pp. 19–24. [all in Russian]
32. [S. Destunis], 1876, I, 19, 103, p. 268; A. Klotz, SS. 608–610; Z. Avalachvili, pp. 280–283; K. Kekelidze, pp. 127–129 [in Georgian]; N. V. Pigulevskaya, 1951, pp. 115–126, 408–410 [in Russian]; J. Desanges, pp. 144–158.
33. See the footnote of Gavrilius Destunis to the translation of Procopius' book ([S. Destunis], 1876, p. 268). Professor N. V. Pigulevskaya mistakenly translates the *Travelers* reference to "Hellenes and Christians" among the Axumites as "Greeks and Christians" (N. V. Pigulevskaya, 1951, pp. 409, 117 [in Russian]). Nevertheless, here the contrast is evidently according to religion.
34. J. Bruce, v. II, chap. III.
35. See U. Monneret de Villard, 1935, *Aksum*, p. 133; C. Conti-Rossini, 1928, *Storia*, pl. XII, no. 46, 47; B. Van de Walle, pp. 238–247.
36. R. Paribeni, p. 455, fig. 3.
37. H. de Contenson, 1963, *Les fouilles à Haoulti en 1959*, p. 48, pl. XLIX, b–c.
38. J. Leclant, 1965.
39. F. Anfray, 1972, p. 71, pl. VI.
40. A. Polera, *Lo stato etiopico e la sua chiesa*, p. 316 (quoted according to A. J. Drewes, 1962, p. 59).
41. A. J. Drewes, 1962, p. 62.
42. W. Munziger, p. 500.
43. A. J. Drewes, 1962, p. 62; Texts A, 19–20; A, 11–12.
44. *DAE*, IV, no. 10, 29–30.
45. A. J. Drewes, 1962, p. 50.
46. Text B, 4.
47. A. J. Drewes, 1954, pp. 185, 186.
48. A. J. Drewes, 1962, pp. 27–29, pl. VI, XXI.
49. I. Yu. Krachkovsky, 1931, pp. 401–408. [in Russian]
50. *RES*, 3956; vol. VI, 1950.
51. G. Ryckmans, 1962, p. 466.
52. [E. O. Winstedt], p. 77.
53. *DAE*, IV, no. 10, 29–30. Littmann proposes that the juxtaposition of bulls

and captives indicates the offering of sacrifice and not a simple donation (*DAE*, IV, S. 32). In general this is true. Attention should be paid to the specificity of the "gift" to the god: not jewels, not land, but only "meat" (people and bulls), which makes Littmann's proposition very highly probable.

54. Heliodorus, IX, I, 25; X, 2, 6, 7, 9, etc.

55. [S. Destunis], 1876, I, 19, 103, p. 268.

56. B. A. Turayev, 1906, *Some lives*, pp. 318–319. [in Russian]

57. C. Conti-Rossini, 1909, *Notes sur l'Abyssinie*, p. 145, note 1; H. von Wissmann, 1964, *Himyar*, p. 484.

58. *DAE*, IV, S. 53, no. 22.

59. R. Basset, p. 410. Also see note 39, Chapter IV.

60. Rodinson, whose report was printed after the writing of the present book, disputed this widespread opinion. Rodinson cites only a part of the possible arguments against the myth of "the Jewish influence" on Ethiopia (M. Rodinson, pp. 11–19).

61. See A. G. Loundine, 1961, pp. 116–119; V. V. Barthold, 1925, *Muslimism*, pp. 483–512; K. S. Kashtaleva, pp. 157–162, etc. [all in Russian]

62. B. A. Turayev, 1914, *History*, pp. 354, 355. [in Russian]

63. *DAE*, IV, SS. 34, 35.

64. *MAB*, II, 1950, SS. 125, 126.

65. Compare *DAE*, IV, no. 17, S. 49.

66. At the same time the similarity of this name for god to the name of the Jewish god, in particular in the Jewish-Himyarite inscriptions (*Ry*, 507, 10–11; *Ry*, 508, 10; *Ja*, 1028, I, etc.), attracts one's attention.

67. F. Anfray, A. Caquot, et P. Nautin, 1970, *Une inscription*.

68. E. Littmann, 1954, *On the old Ethiopic inscription*, pp. 120, 121.

69. H. de Contenson, 1961, *Les fouilles à Ouchatei-Gulo*, pp. 3–7, pl. I–VII.

70. H. de Contenson, 1963, *Les fouilles à Axoum en 1958*, p. 5, pl. XIC, f, g. Tecle Tsadik Mekouria in his extremely valuable monograph on Ethiopian onomastics considers the formula *Krsts msln* a "sorte de surnom exposé sur une longue phrase"—it is truely not typical of ancient Axumites. (Mekouria, p. 64.) If this is the case then we have before us a ritual name-motto especially characteristic for Mahadayas.

71. F. Anfray et G. Annequin, 1965, p. 65; F. Anfray, 1964, pp. 756–757.

72. L. E. Kubbel and V. V. Matveev, 1960, p. 62 (Arabic text), p. 81 (Russian translation).

73. C. Conti-Rossini, 1928, *Storia*, p. 274.

74. A. Anzani, 1926, pp. 59–63, 75–78, 95.

75. A. Mordini, 1959, p. 181. Mordini mistakenly reads *I* (Λ) as *g* (Ꭺ). Both in this and the above cited cases, the opinion of Tecle Tsadik Mekouria on the role of such kinds of slogans as names (one might better say ritual name-mottoes) of the Axumite kings should be considered.

76. A. Anzani, 1926, p. 74.

77. A. Mordini, 1959, p. 182.

78. A. Anzani, 1926, pp. 88, 90, 92.

79. N. V. Pigulevskaya, 1951, pp. 247–259.

80. Yu. M. Kobishchanov, 1964, *Among the sources*. [in Russian]

81. See Yu. M. Kobishchanov, 1962, *Legend*. [in Russian]

82. S. A. Kaufman, 1964. [in Russian]

83. Yu. M. Kobishchanov, 1964, *Ancient Axum*, p. 15. [in Russian]

84. [L. Dindorff], p. 457.

85. B. A. Turayev, 1936, pp. 68, 69. [in Russian]

86. A. Dillmann, 1950, pp. 34–36; B. A. Turayev, 1905, pp. 1–8. [in Russian]

Appendix. Sources on the History of Axum

1. J. Ryckmans, 1955, p. 3, note 7.

2. F. Altheim und Ruth Stiehl, 1961, *Die Daterung*, SS. 234–248.

3. J. Harmatta, 1974, pp. 101 ff.

4. Jacqueline Pirenne, 1975, pp. 49–60.

5. Ibid.

6. J. Pirenne, 1961, *Une problème-clef.*

7. Arturo Anzani, 1941; A. Anzani, 1926; A. Anzani, 1928–1929.

8. F. Vaccaro, 1967.

9. J. Pirenne, 1975.

10. *DAE*, IV, no. 7–11.

11. Th. Nöldeke, 1904.

12. E. Littmann, 1950, SS. 97–127.

13. Roger Schneider, 1974, pp. 767–770.

14. Francis Anfray, André Caquot, et Pierre Nautin, pp. 260–274.

15. R. Schneider, 1974, pp. 770–777.

16. Ibid., pp. 777–786.

17. Murad Kamil, "An Ethiopic Inscription Found at Marib," *Journal of Semitic Studies*, IX, 1964, pp. 56–57.

18. A. Caquot, 1965, pp. 223–228.

19. *DAE*, IV, no. 12–14.

20. Yu. M. Kobishchanov, 1962, *Legend*, pp. 119–125. [in Russian]

21. C. Conti-Rossini, 1896, pp. 250–253.

22. *DAE*, IV, no. 34, S. 61.

23. E. Ullendorff, 1945, pp. 75–80.

24. A. J. Drewes, 1962, p. 68.

25. Ibid., p. 85.

26. C. Conti-Rossini, 1942, pp. 21–28; A. J. Drewes, 1962, pp. 65–67.

27. Enrico Cerulli, 1960, p. 9.

28. A. J. Drewes et A. Caquot, pp. 32–38.

29. Ibid.

30. A. Jamme, 1957, *Ethiopia*, p. 80.

31. A. J. Drewes, 1962, p. 1, VII–VIII, XXIII–XXIV, p. 30 sq.

32. G. Ryckmans (1962, p. 460) dates it to the second half of the III century A.D., since it is undoubtedly younger than Gedara's inscription. Actually it is *far* younger than Gedara's inscription.

33. [E. O. Winstedt], pp. 74–77.

34. A. Dillmann, 1878, SS. 200, 202–203.

35. E. Drouin, p. 155.

36. E. Glaser, 1891, SS. 202–212.

37. J. Pirenne, 1956, no. 2.

38. A. J. Drewes, 1962, p. 106.

39. R. Sundström, in E. Littmann, *Preliminary Report*, S. 170.

40. *DAE*, IV, no. 3, S. 3.

41. Ibid., no. 2.

42. A. H. Sayce, pp. 189–190.

43. *DAE*, IV, no. 5, S. 8.

44. Ibid., no. 21, 22, S. 52.
45. Ibid., no. 19, SS. 51–52.
46. E. Rüppel, 1840, Bd. II, S. 277.
47. Th. Lefebvre, vol. III, p. 435.
48. A. Dillmann, 1878, S. 232.
49. *DAE*, IV, no. 18, SS. 50–51.
50. A. J. Drewes, 1962, p. 68.
51. G. Ryckmans, 1962, p. 461.
52. A. J. Drewes, 1962, p. 85.
53. R. Lepsius, SS. 13, 1.
54. *DAE*, I, S. 50.
55. M. F. Laming-Macadam, pp. 117–118.
56. E. Littmann, 1954, *On the old Ethiopic inscription*, pp. 119–123.
57. U. Monneret de Villard, 1940, pp. 61–68.
58. C. Conti-Rossini, 1928, *Storia*, tav. LV, no. 176.
59. A. J. Drewes, 1962, p. 29, pl. VI, XX.
60. One of the inscriptions was first published by L. Ricci (1955–1958, pp. 58–68). He correctly determined certain letters but was unable to determine the direction of the writing and to give a satisfactory translation. A. J. Drewes (1962, pp. 27–28 identified all of the letters and the lexical and grammatical elements, and gave a translation of the inscription. The other inscription was published by Drewes in *Annales d'Ethiopie*, vol. III, 1959, pp. 95–96.
61. A. J. Drewes et R. Schneider, 1967, p. 96.
62. Ibid., pp. 100–102.
63. R. Schneider, 1965, pp. 91–92.
64. C. Conti-Rossini, 1928, *Storia*, fig. 185.
65. *CIH*, 1920, no. 308, 308 bis.
66. I am using the opportunity to convey thanks to G. Bauer for the translation of separate parts of the inscription. Heinrich Müller [1894] paraphrased the inscription in English in 1893 and Conti-Rossini [1921] in French in 1920.
67. *CIH*, no. 350.
68. C. Conti-Rossini, 1921, pp. 11–12.
69. *CIH*, no. 314 + 954.
70. C. Conti-Rossini, 1921.
71. Kh. Y. Nami, 1943, 1947. [in Arabic]
72. A. Fakhry, 1951–1952.
73. H. St. J. Philby, 1952.
74. A. Jamme, 1962, pp. 64 ff., 67 ff., 189 ff.
75. According to the newest chronology of A. G. Loundine and Jacques Ryckmans (A. Loundine et J. Ryckmans, pp. 407–424).
76. G. Ryckmans, 1955, *Inscriptions sud-arabes*, sér. X, pp. 238, 303.
77. G. Ryckmans, 1956, *Inscriptions sud-arabes*, ser. XIII, 1956, no. 1–2, pp. 139–163; sér. XIV, no. 3–4, pp. 369–389.
78. A. Jamme, 1962. This expedition was organized by the late Wendell Phillips, the president of the American Foundation for the Study of Man and a person of remarkable energy and breadth of scientific interests. A series of prominent scholars —including Richard Le Baron Bowen, Frank P. Albright, Albert Jamme, Berta Segall, and others—participated in the expedition. First, systematic excavations were carried out in South Arabia: of the town of Timna, capital of the ancient Qataban kingdom; of the famous temple at Marib; of the ancient Qataban irrigation systems (Wadi Beiḥân); and of Sheba (Marib). A more detailed description

of this expedition is given in a whole series of reports, of which the most important
is Bowen and Albright, 1958.

79. J. R. Wellstedt, pp. 554–556; *CIH*, no. 621.
80. A. G. Loundine, 1954, pp. 3–24. [in Russian]
81. G. Ryckmans, 1929, *RES*, no. 3904.
82. G. Ryckmans, 1956, *Inscriptions sud-arabes*, sér. X, t. LXVIII, 1955, no. 3–4,
pp. 267–317; A. Jamme, 1962; A. Jamme, 1966, pp. 39–55.
83. J. P. Migne, 1834, pp. 635 sq.
84. [L. Dindorff], SS. 457–458.
85. Theophanes, *Chronographia*, ed. De Boor.
86. I. Guidi, 1881, p. 4; N. V. Pigulevskaya, 1951, pp. 230–231. [in Russian]
87. Tabari, ed. M. J. de Goeje, ser. I, text Arab., pp. 1569–1570.
88. D. M. Dunlop, *Another "Prophetic Letter," JRAS*, 1940, 56 ff.
89. A. d'Emilia, 1948, pp. 54–57; N. V. Pigulevskaya, 1951, pp. 242–559;
N. V. Pigulevskaya, 1950, pp. 51–61. [both Pigulevskaya works in Russian]
90. J. P. Migne, 1834, pp. 631 sq.
91. V. V. Bolotov, 1907, p. 270. [in Russian]
92. Christian Lacomrade, 1951.
93. See A. Caquot et J. Leclant, 1959, p. 174.
94. Ibid., pp. 173–177.
95. I. Guidi, 1881, pp. 1–39.
96. P. Devos, pp. 107–116.
97. R. Schröter, 1877, SS. 360–399; N. V. Pigulevskaya, 1951, p. 277. [in
Russian]
98. R. Schröter, 1877, SS. 400–405; N. V. Pigulevskaya, 1951, p. 277. [in
Russian]
99. Ibid.
100. [A. Møberg], 1924.
101. The investigations of the monument by Møberg himself in his edition of
The Book of the Himyarites and by N. V. Pigulevskaya (N. V. Pigulevskaya, 1951,
pp. 233–238, 275–381 [in Russian]) have the utmost significance.
102. J. P. Migne, 1866, pars I, col. 621–784; N. V. Pigulevskaya, 1951, pp.
246–249. [in Russian]
103. E. M. Shtaerman, pp. 233–245; A. I. Dovatur, 1957, *History*, pp. 245–256.
[in Russian]
104. Flavius Vopiscus the Syracusan, tr. A. I. Dovatur, pp. 235, 237. [in Russian]
105. [S. Destunis], 1876, book I, pp. 243–281; [J. Haury], v. 1, pp. 100–110.
106. *De bello Persico*, II, 1, 1; [J. Haury], p. 149; N. V. Pigulevskaya, 1964,
The policy of Byzantium, p. 83. [in Russian]
107. Quoted according to A. Rozov, p. 97. [in Russian]
108. [L. Dindorff], pp. 432–433, 456–460.
109. C. Mullerus, 1851, pp. 178–180; [S. Destunis], 1861, pp. 483 ff.
110. Theophanes, *Chronographia*, ed. De Boor, SS. 244–245.
111. J. H. Mordtmann, S. 702; N. V. Pigulevskaya, 1951, pp. 312–313 and
footnotes; N. V. Pigulevskaya, 1964, *The policy of Byzantium*, pp. 74–85. [both
Pigulevskaya works in Russian]
112. See N. V. Pigulevskaya, 1964, *The policy of Byzantium*, p. 75. [in Russian]
113. Theophanes, *Chronographia*.
114. J. H. Mordtmann, SS. 693–710; N. V. Pigulevskaya, 1951, pp. 224–226.
[in Russian]
115. [J. B. Chabot], p. 54.

116. [L. Dindorff], p. 429.
117. Theophanes, *Chronographia*, ed. De Boor, p. 244.
118. J. Halévy, 1896, p. 169.
119. N. V. Pigulevskaya, 1951, p. 268. [in Russian]
120. J. Harmatta, 1974, p. 102.
121. J. Pirenne, 1975, p. 54 s.
122. [J. B. Chabot], 1933.
123. Joannes Ephesius, 1904.
124. Quoted according to A. Rozov, p. 14. [in Russian]
125. Abbeloos and Lamy, 1877, p. 125.
126. V. V. Bolotov, 1907, pp. 267–269. [in Russian]
127. Nikephoros Kallistos, *Historia ecclesiastica*, lib. VIII, cap. 35 (cited according to P. Migne, *Patrologia graecae*, Paris, t. 46, 1865, p. 131).
128. See R. Hennig, 1961, p. 35. [in Russian]
129. [J. Bidez], pp. CVI, CXXXII; N. V. Pigulevskaya, 1951, pp. 71–72. [in Russian]
130. A. Scher, 1906, p. 218.
131. A. G. Loundine, 1961, p. 11. [in Russian]
132. Tabari, 1881–1882.
133. L. E. Kubbel and V. V. Matveev, 1960, pp. 96–105. [in Russian]
134. See I. Yu. Krachkovsky, p. 168; A. G. Loundine, 1961, p. 10, note 4. [both in Russian]
135. [M. J. de Göeje], 1886.
136. L. E. Kubbel and V. V. Matveev, 1960, p. 24 and following. [in Russian]
137. J. Pirenne, 1961, *Une problème-clef*, pp. 441–460.
138. *Periplus*, pp. 244 ff.; H. Frisk, 1927.
139. G. Lumbroso, 1898, pp. 124–168; A. A. Vasiliev, 1936; N. V. Pigulevskaya, 1951, pp. 33–40, 115–127. [in Russian]
140. Z. Avalichvili, pp. 280–283.
141. A. Klotz, SS. 608–610.
142. N. V. Pigulevskaya, 1951, pp. 115 ff., 408, 410. [in Russian]
143. The expression "Hellenes and Christians" is understood literally by N. V. Pigulevskaya and translated in one instance even as "Christians and Greeks" (see N. V. Pigulevskaya, 1951, p. 409). However, "Hellenes" is used here in the sense of "pagans."
144. [D. Detlefsen], *Plinii Secundi Naturalis historia*; [B. H. Rackham], *Plinius Secundus. Natural History*.
145. C. Mullerus, 1861.
146. [S. G. Yeremian], 1968, *Ashkharatsuits*. An outstanding monument of geography and cartography of the ancient world.
147. L. E. Kubbel and V. V. Matveev, 1965, pp. 269 ff. [in Russian]
148. Ibid., pp. 300 ff. [in Russian]
149. Ibid., pp. 272–273, 301–302. [in Russian]
150. [E. O. Winstedt], *The Christian topography*.
151. Ibid., p. 321.
152. Ibid., p. 72.
153. Ibid.
154. Ibid., p. 38.
155. [O. Günther], *Epiphanius*, pp. 748–749 (*Corpus scriptores ecclesiasticorum latinorum*).
156. [R. P. Blake and H. de Vis], *Epiphanius*, pp. 117–139.

157. Irfân Shahîd, 1971, pp. 181–230; M. van Esbroeck, pp. 125–129.
158. I. Shahîd, 1971, pp. 181–230; M. van Esbroeck, p. 125 s.
159. N. V. Pigulevskaya, 1951, pp. 238–239. [in Russian]
160. Ibid., p. 239. [in Russian]
161. Ibid., pp. 239–240. [in Russian]
162. Carpantier, 1861, *Martyrium sancti Arethae*, 691 sq.
163. Estevão Pereira, *Historia*.
164. N. V. Pigulevskaya, 1951, p. 246. [in Russian]
165. A. V. Vasiliev, 1907, pp. 33–66. [in Russian]
166. C. Schmidt, c. CXXXVII.
167. Heliodorus, p. 479 (X, 41).
168. C. Mullerus, 1846; V. Priaulx, pp. 277–278.
169. M. Schanz und C. Hosins, SS. 47–50.
170. I. N. Golenishchev-Kutuzov, p. 77. [in Russian]
171. Jules Perruchon, 1889, pp. 318–323, 359–362.
172. Mariano Vittorio, 1552.
173. Joseph Tubiana, 1961, pp. 495–498.
174. M. E. Drouin, pp. 99–224.
175. Carlo Conti-Rossini, 1909, *Les listes*, pp. 259–320.
176. C. Conti-Rossini, 1895.
177. C. Mondon-Vidailhet, 1904, pp. 259–268.
178. H. St. J. Philby, 1960, pp. 395–417.

References and Selected Bibliography

Abbadie, Antoine d'. *Observations sur les monnaies éthiopiennes. RN*, XIII, 1868.

Abbeloos, J. B., et Th. J. Lamy. *Gregorii Barhebraei Chronicon ecclesiasticum.* Paris, 1877.

Abu'l Fida. *Geographic description of Arabia.* Translated from the Arabic. Kazan, 1891. In Russian.

Ademassou, Shiferau. *Exposition de la section d'archéologie Addis Ababa. BO*, XIII, 1956.

Alliot, A. *Pount-Pwane, l'Oponé du géographe Ptolémée. Revue d'Egyptologie*, VIII, 1951.

Altheim, F. *Geschichte der Hunnen*, Bd. V. Berlin, 1962.

Altheim, F., und Ruth Stiehl. *'Ēzānā von Aksum. Klio*, 39, 1961.

Altheim, F., und Ruth Stiehl. *Die Daterung des Königs 'Ezana von Aksum. Klio*, 39, 1961.

Altheim, F., und Ruth Stiehl. *Die Araber in der Alten Welt*, Bd. I. Berlin, 1963.

Altheim, F., und Ruth Stiehl. *Die Anfänges der Königreiches Aksum. Klio*, 42, 1964.

Altheim, F., und Ruth Stiehl. *Der Name E'zānā: Festschrift für Wilhelm Eilers.* Wiesbaden, 1969.

Ammianus Marcellinus. See J. Eyssenhardt.

Anfray, Francis. *Une campagne de fouilles à Yeḥā (février-mars 1960). AE*, V, 1963.

Anfray, Francis. *La première campagne de fouilles à Maṭarā. AE*, V, 1963.

Anfray, Francis. *Note sur quelques poteries axoumites. AE*, VI, 1965.

Anfray, Francis. *Matarā. AE*, VII, 1967, pp. 33–88.

Anfray, Francis. *La poterie de Matarā. Esquisse typologique. Rase*, XXII, 1968, pp.1–74.

Anfray, Francis. *L'archéologie d'Axoum en 1972. Paideuma Mitteilungen zur Kulturkunde*, VIII, 1972, SS. 60–76.

Anfray, Francis. *Deux villes axoumites: Adoulis et Matarā.* IV Congresso Internazionale di Studi Etiopici (Rome, 1972), 1974, pl. IV, fig. 1–2.

Anfray, Francis, et Guy Annequin. *Matarā: Deuxième, troisième, et quatrième campagnes de fouilles. AE*, VI, 1965.

Anfray, Francis, André Caquot, et Pierre Nautin. *Une nouvelle inscription grecque d'Ezana, roi d'Axoum. Journal des Savants*, octobre-décembre 1970 (Paris).

Anzani, Arturo. *Numismatica aksumita. RINSA*, ser. 3, vol. III, 1926.

Anzani, Arturo. *Numismatica e storia d'Etiopia. RINSA*, ser. 3, vol. V–VI, 1928–1929.

Anzani, Arturo. *Monete dei re d'Aksum (Studi supplimentari). RINSA*, ser. 5, vol. I, 1941.

Arkell, A. F. J. A. Wainwright, "Cosmas and the gold trade of Fazogl. Man*, 44, 1944.

Arkell, A. F. *Meroe and India—Aspects of archeology in Britain and beyond.* London, 1951.

Arkell, A. F. *A History of Sudan to 1820 A.D.* London, 1955.

Avalichvili, A. *Géographie et légende dans un récit apocriphe de St. Basil. Revue d'Orient chrétien*, sér. 3, vol. VI (26), 1927–1928.

Barhebraeus. *Gregorii Barhebaeii Chronicon Ecclesiasticum*. Paris, 1877.

Barthold, V. V. *The Koran and the sea. Notes of the Board of Orientalists of the Asian Museum of the Russian Academy of Sciences*, vol. I. Leningrad, 1925. In Russian.

Barthold, V. V. *Muslimism. Proceedings of the Russian Academy of Sciences*. Leningrad, 1925. In Russian.

Basset, R. *Etudes sur l'histoire d'Ethiopie. JA*, XVII–XVIII, 1881.

[Bechingham, C. F., and G. W. Huntingford]. *Some records of Ethiopia (1593–1646)*. London, 1954.

Beeston, A. F. L. "Abreha." *TEI* (new edition).

Beeston, A. F. L. *Problems of Sabaean chronology. BSOAS*, 16, 1954.

Bent, James Theodore. *The Sacred city of the Ethiopians being a record of Travel and Research in Abyssinia in 1893. With a Chapter by Prof. H. D. Müller on the Inscriptions from Jeha and Aksum....* London, 1893.

Berger, P. M. *Histoire de l'écriture dans l'antiquité*. Paris, 1891.

[Bezold, C.]. *Kebra Nagast. Die Herrlichkeit der Könige*. Munich, 1905.

[Bidez, Joseph]. *Philostorgius, Historia ecclesiastica*. Leipzig, 1913.

[Blake, R. P., and H. de Vis]. *Epiphanius. De XII Gemmis. The Old Georgian version and the fragments of the Armenian version* [ed. Blake] *and the Coptic-Sahidic fragments* [ed. de Vis]. London, 1934.

Bolotov, V. V. *Several pages from the church history of Ethiopia. Christian Reading*, no. 1–2, 7–8, 11–12, 1888. In Russian.

Bolotov, V. V. *Ethiopian historiography. Lectures on the history of the ancient church*, vol. II. St. Petersburg, 1907. In Russian.

Book of the Himyarites, The. See [Axel Møberg].

[Boor, Carolus De]. *Theophanes, Chronographia*. Leipzig, 1883.

Bowen, Richard Le Baron, and Frank P. Albright. *Archaeological Discoveries in South Arabia*, vols. I–II. With contributions by Berta Segall, J. Ternbach, A. Jamme, H. Comfort, and Gus W. Van Beck. Foreword by Wendell Phillips. Baltimore, 1958.

Bruce, James. *Travels to Discover the Sources of the Nile in Years 1768–1773*, vol. I–III. Edinburgh, 1790.

Brugsch, Heinrich Karl. *The history of the pharaohs*. Translated from German. St. Petersburg, 1891. In Russian.

Budge, A. E. Wallis. *Annals of the Nubian Kings. With a Sketch of the History of the Nubian Kingdom of Napata*. London, 1912.

Budge, A. E. Wallis. *The Book of the Saints of the Ethiopian Church*. Cambridge, 1928.

Budge, A. E. Wallis. *A History of Ethiopia, Nubia and Abyssinia*, vol. I. London, 1928.

Buhl, F. "Abreha." *EI*, I.

Buhl, F. "Abreha." *TEI*, I.

Bury, J. B. *A History of the Later Roman Empire*, vols. I–II. Oxford, 1922–1923.

Buxton, David R. *Ethiopian Rock-Hewn churches*, vol. XX. Oxford, 1946.

Buxton, David R. *The Christian antiquities of Northern Ethiopia. Ar*, XCII, 1947.

Buxton, David. R. *Travels in Ethiopia*. London, 1949.

Buxton, David R. *Ethiopian medieval architecture. ES*, 1963, pp. 239–244.

Calderini, A. *Documenti per la storia degli etiopi e dei loro rapporti col mondo romano. Atti IV Congresso di studi romani*, vol. II, Rome, 1938.

Caquot, André. *Aperçu préliminaire sur le Maṣḥafa Ṭēfut de Gechen Amba. AE*, I, 1955.

Caquot, André. *La Reine de Saba et le bois de la croix selon une tradition éthiopienne. AE*,

I, 1955.

Caquot, André. *Les chroniques abrégées d'Éthiopie. AE*, II, 1957.

Caquot, André. *La royauté sacrale en Ethiopie. AE*, II, 1957.

Caquot, André. *L'inscription éthiopienne de Marib. AE*, VI, 1965.

Caquot, André, et A. J. Drewes. *Les monuments recueillis à Maqallé (Tigré). AE*, I, 1955.

Caquot, André, et J. Leclant. *Arabe du Sud et Afrique. Examen d'une hypotèse récente. AE*, I, 1955.

Caquot, André, et J. Leclant. *Sur les traces des Axoumites. Annales publiées par la Faculté des Lettres de l'Université de Toulouse*, fasc. 3, 1955.

Caquot, André, et J. Leclant. *Rapport sur les récentes travaux de la Section d'Archéologie. Comptes Rendus de l'Académie des Inscriptions et Belles-Lettres*. Paris, 1956.

Caquot, André, et J. Leclant. *Ethiopie et Cyrénaïque. A propos d'une texte de Synésius. AE*, III, 1959.

Carpantier. *Martyrium sancti Arethae et sociorum in civitate Negran. Cum commentarium praevis. Acta Sanctorum*, X, octobris 1861 (Brussels).

Cascel, W. *'Ajam al-'Arab. Studien zur altarabischen epik. Islamica*, 3, f. 5, 1930.

Cascel, W. *Entdeckungen in Arabien*. Cologne, 1954.

Caussin de Perceval, A.–P. *Essai sur l'histoire des Arabes*, t. I. Paris, 1847.

Cerulli, Enrico. *Recensione della "Storia d'Etiopia" del Conti-Rossini. RSO*, XII, fasc. III, 1929.

Cerulli, Enrico. *Etiopi in Palestina*, vol. I. Rome, 1943.

Cerulli, Enrico. *L'Etiopia medioevale in alcuni brani di scrittori arabi. RaSE*, III, 1943.

Cerulli, Enrico. *La Nubia cristiana, i Baria ed i Cunama, nel X secolo d. Cr., secondo Ibn Hawqal, geografo arabo. Annali dell'Instituto Universitario Orientale di Napoli. Nuova serie*, III, 1949 (Rome).

Cerulli, Enrico. *Storia della letteratura etiopica. Cap. I. Il periodo aksumita*. Milan, 1956.

Cerulli, Enrico. *Punti di vista sulla storia dell' Etiopia. Discorso inaugurale. ACISE*, 1960.

Cerulli, Ernesta. *Peoples of South-West Ethiopia and its Borderlands*. London, 1956.

[Chabot, J. B.]. *Chronicon Pseudo-Dionysianum vulgo dictam. (Corpus Scriptores Christianorum Orientalium. Scriptores syri, ser. III)*, vol. III. Paris, 1933.

Clark, J. Desmond. *The spread of food production in Sub-Saharan Africa. JAH*, III, 1962.

Clark, W. L. *Coins from Axum. Museum Notes*, no. 3, 1948 (American Numismatic Society, New York).

Cleret, Maxime. *Ethiopie, fidèle à la croix*. Paris, 1957.

Codex Justinianus. Corpus Iuris Civilis, vol. II. Edited by Th. Mommsen, P. Krüger, R. Schöll, G. Kroll. Berlin, 1959.

Codex Theodosianus cum perpetuis commentariis Iacobi Gothofredi. Lyons, 1665.

Complete Description of the World and Its Peoples. See G. Lumbroso, 1898; A. A. Vasiliev, 1936.

Contenson, Henri de. *Aperçus sur les fouilles à Axoum et dans la région d'Axoum en 1958 et 1959. AE*, III, 1959.

Contenson, Henri de. *Les fouilles à Axoum en 1957. Rapport préliminaire. AE*, III, 1959.

Contenson, Henri de. *Les premiers rois d'Axoum d'après les découvertes récentes. JA*, CCXLVII, fasc. I, 1960.

Contenson, Henri de. *Les fouilles à Haoulti-Melazo en 1958. AE*, IV, 1961.

Contenson, Henri de. *Les fouilles à Ouchatei-Gulo, près d'Axoum, en 1958. AE*, IV, 1961.

Contenson, Henri de. *Les principales étapes de l'Ethiopie antique. CEA*, 5, vol. II, 1961.

Contenson, Henri de. *Trouvailles fortuites aux environs d'Axoum (1957–1959). AE*, IV, 1961.

Contenson, Henri de. *Les monuments d'art sud-arabe découverts sur le site de Haoulti (Ethiopie) en 1959. Syria*, XXXIX, no. 1–2, 1962.

Contenson, Henri de. *Les fouilles à Axoum en 1958. Rapport préliminaire. AE*, V, 1963.

Contenson, Henri de. *Les fouilles à Haoulti en 1959. Rapport préliminaire. AE*, V, 1963.

Conti-Rossini, Carlo. *Di un nuovo codice della Cronaca Etiopia. RRAL*, ser. 5, vol. II, 1893.

Conti-Rossini, Carlo. *Donazioni reali alla cattedrale d'Aksum. L'Oriente*, II, 1895, no. 1–2 (Rome).

Conti-Rossini, Carlo. *L'inscrizione dell' obelisco presso Maṭarā. RRAL*, ser. 5, vol. V, 1896.

Conti-Rossini, Carlo. *Note etiopiche. — Leggenda tigray su Abreha e Asbeha. Giornale della Società asiatica italiana*, X, 1896–1897 (Rome).

Conti-Rossini, Carlo. *La leggenda etiopica di re Arwé. Archivio per le tradizioni popolari*, I, 1897 (Rome).

Conti-Rossini, Carlo. *Note etiopiche. I. Una guerra fra la Nubia e l'Etiopia nel secolo VII. II. Leggende tigrai. III. Sovra una tradizione Bilin.* Rome, 1897.

Conti-Rossini, Carlo. *L'omilia di Yohannes, vescovo di Axum in onore di Garima. Actes du XIe Congrès International des Orientalistes,* 4e Section. Paris, 1898.

Conti-Rossini, Carlo. *Note per la storia letteraria abissina. RRAL*, ser. 5, vol. VIII, 1899.

Conti-Rossini, Carlo. *Ricerche e studi sull' Etiopia. BSGI*, ser. IV, vol. I (XXXVII), 1900.

Conti-Rossini, Carlo. *L'evangelio d'oro di Dabra-Libanos. RRAL*, ser. 5, vol. X, fasc. 5–6, 1901.

Conti-Rossini, Carlo. *Documenti per l'archeologia d'Eritrea nella bassa valle del Barca. RRAL*, ser. 5, vol. XII, 1903.

Conti-Rossini, Carlo. *Sugli Habašāt. RRAL*, ser. 5, vol. XV, 1906.

Conti-Rossini, Carlo. *Les listes des rois d'Aksoum. JA*, XIV, 10 septembre 1909.

Conti-Rossini, Carlo. *Notes sur l'Abyssinie avant les Sémites. Florilegium Melchior de Vogüé,* Paris, 1909.

Conti-Rossini, Carlo. *Liber Aksum.* Paris, 1910.

Conti-Rossini, Carlo. *Un documento sul christianismo nello Yemen ai tempi del re Saräḥbil Yakkuf. RRAL*, ser. 5, vol. XIX, 1911.

Conti-Rossini, Carlo. *"Goodspeed, Edgar J. The Conflict of Severus, patriarch of Antiochia by Athanasius* (Ethiopic text and translation)." Paris, 1911.

Conti-Rossini, Carlo. *Picoli studi etiopici. 2. Soba-Noba nella tradizione abissina. ZA,* 1912.

Conti-Rossini, Carlo. *Principi di diritto consuetudinario dell'Eritrea.* Rome, 1916 (Manueli Coloniali).

Conti-Rossini, Carlo. *Meroe ed Aksum nel romanzo di Eliodoro. RSO*, VIII, 1919.

Conti-Rossini, Carlo. *Expéditions et possessions des Habašāt en Arabie. JA*, sér. II, t. XVIII, 1921.

Conti-Rossini, Carlo. *Egitto ed Etiopia nei tempi antichi e nell' età di mezzo. Aeg*, III, 1922.

Conti-Rossini, Carlo. *Commenti e notizie di geografi classici sovra il Sudan Egiziano e l'Etiopia. Aeg*, V, 1925.

Conti-Rossini, Carlo. *Leggende geografiche giudaiche del IX secolo. BSGI*, fasc. I–II, 1925.

Conti-Rossini, Carlo. *Monete aksumite. AE*, I, 1927.

Conti-Rossini, Carlo. *Gad e il dio Luna in Etiopia. SMSR*, 1928.

Conti-Rossini, Carlo. *Storia d'Etiopia*, t. I. Bergamo, 1928.

Conti Rossini, Carlo. *Aksum. Enciclopedia Italiana di scienze, ed arti*, vol. II. Rome, 1929, pp. 46–47.

Conti-Rossini, Carlo. *Chrestomathia Arabica Meridionalis Epigraphica*. Rome, 1931.

Conti-Rossini, Carlo. *Necropoli musulmana ed antica chiesa christiana presso Uogri Hariba nell' Enderta*. RSO, XVII, 1937–1938.

Conti-Rossini, Carlo. *Un' inscrizione etiopica di Ham*. RRAL, I, 1939.

Conti-Rossini, Carlo. *Pergamene di Dabra Dammo*. RSO, I, fasc. I, 1940.

Conti-Rossini, Carlo. *Un' inscrizione sul obelisco di Anzà*. RaSE, II, 1942.

Conti-Rossini, Carlo. *La regalità sacra in Abissinia e nei regni del Africa centrale ed occidentale*. SMSR, 21, 1947–1948.

Conti-Rossini, Carlo, e L. Ricci. *Consuetudini giuridiche del Seraé*. Asmara, 1938.

Cosmas Indicopleustes. *See* [E. O. Winstedt].

Cossar, B. *Necropoli precristiani di Seleclaca. Studi etiopici*. Rome, 1945.

Coulbeaux, J. B. *Histoire politique et religieuse de l'Abyssinie, depuis les temps plus reculés jusqu'à l'avènement de Menelik II*, t. I. Paris, 1929.

Crowfoot, J. W. *Nuba Pots in the Gordon College*. SNR, VII, 1959.

Davidson, Basil. *New discovery of ancient Africa*. Translated from English. Moscow, 1962. In Russian. (English title, 1959, *Old Africa Rediscovered*; United States title, 1959, *Lost Cities of Africa*.)

Desanges, Jehan. *Une mention alterée d'Axoum dans l'Exposition totius mundi et gentium*. AE, VII, 1967.

[Destunis, Spyridon]. *Byzantine historians: Dexippus, Eunapius, Olympiodorus, Malchus, Peter Patricius Menander, Candide, Nonnus, and Theophanes the Byzantine*. Translated from the Greek by S. Destunis. St. Petersburg, 1861. In Russian.

[Destunis, Spyridon]. *Procopius Caesarensis. History of the wars of the Romans with the Persians, Goths, and Vandals*. Translation of Spyridon Destunis from notes of Gavrilius Destunis. St. Petersburg, 1876. In Russian.

[Detlefsen, D.]. *C. Plinii Secundi Naturalis historia*, vols. I–IV. Berlin, 1866–1871.

Deutsche Aksum-Expedition. Berlin, 1913. Bd. I, Bd. IV, *see* Enno Littman; Bd. II, *see* D. Krencker; Bd. III, *see* Th. von Lüpke.

Devos, Paul. *Quelques aspects de la nouvelle lettre récemment découverte, de Siméon de Bêth-Arsâm sur les martyrs himyarites*. IV Congresso Internazionale di Studi Etiopici (Rome 1972), vol. I. Rome, 1974.

Diakonov, A. P. *Joannes Ephesius and his church-historical works*. St. Petersburg, 1909. In Russian.

Dihle, A. *Umstri tene Daten, Untersuchungen zum Auftreten der Griechen am Roten Meer*. Cologne and Opladen, 1965.

Dillmann, A. *Lexicon linguae aethiopicae*. Leipzig, 1865.

Dillmann, August. *Über die Anfänge des Axumitischen Reiches*. APAW, 1878.

Dillmann, August. *Zur Geschichte des Axumitischen Reiches im vierten bis sechsten Jahrhundert*. APAW, Abh. I, 1880.

Dillmann, August. *Über die Regierung und insbesondere die Kirchenordnung des Königs Zar'a Jacob*. Berlin, 1884.

Dillmann, August. *Chrestomathia Aethiopica*, 3d ed. Berlin, 1950 (1st ed. Leipzig, 1841; 2d ed. Leipzig, 1866).

Dinawari, Ad. *See* V. Guirgass.

[Dindorff, Ludwig]. *Ioannes Malalae Chronographia*. Bonn, 1831.

Diodori Bibliotheca historica. Ed. Imm. Becker, L. Dindorff, recognovit F. Vogel. Leipzig, 1888.

Diodorus of Sicily. With an English translation, ed. C. H. Oldfather. London, 1946.

Doresse, Jean. *Au pays de la reine de Saba: L'Ethiopie antique et moderne*. Paris, 1956.

Doresse, Jean. *Les premiers monuments chrétiens de l'Ethiopie et l'église archaïque de Yeḥā. Novum Testamentum*, X, no. 3, 1956.

Doresse, Jean. *Découvertes en Ethiopie et découverte de l'Ethiopie. BO*, XIV, 1957.

Doresse, Jean. *L'empire du Prêtre-Jean*, vol. I–II. Paris. 1957.

Doresse, Jean. *L'Ethiopie et l'Arabie méridionale aux IIIe et IVe siècles A.D. d'après les découvertes récentes. Kush*, VI, 1957.

Doresse, Jean. *La découverte d'Aṣbi-Derà. ACISE*, 1960.

Dovatur, A. I. *History of research "Scriptores historiae Augustae." MAH*, no. 1, 1957. In Russian.

[Dovatur, A. I.]. *Scriptores historiae Augustae*, XXVI. *MAH*, no. 1, 1957. In Russian.

Drewes, A. J. *The inscription from Dibdib in Erithrea. BO*, XI, 1954.

Drewes, A. J. *Problèmes de paléographie éthiopienne. AE*, I, 1955.

Drewes, A. J. *Les nouvelles inscriptions de l'Ethiopie. BO*, XIV, 1956.

Drewes, A. J. *Les Inscriptions de Melazo. AE*, III, 1959.

Drewes, A. J. *Inscriptions de l'Ethiopie antique.* Leiden, 1962.

Drewes, A. J., et A. Caquot. *Les monuments recueillis à Maqallé (Tigré). AE*, I, 1955.

Drewes, A. J., et R. Schneider. *Documents épigraphiques de l'Ethiopie—I. AE*, VII, 1967, pp. 89–106.

Drouin, M. E. *Les listes royales éthiopiennes et leur autorité historique. RA*, août-octobre, 1882.

Dunlop, D. M. *Another "Prophetic Letter." JRAS*, 1940.

Emilia, A. d'. *Intorno ai* Νόμοι τὸν Ὁμηριτῶν. *RaSE*, VII, 1948.

Epiphanius Constantiensis. *See* [R. P. Blake and H. de Vis]; [O. Günther].

Esbroeck, M. van. *L'Ethiopie à l'époque de Justinien: S. Arethas de Neğrān et S. Athanase de Clysma.* IV Congresso Internazionale di Studi Etiopici (Rome, 1972), vol. I. Rome, 1974, pp. 115–139.

Evans-Pritchard, E. E. *The Divine Kingship of the Shilluk of the Nilotic Sudan.* Cambridge, 1948.

Expositio totius mundi. See A. A. Vasiliev, 1936; G. Lumbroso, 1898.

[Eyssenhardt, J.]. *Ammianus Marcellinus, Rerum gestarum libri qui supersunt.* Berlin, 1871.

Fakhry, A. *An Archeological Journey to Yemen (March–May 1947)*, vol. I–III. Cairo, 1951.

[Faris, N. A.]. *The Antiquities of South Arabia, being a translation . . . of the eighth book of al Hamdānī's al-Iklil.* Princeton, 1938.

Fell, Winand. *Die Christenverfolgung in Südarabien und die himjarischäthiopischen Kriege nach abessinischer Überliferung. ZDMG*, 35, 1881.

Feteḥ Mahāri. *See* M. Hofner, 1959.

Flavius Vopiscus the Syracusan. *Divine Aurelian.* Translated from the Latin by S. P. Dovatur. *MAH*, no. 4, 1959. In Russian.

Fleischer, H. L. *Abulfidae Historia anteislamica.* Leipzig, 1831.

Forrer, L. *Südarabien nach al-Hamdānis Beschreibung der Arabischen Halbinsel.* Leipzig, 1942.

Foti, C. *La Cronaca Abbreviata dei re d'Abissinia in un manoscritto di Dabra Berhan di Gondar. RaSE*, I, 1941.

Franchini, V. *Ritrovamenti archeologici di Dibdib. Bol.*

Franchini, V. *La zona archeologica di Macheda. Bol.*

Franchini, V. *Ritrovamenti archeologici in Eritrea. RaSE*, XII, 1954.

Franchini, V. *Altre pitture rupestri nell' Akkele-Guzay. Bol*, II, 1957.

Franchini, V. *Notizie su alcune pitture ed incisione recemente ritrovati in Eritrea. ACISE*, 1959.

Franchini, V. *Nuova ritrovamenti di pitture rupestri e graffiti in Eritrea. RSE*, XX, 1964.

Frisk, H. *Le périple de la mer Erythrée*. Gothenburg, 1927.

Gabriel, Gavino. *Il Museo Archeologico di Asmara. Bol.*

Gaudio, Attilio. *Quattro ritrovamenti archeologici e paleografici in Eritrea. Bol.*

Gaudefroy-Demombynes, M. *Mahomet*. Paris, 1957.

Gesenius, W. *Hebräische und Aramäisches Handwertenbuch*. Leipzig, 1921.

Glaser, Eduard. *Skizze des Geschichte Arabiens*, Bd. I. Berlin, 1888.

Glaser, Eduard. *Nochmals die Adulitanische Inschrift. Das Ausland*, 1891.

Glaser, Eduard. *Die Abessinier in Arabien und Afrika*. Munich, 1895.

Glaser, Eduard. *Zwei Inschriften über den Dammbruch von Mârib*. Berlin, 1897.

[Goeje, M. J.]. *Annales quos scripsit Abu Djafar Mohammed Ibn Djarir at-Tabari*, cum alis ed. M. J. de Goeje, ser. I. Leiden, 1881.

[Göeje, M. J. de]. *Liber expurgationis regionum, auctore Imamo Ahmed Ibn Jahja Ibn Djabir al Beladsori*. Leiden, 1886.

Golenishchev-Kutuzov, I. N. *The influence of Latin literature of the IV–V centuries on medieval and renaissance literature. MAH*, no. 1, 1964. In Russian.

Graziosi, Paolo. *Le pitture rupestri dell' Amba-Focadà (Eritrea). RaSE*, I, 1941.

Grohmann, A. *Über den Ursprung und die Entwicklung der äthiopischen Schrift. Archiv für Schriftkunde*, Jahre I, no. 2–3, 1915 (Leipzig).

Guidi, Ignazio. *La lettera di Simeone vescovo di Beth-Aršam sopra i martiri omeriti. Memorie della Reale Accademia dei Lincei (Classe scienze morale, storiche e filologiche)*, ser. 3, vol. VII, 1881.

Guidi, Ignazio. *Ostsyrische Bischöfe und Bischofssitze im V, VI, und VII Jahrhundert. ZDMG*, 43, 1889.

Guidi, Ignazio. *Di due frammenti relativi alla storia di Abissinia. RRAL*, ser. 5, vol. II, 1893.

Guidi, Ignazio. *Bahrey, Historia gentis Galla. (Scriptores aethiopici versio*, ser. altera, t. III, *Historia regis Sarsa Dengel)*. Paris, 1907.

Guidi, Ignazio. *Bizanzio e il regno di Aksum. Studi bizantini*, 1924 (Rome).

Guidi, Ignazio. *Due nuovi manoscritti della "Cronaca abbreviata" di Abissinia. RRAL*, ser. 6, 1926.

Guidi, Ignazio. *Storia della letteratura etiopica*. Rome, 1932.

[Guirgass, Vladimir]. *Abû Ḥanîfa ad-Dinawerî, Kitáb al-aḫbâr aṭ-tiwâl*. Leiden, 1888.

Gumilev, L. N. *Ancient Mongolian religion. Reports of the section and commission for the Geographic Society of the USSR*, issue 5, *Ethnography*. Leningrad, 1968. In Russian.

Gumilev, L. N. *Searches for the imaginary kingdom (the legend of the "land of presbyter Ioannes")*. Moscow, 1970. In Russian.

Gumilev, L. N. *Staroburyat painting. Historical subjects in the iconography of Agin datsan*. Moscow, 1975. In Russian.

[Günther, O.]. *Epiphanius. De duodecim gemmis. Corpus scriptores ecclesiasticorum latinorum*, t. XXXV, pars II. Vienna, 1861.

Hable-Sellassie, Sergew. *Church and State in the Aksumite Period. Proceedings of the Third International Conference of Ethiopian Studies* (Addis Ababa, 1966), vol. I. Addis Ababa, 1969, pp. 5–8.

Hailemariam, Ato Gezau. *Objects found on the neighborhood of Axum. AE*, I, 1955.

Halévy, J. *Examen critique des sources relatives à la persécution des chrétiens de Nedjran par le roi juif des Himyarites. RS*, 1896.

Hallpike, C. S. *The Konso of Ethiopia: A Study of the Values of a Cushitic People*. London, 1972.

Harmatta, Janos. *The Struggle for Possession of South Arabia between Aksum and the*

Sassanians. IV Congresso Internazionale di Studi Etiopici (Rome, 10–15 aprile 1972), vol. I. Rome, 1974.

Harris, W. C. *The Highlands of Aethiopia,* vol. I–III. London, 1842–1844.

Hartmann, M. *Der Najasi Aschama und sein Sohn Arma. ZDMG,* 49, 1895.

[Haury, J.]. *Procopius Caesarensis, Opera omnia,* vol. I. Leipzig, 1905.

Heliodorus. *An Aethiopian Romance,* tr. Thomas Underdowne [anno 1587]. London and New York, 1927.

Heliodorus. *Ethiopica.* Translated from the Greek. Moscow-Leningrad, 1936. In Russian.

Hennig, R. *Terrae incognitae,* Bd. II. Leiden, 1937.

Hennig, Richard. *Unknown lands,* vol. 1–2. Translated from German. Moscow, 1961. In Russian.

[Henri, René]. *Photius. Bibliotheque,* vol. I. Paris, 1960. (Texte établi et traduit par René Henri.)

Hergenröther, J. J. *Handbuch der algemeinen Kirkengeschichte,* Bd. II. Freiburg, 1904.

Herodotus. *Herodoti Historiae.* Recognovit Carolus Hude. Oxford, 1903.

Herrmann, A. *Die alten Verkehrswege zwischen Indien und Südchina. Zeitschrift der Berliner Gesellschaft für Erdkunde,* 1913, SS. 771 usw.

Herrmann, A. *Ein Seeverkehr zwischen Abessinien und Südchina zu Beginn unser Zeitrechnung. Zeitschrift der Berliner Gesellschaft für Erdkunde,* 1913.

Heuglin, Theodor von. *Beschreibung einiger äthiopischen Kupfermünzen (Adoa, 1861). ZDMG,* I, 1863.

Heuglin, Theodor von. *Reise nach Abessinien.* Jena, 1868.

Heyd, W. *Histoire du commerce du Levant au moyen-age,* vol. I. Leipzig, 1885–1886.

Hirschenberg, J. W. *Nestorian sources of North-Arabic traditions on the establishment and persecution of Christianity in Yemen. BO,* 15.

Hitti, Philip K. *A History of the Arabs,* 4th ed. London, 1949.

Hofmayr, W. *Die Schilluk. Geschichte, Religion und Leben eines Nilotenstammes.* Mödling, 1925.

[Höfner, Maria]. *Feteh Mahāri.* Mainz, 1959.

Höfner, Maria. *Über sprachliche und kulturelle Beziehungen zwischen Südarabien und Äthiopien im Altertum. ACISE,* 1960.

Höfner, Maria. *Die Semitien Äthiopiens. Wörterbuch der Mythologie.* Stuttgart, 1962.

Holm, Henrietta M. *The Agricultural Economy of Ethiopia.* Washington, 1956.

Honigmann, E. *Un Evêque d'Adoulis au Concile de Chalcedon.* Istanbul, 1950.

Honigmann, Ernest, et André Moricq. *Recherches sur les Res Gestae Divi Saporis.* Brussels, 1953.

Hornung, M. B. *Axumite Coins. Communications of the State Hermitage* [Museum], XXXVII, 1973 (Leningrad). In Russian.

Hudūd al-'Alam (The Regions of the World). See V. Minorsky.

Huntingford, C. E. *The Galla of Ethiopia. The Kingdoms of Kafa and Janjero.* London, 1955.

Ioannes. See Joannes.

Istrin, V. *The revelations of Methodius Patarus and the apocryphal visions of Daniel in Byzantine and Slavo-Russian Literatures.* Moscow, 1897.

Jamme, A. *Ethiopia. AE,* I; *BO,* XV, 1957.

Jamme, A. *On a drastic current reduction of South-Arabic chronology. BSOAS,* no. 145, 1957.

Jamme, A. *Sabaean inscriptions from Maḥram Bilqîs (Mârib).* Baltimore, 1962.

Jamme, A. *Research on Sabaean Rock Inscriptions from Southwestern Saudi Arabia.* Washington, 1965.

Jamme, A. *Sabaean and Hasaean Inscriptions from Saudi Arabia.* New York, 1966.

Jensen, A. E. *Elementi della cultura spirituale dei Conso nell' Etiopia meridionale. RaSE,* II, 1942.

Jensen, A. E. "Neuere Notizen über das Gada System." *Paideuma,* II, no. 1–2, 1941.

Joannes Ephesius. *Historia ecclesiastica.* Pars terta, liber IV, vol. 5–8. *CSCO, Scriptores syri,* ser. terta, t. III. Paris, 1904.

Joannes (Ioannes) Malalae. *See* Dindorff.

John of Ephesus. *Lives of the Eastern Saints.* Syriac text, ed. and tr. E. W. Brooks. *PO,* XVIII (t. I, 1923); XIX (t. III, 1926).

Jones, A. H. M., and Elizabeth Munroe. *A History of Abyssinia.* Oxford, 1935.

Jones, A. H. M., and Elizabeth Munroe. *A History of Ethiopia.* Oxford, 1955.

Jones, W. *On Asiatic History, Civil and Natural. Asiatic Researches,* 1973.

Kamil, Murad. *An Ethiopic Inscription Found at Marib. Journal of Semitic Studies,* IX, 1964; *Ethiopian Studies,* 1963.

Kammerer, Albert. *Essai sur l'histoire antique d'Abyssinie. Le royaume d'Aksoum et ses voisins d'Arabie et de Meroë.* Paris, 1926.

Kammerer, Albert. *Les monnaies abyssines de la collection Moucharjée, d'Aden.* Paris, 1926.

Kammerer, Albert. *La mer Rouge, l'Abyssinie et l'Arabie depuis l'antiquité,* t. I. *Les pays de la mer Erythrée jusqu'à la fin du Moyen-Age.* Le Caire, 1929.

Kashtaleva, K. S. *The term Hanif in the Koran. Reports of the Academy of Sciences of the USSR,* ser. 3, no. 8, 1928. In Russian.

Katsnelson, I. S. *The Nubian State. Reports and Communications of the History Faculty of Moscow State University,* issue 8, 1949. In Russian.

Katsnelson, I. S. *Some features of the government structure of Nubia in the VI-IV centuries B.C.* XXV International Congress of Orientalists. Moscow, 1960. In Russian.

Kaufman, S. A. *The art of ancient Ethiopia.* Manuscript. Moscow, 1964. In Russian.

Kawar, J. *Byzantium und Kinda. Byzantinische Zeitschrift,* 53. 1960.

Kebra Nagast. See Strelcyn.

Kekelidze, K. *Etudiebi jveli Kartuli literaturis istoriidan,* t, II. Tiflis, 1945. In Georgian.

Kenner, Friedrich. *Über das Münzrecht und die Goldpräge der Könige der Axumiten. Sitzungberichte der phil.-hist. Klasse der K. Akademie der Wissenschafter,* Bd. XXXIX. Vienna, 1862.

Khvostov, M. M. *History of eastern trade of Graeco-Roman Egypt.* Kazan, 1902. In Russian.

Kirwan, L. P. *Oxford University excavations at Firka.* Oxford, 1959.

Kirwan, L. P. *Tanqasi and the Noba. Kush,* V, 1957.

Kirwan, L. P. *The decline and fall of Meroe. Kush,* VIII, 1960.

Klotz, A. *Odoiporai apo Edem. Rheinisches Museum für Filologie,* 65, 1910.

Kobishchanov, Yu. M. *Political significance of "The Investigation of Zara Yaqob." Problems of Oriental Studies,* no. 1, 1960. In Russian.

Kobishchanov, Yu. M. *The "armies" of king 'Ēzāna (Remnants of a military democracy in ancient Axum). MAH,* no. 1, 1962. In Russian.

Kobishchanov, Yu. M. "Review of A. G. Loundine's book *South Arabia in the VI century." PAA,* no. 4, 1962. In Russian.

Kobishchanov, Yu. M. *Legend about the campaign of Hadāni Dan'ēl (Epic inscription of late Axum). PAA,* no. 6, 1962. In Russian.

Kobishchanov, Yu. M. *Communications of medieval Ethiopian sources on Christian Nubia. PC,* issue 7(70), 1962. In Russian.

Kobishchanov, Yu. M. *The election of the king in ancient Axum. MAH,* no. 4, 1963.

324   REFERENCES AND BIBLIOGRAPHY

In Russian.

Kobishchanov, Yu. M. *Social relationships in the Axumite kingdom. AEC*, V, 1963. In Russian.

Kobishchanov, Yu. M. *Ancient Axum. The Axumite kingdom in the period of emergence and of florescence (III–VII centuries)*. Author's abstract of his candidate dissertation, Moscow, 1964. In Russian.

Kobishchanow, Yu. M. *Aksum—ancient African civilization. Moscow News*, 1964, no. 13 (692); no. 14 (693).

Kobishchanow, Yu. M. *Aksum, antique civilization africaine. Les Nouvelles de Moscou*, 1964, no. 13 (692); no. 14 (693).

Kobishchanov, Yu. M. *The gold-bearing country of Sasu. PC*, issue 11 (74), 1964. In Russian.

Kobishchanov, Yu. M. *Who killed Dhu-Nuwas? BA*, XXV, 1964. In Russian.

Kobishchanov, Yu. M. *Among the sources of Ethiopian literature (Axumite literature). Literature of the countries of Africa*, collection 1, Moscow, 1964. In Russian.

Kobishchanow, Yu. M. *Les données primordiales sur les chasseurs-cueilleurs de l'Ethiopie.* Communication sur le VII Congrès international des sciences anthropologiques et ethnologiques, Moscou, 1964.

Kobishchanov, Yu. M. *Early information on hunter-gatherers of Ethiopia.* VII International Congress of Anthropological and Ethnographical Sciences, Moscow, 1964. In Russian.

Kobishchanow, Yu. M. *On the problem of sea voyages of ancient Africans in the Indian Ocean. JAH*, 6, no. 2, 1965.

Kobishchanow, Yu. M. *Extraite de l'histoire des rapports entre les peuples de l'Empire Russe et de l'Ethiopie. La Russie et l'Afrique*, 1966 (Moscou).

Kobishchanow, Yu. M. *From the history of relations between the peoples of Russia and Ethiopia. Russia and Ethiopia*, 1966 (Moscow).

Kobishchanow, Yu. M. *The sea voyages of ancient Ethiopians in the Indian Ocean.* III International Conference of Ethiopian Studies, Addis Ababa, 1966.

Kobishchanov, Yu. M. *Personal tribute collection in tropical Africa. PAA*, 1972, pp. 65–78. In Russian.

Kobishchanov, Yu. M. *Africa: origin of backwardness and paths of development.* Moscow, 1974. In Russian.

Kobishchanov, Yu. M., and V. P. Starinin. *"African ethnographic collection IV"* (review). *PAA*, no. 6, 1963. In Russian.

Krachovsky, I. Yu. *Two South Arabian inscriptions in Leningrad.* Leningrad, 1931. In Russian.

Krachovsky, I. Yu. *Introduction to Ethiopian philology.* Leningrad, 1955. In Russian.

Krachovsky, I. Yu. *Arabic geographic literature. Selected Communications*, vol. IV. Moscow-Leningrad, 1957. In Russian.

Kraft, J. L. *Travels, Researches and Missionary Labours in East Africa.* London, 1860.

Krencker, Daniel. *Deutsche Axum-Expedition*, Bd. II. *Ältere Denkmäler Nordabessiniens.* Berlin, 1913.

Krencker, Daniel. *Die grossen Stelen in Aksum. FF*, 12 Jahrg., 1936.

Krimsky, A. E. *Ancient history of South Arabia from ancient Babylonian times to [the time of] the subjugation of the country to Muhammad. Eastern Antiquities*, IV, 1913 (Moscow). In Russian.

Krimsky, A. E. *"Ethiopian literature and language." Encyclopedic Dictionary "Garnet,"* edition 7, vol. 54, Moscow, 1948. In Russian.

Krivov, M. V. *Ethiopia in the revelations of Pseudo-Methodius Patarus. BA*, 38, 1977. In Russian.

Kubbel, L. E., and V. V. Matveev. *Arabic sources of the VII–X centuries on the ethnography and history of Africa south of the Sahara.* (Preparation of texts and translation.) Moscow-Leningrad, 1960. In Russian and Arabic.

Kubbel, L. E., and V. V. Matveev. *Arabic sources of the X–XII centuries on the ethnography and history of Africa south of the Sahara.* (Preparation of texts and translation.) Moscow-Leningrad, 1965. In Russian and Arabic.

Kuznetsov, B. I., and L. N. Gumilev. *Bon (an ancient Tibetan religion). Reports of the section and commission for the Geographic Society of the USSR,* issue 15, Leningrad, 1970. In Russian.

Lacomrade, Christian. *Synésios de Cyrène, hellène et chrétien.* Paris, 1951.

Laming-Macadam, M. F. *The Temples of Kawa. I. The Inscriptions.* London, 1949.

Lammens, H. *Les "'Aḥābiš" et l'organisation militaire de La Mecque au siècle de l'hégire. JA,* sér. 8, vol. VIII, 1926, pp. 425–482.

Leclant, Jean. *Egypte-Afrique. Bulletin de la Société française d'Egyptologie,* no. 21, 1956.

Leclant, Jean. *Les fouilles à Axoum en 1955–1956. Rapport préliminaire. AE,* III, 1959.

Leclant, Jean *Note sur l'amulette en cornaline. J.E., 2832. AE,* VI, 1965.

Leclant, Jean, et André Miquel. *Reconnaissances dans l'Agamé: Goulo-Makedā et Sabéa (octobre 1955–avril 1956). AE,* III, 1959.

Lefebvre, Théophile. *Voyage en Abyssinie executé pendant les années 1839–1843,* vol. I–III. Paris, 1845.

Leggese, A. *Class Systems Based on Time. Journal of Ethiopian Studies,* I, no. 2, 1963 (Addis Ababa).

Lepsius, Richard. *Briefe aus Ägypten, Äthiopien und des Sinai.* Berlin, 1852.

Lepsius, Richard. *Denkmäler aus Ägypten und Äthiopien,* Bd. V. Berlin, 1913.

Leroy, Jules. *Les "Ethiopiens" de Persépolis. AE,* V, 1963.

Lesquier, J. *L'armée romain d'Egypte.* Paris, 1951.

Letronne, A. J. *Histoire du christianisme en Egypte, en Nubie et en Abyssinie. Oeuvres choisies,* I, 1881.

Littmann, Enno. *The Legend of the Queen of Sheba in the Tradition of Axum.* Princeton, 1904.

Littmann, E. *Preliminary report on the Princeton University expedition to Abyssinia. ZA,* XX, 1907.

Littmann, Enno. *Geschichte der äthiopische Litteratur. Geschichte der christianischen Litteraturen des Orients.* Leipzig, 1907.

Littmann, Enno. *Sternensagen und Astrologisches aus Nordabessinien. Archiv für Religionswissenschaft,* XI, Heft II, 1908.

Littmann, Enno. *Abessinische Parallelen zu einigen altarabischen Gebräuchen und Vorstellungen. Beiträge zur Kentnis des Orients,* VI, 1908 (Berlin).

Littmann, Enno. *Deutsche Aksum-Expedition,* Bd. I. *Reisebericht der Expedition / Topographie und Geschichte Aksums.* Berlin, 1913.

Littmann, Enno. *Deutsche Aksum-Expedition,* Bd. IV. *Sabäische, Griechische, und Altabessinische Inschriften.* Berlin, 1913.

Littmann, Enno. "Adulis." "Aksum." *Paulys Realenzyklopädie der classischen Altertumswissenschaft.* Stuttgart, 1919.

Littmann, Enno. *Eine neue Goldmünze des Königs Israel von Aksum. Zeitschrift der Numismatik,* 35, no. 4, 1925.

Littmann, Enno. *Indien und Abessinien. Beiträge zur Litteraturwissenschaft und Geistesgeschichte Indiens.* Berlin, 1925.

Littmann, Enno. *La leggenda del Dragone di Axum in lingua tigrai. RaSE,* VI, 1947–1948, 1949.

Littmann, Enno. *Äthiopische Inschriften. MAB,* II, Berlin, 1950.

Littmann, Enno. *L'inscrizione di Anzà. RaSE*, XI, 1953.

Littmann, Enno. *Aus dem alten Abessinien. Serta Cantabrigensis*, Wiesbaden, 1954.

Littmann, Enno. *On the old Ethiopic inscription from the Berenice road. JRAS*, 1954.

Littmann, Enno, und D. Krencker. *Vorbericht der Deutschen Aksum-Expedition. APAW*, 1906.

Longpérier, Adrien de. *Monnaies des Homerites frappées à Raidan (Arabie Méridionale). RN*, XIII, 1868.

Longpérier, Adrien de. *Monnaies des rois d'Ethiopie (Nagast d'Aksum en Abyssinie). RN*, XIII, 1868.

Loundine, A. G. *A South Arabian historical inscription of the VI century from Marib. Epigraphics of the East*, issue IX, 1954. In Russian.

Loundine, A. G. *From the history of Arabia at the beginning of the VI century A.D. PC*, issue 2(65), 1956. In Russian.

Loundine, A. G. *Review of Sidney Smith['s] "Events in Arabia in the 6-th century." PAA*, no. 1, 1957. In Russian.

Loundine, A. G. *The question of the chronology of Himyarite inscriptions. PC*, issue 3(66), 1958. In Russian.

Loundine, A. G. *A South Arabian construction inscription of the beginning of the VI century. Ethographics of the East*, issue XIII, 1960. In Russian.

Loundine, A. G. *"The Axoumite Kingdom." SHE*, vol. I, p. 311. Moscow, 1961. In Russian.

Loundine, A. G. *South Arabia in the VI century. PC*, issue 8, 1961. In Russian.

Loundine, A. G. *Sabaean civil servant and diplomat of the III century A.D. PC*, issue 25(88), 1974.

Loundine, A. G., et J. Ryckmans. *Nouvelles données sur la chronologie des rois de Saba et Ḏū Raydān. Mus*, t LXXVII, no. 3–4, 1964.

Lukas, A. *Materials and handicraft productions of Ancient Egypt*. Translated from English. Moscow, 1958. In Russian.

Luknitsky, K. N. *Abyssinia from ancient times to the epoch of imperialism. Abyssinia (Ethiopia) Collection of Articles*, Moscow-Leningrad, 1936. In Russian.

Lumbroso, G. *L'Egitto dei Greci e dei Romani*. Rome, 1895.

Lumbroso, G. *L'Expositio totius mundi et gentium annotata. Atti della Reale Accademia dei Lincei*, ser. 5, vol. VI, pt. I, 1898.

Lüpke, Theodor von. *Deutsche Aksum-Expedition*, Bd. III. *Profan- und Kultbauten Nordabessiniens aus älterer und neuerer Zeit*. Berlin, 1913.

Lyalkina, M. A. *Theodore Bent's Abyssinian journey in 1893*. St. Petersburg, 1896. In Russian.

McCrindle, J. W. *The Christian topography of Cosmas*. London, 1897.

McMichael, H. A. *A History of the Arabs of the Sudan and some account of the peoples who preceded them and the tribes inhabiting Darfur*, vol. I. Cambridge, 1952.

Mani. *See* C. Schmidt.

Mannert, K. *Geographie der Griechen und Römer*, Bd. I–XII. Nuremberg-Leipzig, 1795–1825.

Mantel-Niecko, M. *Staroamharskie pieśni królewskie. Przegląd Orientalny*, .no. 3(23), 1957.

Manzi, Luigi. *Il commercio in Etiopia, Nubia, Abissinia, Sudan dai primordi alla dominazione musulmana*. Roma, 1886.

Margolin, P. *Three Jewish travelers of the IX–XII centuries: Eldad Danit, R. Benjamin Tudelsky, and R. Petahi Regensburgsky*. Hebrew text with Russian translation. St. Petersburg, 1881.

Marquart, J. *Die Benin-Sammlung des Reichsmuseums für Volkskunde in Leiden*. Leiden,

1913.

Maspero, J. *Histoire des patriarches d'Alexandrie* ... (518–616). Paris, 1923.

Matthews, D., and Mordini, A. *The Monastery of Debre-Damo, Ethiopia. Ar*, XCVII, 1959.

Mekouria, Teclé Tsadik. *Les noms propres de bâptême et l'étude généalogique des rois d'Ethiopie (XIII–XXᵉ siècles) à travers leurs noms patronymiques.* Belgrade, 1966.

Migne, J. P. *Patrologiae grecae*, t. 25, Paris, 1834; t. 65, 1862; t. 86, 1864; t. 88, 1866.

Mikhalovsky, K. *Does the riddle of group X remain as before? MAH*, no. 2, 1967. In Russian.

[Minorsky, V.]. *Ḥudūd al-ʿAalam (The Regions of the World)*, Persian geography 372 *A.H.–982 A.D.* London, 1937.

Mlaker, K. *Die Inschrift von Ḥuṣn al-Gurāb. Wiener Zeitschrift fur Semitistick*, no. 7, 1929.

[Møberg, Axel]. *The Book of the Himyarites.* Lund, 1924. (Cited as *BH*.)

Mommsen, Theodor. *Römische Geschichte*, Bd. V. *Die Provinzien von Caesar bis Diocletian.* Berlin, 1893.

Mommsen, Theodor. *History of Rome*, vol. V. *The Provinces from Caesar to Diocletian.* Translated from the German. Moscow, 1949. In Russian.

Mondon-Vidailhet, C. *Une tradition éthiopienne. RS*, XII, 1904.

Monneret de Villard, U. *Aksum. Ricerche di topographia generale.* Pontificium Institutum Biblicum, *Analecta orientalia, 16*, Rome, 1935.

Monneret de Villard, U. *Un tipo di chiesa abissina. AE*, VI, 1935.

Monneret de Villard, U. *L'origine dei piu antichi tipi di chiese abissine. Atti del III Congresso di Studi Coloniali*, Florence, 1937.

Monneret de Villard, U. *Note sulle influenze asiatiche nell' Africa Orientale. RSO*, XVIII, 1938.

Monneret de Villard, U. *L'inscrizione etiopiche di Ham e l'epigrafia meroitica. Aeg*, XX, 1940.

Monneret de Villard, U. *Storia della Nubia cristiana.* Rome, 1938.

Monneret de Villard, U. *Perchè la chiesa abissina dependeva dal patriarchato d'Alessandria. Oriente Moderno*, XXIII, 1943.

Monneret de Villard, U. *Mosé vescovo di Adulis. Oriente Cristiana Periodico*, XIII, 1947.

Monneret de Villard, U. *Aksum e i quattro re del mondo. Annali Lateranensis*, XII, 1948 (Vatican).

Montfaucon, Bernard de. *Patrum et scriptorum graecorum nova collection*, vol. II. Paris, 1706.

Mordini, Antonio. *Un riporto sotto roccia con pitture rupestri nell' Amba-Focada. RSE*, I, 1941.

Mordini, Antonio. *Informazioni preliminari sui resultati delle mie ricerche in Etiopia dal 1939 al 1944. RaSE*, IV, 1946.

Mordini, Antonio. *Su di un nuovo titulo regale aksumita. RaSE*, VIII, 1949.

Mordini, Antonio. *Un vasetto con figurazione votive proveniente de Daroca (Tigrai). Bol.*

Mordini, Antonio. *Appunti di numismatica aksumita. AE*, III, 1959.

Mordini, Antonio. *Gli aurei Kushāna del convento di Dabra-Dāmmo. Un'indizio sui rapporti commerciale fra India e l'Etiopia nel primi secoli dell'era volgare. ACISE*, 1960.

Mordini, Antonio. *Gli aurei Kushāna del convento di Dabra-Dāmmo.* Accademia Nazionale dei Lincei, 1960.

Mordini, Antonio. *I tessili medioevali del convento di Dabra-Dāmmo. ACISE*, 1960.

Mordini, Antonio. *Storia della letteratura etiopica.* Rome, 1961.

Mordtmann, J. H. *Die himjarische-ätiopische Kriege noch einmal. ZDMG*, 35, 1881.

Mordtmann, J. H. *Himjarische Inschriften und Altertumer.* Berlin, 1893.

Moscati, Sabatino. *Ancient semitic civilizations.* London, 1957.

Müller, Heinrich D. *Epigraphische Denkmäler aus Abessinien.* Berlin, 1894.

Mullerus, C. *Anabasis Pseudo-Kallisthenes. Indica.* Paris, 1846.

Mullerus, C. *Fragmenta historicorum graecorum,* t. IV. Paris, 1851.

Mullerus, C. *Geographi graeci minores,* vol. I–II. Paris, 1855, 1861.

Mullerus, C. *Claudii Ptolemaei Geographicae enarrationis.* Paris, 1879.

Munziger, W. *Ostafrikanische Studien.* Schaffhausen, 1864.

Nami, Kh. Y. *Našr nuqūš sāmiya qadīma min junūb bilād al-'Arab wa šaraḥuhā.* Cairo, 1943.

Nami, Kh. Y. *Nuqūš 'arabiyya junūbiyya (South Arabic Inscriptions).* Majallat Kulliyyat al-Ādāb (*Revue de la Faculté des Lettres, Université Fouad I*), IX, no. 1, 1947 (Cairo).

Niebuhr, B. G. *Über das Älter der zweiten Hälfte der adulitischen Inschrift.* Berlin, 1810.

Nielsen, Ditmar. *Die äthiopischen Götter. ZDMG,* 66, 1912.

Nielsen, Ditmar. *Handbuch der altarabische Altertumskunde.* Paris-Copenhagen-Leipzig, 1927.

Nielsen, Ditmar. *Biblical religion in the light of the latest archaeological excavations. MAH,* no. 1, 1937. In Russian.

Nöldeke, Th. *Beiträge zur Semitischen Sprachwissenschaft.* Stuttgart, 1904.

Olderogge, D. A. *L'Arménie et l'Ethiopie au IV siècle (à propos des sources de l'alphabet arménien.* IV Congresso Internazionale di Studi Etiopici (Rome, 1972), vol. I. Rome, 1974.

Olympiodorus. *See* E. U. Skrzhinskaya.

Pankhurst, Richard. *An Introduction to the economic history of Ethiopia. From early times to 1800, with a foreword by K. M. Pannikar.* (Essex), Lalibela House, 1961.

Pankhurst, Sylvia. *Ethiopia. A cultural history.* (Essex), Lalibela House, 1955.

Paribeni, R. *Ricerche nel luogo dell'antica Adulis.* Rome, 1908.

Paul, Andrew. *A History of the Beja Tribes of the Sudan.* Cambridge, 1954.

Peoples of Africa. Under the editorship of D. A. Olderogge and I. I. Potekhin. Moscow, 1954. In Russian.

Pereira, Estevão. *Historia dos martyres de Nagran.* Lisbon, 1899.

Periplus. See Pseudo Arrian. *Also see* W. H. Schoff; *and see* William Vincent for an English-language version.

Perruchon, Jules. *Histoire des guerres d'Amda-Ṣyon roi d'Ethiopie. JA,* XIV, 1889.

Perruchon, Jules. *Les chroniques de Zar'a Yâ'eqôb et de Ba'eda-Mâryâm, rois d'Ethiopie.* Paris, 1893.

Philby, H. St. J. *Note on the Kings of Saba. Mus,* 63, no. 3–4, 1950.

Philby, H. St. J. *Arabian Highlands.* New York, 1952.

Philby, H. St. J. *Note on "Ryckmans 535." Mus,* 73, no. 3–4, 1960.

Philostorgius. *See* J. Bidez.

Philostratus. *Life of Apollonius.* Tr. C. P. Jones; edited, abridged, and introduced by G. W. Bowersock. Harmondsworth, 1970.

Pietschmann, Richard. "Adule." "Axomis." *Realencyclopädie der Klassischen Alter-tumswissenschaft von Pauly-Wissowa,* vol. II. Stuttgart, 1893, 1896.

Pigulevskaya, N. V. *Byzantium and Iran at the juncture of the VI and VII centuries.* Leningrad, 1946.

Pigulevskaya, N. V. *Byzantine diplomacy and the silk trade in the V–VII centuries. BA,* I (XXVI), 1947. In Russian.

Pigulevskaya, N. V. *Ethiopia and Himyar in their mutual relationships with the Eastern Roman Empire. MAH,* no. 1, 1948. In Russian.

Pigulevskaya, N. V. *Origins of Kushite-Himyarite wars. BA,* II (XXVII), 1949. In Russian.

Pigulevskaya, N. V. *The laws of the Himyarites. BA,* III, 1950. In Russian.

Pigulevskaya, N. V. *Byzantium and the routes to India*. Leningrad, 1951. In Russian. (German translation: *see* N. W. Pigulewskaja.)

Pigulevskaya, N. V. *The question of "literate" peoples of antiquity. The Ancient World (Collection in honor of V. V. Struve)*. Moscow-Leningrad, 1961. In Russian.

Pigulevskaya, N. V. *Kindites and Lahmides in the V and the beginning of the VI centuries. PC*, issue 9, 1963. In Russian.

Pigulevskaya, N. V. *Arabs at the boundaries of Byzantium and Iran in the IV–VI centuries*. Moscow-Leningrad, 1964. In Russian.

Pigulevskaya, N. V. *The policy of Byzantium on the Eritrean Sea. PC*, issue 11, 1964. In Russian.

Pigulewskaja, N. W. *Byzanz aus den Wegen nach Indien*. Berlin, 1969.

Pirenne, Jacqueline. *L'inscription "Ryckmans 535" et la chronologie sud-arabe. Mus*, LXIX, no. 1–2, 1956.

Pirenne, Jacqueline. *Chronique d'archéologie sud-arabe (1955–1956). AE*, II, 1957.

Pirenne, Jacqueline. *Une problème-clef pour la chronologie de l'Orient: la date du "Périple de la mer Erythrée." JA*, CCXLIX, fasc. 4, 1961.

Pirenne, Jacqueline. *Le royaume sud-arabe de Qataban et sa datation, d'après l'archéologie et les sources classiques, jusqu'au Périple de la mer Erythrée*. Louvain, 1961.

Pirenne, Jacqueline. *De la chronologie des inscriptions sud-arabes après la fouille du temple de Marib. BO*, XXVI, 1969.

Pirenne, Jacqueline. *L'imbroglio de trois siècles de chronologie aksumite: IVe–VIe s. Documents pour servir à l'histoire des civilisations éthiopiennes*. Fasc. 6, 1975. Addis Ababa, Centre National de la Recherche Scientifique, 1975.

Piva, A. *Una civiltà scomparsa dell'Eritrea. E gli scavi archeologici di Cheren*. Rome, 1907.

Platonov, V. M. *Brief Chronicle of Alaka Lemlem According to the Manuscript LO MNA Eth. 30, Africana*. Culture and Languages of the Peoples of Africa. Moscow-Leningrad, 1966. In Russian.

Pliny. *See* D. Detlefsen *or* B. H. Rackham.

Portères, Roland. *Berceaux agricoles primaires sur le continent africain. JAH*, III, no. 2, 1962.

Prasolov, L. I. *Soils of Abyssinia and Eritrea. Soil Science*, no. 28, 1933. In Russian.

Priaulx, B. *On the Indian Embassies to Rome, from the Reign of Claudius to the Death of Justinian. JRAS*, XX, 1863.

Prideaux, W. F. *Coins of the Axumite Dynasty. NCH*, ser. 3, vol. IV, 1884; vol. V, 1885.

Princeton Expedition. *See* E. Littman, *Preliminary Report*; R. Sundström.

Procopius Caesarensis. *See* [S. Destunis], 1876; [J. Haury].

Pseudo Arrian. *Sailing around the Erythrean Sea*. Translated by S. P. Kondratiev. *MAH*, no. 2, 1940. In Russian. Cited as *Periplus*. *Also see* W. H. Schoff; William Vincent.

Ptolemaeus, Claudius. *See* C. Mullerus, 1861, 1879; *also see* P. Schnabel.

Quatremère, M. *Mémoire géographique et historique sur l'Egypte et la Nubie*. Paris, 1811.

[Rackham, B. H.]. *Plinius Secundus. Natural History*. London, 1947–1956.

Rathjens, C. *Kulturelle Einflusse in Süd West Arabien. Jahrbuch für Kleinasiatische Forschung*, I, 1950.

Raunig, W. *Die Versuche einer Datierung des Periplus maris Erythraei. Mitteilungen der anthropologischen Gessellschaft in Wien*, 100, 1970, SS. 231–242.

Redin, E. K. *Historical monuments of the town of Adulis (in Africa) in personal manuscripts of Cosmas Indicopleustes' communications*. Collection of articles on Slavic studies dedicated to M. S. Dromov. Kharkov, 1905. In Russian.

Redin, E. K. *Countries and peoples after Ephoros in the personal notes of Cosmas Indicopleustes' communications. BA*, XIII, 1906. In Russian.

Renouvin, P. *Histoire des peuples d'Afrique Noire*. Paris, 1960.

Ricci, L. *Ritrovamenti archeologici in Eritrea*. *RaSE*, XIV, 1955–1958.

Ricci, L. *Notizie archeologiche*. *RaSE*, XV, 1959.

Rodén, K. G. *Le tribú dei Mensa*. Rome, 1940.

Rodinson, Maxime. *Sur la question des "influences juives" en Ethiopie*. *ES*, 1963.

Rodinson, Maxime. Éthiopien et sudarabique. Rapports sur les conférences. *École pratique des hautes études. IVᵉ Section, sciences historiques et philologiques. Annuaire*, 1965 / 1966, pp. 125–141; 1966 / 1967, pp. 121–139; 1968 / 1969, pp. 161–182; 1974 / 1975, pp. 209–247 (Paris).

Rodinson, Maxime. *Sur une nouvelle inscription du régne de Dhoû Nowâs. Bibliotheca Orientalis*, XXVI, no. 1, 1969.

Rodinson, Maxime. *Notes sur la texte de Jean de Nikiou*. *IV Congresso Internationale di Studi Etiopici* (Rome, 1972), vol. II. Rome, 1974.

Rodinson, Maxime. Éthiopien et sudarabique. Rapports sur les conférences. Le Periple de la Mer Érythrée. *École pratique des hautes études. IVᵉ Section, sciences historiques et philologiques. Annuaire*, 1974 / 1975, pp. 210–238; 1975 / 1976, pp. 201–219 (Paris).

Rozov, A. *Christian Nubia*, part I. Kiev, 1890. In Russian.

Rubin, B. *Prokopius von Kaisareia*. Stuttgart, 1955.

Rubin, B. *Das Zeitalter Justinians*. Berlin, 1960.

Rufinus, Tyrranius. *See* R. Hennig.

Rüppel, E. *Reise in Abessinien*, Bd. 1–2. Frankfurt-am-Main, 1838–1840.

Rüppel, E. *On an Unedited Coin of one of the Early Kings of Abyssinia*. *NCh*, ser. 1, vol. VIII, 1845–1846.

Ryckmans, G. *Inscriptions sud-arabes*: sér. X, no. 506–508, 515, *Mus*, t. LXVI, no. 3–4, 1953; sér. XII, No. 533, *Mus*, t. LXVIII, no. 3–4, 1955; sér. XIII, no. 535, *Mus*, t. LXIX, no. 1–2, 1956; sér. XIV, no. 539, *Mus*, t. LXIX, no. 3–4, 1956.

Ryckmans, G. *Notes épigraphiques, sixième série, IX. Une contribution à l'épigraphie et l'histoire de l'Ethiopie antique*. *Mus*, LXXXV, no. 3–4, 1962.

Ryckmans, J. *Inscriptions historiques sabéennes de l'Arabie centrale*. *Mus*, LXVI, no. 3–4, 1953.

Ryckmans, J. *La chronologie sud-arabe du premier siècle avant notre ère*. *BO*, X, 1953.

Ryckmans, J. *L'origine et l'ordre des lettres de l'alphabet éthiopien*. *BO*, XII, no. 1, 1955.

Ryckmans, J. *La persécution des chrétiens himyarites au sixième siècle*. Istanbul, 1956.

Ryckmans, J. *"A. Jamme, Sabaean inscriptions from Maḥram Bilqîs."* *BO*, XXI, no. 1–2, 1964.

Ryckmans, J. *Les rois de Hadramawt mentionnés à 'Uqla*. *BO*, XXI, no. 5–6, 1964.

Saint-Martin, L. Vivien de. *Eclaircissements géographiques et historiques sur l'inscription d'Adulis et sur quelques points des inscriptions d'Axum*. *JA*, II, 1863.

Salt, H. *A voyage to Abyssinia and travels into the interior part of that country*. London, 1814.

Sapeto, G. *Viaggio e missione cattolica fra i Mensa, i Bogos e gli Habab*. Rome, 1857.

Sauter, Roger. *Où est notre connaissance des églises rupestres d'Ethiopie*. *AE*, V, 1963.

Sayce, A. H. *A Greek inscription of a King of Axum found at Meroë*. *Proceedings of the Society of Biblical Archeology*, XXXI, 1909.

Schanz, M., und C. Hosins. *Geschichte der Römischen Literatur*, Bd. IV. Munich, 1959.

Scher, A. *Histoire nestorienne (Chronique de Seert)*. *PO*, sér. 4, t. 3, 1906.

Schlumberger, G. *Le trésor de Sana (Monnaies himyaritiques)*. Paris, 1880.

Schlumberger, G. *Monnaies inédites d'éthiopiens et des homérites*. *RN*, sér. 3, t. IV, 1886.

Schmidt, C. *Manichäische Handschriften der Staatlichen Museen von Berlin*, Bd. I.

Kephalaia. Stuttgart, 1940.

Schnabel, P. *Text und Karten des Ptolemaeus.* Leipzig, 1938.

Schneider, Roger. *Une page du Gadla-Sadgān. AE,* IV, 1963.

Schneider, Roger. *Notes épigraphiques sur les découvertes de Matara. AE,* VI, 1965.

Schneider, Roger. *Trois nouvelles inscriptions royales d'Axoum.* IV Congresso Internazionale di Studi Etiopici (Rome, 1972). Rome, 1974.

Schoff, W. H. *Periplus maris Erythraei.* London, 1912.

Schoff, W. H. *The Periplus of the Erythraean Sea.* New York, 1912.

Schröter, R. *Trostschreiben Jacob's von Serug an die himjarischen Christen. ZDMG,* 31, 1877.

Schwartz, E. *Ein Bischof der Römischen Reichskkirche im Abessinien. Philologus,* no. 91, 1936.

Seligmann, C. C., and B. Z. Seligmann. *Pagan tribes of the Nilotic Sudan.* London, 1932.

Sethe, K. *Urkunden des Alten Reiches,* Bd. IV. Leipzig, 1932.

Sevak, Gurgen. *Mesrop Mashtots, the creation of the Armenian scripts and philology.* Yerevan, 1962. In Armenian.

Shahîd, Irfân. *The Martyrs of Najrân. New Documents (Subsidia hagiographica,* 49). Brussels, 1971.

Shahîd, Irfân. *The Kebra Nagast in the light of recent research. Le Muséon,* LXXXIX, fasc. 1–2, 1976.

Shinnie, P. L. *Excavations at Tanqasi 1953. Kush,* II, 1954.

Shinnie, P. L. *The Fall of Meroë. Kush,* VI, 1957.

Shtaerman, E. M. *Scriptores historiae Augustae as an historical source. MAH,* no. 1, 1957. In Russian.

Simoons, Frederick J. *Northwest Ethiopia. Peoples and economy.* Madison, 1960.

Sinko, T. *Die Discriptio orbis terrae, eine Handelsgeographie aus dem IV Jahrhundert. Archiv für latinische Lexicographie und Grammatik,* XIII, 1904.

Skrzhinskaya, E. Ch. *The Historia of Olympiodorus. Byzantine Messenger,* 8, 1956. In Russian.

Smirnov, S. R. *Education and the paths of development of North Sudanese nationality. AEC,* no. 1, 1956. In Russian.

Smith, Sidney. *Events in Arabia in the 6th century A.D. BSOAS,* XVI, pt. 3, 1954.

Snowden, J. D. *The Cultivated Races of Sorghum.* London, 1936.

Solà Solé, J. M. *La inscripción G1 389 y los comienzos del monoteismo en Sudarabia. Mus,* LXXII, no. 1–2, 1959.

Solovyev, M. *"The Sacred city of Ethiopia" by Theodore Bent. Russian Messenger,* June 1894. In Russian.

Sreznevsky, I. *The Christian topography of Cosmas Indicopleustes. A comparison of the Slavic translation with the Greek original as to content. Notes of the Imperial Academy of Sciences,* vol. 9:3, 1866 (St. Petersburg). In Russian.

Stein, E. *Histoire du Bas Empire,* t. II. Paris, 1949.

Stiehler, W. *Landwirtschafts und Siedlungsgeographie Äthiopiens. Erdkunde,* 2, 1948.

Strabo. *Geography.* Translated by F. G. Mishchenk. Moscow, 1879. In Russian.

[Strelcyn, Stefan]. *Kebra Nagast szyli Chwala Królów Abisynii.* Warsaw, 1956.

Sundström, R. "Report of an expedition to Adulis." In E. Littman, ed., *Preliminary report on the Princeton University expedition to Abyssinia.*

Svet, Ya. M. *Having Traversed a Hundred Thousand Li.* Moscow, 1960. In Russian.

Synesius of Cyrene. *See* C. Lacomrade.

Tabari, At. *Annales quos scripsit Abu Djafar Mohammed Ibn Djarir at-Tabari, cum alis ed. M. J. Goeje,* ser. I. Leiden, 1881.

Tedesco-Zammarano, V. *Contributo alla numismatica aksumita. Numismatica*, XIII, 1947 (Rome).

Tertullianus, Quintus Septimus Florens. *Opera. Ad Nationes.* Turnhout, 1953.

Theophanes. *Chronographia*, ed. C. De Boor. Leipzig, 1883.

Theophanes the Confessor. *Chronicle of Theophanes the Byzantine from Diocletian to king Michael and his son Theophilactes.* Translated from the Greek by V. I. Obolensky and F. A. Ternovsky. Moscow, 1884. In Russian.

Thompson, J. *The history of ancient geography.* Translated from English. Moscow, 1953. In Russian.

Trimingham, J. Spencer. *Islam in Ethiopia.* London, 1952.

Tringali, G. *Cenni sulle "'ona" di Asmara e dintorni. AE*, VI, 1965, pp. 143–161.

Tubiana, Joseph. *Eléments de toponimie éthiopienne (Tigré). JA*, 244, fasc. 1, 1956.

Tubiana, Joseph. *Quatre généalogies royales éthiopiennes. CEA*, 7, 1961.

Turayev, B. A.ብዕል : ፺ውጉ•ት :*"The Wealth of kings." A treatise about dynastic overthrow in Abyssinia in the VIII century. Notes of the Eastern Division of the (Imperial) Russian Archaeological Society*, XIII, 1901. In Russian.

Turayev, B. A. *Two Axumite coins in the Imperial Hermitage. Notes of the Classical Division of the (Imperial) Russian Archaeological Society*, I, 1901. In Russian.

Turayev, B. A. *An investigation in the area of hagiological sources of the history of Ethiopia.* St. Petersburg, 1902. In Russian.

Turayev, B. A. *Carlo Conti-Rossini, "L'evangelio d'oro di Dabra-Libanos"* (review). *Notes of the Eastern Division of the (Imperial) Russian Archaeological Society*, XIV (1901), 1902. In Russian.

Turayev, B. A. *"Christianity in Abyssinia." Encyclopedic Dictionary of Brockhaus and Effron*, vol. XXXVII, A, book 74. St. Petersburg, 1903. In Russian.

Turayev, B. A. *Hagiological tale about the fall of the Axumite kingdom. Collection in honor of V. I. Lamainsky.* St. Petersburg, 1905. In Russian.

Turayev, B. A. *Ethiopian Manuscripts in St. Petersburg.* St. Petersburg, 1906. In Russian.

Turayev, B. A. *Some lives of Ethiopian saints. BA*, XIII, 1906. In Russian.

Turayev, B. A. *Tale about Dabra-Libanos monastery. BA*, XIII, issue 2–3, 1906. In Russian.

Turayev, B. A. *Notes to a Brief Ethiopian Chronicle of V. V. Bolotov. BA*, XVIII, 1910. In Russian.

Turayev, B. A. *"Aksum." New Encyclopedic Dictionary of Brockhaus and Effron*, vol. I. St. Petersburg, 1911. In Russian.

Turayev, B. A. *"Aethiopica" for 1912–1914. Bibliographia*, III, issue 2, 1914 (Prague). In Russian.

Turayev, B. A. *History of the Ancient East*, part II. Prague, 1914. In Russian.

Turayev, B. A. *Abyssinian chronicles of the XIV–XVI centuries.* Moscow-Leningrad, 1936. In Russian.

Ullendorf, E. M. *Exploration and study of Abyssinia. A Brief Survey. With an appendix on "The Obelisk of Matara."* Asmara, 1945.

Ullendorff, E. M. *Note on the introduction of Christianity into Ethiopia. Africa*, no. 19, 1949.

Ullendorff, E. M. *The Semitic languages of Ethiopia.* New York, 1949.

Ullendorff, E. M. *The Obelisk of Matara. JRAS*, 1951.

Ullendorff, E. M. *An Ethiopic Inscription from Egypt. JRAS*, 1955.

Ullendorff, E. M. *Hebraic-Jewish elements in Abyssinian (Monophysite) Christianity. Journal of Semitic Studies*, July 1956.

Ullendorff, E. M. *The Ethiopians. An Introduction to Country and People.* London, 1960.

Urvoy, M. L. *Histoire de l'empire du Bornou.* Paris, 1949.
Uspensky, F. I. *History of the Byzantine empire*, vols. I–II. St. Petersburg, 1914–1918. In Russian.
Uspensky, K. N. *Essays on the history of the iconoclastic movement in the Byantine empire in the VIII–IX centuries. Theophanes and his chronography. BA*, 3, 1950; 4, 1951. In Russian.
Vaccaro, F. *Le monete di Aksum.* Casteldario, 1967.
Vaccaro, F. *Monete aksumite. Bol.*
Vaccaro, F. *Monete sudarabici di Museo del Asmara. Bol.*
Vallon, A. *History of slavery in the ancient world.* Translated from the French. Appendix [by] W. Westermann: *Slavery in the Roman empire.* Moscow, 1941. In Russian.
Van de Walle, B. "Le cippe d'Horus découverte par J. Bruce à Axoum." *Chronique d'Egypte*, no. 56, 1953.
Vasiliev, A. A. *The Life of [St.] Grigentius, the Omerite bishop. BA*, XIV, 1907. In Russian.
Vasiliev, A. A. *Kaiser Justin I (518–527) und Abessinien. Bizantinische Zeitschrift*, XXXIII, 1933.
Vasiliev, A. A. *Expositio totius mundi. An anonymous geographic treatise of the fourth century A.D.* New York, 1936.
Vasiliev, A. A. *Justin the First. An introduction to the epoch of Justinian the Great.* Cambridge, Mass., 1950.
Vavilov, N. I. *Wheats of Abyssinia and their place in the overall system of wheats.* Leningrad, 1931. In Russian.
Vavilov, N. I. *Bases théoriques de la sélection des plantes*, t. I. *Sélection générale.* Moscow-Leningrad, 1935.
Vavilov, N. I. *World-wide origins of the most important cultivated plants. Selected Works*, vol. II. Moscow-Leningrad, 1962. In Russian.
Vincent, William. *The Commerce and Navigation of the Ancients in the Indian Ocean*, vol. II. *The Periplus of the Erythrean Sea.* London, 1807.
Vycichl, Werner. *Le titre de Roi des Rois* שׁוּר : יוּיּר : *Etude historique et comparative sur la monarchie en Ethiopie. AE*, II, 1957.
Vycichl, Werner. *Egzi'abḥēr "Dieu." AE*, II, 1957.
Vycichl, Werner. *Le pays de Kush dans une inscription éthiopienne. AE*, II, 1957.
Wainwright, J. A. *Cosmas and the gold trade of Fazogl. Man*, 42, 1942.
Wellstedt, J. R. *Account of Some Inscriptions in the Abyssinian Character. JRAS*, III, 1834.
Westermann, D. *Geschichte Afrikas.* Cologne, 1952.
Winckler, H. *Altorientalische Forschungen*, Bd. I–II. Leipzig, 1893–1894.
Winckler, H. *Die Sabäische Inschriften der Zeit Alhan Nafans. Mitteilungen der Vordasiatischen Gesellschaft*, 5, 1897.
Winckler, H. *Zur alten Geschichte Jemens und Abessiniens. Orientalische Skizzen*, I, 1899 (Leipzig).
Winckler, Hugo, Karl Niebuhr, and Heinrich Schultz. *History of humanity. Universal History*, vol. XII, translated from German under the editorship of V. V. Barthold and B. A. Turayev. St. Petersburg, 1903. In Russian.
[Winstedt, E. O.] *The Christian topography of Cosmas Indicopleustes.* Cambridge, 1899.
Wissmann, H. von. *De mari Erythreo. Stuttgarter Geographische Studien*, Bd. 69 (Lautensach Festschrift), 1957.
Wissmann, H. von. *Zur Geschichte und Landeskunde von Alt-Südarabien. Sitzungsberichte der Osterreichische Akademie den Wissenschaften, phil.-hist. Klasse*, 246, 1964.
Wissmann, H. von. *Himyar. Ancient history. Mus*, XXVI, no. 3–4, 1964.
Wissmann, H. von, und M. Höfner. *Beiträge zur historischen Geographie der voris-*

lamischen Südarabiens. Mainz, 1963.

Wohlenberg, H., und A. E. Jensen. *Im Lande des Gada: Wanderungen zwischen Volkstrümmern Südabessiniens.* Stuttgart, 1936.

Woolley, C. L., and D. Randall-MacIver. *Karanóg. The Romano-Nubian cemetery.* Philadelphia, 1910.

World History, vol. II. Under the editorship of S. L. Utchenko. Moscow, 1956. In Russian.

[Yeremian, S. G.] *Ashkaratsuits (an Armenian geography of the VII century). Messenger of the Social Sciences of the Academy of Sciences of the Armenian Socialist Soviet Republic.* Yerevan, 1968, no. 5. In Armenian.

Zotenberg, H. "Mémoire sur la chronique byzantine de Jean, évêque de Nikiou," *JA,* sér. 7, t. 13, 1879.

Index

Yuri M. Kobishchanov was born in 1934, in Kharkov (the Ukraine). He was educated in Moscow, and in 1963 he received an advanced degree in historical sciences from the Institute of Asia and Africa of the Moscow University. Mr. Kobishchanov specialized in ancient and medieval history, with particular interest in feudalism. His interest in the history of Axum, which began at an early point in his career, is only one of several areas of scholarship in which he has made notable contributions. Mr. Kobishchanov has also published extensively on Medieval Nubia, Precolonial African Society, and Ancient Ethiopian Literature. Mr. Kobishchanov is employed by the Africa Institute of the Academy of Sciences of the U.S.S.R.

AXUM

Yuri M. Kobishchanov
Translated by Lorraine T. Kapitanoff
Edited by Joseph W. Michels

Since its publication in the Soviet Union this work has been highly praised by historians and archaeologists around the world. This English translation now makes it available to a wider audience. The author worked closely with the editor and translator, adding much new material, to make this an expanded and revised edition, not just a translation. It is now the most up-to-date and authoritative work available in any language on the history and culture of the Axumite civilization of highland Ethiopia.

The Axumites played a major role in trade between the classical world of the Mediterranean and countries bordering the Red Sea and the Indian Ocean. With its origins in the civilization of South Arabia, the Axumite Kingdom evolved by the fourth century A.D. into one of the most powerful states in contact with the classical world. It took a thousand years for the Axumite Kingdom to run its course. Although it collapsed with the onset of the Medieval period, it profoundly affected the more recent history of Ethiopia.

Kobishchanov covers such major topics as political history, political and economic organization, ideology, and the social system. The section on political history reveals unexpected and fascinating details regarding relations between Axum and such major powers as Rome, Byzantium, and Persia. He vividly reports the military expeditions which enabled Axum to carve out an empire extending from Nubia to Somalia, and South Arabia to southern Ethiopia — by which Axum secured total hegemony over the southern half of the Red Sea.

With a broad anthropological perspective, the author reconstructs from ancient historical texts the structure and functioning of Axumite culture. In addition to adding new material to various parts of the book, the